Doing the Media

Center for Understanding Media

Doing the Media

A Portfolio of Activities, Ideas and Resources

New revised edition

Edited by

Kit Laybourne
Pauline Cianciolo

A DANTREE PRESS BOOK

McGRAW-HILL BOOK COMPANY

New York   St. Louis   San Francisco   Auckland   Bogotá   Düsseldorf
Johannesburg   London   Madrid   Mexico   Montreal   New Delhi
Panama   Paris   São Paulo   Singapore   Sydney   Tokyo   Toronto

Printed in the United States of America

First printing 1978
1234567890 MUMU 7832109

Library of Congress Cataloging in Publication Data

Center for Understanding Media.
 Doing the Media.

 Bibliography: p.
 Includes index.
 1. Audio-visual education. 2. Media
programs (Education) I. Laybourne, Kit.
II. Cianciolo, Pauline. III. Title.
LB1043.C4   1978a   371.33   78–9076
ISBN 0–8389–0275–8 lib. ed.
ISBN 0–89560–027–7 trade ed.
ISBN 0–07–010336–4 pbk.

ACKNOWLEDGMENTS

John Culkin, "A Schoolman's Guide to Marshall McLuhan," *Saturday Review,* March 18, 1967. Copyright © 1967 Saturday Review. Adapted by permission for the author's chapter, "Doing the Truth."

The Workshop for Learning Things, Watertown, Mass.; George Cope, Director. For support of photographic ideas developed by Bobbi Carrey, Ann Mandelbaum, and others.

Susan Rice and Rose Mukerji, guest editors, *Children are Centers of Understanding Media,* published by the Association of Childhood International in collaboration with the Center for Understanding Media. Copyright © 1973 Association for Childhood International, Monroe D. Cohen, Director of Publications. Portions of chapters on film, video making, and other media excerpted and adapted with permission.

Susan Rice, "Children's Film Theater: An Eye for an I," *Sightlines,* Fall 1974. Copyright © 1974 Educational Film Library Association. Revised and reprinted with the permission of Nadine Covert, Administrative Director of EFLA.

Yvonne Andersen, *Teaching Film Animation to Children.* Copyright © 1970 Van Nostrand Reinhold Company. Illustration reprinted with permission of the author and the publisher.

Yvonne Andersen, *Make Your Own Animated Movies.* Copyright © 1970 Little, Brown and Company. Illustration with text reprinted with permission of the author and the publisher.

Kit Laybourne, "Now You See Me . . . Now I See Myself," *K-eight* magazine, Jan.–Feb. 1972, edited by Susan Rice. Copyright 1972 North American Publishing Company. Excerpted, revised and adapted by permission of the author and publisher for the author's chapters on video making.

Don Kaplan, "The Joys of Noise, Part 1," *Music Educators Journal,* Feb, 1976. Copyright 1976 Music Educators National Conference. Revised and used with permission for the author's chapter, "Emancipating Noise."

Miller-Brody Productions, Inc., producers of Newbery Award Records. For reproduction of the photo on page 165, courtesy of Miller-Brody Productions, Inc. Copyright © 1978.

Design: Robert Reed; Production: George Disabato.

PHOTO AND ART CREDITS

Chuck Anderson, pages 44, 78, 82, 85 (top left and right), 107 (top), 115 (bottom), 119 (left), 133 (bottom).

Ellie Waterson Bartow, page 49.

Irwin Belofsky, pages 104 (top), 107 (bottom), 108 (bottom), 111 (top), 117, 118.

Bruce Cost, pages 109 (top), 102.

Milo Dalbey, pages 26, 27, 40.

Helen Eisenman, pages 18 (top), 32, 45, 80 (bottom), 83, 86, 90, 130, 131, 163.

Todd Flinchbaugh, 85 (lower left), 86 (top).

Marlene Hazzikosta, page 152.

Kit Laybourne, pages 58, 59, 60, 61, 63, 64, 65, 67, 69, 75, 77, 79 (bottom), 80 (top).

John LeBaron, page 115 (top).

Ann Mandelbaum, i, ix, 19, 21 (top), 30 (right), 31 (top), 37, 142. 37, 142.

Darryl Savilla, page 72.

Mary Sheridan, pages 95 (top), 113.

Georgeann Spencer, pages 143, 144 (bottom), 145.

Foxfire Fund, page 108 (top).

Media Center for Children, pages 96, 98, 99.

WNVT Channel 53, Loudon County, Va., page 109 (bottom).

All other photographs are taken from the photograph collection of the Center for Understanding Media and include the work of Bruce Ackerly, Yvonne Andersen, Chuck Anderson, Ellie Waterson Bartow, Irwin Belofsky, Bobbi Carrey, Bruce Cost, Milo Dalbey, Charles Marden Fitch, Peter Haratonik, John LeBaron, Ann Mandelbaum, Darryl Savilla, Calvin E. Schlick III, Mary Sheridan.

Children's art from the Children's Film Theater.

Contents

Preface   vii

Part 1. Introduction to Media Studies

1   Doing the Truth
by John Culkin   3

2   Guidelines for Film and Media Programs
by Robert Geller and Kit Laybourne   7

Part 2. Photography

3   Doing Photography
by Ann Mandelbaum   14

4   A Photographic Yellow Pages
by Bobbi Carrey   37

5   A Developmental Perspective
by Ellie Waterston Bartow   41

Part 3. Film

6   Doing Super 8
by Ellie Waterston Bartow   48

7   A Filmmaking Course
by Jon Dunn and Kit Laybourne   56

8   Doing Animation
by Kit Laybourne   73

9   Talking about Movies: Subverting
The Old School Game
by Richard A. Lacey   88

10   Children's Film Theater: An Eye
for an I
by Susan Rice   93

11   Is What You See All You Get?
by Kay Weidemann, Gerry Laybourne, and
Maureen Gaffney   96

Part 4. Video

12   Doing Videotape
by Kit Laybourne   103

13 Studio Television
     by Jean Baity   113

14 Television Studies
     by Kit Laybourne   119

Part 5. Sound

15 Sound Study
     by Louis Giansante   126

16 Doing Audiotape
     by Louis Giansante   131

17 Emancipating Noise
     by Don Kaplan   135

Part 6. Other Media

18 Animating the Overhead
     by Georgeanna Spencer   142

19 Media Bag
     by Milo Dalbey   147

Part 7. Curriculum Design

20 Taming King Kong: Lessons of the
     Recent Past
     by Richard A. Lacey   152

21 Approaches to Curriculum Design
     by Kit Laybourne   155

22 An Integrated Media Arts Curriculum
     by Milo Dalbey   159

Resources

Books and Nonprint Materials   167

Periodicals   187

Organizations   189

Media Distributors   192

About the Contributors   203

Index   205

This is a second generation volume of *Doing the Media*. A preliminary version emerged in 1972 as a published report by the Center for Understanding Media of its eighteen month research project with the Mamaroneck, New York, Public School System. The Mamaroneck Media Project, funded by a grant from the Ford Foundation, developed many of the curricular approaches described both in the preliminary edition and in this new and expanded edition, though this volume goes beyond the initial project.

The objects of that original media studies project are best expressed in the proposal to the Ford Foundation: "The timing is right ... for a study of the best thinking and teaching which is currently available and for the development of a series of flexible curriculum designs to serve as models in the elementary and secondary schools. Add the training of teachers and the development of teaching material and you have our proposed project."

The ideas and concerns expressed in the proposal and demonstrated in the project proved compelling enough to have kept the authors engaged in this edition for over six years. During that time the substance of this volume has caught the interest of many others, some of whom became contributors to this edition, and some of whom published their draft pieces in journals and magazines.

Growing out of the Mamaroneck program and extending beyond that earlier report published by the Center, this edition of *Doing the Media* is a completely revised and reorganized work which includes additional articles as well as revised and rewritten selections from the previous report. It is intended to serve as both a practical text in media education courses and as a portfolio of ideas for the professional teacher, media specialist, librarian, and others engaged in formal or informal educational activities. It is a lively and thoughtful collection of media philosophy, activities, and goals designed for use in elementary and secondary school levels. As an aid for teachers and child caregivers who share a concern for bringing the real world of students in their classrooms or under their care, and for better preparing those children and young people for the challenges of their media-dominated culture, this edition is offered as a book publication in response to expressed needs and interest.

Doing the Media had its genesis in the experimental atmosphere of the late nineteen sixties and early seventies, when healthy national debate was still a possibility: opposing sides on educational issues were not clearly drawn; there was more listening going on, and fewer nonproductive accusing voices had a monopoly on our attention; and libraries were well funded (in great part with federal programs), and school libraries became media centers. But with the rapidity which characterizes our modern culture, yesterday's dialogues have been replaced by today's complaints: "Academic achievement is declining!" and "Why can't we just take our students *back to basics!*"

What is the place for a book which explores the potential role of media studies in our schools? And how do media educators and librarians answer the challenge of the *back to basics* adherents? The authors and sponsors of this book, as concerned educators, refuse to allow media studies to be characterized as a costly and expendable extra-curricular activity. The bombarding media, they remind us, have become an integral part of the sizeable portion of American education that occurs outside the classroom walls. Media *educate* and *miseducate* us everyday. The schools have a responsibility to insure that we and our children are an audience of enlightened, selective consumers of media, equipped to decode the complex and easily misleading messages of the media. In doing this, the schools would be carrying on the American educational tradition of bringing flexibility and relevance to the curriculum. The necessity for understanding and doing the media would undoubtedly be discerned by John Dewey himself, who in 1897 noted, "I believe that the school must represent present life—life as real and vital to the child as that which he carries on in the home, in the neighborhood, or in the playground." In concurring, we would say that no aspect of contemporary life deserves more attention in the school life than media in their varied forms.

For the educator who has caught the message and spirit of *Doing the Media,* what practical role can this book be expected to play? As a resource in itself and a guide to other resources, it provides an invaluable reference for creating an expansive and enjoyable program for media education from elementary through senior high school. Its performance-based lessons—with emphasis on processes rather than on products or equipment—include everything from the creation of a storyboard to the production of a mixed media festival. The book speaks both to the teacher with no media background who is looking for a place to begin and to the experienced media instructor seeking fresh, innovative ideas. Above all, the book is a joyful creation of people who relish and want to share their mandate to close the gap between the media culture and the world of the classroom.

Acknowledgements

Doing the Media was made possible through grants from the following organizations: The Ford Foundation, The National Endowment for the Arts, The U.S. Office of Education, The New York State Council on the Arts, The Henry Nias Foundation, and the Edward E. Ford Foundation.

Many of the individuals who worked with the original Mamaroneck Media Project appear in the photographs through this volume. We list their names here, and say thank you once again to: teachers—Helen Boyle, Patsy Brennan, Steve Christos, Trish Coyle, Diane Dermer, Angel Diakopoulos, Pat Fanning, Kathy Farrell, Bonnie Feldman, Madeline Gilbert, Tom Krawczyk, Sy Kushner, Joan Landesco, George Langenauer, Frank Lifrieri, Joan Pappalardo, Helen Rittenberg, Carol Scannell, Joanne Shapoff, Sally Soyka, Marilyn Sykes, and Dom Tedesco; community volunteers—Donna Adler, Jean Baity, Lisa Karnofsky, June Katz, Katy Moody, Mary Ann Mumma, Margaret Nichol, Tony Pisacane, Judy Rosbe, Susan Schmidt, Lily Towey; student volunteers—Dan Coplan, Dan Edelman, Jon Edelman, Lisa Nichol, Cal Schlick. Our gratitude is extended also to the staff of the Mamaroneck School System, in particular, to Virginia Magee, Gloria Pritts and Jack Seligman—all of the Mamaroneck Instructional Center; Bruce Ackerly, project technician; Bob Krause and Walt Coupe, the administration of Mamaroneck Avenue School; Dr. Otty Norwood and Dr. Cal Schlick of the Mamaroneck School District.

Thanks are extended to people at the Center for Understanding Media: consultants Yvonne Andersen, Dr. Joseph Colmen, Tom McDonough, Bobbi Carrey, Mary Sheridan, Susan Rice, Dr. Andreas Steinmetz; project staff members Robert Geller, Milo Dalbey, Ellie Waterston Bartow, and Barbara Ludlum; and, of course, the man behind it all, John Culkin, founder and director.

The following colleagues and friends are thanked for meeting their deadlines with such exciting materials for this new edition that they forced earlier contributors to extend their deadlines in order to match the infusion of new ideas and energies: Deirdre Boyle, Jon Dunn, Todd Flinchbaugh, Maureen Gaffney, Louis Giansante, Peter Haratonik, Don Kaplan, Richard Lacey, Gerry Laybourne, Ann Mandelbaum, Georgeanna Spencer, Kay Weidemann. The authors who reworked their articles from the preliminary edition and contributed new ones are also gratefully acknowledged for those contributions: Jean Baity, Bobbi Carrey, John Culkin, Milo Dalbey, and Susan Rice.

A special thanks is extended to those at the Center for Understanding Media who worked on the production of this work: Lynn Garrett, Susan Svigoon, and Martha Svigoon.

This edition of *Doing the Media* exists because of the care and gumption invested in it by Pauline Cianciolo, president, and Jacqueline Peterson, house editor, of Dantree Press. All who worked on the original project and on this volume would save the final and biggest thanks to Polly and Jackie.

Kit Laybourne, Editor

Doing the Media

Part 1
Introduction to Media Studies

A media collage

Chapter One

Doing the Truth

by John Culkin

Education, John Culkin was once assured by a seven-year-old, is "how kids learn stuff." That definition needs no improvement. In this chapter the author shows that the whole process of formal schooling is now wrapped inside an environment of speeded-up technological change which is constantly influencing *kids* and *learning* and *stuff*. Exploring some of the philosophies behind the expanded education envisaged in this book, he presents here a perfect starting point for reader seeking a firm, educative platform on which to build a media program.

"Japanese children speak Japanese."

The realization of this simple truth led the Japanese educator Suzuki to a new respect for the potential of the child and to a new form of education which would focus on creating proper environments for learning. Portuguese children don't speak Japanese. It has nothing to do with their learning potential and everything to do with their learning environment. Children learn the language and symbol systems of their own culture. All of this seems platitudinous enough until we realize how many "languages" and symbol systems there are today in the world of young children.

Today's children are immersed in a sea of communications. They live in a society whose citizens annually spend more than 31,000,000 years of human time watching television. They themselves see more of television than they do of schoolrooms. One doesn't have to be a card-carrying McLuhanite to acknowledge the pervasive presence of media and messages of all kinds. There is the station-to-person world of television, radio, film, book, stereo, telephone, photograph, comics, tape recorder, magazine, and computer. There is the person-to-person world of word, gesture, expression, smell, tone, and touch. Each of these symbolic codes interacts with the sensory and psychic apparatus of the child to help him define himself and his environment. The reknowned anthropologist Dr. Edmund Carpenter has stressed the importance of understanding the nature of these new forms of communications:

> English is a mass medium. All languages are mass media. The new mass media—film, radio, TV—are new languages, their grammars as yet unknown. Each codifies reality differently, each conceals a unique metaphysics. Linguists tell us that it's possible to say anything in any language if you use enough words or images, but there's rarely time; the natural course is for a culture to exploit its media biases.[1]

The media and the arts are not merely envelopes which carry all messages indifferently; they shape both the message and the perceiver.

When we are talking about our sensory life, we are automatically talking about what is *basic* in education. The complex and creative act of knowing that moves

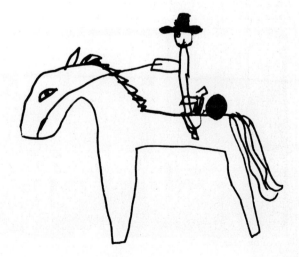

through sensation, perception, and cognition depends directly on our sensory apparatus. The quality of our sensorium influences the quality of our knowledge. This may all seem obvious enough until we reflect on the fact that most schools do very little to consciously train the senses. The environment, on the other hand, is constantly shaping the senses at random. Philosopher Susan Sontag suggests a positive approach to dealing with the buzzing confusion of the media environment:

> Ours is a culture based on excess, on overproduction;.the result is a steady loss of sharpness in our sensory experience. All the conditions of modern life—its material plenitude, its sheer crowdedness—conjoin to dull our sensory faculties. What is important now is to recover our senses. We must learn to *see* more, to *hear* more, to *feel* more.[2]

The work of the Canadian scholar Marshall McLuhan has alerted our age to this shaping power of the media. He is quick to point out that this has always been true and that the effects are no longer inevitable if we are willing to understand and intervene. McLuhan's major work is *Understanding Media,* and it provides much of the stimulus for *Doing the Media.* I would like to consciously acknowledge that connection by offering a synopsis of those theories of McLuhan which deal with the influence of the environment on the senses.

What follows is one man's McLuhan served up in barbarously brief form. Five postulates, spanning 4000 years, will serve as the fingers in this endeavor to grasp what is essential of McLuhan.

1) *1978 B.C.—All the senses get into the act.* A conveniently symmetrical year for a thesis which is partially cyclic, 1978 B.C. gets us back to man before the Phoenician alphabet. We know from our contemporary ancestors in the jungles of New Guinea and the wastes of the Arctic that preliterate man lives in an all-at-once sense world. The reality which bombards him from all directions is picked up with the omnidirectional antennae of sight, hearing, touch, smell, and taste. Films such as *The Hunters* and *Nanook of the North* depict primitive men tracking game with an across-the-board sensitivity which mystifies literate Western man. We mystify them too. And it is this cross-mystification which makes intercultural abrasions so worthwhile.

Each culture develops its own balance of the senses in response to the demands of its environment. The most generalized formulation of the theory would maintain that the individual's modes of cognition and perception are influenced by the culture he is in, the language he speaks, and the media to which he is exposed. Each culture, as it were, provides its constituents with a custom-made set of goggles. The differences in perception are a question of degree. Some cultures are close enough to each other in perceptual patterns so that the differences pass unnoticed. Other cultural groups, such as the Eskimo and the American teenager, are far enough apart to provide a firm basis for comparison.

2) *Art imitates life.* In *The Silent Language* Edward T. Hall offers the thesis that all art and technology is an extension of some physical or psychic element of man. Today man has developed extensions for practically everything he used to do with his body: axe for hand, wheel for foot, glasses for eyes, radio for voice and ears. Money is a way of storing energy. This externalizing of individual, specialized functions is now, by definition, at its most advanced stage. Through the electronic media of telegraph, telephone, radio, and television, man has now equipped his world with a nervous system similar to the one within his own body. President Kennedy is shot and the world instantaneously reels from the impact of the bullets. Space and time dissolve under electronic conditions. Current concern for the United Nations, the Common Market, ecumenism, reflects the organic thrust toward the new convergence and unity which is "blowing in the wind." Now in the electric age, our extended faculties and senses constitute a single instantaneous and coexistent field of experience. It's all-at-once. It's shared-by-all. McLuhan calls the world "a global village."

3) *Life imitates art.* We shape our tools and thereafter they shape us. These extensions of our senses begin to interact with our senses. These media become a massage. The new change in the environment creates a new balance among the senses. No sense operates in isolation. The full sensorium seeks fulfillment in almost every sense experience. And since there is a limited quantum of energy available for any sensory experience, the sense-ratio will differ for different media.

The nature of the sensory effect will be determined by the medium used. McLuhan divides the media according to the quality or definition of their physical signal. The content is not relevant in this kind of analysis. The same picture from the same camera can appear as a glossy

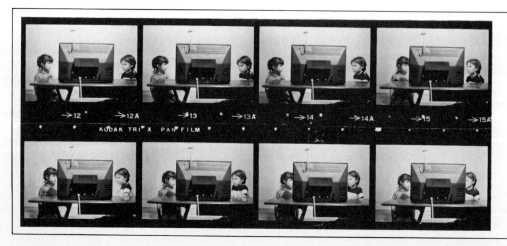

Television is cool–
it invites participation
and involvement.

photograph or as a newspaper wire-photo. The glossy photograph is well-defined, of excellent pictorial quality, hi-fi within its own medium. McLuhan calls this kind of medium "hot." The newspaper photo is grainy, made up of little dots, low definition. McLuhan calls this kind of medium "cool." Film is hot; television is cool. Radio is hot; telephone is cool. The cool medium invites participation and involvement. It leaves room for the response of the consumer. A lecture is hot; all the work is done. A seminar is cool; it gets everyone into the game. Whether all the connections are casual may be debated, but it's interesting that the kids of the cool TV generation want to be so involved and so much a part of what's happening.

4) *We shaped the alphabet and it shaped us.* In keeping with the postulate that "the medium is the message," a literate culture should be more than mildly eager to know what books do to people. Everyone is familiar enough with all the enrichment to living mediated through fine books to allow us to pass on to the subtler effects which might be attributed to the print medium, independent of the content involved. Whether one uses the medium to say that God is dead or that God is love the structure of the medium itself remains unchanged:

Nine little black marks with no intrinsic meaning of their own are strung along a line with spaces left after the third and fifth marks. It is this stripping away of meaning which allows us to X-ray the form itself.

As an example, while lecturing to a large audience in a modern hotel in Chicago, a distinguished professor is bitten in the leg by a cobra. The whole experience takes three seconds. He is affected through the touch of the reptile, the gasp of the crowd, the swimming sights before his eyes. His memory, imagination, and emotions come into emergency action. A lot of things happen in three seconds. Two weeks later he is fully recovered and wants to write up the experience in a letter to a colleague. To communicate this experience through print means that it must first be broken down into parts and then mediated, eyedropper fashion, one thing at a time, in an abstract, linear, fragmented, sequential way. That is the essential structure of print. And once a culture uses such a medium for a few centuries, it begins to perceive the world in a one-thing-at-a-time, abstract, linear, fragmented, sequential way. And it shapes its organizations and schools according to the same premises. The form of print has become the form of thought. The medium has become the message.

For centuries now, according to McLuhan, the straight line has been the hidden metaphor of literate man. It was unconsciously but inexorably used as the measure of things. It went unnoticed, unquestioned. It was presumed as natural and universal. It is neither. Like everything else it is good for the things it is good for. To say that it is not everything is not to say that it is nothing. The electronic media have broken the monopoly of print; they have altered our sensory profiles by heightening our awareness of aural, tactile, and kinetic values.

5) *1978 A.D.—All the senses want to get into the act.* Print repressed most sense-life in favor of the visual. The end of print's monopoly also marks the end of a visual monopoly. As the early warning system of art and popular culture indicates, all the senses want to get into the act. Some of the excesses in the current excursions into aural, oral, tactile, and kinetic experience may in fact be directly

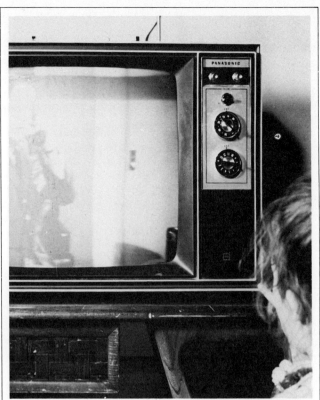

Information levels are now higher outside the classroom. Schools must enable children to master media's codes and to control media's impact.

responsive to the sensory deprivation of the print culture. Nature abhors a vacuum.

Television is not merely a leisure time activity. For better or for worse, it is a rival educator competing with the teacher for the attention of the child. While a classroom teacher devotes small periods of time to teaching nutrition, the television set is spangled with commercials selling sugar-saturated, low quality breakfast cereals. TV preaches the lie that almost any headache or heartache can be solved in a thirty-second commercial or a thirty-minute drama. No room here for deferred gratification. The medium, through its use of quick editing, reinforces the short attention span of the viewer. It jumbles our sense of time and place by whizzing us from 1,000,000 B.C. to the year 2001 through a flick of the dial. All times and all places are present in the present tense on the television screen.

Today's students are world citizens because of their televised visits to all the peoples and countries of the world. They have been to the moon, to Sesame Street, to assassinations, to wars—to almost everything that is part of human experience. Any program watched by a child is children's telvision. This is why our efforts in the schools must be directed at strengthening the child's ability to deal with what is. It is growing increasingly difficult to protect the child from an outside environment over which we have little control. Today the only way to make people selective consumers is to make them smart.

For the first time in history the information levels are higher outside the classroom than in it. It has always made good sense for people who live on water to learn how to swim. Swimming in the electronic environment means recognizing its importance, understanding it, and gaining control over it. The schools must acknowledge the existence and influence of this new media culture and enable the child to master its codes and to control its impact. We should want today's students to be active, intelligent, tough-minded, and selective consumers of the total media culture just as in the past we have tried to develop taste and discrimination for the traditional literary, dramatic, and artistic culture.

In practice this would mean that children would view and discuss a variety of films and television programs; that they would create their own films, videotapes, audiotapes, and photographs; that exercises in writing, painting, dance, and drama would deal with themes from the popular culture; that the new media would be used as active agents in developing the sensory life of the child.

There is a nice phrase somewhere in St. Paul where he encourages his audience to be "doers of the truth." This is apposite here. Communications is a relatively new field. It deals with a phenomenon so pervasive and so rapidly changing that it is often impossible to get a clean research fix on the data. The theory will almost always lag behind the realities of the child's daily media experience. The "doers of truth" will recognize this. Their response will be a simple one. Anything which helps the child to understand and control the media environment is a good thing. Any way the media can help the child to define himself and his relation with others is a good thing.

Be ye doers of the truth.

NOTES

1. Edmund Carpenter, *Explorations in Communication,* ed. by Edmund Carpenter and Marshall McLuhan (Boston: Beacon Press, 1960), p. 162.
2. Susan Sontag, *Against Interpretation* (New York: Dell Publishing Co., 1967), pp. 13–14.

A school media festival

Guidelines for Film and Media Programs

by Robert Geller and
Kit Laybourne

The authors present a brief overview of the
current media environment and the rationale for
teaching film and media studies in today's schools.
They offer some basic strategies for setting up and
sustaining media programs, and introduce some of
the activities and ideas that are treated in the
following chapters. The future of media studies,
they show, begins now.

Chapter Two

THE SEEING PART

Rationale

It's unlikely that endless coercion tactics for change will
be needed to get film and media teaching into your
schools. Most communities are aware that newspapers,
radio, movies, and television have a strong impact on how
we perceive ourselves and our environment. One problem
may be that, while we take for granted the importance of
such inputs, we don't seem to find the time to plan for
integrating media analysis into traditional learnings.

Schooling aims at providing children with those "skills"
society deems requisite to a full and effective life. As times
change so should basic skills. Understanding media is a
twentieth century tool for survival. Our children need to
develop a critical approach to the media and creative experience with it if they are to function effectively within
contemporary culture. It makes sense to introduce this
experience as early as kindergarten.

Most five-year-olds come to school in September with
well over 1500 hours of television watching. The latest
census reports indicate the television set is on for 6.2
hours a day in the average American home. On Saturday
mornings the kids see a commercial on the average of
every 2.8 minutes. In the elementary grades the average
student watches the tube for more than 25 hours a week.
The statistics run even higher for children of the poor.

There has to be a way to treat these experiences as more
than a glimpse at pop culture. This doesn't mean assess-
ing film, radio, and video as destroyers of our past and
underminers of our humanity. Quite the contrary, the
enlightened audience of parents, teachers, and students
can demand the most of the media and essentially become
the "producers of their own experiences." They can do
this by seeing and listening perceptively, by actually
working with the technology that creates the media environment. There is more than a vague premise that new
technologies can actually sensitize us and improve our
world—if we care enough to understand and shape them.

levels of learning and teaching. Also, new skills in arrangement and ordering, selectivity and editing, and perception and creating become very apparent.

Getting Started

Some part of the summer should be given over to a working experience involving teachers, librarians and other media specialists, parents, and a helpful administrator with contemporary ideas. As in all sustained innovations, the principal's or superintendent's involvement is essential. There are numerous institutes and seminars for teachers throughout the country. For help in locating a summer program in your area, write the Center for Understanding Media or the American Library Association (see the list of organizations in the Resources section at the end of this book).

There is also a wide variety of courses and workshops in film and media given during the regular school year at most community colleges, liberal arts colleges, and universities, very often in the evenings or on Saturdays to accommodate the schedules of working teachers. In addition, many institutions will offer special off-campus courses for school systems or teacher groups upon request, especially if a specified minimum class-size can be guaranteed.

If traveling or funding for summer or evening study is impossible, it makes sense to preview a whole bunch of films, both shorts and features, during a week or two in July. Invite teachers from as many departments and grade levels as possible. Attempt to find a local filmmaker or college student with a good film background to help you make an 8mm film as a group. The seeing and doing are fine complements.

If possible, we also suggest evening screenings which involve community and students. Such screenings can engender parental support and get kids and parents talking about a common heritage that is seldom shared. Monthly workshops in filmmaking, videotaping, and photography could supplement the screenings of TV programs shared earlier. Also, more and more schools are using the sixty-minute lunch period for film viewing, sound-and-light programs, or video viewing. It sure beats counting the flying milk containers.

The local theater exhibitor can be a valuable ally. His theater is usually vacant during morning and afternoon

Assessing the Impact

It's foolish to plunge headlong into a media program. Planning time is needed to locate and integrate the media that will be both pertinent and of fine quality.

Careful attention should also be paid to specific objectives for film and other media seminars or workshops and to a choice of consultants who are flexible, knowledgeable, and at ease with the school structures. Whenever possible, in-service programs for students, teachers, administrators, and parents should precede the actual project. While there is sufficient urgency to teach film and media experiences for their own sake, it is helpful to have teachers from various grade levels and subject areas begin thinking about ways that film and TV viewing and production workshops can be integrated into their own teaching.

A caution is offered, however, to avoid plunging too quickly into rigid measurement approaches and fixed categories; these kill the excitement and fun of innovative learning and can hinge all experiences to desperately anticipated outcomes. This does not preclude the need to carefully define the why and how of media learning.

No hard research exists yet to prove that students read better, do arithmetic better, or think better after seeing films or making their own. Empirical observations do show that community members, teachers, and students thrive in the open environment that film and media create, that high motivational levels carry over to all other

Teachers meet with media specialists and visiting media practitioners to learn new skills and to do the media themselves.

hours. He might be eager to help program classics, silent films, films that tie into ongoing courses or field trips, or films for younger kids. It would make sense to involve him, wherever possible, in plans for film clubs or film societies so that he might know in advance what monthly screenings were being planned. For example, a school screening of *Treasure of Sierre Madre* might lead nicely to a Bogart week at the local theater. The possibilities are limitless.

Start to build your own library of resource material to supplement and enhance knowledge gained through direct media exposure. (Consult the Resources section for a selective, annotated bibliography.) Involve your school librarian in building your school's collection of professional materials, and offer your assistance in selecting, reviewing and evaluating both book and nonbook materials for that collection, as well as for the general central library media center.

The more you do film and media planning the less you'll feel the need to structure things. But, at the beginning, you may find security in working with a unit organized by subject. Some tested examples are: film history; films and themes (love, war, adolescence); genre films like the Western; films by one director; films that went from novel to films; films on one theme treated differently by different countries; films of one decade (with some guesses about how events shape film); films that are visually exciting and without linear or narrative design.

With younger kids, we suggest less concern for packaging. Let the kids view films and encourage them to react to what they see by drawing, clapping hands, writing a story, talking about themselves. Let your students explore their own film experiences (see chapter 9), and expand their learning and activities with both pre-screening and post-screening experiences (see chapters 10 and 11).

Starting a film or media program without funding is a little shy of wisdom. But starting a program without a lot of money is quite possible. Film catalogs list on a wide scale, depending on such factors as film length, source of film, and audience range. Short films cost less and can be shown more often. But don't ignore the feature film when making up your budget; remember that these features generally represent a more sophisticated filmmaking and can elicit a wide range of post-screening response. Older films cost less but may be harder to sustain excitement about at first. A full-year film rental budget of $750 is sparse and lean, but certainly manageable. If at least 750 kids get involved, that one dollar a year per student would buy a lot of learning. Cookie sales, car washes, film festivals, and theater screenings are additional ways to raise money.

THE DOING PART

Who Should Participate

In the past, English and Social Studies departments got into film and media study earlier than other departments. It is time for others to become involved. Film and TV documentaries often fit splendidly into science and psychology courses. The art teacher should be a vital part of any media program; he or she is trained to see and help others understand the excitement of imaging and selecting and compressing things. On the elementary level the involvement of as many grades as possible is encouraged. This kind of extended participation means more enthusiasm, more kids, more shared budgets—an eventual breakdown of rigidity in curriculum.

But every media program, whether it involves one class or many, needs the support and participation of the school's audiovisual department and library media center staff. These people make the difference between a media studies project that is well equipped, and rich in resource material, and one that is almost certainly doomed to uneven quality because the unsupported media teacher is over-extended.

Beginning Now

Start with things you are really excited about and projects that you feel comfortable with. As obvious as that piece of advice is, it needs saying. We've known too many teachers who thought, for example, that filmmaking was the only place to begin and then got ensnarled in logistics, procedures, and frustrations that neither they nor their students needed. Let the beginning be manageable. Choose an area you like, and carefully try out every activity before your students do.

We suggest you start with media-making activities that are easy and inexpensive to organize. Your school audiovisual department may have equipment you didn't know about. The athletic departments of most large schools, for example, have cameras to film their football games. If you're interested in filmmaking and can use the athletic department's equipment, start your activity "off season." Often your students or their parents will have access to equipment that you can borrow. Media teachers learn to be con-artists. But no matter how well you can borrow or requisition items of hardware or software, invariably you will buy an item or two yourself. So get to know your local media merchants, such as the camera or photo supply storekeeper or salesman. A lot of good second-hand equipment is available.

"How you teach is what you teach; the medium of instruction is the message of learning." That aphorism is aimed at reminding you to give real thought to the way you design your media-making activities. Presumptuous, perhaps. But here are some ideas we'd urge you to think about: consider the differences between cheap, fast projects and the more costly, slower ones; between large group orientation and work by individuals or small groups; between inductive and deductive learning; between activity-based, student-selected teaching and that which is lecture-oriented and teacher-selected; between an emphasis on the "process" of media making and on the "product" of media making. Challenge *any* pre-established scheme for *any* portion of instruction.

There are things you can do with existing hardware and readily available materials: scratch-and-doodle filmmaking to introduce the principles and techniques of animation (see chapter 8); resuscitating opaque and overhead projectors and recycling old photographs and magazine pictures to experiment with framing, new forms, and movement (see chapter 18); devising creative and documentary projects with tape recorders and found sound (see chapters 15, 16, and 17); introducing slidemaking and storyboarding for filmmaking by recycling "spoiled" film and old pictures (see chapters 8 and 19); doing photogra-

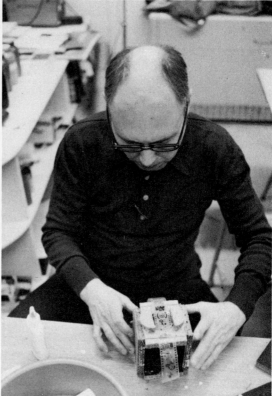

Trying out—doing the media—before teaching. *Above left*, animating the overhead; *right*, making a filmstrip projector; below *left*, mastering video; *right*, unloading film in changing bag.

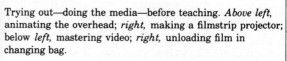

phy without a camera, and expanding the homemade camera into a slide viewer, lumiere, kaleidoscope, filmstrip viewer, and reflex camera (see chapters 3 and 4); and using all sorts of existing non-electronic hardware to create multi-media forms, communication cubes, and pleasure domes (see chapters 18 and 19).

Of course, some activities require equipment and software that may not be readily available in your school's audiovisual closet. Still, you don't have to be rich to get started. There are many inexpensive ways to introduce photography (see chapters 3 and 4), and a simple plastic camera can be purchased for under two dollars.

A much underrated and underutilized medium is the slide tape, a series of 35mm slides projected through a carousel unit joined to a stereo tape recorder by a synchronizer. This relatively inexpensive system can serve as an introduction to motion pictures, for both media have many of the same problems and effects. You can also combine photographic activities (see chapters 3, 4, and 5) with slide making and filmmaking (see chapters 7 and 8).

The inexpensive Super 8 camera (see chapter 6) has become popular in schools and among amateur filmmakers. It presents endless options for: organization (from 30-second assignments by individuals to full-class epics); different kinds of films (documentary, narrative, design, experimental, animation); various levels of sophistication in production (from movies that are edited in-camera to movies shot with complicated interior lighting). The amount of equipment available, your budget, the age and interest of your students, and the kind of film you feel most comfortable trying will determine the nature and extent of the projects you and your students undertake.

Feel a little shaky about teaching filmmaking? We suggest you begin with animation (see chapter 8), which requires little film, can be done in the classroom, needs little editing, and provides a nice ratio between planning time and shooting time. Kids' animated movies are almost always great to look at. And that is an important factor if you are trying to urge a principal or community to support your program.

Until recently too little creative energy has been expended on school videotape systems. The non-portable, complicated, fragile, and expensive one-inch VTR complexes remained in the hands of technicians and special-ists. Both machines and audiovisual experts were limited to canning lectures, taping "redeeming" educational broadcasts from the other media, and, at best, producing formal, studio-found programs by students. In the past few years, however, a new kind of VTR has been finding its way into the schools. The medium is now portable, thanks to half-inch technology. It is simple to operate, rugged, and inexpensive. Activities with this VTR system are limitless (see chapters 12, 13, and 14).

Media Studies for the Future

We have found that media making leads to more discriminating media viewing; the reverse is also true. By encouraging students to participate with the media that dominate so much of their lives and their interest, we believe educators can help young people learn to control that most complex and critical of all media—the changing environment.

More and more the media and their messages have *become* our world. The students you have in school today will be running our society by the end of the century, a time when the media will have an even greater hand in determining what they will think, feel, and know about the world. If they are to cope with the changes ahead, they will have to develop new critical attitudes toward the media. For them especially, understanding the media will be more than an intellectual exercise, and doing the media will be more than an activity. Understanding and doing will be survival skills. Chapters 9, 10, and 11, for example, present ideas, activities and resources for film literacy and critical film viewing/thinking.

In the final chapters (chapters 20, 21, and 22) the need for a media-oriented education is reviewed and a media studies program proposed. Our underlying assumption throughout this book, of course, is that every school—from primary through college—has its own library media center staffed with professional librarians and other media specialists. That issue, we believe, has itself not been adequately faced by the educational community or by the funding bodies that determine support for the essential services of the centralized media library and its staff. But that is the subject best left to other books. We have purposely limited our concern here to *doing the media*.

Part 2
Photography

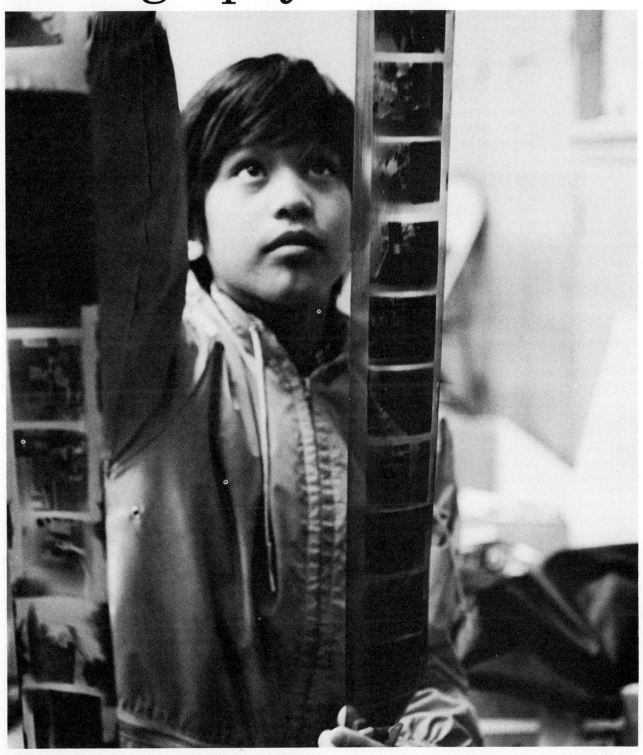

Doing Photography

by Ann Mandelbaum

Based on a series of workshops developed by Bobbi Carrey, consultant for the Center for Understanding Media and a professional free-lance photographer, this chapter shows how doing photography in a media program means much more than snapping pelicans at the zoo on a camera club field trip. Here Ann Mandelbaum provides detailed instructions for everything from the "primitive" pinhole camera to photographic painting. To all weekend photographers who think of film as something to be developed at the drugstore, she provides some remarkable educational surprises. Here then is an A to Z introduction to photography.

Chapter Three

Photography bombards us hourly, from the souped-up commercial image in advertising to the family snapshot. It can seem so illusive, so much a part of the perfected machine age. The magic is inside each one of us; the pictures come from people not from cameras. With the following ideas and activities we hope to bring this often overlooked premise closer to home. Our concern extends to an understanding of photographic principles and techniques as practical necessities. The emphasis here falls on photography as: a means of replacing *looking* with *seeing;* a way to go beyond the physical limits of an object and its word label; and a beautifully subjective medium allowing for personal interpretation.

THE PHOTOGRAM

The best way to convince students of their creative worth is to offer an on the spot, finger-in-the-pie means of involvement. It therefore makes sense to introduce photography without complex machinery, to substitute the hand for the camera. This can be done most simply through "light drawings," or photograms—photographic prints of light and shadow made without camera or negative. The process is clear, quick, and inexpensive.

The materials used can range from the absolute minimum to the very complex. To begin, arrange a variety of objects on light-sensitive paper. Light-sensitive paper is readily available in photo and art supply stores. It is chemically coated so that its shiny surface, or emulsion, responds to light. To "take a picture," simply expose the object or composition of objects to a light source and process the latent photographic image with the appropriate chemicals. Where light hits, the paper becomes dark; where light is blocked or partially blocked, the paper stays white or turns grey.

The processing of the paper varies according to what is used for the image and the kind of light-sensitive paper used for the "photograph." A huge bonus is that there is

Making sun-prints of small objects on studio proof paper. To review: *expose* to sun or photoflood bulb; *develop* simultaneously in same; *fix* image by keeping photogram in dark place or dipping it quickly in hypo solution.

a limitless choice of techniques and materials. Sun-print photographs, developed by means of the sun's rays, offer beginners creative exposure to the basics of photography without need of a darkroom. Adding standard photographic methods and a few basic pieces of equipment, however, provides a wide open field for more advanced work. In all cases, with minimum hassle, the photographic concepts of light and dark, space, tone, and shape can be clearly presented.

This is a good place to mention the merits of that ubiquitous school supply, construction paper. It isn't photographic, but because sunlight acts on it fairly quickly, it is a ready-made printing material for photograms. A few hours to a day's exposure will produce an image that is permanent when the photogram is kept out of further sunlight.

One of the first considerations is the subject of the image. Objects should be selected for their uniqueness. Strangely shaped opaque forms make interesting silhouettes. Transparent or semi-transparent materials will produce a variety of grey tones. Three-D objects create depth and shadowy outlines. Textured surfaces also add strange effects. The materials are many and varied.

Solid objects such as keys and coins are easiest to handle because they don't require critically accurate exposure times. Once the specific light conditions are under control, objects producing more subtle tones, such as plants, patterned glass, and packaging materials, can be tried. The choice of objects and their potential arrangement should be well thought out ahead of time. Indecision will result in unclear images or fogged paper once the lighting process has begun.

The effects created, the amount and kind of light, and the chemical processing vary with the kind of light-sensitive paper used. The papers available, and the methods and effects, are described below.

Sunlight or Room Light-Sensitive Papers

These papers require a *lot of light* to make them work (*or less light but a lot of time*). They can be conveniently used in any ordinary room instead of in a darkroom. When there is insufficient sunlight, you can use a gooseneck lamp or a sunlamp equipped with a very bright bulb shining not very far away from the print.

Hair and hands make interesting photograms.

Printing-out paper (Kodak Studio Proof F, Agfa P.O.P.). This is *slow* paper—that is, it is not very sensitive to normal room light but it is still light-sensitive. It is exposed and developed simultaneously, most commonly by sunlight. It also reacts to artificial light, such as sunlamp or photoflood bulb #1 placed at a distance of one foot. Where light strikes the paper, the paper turns dark; where light is obstructed by a two- or three-dimensional object, the paper remains white. The length of exposure will depend on light conditions and the desired degree of development. Exposure (and simultaneous development) can range anywhere from 2–10 minutes. The developed image, which is plum purple on white, can be kept from darkening in a lightproof box. But immersion in a fixer solution (5 tablespoons of sodium theosulphate crystals in 32 ounces of cool water) for 10 minutes and a wash in plain water for an hour will make the photogram permanent. The image will lighten after fixing and washing, so when

SUGGESTED OBJECTS FOR PHOTOGRAMS

pocketbook items, *e.g.*, keys, combs
coins and buttons
matchsticks
pins and paperclips
nuts, bolts, screws   crocheted items/parts
patterned glass objects   lace
cutouts, *e.g.*, numbers, letters   tape/film reels
screens   light bulbs/switches
scissors   feathers
packaging materials   leaves & ferns
Saran wrap, crumpled   flowers
Scotch tape, crumpled   cookie cutters
corrugated plastic   wire scrubbers
bandaging   knives, forks, spoons
knitted fabrics   feet and hands
                                hair

Making sun-print of cutouts on construction paper

Room light-sensitive papers are conveniently used in ordinary room with a sunlamp or photoflood or with a gooseneck lamp.

deciding on exposure time you should make allowance by "overcompensating" the exposure/development. Also, remember to make all exposures with the shiny side up, for that is the light-sensitive surface.

Blueprint paper. Low cost and large size are the main attractions of this readily available architectural paper. It can be purchased in 24"–36" × 50' rolls for approximately 10¢ per square foot. And, as with printing-out paper, it is usable in ordinary room light. But it does have a relatively short shelf life and therefore should be protected from light and air when stored. Exposure is made with the blue side facing up, producing a white image on a blue background. Partial development occurs simultaneously with exposure to sunlight or to sunlamp or photoflood bulb #2 for 1–2 minutes. Full development—when the exposed areas turn bright blue—occurs after a few seconds of immersion in fixer, a solution of 8 parts of water to 1 part Clorox or 3% hydrogen peroxide. (A tip to the wise: Clorox seems to have a longer shelf life.) A few minutes in a rinse of plain water will prepare the print for drying. A large inexpensive tray for developing can be built from triple-thick corrugated cardboard (Tri-Wall) lined with mylar, or you can purchase inexpensive plastic trays. At home, of course, the bathtub can be used.

Repro-negative paper. This graphic arts paper reacts faster to light than do printing-out or blueprint papers, but it can nonetheless be used in the classroom under ordinary roomlight conditions. Turning off lights and pulling down shades temporarily will allow for even more organizing time. Precise exposure is determined through trial and error, depending on the amount and distance of the light source and on the paper being used. A 100-watt bulb is fine for most materials and can be easily controlled. The black-and-white (and intermediate greys) image produced by the paper requires the regular three-tray photographic development procedure: *developer, stop bath, and fixer.* The *developer* (Dektol and water) makes the image visible; the *stop bath* (28% acetic acid and water or plain water) stops the action of the developer; and the *fixer* (diluted solution of hypo-fixer) makes the image permanent even when exposed to additional light. All of these chemicals should be mixed at room temperature in accordance with their respective container instructions, and trays containing the mixed chemicals should be set out in processing order with a "name label" written in

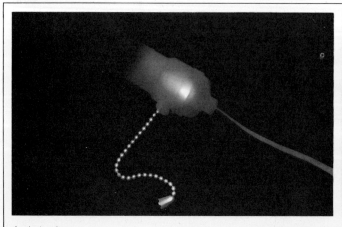

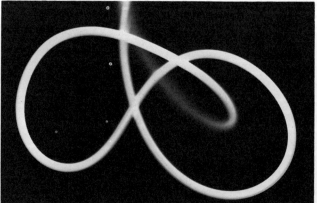

Artistic photograms made by older students: *left,* light-bulb/switch; *right,* light stream

front or painted on the bottom of each tray. Development time will vary according to the effect desired. Stop-bath immersion requires only 30 seconds, and fixing time is 5–10 minutes. After a wash of 30 minutes in plain water, prints are ready to be dried.

Regular Photographic Papers

This category of papers offers an extensive choice of color, texture, and contrast. The papers are usable mainly under darkroom (safelight) conditions, but development can be made in the printing-out fashion (exposed to sunlight or photoflood to produce the image) instead of with a liquid developer in the darkroom. The main problem is that exposure to light must be at least one hour. Even then the photogram is very light in tone and still requires a fixing solution and wash to make the image permanent.

Projection paper. Commonly known as enlarging paper, (such as Kodabromide or Agfa Brovira) is extremely sensitive to light. As a result it should be kept protected, even under safelight conditions, to prevent fogging. Average exposure to enlarger light is 2 seconds under a 100-watt bulb set 3 feet away.

Contact paper. Its common use is to make prints or contact sheets by being placed in direct contact with negatives. Because it is less sensitive than enlarging paper, using it under the enlarger is quite time consuming. Instead it should be exposed in the darkroom to a 100-watt bulb set 2 feet away for 5 seconds.

For the image to appear and remain permanent, both contact and projection papers need the same three-tray development and wash processing, as described above in the repro-negative paper section: 1) developer, 2) stop bath, 3) fixer.

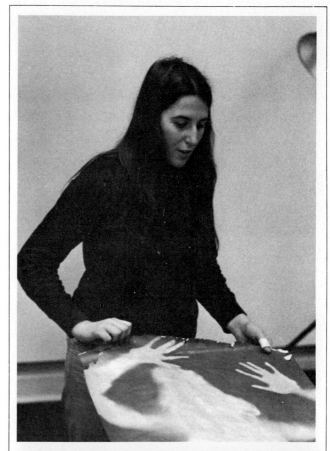

The preceding instructions are deceptively complex, but the actual processes are easy to master. In fact, your students will very quickly pick up the techniques and be ready for testing new ideas. The less sensitive papers offer the most leeway for experimentation. Objects can be moved to give a ghostlike shadow to all objects. Dimension and texture can be created by putting materials on top of each other. An interesting effect can be achieved by putting moving liquid in crumpled cellophane or in a plastic bag over the paper before exposure. And images on printing-out paper can be expanded through coloring in vegetable dye immediately after fixing. Good tone can be achieved by mixing 2 tablespoons of color to a quart of water. Color can also be added to repro-negative and regular printing papers with immersion in standard color toners (available in photo stores) after printing.

Photographic Painting

The rich possibilities of doing photography without a camera can be expanded still further to include a series of exercises in which light-sensitive paper is approached like a canvas. The technique in photographic painting is abstract rather than representational.

One method, using a pocket flashlight as a light source, allows for the creation of shapes and figures as light moves over the paper. Wherever the light hits, the paper turns dark after processing. The same effect can be produced by piercing a sheet of cardboard with a needle, holding it under the enlarger light and over the paper

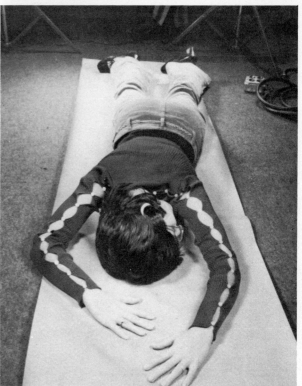

Making blueprint body prints—fun for all ages. To review: *expose* to sunlight or photoflood bulb; *develop* in water and 3% hydrogen peroxide; *rinse* in water and hang to dry.

Cutout photograms made by kindergarteners

Making photograms on photographic paper and repro-negative. To review: *arrange* objects on paper; *expose* to sunlight or artificial light; *develop* in Dektol and *stop bath; fix* in hypo solution; *rinse* and hang to dry.

which has been placed on the base of the enlarger. Evenly executed movement creates lines, while holding the card still results in circles and blobs. The best materials for both methods are contact or enlarging paper. Although they must be used in a darkroom, they are sufficiently sensitive to light so that you won't run the risk of overexposing. Since no part of the image will be visible until development, the act of creation itself is a mystery!

Another process has to do with using the photographic chemicals themselves to paint an image. The printing paper (in this case only the regular photographic papers work) gets an overall exposure from the room light. Selected parts of the paper are then painted with a brush that has been dipped in the chemical or toner, causing development of those parts. This procedure is the exact opposite of normal photogram making, when selected parts of the paper—those not covered by the design objects—are exposed to light and then the total product is developed. Corrugated cardboard, sponges, sneaker treads, swatches of corduroy, and Q-tips can be substituted for a brush. The choice of chemicals includes the following:

Black-and-white developer. This developer can be used in varying dilutions to produce different tones. The developer, however, should be limited to small areas at a time to increase control. In other words, after one corner of a drawing shows the desired effect, the worked corner should be dipped in stop bath so that the design doesn't develop any further. The design should be worked toward the center, with each successive portion submerged in the stop bath. After completion the whole painting is submerged in stop bath for 5 seconds, in fixer for 10 minutes, and is then rinsed in water for an hour. The paper may darken with exposure to light while being painted, but the unpainted background will turn light again after fixing.

Any number of effects are produced by dragging a string soaked with developer over the surface of the paper, by stamping the paper with objects dipped in developer, or by washing a solution of developer over areas already painted to give a wide range of greys. Another variation: overused developer will create a brown image on white, instead of the typical black-grey.

Fixer. The procedure with fixer is much the same as with the developer, but the results are exactly the opposite. Fixer will cause white images to appear against a dark background. Since development can't be stopped in stages, as in painting with developer, the entire design should be decided initially. After the paper has been painted with fixer, it is placed in developer until the desired image and tone appear. No stop bath is necessary, the next steps being fixing for 10 minutes and a water wash for an hour.

Color toner. The procedure with toner is parallel to that of black-and-white developer, but multi-colored designs on a white background are the result. Several types that work well on most contact and enlarging papers are FR Develochrome Direct Toning Developer, Edwal Color Toner, and Kodak Sepia Toner. After painting, the paper is dipped briefly in a tray of clear water, then fixed in color fixer for 3–5 minutes (regular black-and-white fixer has acid in it, and therefore destroys the effect of the dye), and washed in clear water for 5–15 minutes. Overwashing fades color.

Note: in all photogram processes except that with color toner, washing times can be considerably reduced through use of a Hypo Cleaning Agent. See manufacturer's instructions for procedure.

The specifics have been set out for you—dig in. Photography without a camera sets a free, imaginative tone for the introduction of the machine itself. Photograms emphasize how uncontrolled, initially unspecific information really works as an image. They also present a loose approach to the frame of an image, removing emphasis from a tight, restricted rectangular shape. The other aspect: photographic painting has a wonderful tendency of breaking down the mystique surrounding chemicals. All in all, herein the groundwork for the medium can be solidly laid.

THE PINHOLE CAMERA

We have dealt with the way light basically affects sensitized photo materials and with some of the beginning photographic processing steps that will show the results and make them permanent. Of course the creative control of photography doesn't stop at that point, and we are continuously provided with ever more sophisticated tools for that purpose. Putting such innovations in proper perspective, though, will give credit where credit is due—to the "camera obscura" and its rudimentary model the pinhole camera. While it has certain limitations, the pinhole approach provides a cheap, clear, and rapid method of confronting light, film, and the camera. And the marvelous bonus is that the process not only allows total personal involvement but also has enough spunk to produce real, live photographs that are innocently unique.

The Camera

The pinhole camera can be easily built in the classroom, media center, or home. Its basic form is any lightproof, cylindrical or rectangular box or can. Life is made simpler if you just find a well-constructed model with a deep fitting lid, such as Kodak's 4" X 5" film box, but the imagination can produce a wealth of cameras: a 2-lb. coffee can, a clean paint or vegetable shortening can, a cylindrical oatmeal box, a shoe box, etc.

To convert this basic form into a pinhole camera, you need only make a lens opening, a shutter, and a film holder (see figure 1). The materials required are, in addi-

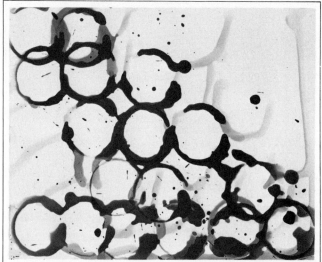

Child's photographic painting: writing with developer on photo paper. Chemical causes black and grey image against white background.

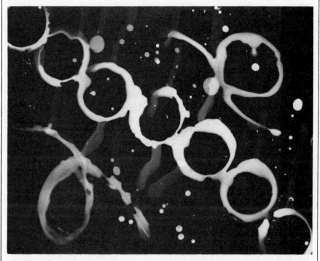

Child's photographic painting: writing with fixer on photo paper. Chemical causes white image against dark background.

Pinhole cameras can be made in many sizes and shapes, each creating its own effect.

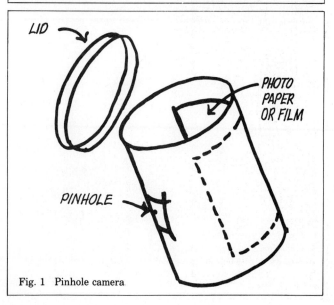

Fig. 1   Pinhole camera

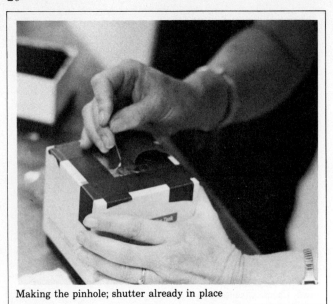

Making the pinhole; shutter already in place

4. To make the film holder, glue cardboard strips on the side opposite the pinhole. This allows the film or photographic paper to be slipped in and held securely in place. Tape, a simpler but less dependable holder, can also be used for each shot.

5. With all cutting and taping done, paint the inside of the box or can a flat black. The best paint is a "Kwik Dry" spray can, lacquer type, but india ink or poster paint will work too.

The Exposure

You can use regular film or photographic projection paper in your pinhole camera. Suggested materials are Kodak Royal Pan Sheet Film 4141, or Kodak Tri-X Pan Film in 120 or 620 size; and fast reacting papers such as Kodabromide F-#2 or Agfa Brovira-#2. To take your picture—that is, to expose the film—take the following steps:

1. Load the camera. If you are using regular film, you must load in total darkness (in a darkroom or in a light-tight closet); if you are using photographic paper, you can load under a safelight. Load the film or tape the paper inside the box directly across the pinhole, with dull side up for film and shiny side up for paper.

2. Close the camera lid, and cover the pinhole and all possible light leaks.

3. Leave the darkroom or safelight loading room and set up your shot. Point the camera at the subject. It is important that the camera remain still during exposure, so give the camera firm support on a steady surface. Tape, a lump of modeling clay underneath, or a heavy rock on top will minimize movement.

4. Lift the "shutter," allowing light to pass in for the alloted time so that it hits the photographic paper or film. Recommended exposures are:

tion to the box or can: tinfoil (or substitute), #10 sewing needle, black photographic tape, opaque paper, and black paint.

The procedure is as follows:

1. Make the "lens opening." It consists of a pinhole most simply formed by gently poking a hole with the very point of a #10 sewing needle into the center of a piece of heavy duty aluminum foil, or the backing paper from Kodak roll film (or other heavy black paper), or thin metal (like brass shim stock available in auto supply stores). It's important to make a clean, perfectly round hole. So for whatever substance you may be using, work on a resilient surface like soft wood or cardboard while "drilling" the hole.

2. Cut out a small square opening from one side of the can or box in that part of the can or box which is opposite to where the film will be ultimately placed. For most photographic effects the hole should be centered. For special effects, described later in this section, the hole can be placed off-center or less directly across from the photographic film. Fasten the "lens opening" with tape over the opening you cut out.

3. The "shutter" consists of a piece of black tape or opaque paper. Attach it above or near the pinhole and use it to cover the opening and to prevent light from entering the camera whenever light isn't desired.

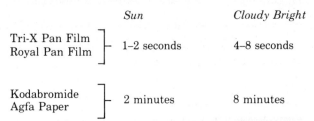

	Sun	*Cloudy Bright*
Tri-X Pan Film Royal Pan Film	1–2 seconds	4–8 seconds
Kodabromide Agfa Paper	2 minutes	8 minutes

These are approximate times, which vary according to the distance from the pinhole to paper or film, the sensitivity of paper or film, and the exact size of the pinhole. Much trial and error will bring more controlled results.

5. Cover the pinhole with the "shutter."

This page and opposite, setting up the shots, with pinhole camera firmly in place

The Processing

You are now ready to process your film:

1. Return with the camera to a light-controlled room, where your chemicals for processing have already been prepared in trays arranged step-by-step. Develop in the three-step process: 1) *developer* (Dektol)—process film according to manufacturer's instructions, process paper for 2 minutes; 2) *stop bath* (water) for 20 seconds minimum; and 3) *fixer* (hypo) for 5–10 minutes. Wash.

2. The printing should take place under safelight conditions. While the film negatives can be exposed to light by placing them in direct contact with paper or under an enlarger, the paper negatives should be printed only in the contact manner, using room light. The paper negatives can be printed dry or wet. In both cases place a piece of unexposed printing paper, emulsion to emulsion or shiny side to shiny side, under the negative. Make the exposure to a 100-watt bulb, 8" away for 3 seconds. When using a wet negative, soak the unexposed paper in water for 1–2 minutes and then place it under the wet negative with the excess water removed. Process the freshly exposed paper, both from the film and paper negatives, through the three-tray method of developer, stop bath, and fixer to make the positive image. The final water wash prepares it for drying.

Variations and Experiments

Not only is the pinhole a great way to explain the basic functionings of a camera, but it also demonstrates in a clear and visible way the basic principles of photography. The variables in pinhole photography are many, and so therefore are the possible problems: under- and over-processing in exposure and in development, fogging, rough or oversized pinholes that produce blurry images, film or paper movement resulting when the tape unsticks, and light leaks. But the rewards are worth the battle.

The pinhole excells as a medium for experimentation in photography and optical devices. Through experimentation and variations one gets a clue to the evolution of photography, and early camera problems become apparent. Below are some of the many variations you might try —but you can experiment with your own ideas too. Most of the materials can be found right around you. Others can be purchased relatively inexpensively. For further advice and materials and publications information you might write to Workshop for Learning Things (5 Bridge Street, Watertown, Mass. 02172), which offers, among other things, an Optical Building Kit containing a set of parts that can be used together in various ways. As a start, though, here are a few ideas for variations in photographic activities and experiments in optical devices:

1. Make multiple exposures by giving two or three exposures, each for one-half or one-third the alloted time, to the same piece of film or paper.

2. Produce interesting distortions with non-pinholes, such as narrow slits.

3. Get multiple images with several pinholes in different patterns.

4. Curve the film or paper around three sides to produce the fisheye or distortion image.

5. Use high contrast paper for a variety of stark, graphic effects.

6. Create homemade emulsions, such as gum bichromate or blueprint, and apply the emulsions to objects of unusual shapes and surfaces (such as the inside of a sliced rubber ball).

Student-made pinhole photos, curved for photographic effect

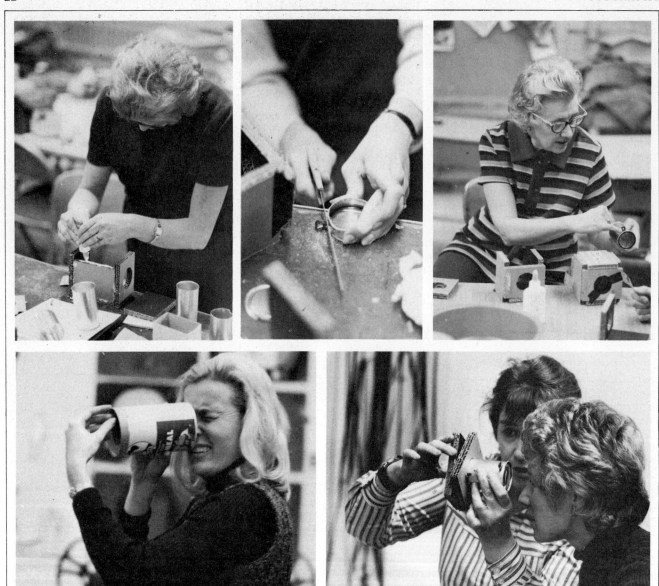

A little manipulation and such cheap materials as magnifying lenses, reflectors, cardboard, boxes, cans, and glue transform pinhole cameras into optical devices.

Then expose the treated object as you would photographic paper.

7. Do self-portraits. Vary the shots and exposures, etc., to make a "statement."

8. Halfway through exposures, add a new object to the scene or take something away. This leads to "ghostlike" images.

9. Rephotograph the negative image. This step will magically produce a positive and can lead to interesting collage ideas.

10. Vary the size of the subject matter by using different sized boxes with the same camera-to-subject distance. The basic box, which has a distance from the pinhole to the opposite end that is equal to the diagonal of the picture format (this distance in a 4" × 5" camera would be 5–6 inches), gives a normal rendering; a flat box creates a wide angle look; a long box produces a telephoto effect; a coffee can or a cylindrical box produces the fisheye. The cylindrical box, especially the Quaker Oats box, is particularly manageable. Not only does

it come in two standard sizes—the 18-oz. size for use with 5" × 7" paper and the 42-oz. for 8" × 10" paper—but it also can produce two distinct images: a pinhole placed on the round side of the box gives a wide angle photo, while an opening on the end of the box will create a telephoto effect.

11. Create distortions with reflectors such as Christmas tree balls or other convex materials.

12. Experiment with the "camera obscura"—transform an entire room to a pinhole camera photographing the scene viewed from the window.

13. Transform the pinhole camera into a slide or filmstrip viewer. This is accomplished simply as follows: replace the pinhole with an empty frozen fruit juice can equipped with a plastic lens (magnifying glass) on one end; on the side opposite the lens cut out a space to serve as a holder for a slide or filmstrip; attach the slide or strip with rubber bands. Lift the box to your eye and look through the lens to the image that is being enlarged by the lens and illuminated when the box is

held up to a window or other light source. Exact focus will require some manipulation of the assembled parts and pieces.

14. For another camera, take your box with the lens (magnifying glass) mounted in the end of the juice can. Put a piece of mirror mylar (glued onto a piece of cardboard so it lies flat) inside the box at a 45 degree angle so that when you look down through a hole covered with tracing paper (or other translucent material) the mirror will reflect the image from the lens onto the viewing surface. (Keep fiddling until it works.) The camera is now usable for viewing, but to take a picture you must make some additional adjustments: photographic paper, lens cap to keep light from hitting the paper before you are ready to take the picture, adjustable lens opening so you can vary the amount of light that will be able to enter, etc. You can make a twin lens camera—one for viewing and one for taking the picture—by putting one box on top of another.

15. With further experimentation, convert the pinhole camera to a kaleidoscope or light box. For any optical device, including the filmstrip viewer, it is recommended that the inside of the box or can be painted with a dull, flat black finish to decrease reflecting light rays.

SLIDE MAKING WITHOUT A CAMERA

Putting aside the need for a camera for the moment, let us consider the process of slides making without a camera. It can be simple and it produces quick yet imaginative results. An entire world of materials and creative tools is readily available.

Slide Surfaces and Design Materials

The choice of the slide surface itself is quite flexible, but all selections have one specific quality—*the ability to allow the passage of light.* All of the following fill the bill with varying degrees of usefulness: cellophane, plastic wrap or bags, wax paper, Scotch tape, glassene or tracing paper, netting, clear or colored acetate, plexiglass, 35mm clear or opaque film leader, filmstrip material (like U-film), and discarded slides, negatives, filmstrips, and 35mm movies.

Each type of slide surface can be adorned with a variety of design materials:

Household items are the most inexpensive and accessible. Practical materials abound, such as plastic wrap and bags, wax paper, Scotch tape, netting. A variety of other basic design materials can also be used: cotton balls, yarn,

Discarded negatives make excellent slide materials for cameraless photographic experiences.

thread, feathers, hair, grain, leaves, small flowers, salt and sugar crystals. These materials can be put between two pieces of the base material or glued to it. They offer exciting collage ideas that can be mounted and viewed as slides.

Sturdier substances—acetate, plexiglass, and clear film leader—have surfaces allowing greater control. Any *opaque* or *translucent markers* can be used to add content to these transparent bases, such as crayons, some inks, Magic Markers, stamp markers, grease pencils, and stick-on imagery.

Easily applied *stick-ons* are instant lettering, or letrasets. These are commercially available letters, numbers, symbols and pictures that are transferred from their papers to the slides by a gentle rubbing action. Lettering kits can be found in many styles and sizes in most art supply and stationery stores, and come in sheets selling for about $3 each.

Crystallizing paint (a paint which crystallizes as it dries) and *glass paint* can be applied in many ways—painted on, dropped with an eye dropper, made thinner with water—and they, too, are commercially available. Crystallizing paint comes in some dozen different colors in two-ounce bottles. They can be purchased (from Edmund Scientific Co., 607 Edscorp Bldg., Barrington, N.J.) for about $5 per six-bottle set. Glass paints are readily found in one-ounce and two-ounce jars in most art supply or hobby shops, as well as from Edmund Scientific Co. and

Inexpensive but functional cameras and slide and filmstrip viewers can be made out of cardboard, rubber bands, and some ingenuity.

other mail order companies. Prices vary according to manufacturer, but they are relatively inexpensive, generally less than a dollar per ounce.

Chartpak pressure sensitive tapes adhere to most surfaces used in slides. They are available in plain transparent colors and in patterns and stripes. Found in many art and drafting supply stores, they vary in price according to size (width) and pattern selected. A reel of transparent tape measuring ¼" thick and 324" long sells for about $1.

U-film filmstrip material comes in 25- and 100-foot rolls (from Hudson Photographic Industries, Irvington on Hudson, N.Y.) which are treated so that they can be marked and then be erased and reused. They can be written on with just about anything—pencil, crayon, grease pen, etc. They can be cut up and are then used in the iron/glue-together slide mounts.

With *35mm clear film leader* two added advantages are apparent: designs can be done side-by-side for easy comparison; and framing decisions are introduced. With unlimited horizontal space available, the slide maker has a choice about keeping the image within the 35mm rectangle frame or cutting it off. This decision must be confronted every time the camera viewfinder is put to the eye, and so this early exercise in framing can prompt thought about what's going on outside of the frame.

Those materials with an emulsion (again, that thin coating of a material that reacts to light)—opaque film leader; discarded slides, negatives, film, and filmstrips—lend themselves more to a taking-away process rather than a putting-on process. Using scissors, straight pins, X-acto knives or any sharp, pointed object on the emulsion side of the film, the slide maker scratches imagery onto the opaque surfaces. If desired, the scratched areas can then be colored or tinted with a translucent marker. Discarded film and slides are great for abstraction and fantasy. Removing portions of the already processed pictures by scratching, punching in holes, bleaching out sections with cotton swabs and household bleach can give an entirely new look to an image. Bleaching or scratching color film and slides is particularly exciting since revealing varied layers of color results in fun distortions and color combinations. Another idea: two frames or negatives can be put in the same mount for superimposition (an exercise in double exposure).

Transparent contact paper merits singling out here. It can be used in its own special activity. The procedure is as follows: A specific image is selected from a magazine or brochure. The image and the contact paper both are cut in 2" squares. The paper backing is peeled from the transparent contact sheet, and the magazine image is pressed face down on the sticky surface. The two are rubbed together to remove air bubbles, and the "sandwich" is then soaked in water for two minutes. The softened wet paper is then peeled away, and the white residue is sponged off. The magazine image becomes an integral part of the contact paper and can be mounted in most of the ways described below. For variety several images can be combined in one mount to give the superimposition effect. The exercise also provides an outside learning experience: the thousands of dots comprising a magazine image will be magnified upon enlargment and give insight into how newspaper and magazine photos are actually made.

Slide Mounts

The slide mount or holder, like the slide surface, also involves a choice. Most types come in either 35mm or superslide size. Both sizes have outside edges measuring 2" square, allowing them to fit into most standard slide projectors. The superslide offers increased working space with an inside area that is 1½" square, compared to the 35mm with its inside areas of 1" X 1½".

Iron/glue-together mounts. These mounts are made of cardboard sealed together with glue or the heat of an iron. They come in many different sizes and prices, depending on the manufacturer, yet are the least expensive choice and remain adaptable to almost all of the materials discussed above.

Slip-in mounts. These are plastic slide holders which have three closed sides and an open fourth side that allows for insertion of materials.

Snap-shut binders. These mounts offer a plastic enclosed area that is sturdy and large enough to give free reign to the imagination. Not only will dry substances like flowers, leaves, lace, insects, coffee grounds, and other small treasures be given a frame, but materials that are sticky or liquidy can also be confined. For examples, oil, whipped cream, shampoo, food coloring, and water do exotic things when affected by the heat of a projector. A workable substitute for the snap-shut binder is clear slides bound carefully together with masking tape, but very wet substances inside must be avoided.

Kodak Ektagraphic write-on slides. This type comes only in the superslide size and can be designed with almost all markers, including pen and pencil.

Plexiglass mounts. These can be found ready-made in 2" squares but are that way the most expensive choice, costing 10¢ each. With the proper saw, however, larger sheets of plexiglass 1/16" thick can be cut to size, also cutting the cost! They are very versatile, able to handle rough scratching and doodling, painting with glass stain, drawing with crayons or grease pencils, and cutting and pasting to the heart's delight.

Although this outline groups certain materials together, the mixing and matching can go on forever. Let your own inclination be your guide, but keep this suggestion in mind: Your plan of attack can be most clearly made by focusing on one type or group of materials. Especially in the case of young students, a wide open choice leads to confusion, whereas focusing energy on smaller concerns will prompt more complete attention. Whatever the specific choices, the gains go much farther than the artistic product. Concepts such as magnification, transparency, color mixing, and elements of design become clear. But the main objective is creative expression, unencumbered by inhibiting materials and equipment. Interaction with these "close to home" objects and forms paves the way for the camera. It frees up sensory response to texture, shape, and abstraction that will later find clear expression through the camera and film.

SLIDE/TAPE MAKING

With such a wealth of imagery prepared in slide form, you're already equipped with raw material for slide/tape

Slide making without a camera is simple and produces quick, imaginative results.

making. The out-of-camera slides can become a unit by themselves or can be creatively combined with slides made with a camera. Arranged in a previsualized sequence and set to a carefully chosen sound track, the slides provide the base for creative media mixing.

The majority of slide series are made with cameras that take 35mm or 126 film. Both color and black-and-white can be used, since Kodak makes a negative/positive developing kit that will process Kodak Panatomic X film into slide form. With the camera and film chosen, some major decision-making comes next. A topic or theme for slide taking and collecting must be chosen. In some cases a strongly favored piece of music or sound track may prompt the topic but, more commonly, the visuals are dealt with first. The possibilities are as varied as the people creating. Main categories include:

1. Giving information or describing a skill—the "how to" genre such as glassblowing, potterymaking, breadbaking.
2. Creating a mood through personalized portraits or exploring nature and the seasons.
3. Telling a story—"a day in the life," the path of an exotic or local trip.
4. Connecting imagery through design by grouping shapes, textures, tones, patterns, moods.

Enough time should be set aside to produce a large selection of images from which to choose and for reshooting pictures that are disappointing. In fact, advising students to take more than one shot of the same subject when unsure of light and framing is a good idea. To avoid holes or gaps in the ultimate sequence, a content outline should be made before shooting. This reduces wasted time, energy, and film; the result is a tighter series.

Once the images are amassed each student turns into a combination director/editor. The creative process has just begun. Working with a sort of storyboarding approach to the slides will put them in an order that creates a smooth connection from one to another. (See section on storyboarding in Chapters 6 and 7). Placing all slides on a light box or area illuminated from below makes editing easier. Unfortunately, artists become quickly attached to their art so that elimination is difficult. But all repetitive and irrelevant images must be weeded out to add a more engrossing feeling to the sequence. At this point, the sound track can be given more specific consideration. Music, voice, and sound effects can be combined, depending on the outcome desired. Juggling both the visual and audio segments by adding or subtracting a slide, changing the pacing of the slides, and increasing or reducing the sound track will result in a neatly synchronized show. A finishing touch to the presentation comes in the form of titling and crediting. This can be done by hand writing on clear slides or photographing with a close-up lens and a copy stand.

Presentation of the slide/tape sequence is the final step. As for the slide projector itself, one that is designed to handle slides in bulk is the best choice. Most types can take adaptors for attaching carousels and other slide changing units, so there shouldn't be much problem. Unfortunately, parts made by one company are not usually compatible with those of another, so consider the purchase of new equipment carefully. Some new projects have built-in fade devices which dissolve one slide into another; some are also equipped with a variety of lenses. This feature fills the need for physically moving the pro-

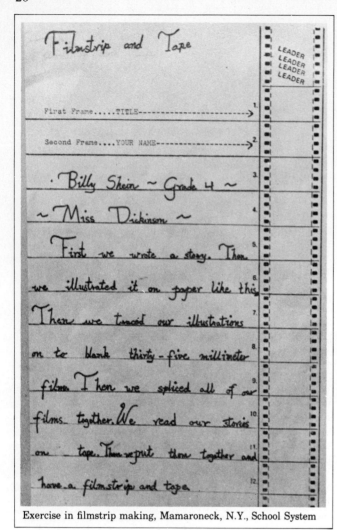

Exercise in filmstrip making, Mamaroneck, N.Y., School System

Script for filmstrip and tape by fourth grader, Mamaroneck, N.Y.

jector back and forth to achieve the desired image size. The ultimate "extra" device is a master console ($50 or so) which will work with two or more separate projectors and permit fancy maneuvering such as timed dissolves, superimpositions, and very subtle overlaps. There are some simple special visual effects to try. Consider irregular spacing of the images, partial masking or covering of slides to create size changes, interspersing of blank or

black slides among the others, projection on textured or curved surfaces or on the ceiling, and creating silhouettes on certain images by obstructing light from the projection.

As for the sound track, a precisely timed tape that has been recorded with the pacing of the slide sequence in mind will work beautifully. Of course, souped-up equipment can add an extra element of control. An automatic

DIRECTIONS FOR MAKING A FILMSTRIP PROJECTOR

George Langenauer, a sixth grade teacher from Mamaroneck, New York, drew up directions for making a filmstrip projector for his class. The directions are given below and should be read in their entirety before you try.

Equipment:
6 pieces of cardboard 4 in. × 3 in.
glue
hole cutter
saw
small cardboard can
magnifying glass
2 rubber bands

Steps:
1. Check to see that you have all the required equipment.
2. On the brown side of the cardboard, number each piece 1,2,3,4,5,6; on each piece, label the corners:

3. Saw can 2 inches from the metal rim.
4. Cut slit in cardboard near rim.
5. Place handle of magnifying glass into slit and ease magnifying glass until flat against metal rim.

slide/tape programming unit allows the preprogramming of a tape with an inaudible signal. This sets off a relay that causes a slide change at the proper moment.

But the show must go on. And with or without fancy side effects, the media mix can be a smash. Just be certain to allow time at the end of the presentations for contemplation and discussion. Allow for going beyond the creation of the individual images to consideration of the whole and how the parts work to give it strong impact. Discussion can personalize the whole process through input by the photographers and feedback from their classmates. Good topics to consider are: Does the choice of sound track enhance the visuals and vice-versa? Is the pacing smooth? How well does the total visual sequence work? Do any particular juxtapositions stand out? Do the special effects used work as an integral part of the whole?

Filmstrips

Filmstrips, a series of drawings or photographs on a strip of 35mm film arranged in a specific order, fall into the same category as slide sequences. They offer a practical medium, especially since most schools have filmstrip projectors on hand, or they can even be made by teachers or students themselves by altering the pinhole camera. As already mentioned previously, filmstrips can be quite simply made by marking on clear film. Such cameraless filmstrips provide a free, uninhibited experience allowing mistakes to be easily corrected and the order of frames to be changed by erasing or by cutting and splicing.

Introducing a camera into the matter adds a more complex element. In a filmstrip created on a single roll of film with camera photography, the order of frames is permanent. Total thought and planning must therefore be done before the shooting. This procedure forces greater consideration of each subject as it is approached with the camera and requires a determination of what each image should add to a sequence. Contrary to its unplanned use in individual slidemaking, the camera in this case functions to make physical connections between the individual images.

There are some obstacles to consider in making photographic filmstrips: it requires special "half frame" 35mm cameras which use regular 35mm film but produce 72 pictures on a 36-exposure roll; the cameras must be used in the same position for every shot so that all images are

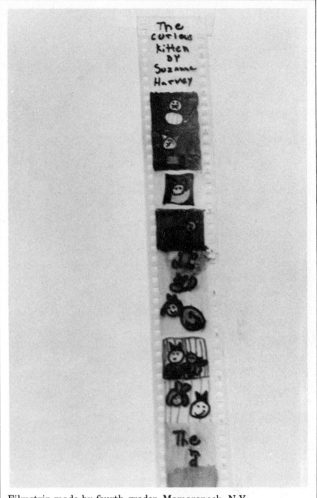

Filmstrip made by fourth grader, Mamaroneck, N.Y.

right side up in the resulting filmstrip; and special processing that returns the film uncut and unmounted must be used.

Nonetheless, filmstrips do deserve consideration for they are compact, easily handled, and always in proper sequence. Their presentation can parallel that of slide/tape shows once the film has been shot. The only difference is that remaining decisions deal only with the accom-

---

6. Cut one hole in the center of piece 5 and piece 6.
7. Put 2 rubber bands on piece 5. One should be around points A B and one around points C D.
8. Cut one circle in half and glue on brown side of 5— one inch apart on circle hole.
9. Take side 6 and magnifying glass in can. Put sawed edge side into black side of cardboard.
10. Place piece 1 with black side up on the desk in front of you with points A D facing you and B C away from you.
11. Place piece 2 with black side to the right and side of B C of 2 standing on side C D of 1. Glue in place.
12. Place piece 3 with black side to the left and side B C of 3 standing on side A B of 1. Glue in place.
13. Place piece 6 with magnifying glass inserted on B C of 1. Make certain black side of 6 is facing you and that A B of 6 is at B C of 1. Glue in place.
14. Place piece 5 with black side away from you at side A D of 1. Make sure side D C of 5 is at A D of 1. Glue in place.
15. Place piece 4 with black side down on top. Make sure A D is facing you and B C is away. Glue in place.

panying sound track, since all visual choices have already been made.

An excellent way to prepare students for cameramade filmstrips is an exercise in sound filmstrip making. It involves both story plotting and frame sequencing—composing or writing out the narrative, drawing the narrative in a strip of frames, and then transposing the drafted sequence of frames onto clear leader. This exercise is fun even if you don't proceed to cameramade filmstrips, and it can be used also as a warm-up for animated filmmaking.

CAMERA PHOTOGRAPHY

Now, to introduce the guest of honor, the ready-made camera itself. It appears in a variety of sizes—miniature to large format view camera; in various constructions—plastic, wood, and metal; and in varying degrees of sophistication—from the plastic one-dollar model to the instant image camera, producing a photograph in 30 seconds. Here's a sketchy description of the general categories:

The Camera

The Plastic Camera. Produced in Hong Kong under a variety of brand names (such as Arrow, Diana, Panax, Rover, Sec, and Windsor), this small camera can be purchased for a $1.50 or less in discount stores or mail ordered from various distribution centers. It takes 120 or

620 film and offers a surprising level of technical control, including a choice of three different lens openings and the capability of focus from three different distances. There are some characteristics basic to the camera that might be considered problematic: it has a parallax limitation, i.e., you don't get exactly what you see; there is a 4–5 foot limit on distance between camera and subject; low light conditions require the use of a flash or other outside light source; the subject must be relatively still to prevent blur, since there is no way to control the speed at which the shutter opens and closes; and the minimal plastic construction often results in a short life and in light leaks. An open mind can accommodate most of these factors and, in fact, put the camera's simplicity to creative use. Multiple exposure—the shooting of two or more pictures on the same piece of film—is not possible with more complicated equipment (a safety feature for photographers who forget to advance film). Here it can be easily used to achieve interesting special effects: "motion" will emerge by the repeated exposure of the same subject on the same frame, with a slight change of the subject's position—make sure to reduce the amount of light, depending on the number of exposures given; images can be overlapped between frames by only partially advancing the film after an exposure and then reshooting; strange juxtapositions can be produced by masking off a portion of the lens, shooting, then masking off the opposite part of the lens and shooting another subject, all on the same frame. In addition, the soft focus of the unsophisticated plastic lens offers an imaginative path for dream-like expression.

The Old Time Box Camera. More commonly known as *the box Brownie* (developed by Kodak but subsequently produced by Ansco, Argus, Agfa), the box camera can be found in almost every attic or closet, or scavenged for a few dollars in local flea markets. Quite often it can be found in very good working condition. Equipped with readily available 620 film, it can be inexpensively used as a standardized classroom camera. The box in this form does share many of the problems with the plastic camera: parallax limitation, inability to stop movement, restricted proximity to subject, inadequacy in low light. In addition, it offers no means of varying lens opening and focus, as does the plastic model. But it does have a construction that is relatively durable and less prone to consistent light leaks. And once the limitations are accepted, it can be used for the same exploration of multiple exposures, the

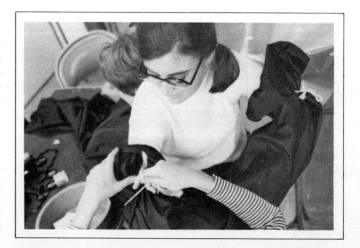

sliding of images between frames, and the soft focus described above.

PROCEDURE. An extra advantage of both the "box Brownie" and the plastic camera is that they can be used to demonstrate the entire photographic process WITHOUT A DARKROOM. Also, because they use more than a miniature format, with resulting negatives of at least 2¼" × 2¼", there is no need for an enlarger to make the pictures clearly visible. The simplest procedure is as follows:

1. Expose the film (that is, snap the pictures), rewind the film, and remove the exposed film from the camera.

2. Set up the chemicals for development in the three-tray procedure learned previously: *developer* (Dektol to make 1 gallon), which reveals the photographic images by making changes on those parts of the film that have been struck by light; *stop bath* (water or 28% acetic acid), which stops continued development; and *hypo-fixer* (to make 2 gallons), which gives permanence to the image on the negative by preventing further changes on the film. (Again, see manufacturer's instructions for mixing details.) For younger children, we suggest a set of five pails and absorbent trays under them to prevent messiness. The pails should be easily washable plastic to hold the developing liquids: 1) water; 2) developer; 3) water; 4) fixer; 5) water. The absorbent trays can be 14" × 18" cardboard trays lined with mylar, or cafeteria trays, although sometimes using just newpapers to absorb splashes may do.

3. Change the film: insert your hands, the rewound exposed film, and a *developing tank* into a *changing bag*. The changing bag is your instant darkroom—it is made of dense, light-proof black cloth, which is tied around the arms. The developing tank is a plastic box cleverly made so that you can pour the developing liquids in and out without letting in any light. Unload the film into the light-tight developing tank, cover the lid, and remove the tank from the changing bag.

4. Develop the film by the three-steps outlined above, rinsing the film in water before development and washing it again afterwards.

5. Wipe the excess water from the film with a sponge and hang the film to dry on a filmdrying line of twine just like you would laundry. For clips use wooden spring-loaded clothespins. Weight the handing roll down with a clothespin clipped to the bottom.

6. With the dry film and one of the printing papers usable in normal roomlight or sunlight (studio proof, blueprint, or repro-negative paper—described previously in the photogram section), make contact prints. To do this, place the negative emulsion side (dull or matte finish) down on the paper, which,

Directions for working with developing tank should be clearly visible, and chemicals already set up in processing order.

in turn, is placed emulsion side (shiny finish) up. Cover both of these with glass, making a tight sandwich. Expose the combination to an outside light source, the length of exposure depending on the strength and distance of the light source, the type of paper being used, and the density or degree of transparency of the negative. Develop and/or fix, depending on the paper (again, review the photogram section for details).

The resulting images are small but provide an exciting end product that satisfies creative energy. And the process can't be beat for use with large groups and limited darkroom space.

The Cartridge Loading "Instamatic." Often provoking a scornful response, the *instamatic* nevertheless can be a real boon to classroom photography. Its disadvantages are like those of the box and plastic cameras mentioned above: fixed focus, parallax limitation, no shutter or light control. But once these are accomodated, the positive factors stress the instamatic's manageability. Available for less than $15, this rugged, compact model allows for carefree handling and can be found in most households. The factory loaded film cassettes, filled with 110 or 126 film, are simply dropped into the camera, eliminating worry about unthreaded film. The small format of the film, a bit smaller than 35mm, precludes the out-of-the-darkroom use. But black-and-white film can be processed with the same equipment used for 35mm development. And color slides via the cartridge camera are compatible with all slide projectors and viewers.

Opposite page, the change bag—an instant darkroom. A fellow student ties and unties the bag for the other to unload the film into the developing tank.

Left, the developing tank—a plastic box into which you put your film for developing. It is cleverly made so that the developing liquids can be poured in and out without letting in light.

It should be mentioned that cartridge cameras come in models with relatively good lenses and with manual control of focus, shutter, and lens opening. But these types class themselves out of most school budgets.

The Instant Image Maker. Originally Polaroid's baby but now also offered by Kodak, the instant camera can be considered inexpensive. While the camera itself can be purchased for less than $20, the film is, unfortunately, very expensive and somewhat messy. Another problem is that getting a negative for reprints of the original pictures requires special film and an extra attachment. It should also be noted that the camera parts and technical photographic process become secondary in using this convenient procedure. But the instant image offers an incomparable advantage: the immediacy of the photograph not only holds attention but it also maintains relevancy. Discussion of the picture can therefore be quickly connected to the picture-taking experience. The relationship between the photographer's intention and what the picture actually reveals—composition, framing, subject matter—is not lost, as so often happens in those other processes when large time intervals are involved between shooting the film and developing prints.

The Adjustable Camera. Generally this camera falls into another price category, the least expensive starting around $50. But the picture-taking boom has significantly affected consumers, and this more sophisticated machine seems to be finding its place in homes nearly as much as the TV set. There are hundreds of different models, and these can be divided into four categories according to the viewing system used:

1. VIEWFINDER OR RANGEFINDER. This is an eye level camera with a peephole for viewing that does not go through the lens. In its crude form (the plastic and cartridge cameras are the most primitive examples), the parallax problem occurs—the image seen only approxi-

mates what the picture will be since the viewfinder is several inches to the left of the lens. The more sophisticated rangefinder models hook up to the lens for accurate focusing and framing. In all cases, this type of camera is particularly useful in low light (viewing systems that go through the lens don't provide as bright an image), and it has the added advantage of a quiet shutter mechanism.

2. THE SINGLE LENS REFLEX (SLR). Since the viewing system of this type functions through the lens, it provides the best means of seeing exactly what the camera will produce. This advantage is made possible by a system of mirrors and prisms. Hand in hand with this feature, though, are the disadvantages of a through the lens/mirror system: the moving mirror creates noise as it falls to allow passage of the light, and visibility is reduced because of the long path of the light—it passes through the lens, bounces off the mirror, and passes through a viewing screen and a prism before reaching the viewer. Again, the good with the bad: the complexity of the SLR produces clear precise pictures, but it necessarily has a heavier, less compact form which is more likely to break down than that of a rangefinder. Nevertheless the SLR, available in sizes to accomodate both 35mm and roll film such as 120, has become the most widely used form for candid photography.

3. THE VIEW CAMERA. Offering a cumbersome, intricate system of photography that is not conducive to most classroom work, this type nevertheless merits mention both historically and technically. It offers the oldest and most direct viewing system: the light passes through the lens in front and hits the ground glass viewing screen behind it; the lens and ground glass are attached in an accordion fashion, focusing achieved by moving the lens back and forth. The advantages are appealing: the large negative size, ranging from 4" × 5" to 11" × 14", allows detailed viewing and produces a high quality image; its through-the-lens viewing eliminates parallax error; and the ad-

Setups for processing without a darkroom: 5 pails or buckets, absorbent trays or newspapers, processing chemicals. In the photo on the right, the setup is in an improvised closet which serves also as a darkroom (note enlarger in background).

justable film plane and lens correct focus and distortion problems. But average camera use is burdened by these disadvantages: the bulkiness of the camera necessitates the use of a tripod; a dark cloth must be draped over the back of the camera so that the image can be viewed; the image appears on the viewing screen upside down and backwards, requiring a practised eye; the film comes in sheets which must be loaded individually by the photographer. The result, then, is that candid photography in uncontrolled light situations must be sacrificed for high quality pictures.

4. TWIN LENS REFLEX. This category is treated last since it embodies characteristics, both good and bad, of the three previous types. The viewing system, particularly, combines all three varieties. As with the view camera, there is a flat ground glass that allows for careful composing. The viewing system, similar to that of the rangefinder, is separate from the camera lens and results in parallax error, but the similarity stops here: as the name indicates, the twin lens camera has two lenses, one for viewing and one for the exposure of the film (see figure 2). The two lenses are coupled mechanically for easy focusing. Like that of the SLR, the viewing lens uses a mirror to reflect the image to the viewer. But since there is a separate lens for shooting and the passage of light, it is not necessary for this matter to move out of the way when exposure is being made. Therefore a more simple, rugged, and quiet construction distinguishes the twin lens reflex from the SLR.

Similarities to other camera types include: a relatively large format (roll film of 120 or 220 yields a 2¼" × 2¼"

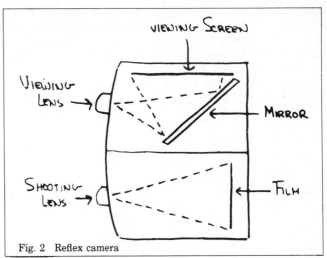

Fig. 2   Reflex camera

negative) which allows for quality enlargement like the view camera but necessitates a more cumbersome form; and the absence of an interchangeable lens, a drawback also basic to most rangefinders.

Camera Activities

A simple and general approach to all varieties of cameras, regardless of degree of complexity, is the best method of introduction. Start with those basic characteristics all cameras share. Such tasks as film loading and advancing and shutter releasing are easy for students to master, and this ease of basic operation builds a critical foundation of self-confidence and competence in the beginning photog-

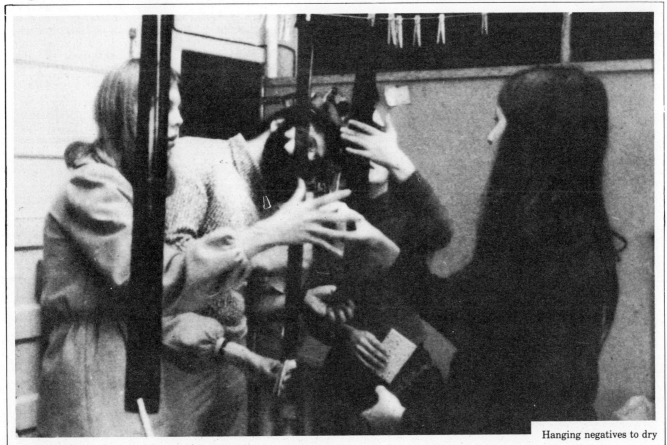

Hanging negatives to dry

rapher. Once students feel comfortable handling their cameras, they can be initiated into more complex manipulations and theory. Try using a pre-set format at first: all cameras can be converted into "instamatics" by setting the focus on infinity, the shutter speed at 1/60–1/125 of a second, and the aperture at F16–F11, depending on the light (film instruction will advise). This approach allows students to concentrate on planning and composing their first shots without care for camera setting.

The following ideas, games, and activities are designed to supplement your own bag of tricks. Try not to use these as strict rules or as assignments but more as guides for a focus. This approach will encourage students to be the source of their own work and to develop their own working vocabularies. Except for the two main categories, the suggestions assume no preconceived order. Feel your own way—some students get itchy fingers more quickly than others.

Pre-camera Warmups

1. In slide or picture form, show a series of ten or more different images of the same object (tree, chair, book, horse, hand, etc.). Discuss the characteristics of each shot. This helps to de-emphasize word labels, focusing instead on sensory perception of shape, texture, size, mood, and gesture. Common objects can be experienced beyond regard for their identity and function.

2. Confront word labeling further with this exercise: blindfold students and, with the suggestion that they "get into their hands," have them identify objects through visual/tactile associations. Things such as fabrics, liquids, and grains can be experienced in terms of space, temperature, texture, size, smell, and shape.

3. Explore the tendency to interpret quickly with only partial information. Look at fragments and abstract shapes and lines, citing as many relationships and definitions as possible. Discuss ambiguous photographs. Hide three-fourths of an image and have the class guess what's going on; encourage jumping to conclusions.

4. To expand attention and observational skills, have students:

a. Look at a slide, scan it for a minute, turn off the projector and try to describe the slide completely.
b. Look at a slide for five minutes, as if it will never be seen again, turn off the projector, talk casually for five minutes, turn the projector back on, discuss the surprises and changes noted.
c. Look at a group of five to ten related images, placed next to each other, for five minutes; then look away and try to remember as much about each as possible or recall how they relate or differ.
d. Use twenty or more adjectives to describe one object.
e. Stay in a small space for a few minutes, observe it, walk away and try to remember it in detail.
f. View a room for five minutes, leave the room while it is rearranged, return, and try to notice changes.
g. Look at a partner for one minute, turn away while several physical changes are made, try to observe the changes. Reverse roles.
h. Listen to a partner tell personal information in one minute and try to do an instant replay. Reverse roles.
i. Using an empty slide mount, spend a half hour making potential pictures by holding it up to the eye and "framing" the world.

j. Shut eyes for thirty seconds and, in a click-click fashion, open and shut them. Describe the image seen and "recorded." Was it ordered? Did it have any meaning? This exercise transfers a sense of the camera process to the body, showing that each shot is a quick record of the instant.
k. Direct attention to shape, form, and tone and their interaction by looking at images through a reducing glass or an unfocused projector (both of these abstract content into shape and tone). Cut paper of different tones into abstract shapes and arrange the pieces in different patterns.

With Camera in Hand

1. Suggest that the first few rolls be shot with a sensitivity to line and shape and their interaction, rather than with strict attention to controlling technique. The camera can even be used initially with tape over the eyepiece, de-emphasizing precise, specific image making and loosening up the whole picture taking experience. Advise students to let the camera find its own place, without too much thought behind it.

2. Encourage students to shoot more than one frame of the same scene or object. The second shot usually offers better *composition* in terms of where to place the camera (camera angle) and when to release the shutter (arrangement of subjects within the frame). Multiple shots also provide for experience in selection and editing.

3. Deal with the frame itself as relevant but not rigid. Suggest that it acts to cut out a slice of life but not to confine the subject. Many successful images reveal parts or fragments at their edges, directing the energy and interest of the viewer outside the frame to the surrounding activity.

4. To explore framing possibilities, make Xerographic or other reproductive copies of the same photograph and give several to each student. The students cut or mark new borders, indicating new framing choices. Or the photograph can be cut into many pictures, showing that each image has the potential for other shots within it, including *zoom* shots and *edited* shots.

5. With framing still in mind, point out the validity of taking photographs in which the subject is less important than the relationship of the objects within the frame. The position of the objects in the rectangle can become the subject matter itself (again, *composition*). Taking a "step back" from the information allows patterns and their interaction to emerge.

6. Study the effect of animate beings within a photograph and the difficulty in taking emphasis away from them.

Turn mistakes into a learning experience. Here an accidental multiple exposure on 120 film made a fantastic neighborhood montage.

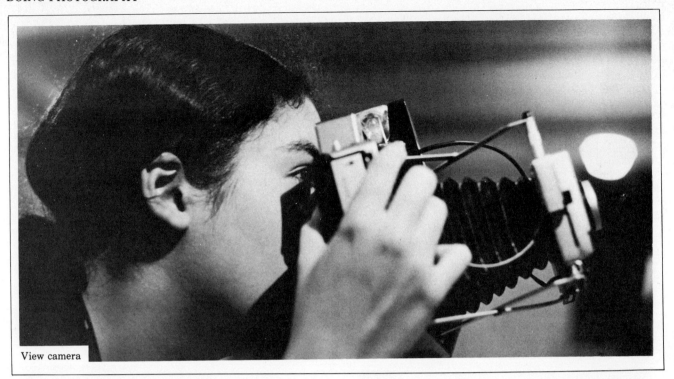

View camera

7. Take advantage of *light* and its many "faces" to instigate discovery and activity:

    a. How many different ways can the same scene or object be lighted?
    b. How do different seasons of the year and hours of the day show light in distinct ways?
    c. How differently does light function as background, side element, source underneath?
    d. How is light affected by objects partially blocking its passage?
    e. What is the difference between light as subject and as illuminator?
    f. Study photos or slides which reveal the varying moods and degrees light can assume: e.g., warm, cold, strong, diffused, clear.
    g. In what ways does the tension between light and dark appear?

8. *Portraiture* in general can be a provocative topic. Students can learn much about themselves and each other by creating self-portraits and taking photos of their classmates. It will become clear that people show a special side when posing and that gesture, body language, and feelings can be readily seen. A good topic for discussion concerns what can be known about a person, even though his or her face isn't visible.

9. Consider the other elements of a portrait such as the distance between subject and photographer, the position and size of the subject within the frame, the camera angle of the photographer (how he/she records the subject and edits the pieces of that photographic recording), the environment surrounding the subject. How is the emotional content of the portrait affected by these elements?

10. Use the "instant image" camera as a quick method for interpersonal relating among students. In rotating pairs they can photograph each other. Through their responses to each other while they photograph and with their discussions of whether the results of the images are representative or not, they often reduce typical peer barriers and pressures.

11. Explore the "instant image" format for its ability to reveal the differences between the original subject and its photographic representation. What does the lens do to change the actual depth and perspective? How does the frame function in isolating the image? How are tone values altered? This process can also be carried out with a regular camera but the result will not be as effective.

12. Try this sequencing exercise: Have students shoot a roll of film (that can eventually be seen in slide form), relating each image to the preceding one. The emphasis should not only be on graphic repetition but also on a recurring general feeling and on spatial and tonal relationships that connect each slide in the series. The learning experience comes both in taking the photographs and in viewing other students' approaches to relating images.

13. Explore the ways in which the "hand" of the photographer is visible. Provocative openers for class discussion can include:

    a. Describe or find a photo which has a reality different from the actual reality of the situation.
    b. Find two images, one stressing emotional content, one showing objective reality.
    c. Think about the shutter and the fact that we don't have to stop the world to look at it!
    d. Deal with under and overexposures: often things *really* look under or over lit!
    e. Consider how a photograph can go beyond the record of a place or thing, adding new information to a common situation?
    f. Discuss how an image can encompass an element of surprise, asking to be seen again and again?

14. Recognize the contact sheet, which contains strips of images that are the same size as the original negatives, as a wonderful means of exploring a photographer's path. The in-

dividual shots, not necessarily important by themselves or worthy of enlarging, will indicate a great deal about each student's approach to the camera.

15. Attempt to play down the "preciousness" of the photographic image, encouraging experimentation and risk taking. General assignments to achieve this effect can include:

a. The shooting by each student of a roll of film which is subsequently developed and printed by a classmate.

b. A negative exchange, in which specific negatives are chosen by the original photographer but then printed by two or more classmates, according to their own interpretations.

c. The hand coloring of black-and-white photographs with a Q-tip dipped in a solution of food coloring, water, and photo-flo (available in all photo stores).

d. Invasion of the surface of a photograph by cutting and pasting, offering great collage potential. The end product can then be given a smooth surface via a copy machine and then further retouched through more hand coloring.

16. Don't neglect the following topics of discussion:

a. Space: how does it become lonely or full?

b. Traces: in what way is meaning derived more from what *was* than what *is*, and more from the part than from the whole?

c. Point of view: how many different identities of one subject emerge when it's viewed from different perspectives and camera angles? How many pictures can you take before its identity is revealed.

d. Pattern: how can a fundamental pattern within the environment be made aesthetically significant?

e. Natural environment: how many ways can nature be experienced? Try to approach it loosely, with quick responses, as in street shooting. Reject the normal tendency to be patient with it.

f. The minimal environment: in what ways can a situation offering little points of departure, such as a parking lot, vacant lot, or baseball field, offer photographic stimulus.

17. Encourage students to go toward a focus or project. Ideas can include any of the above or the following:

a. Personal photo essays, including insights and recent or long past family history.

b. The sudden juxtaposition or abrupt encounter.

c. Making the inanimate appear alive.

d. Expression of an emotion or a mood.

e. Abstraction of familiar objects or landmarks through

Don't just stand there and shoot—stoop...

distortion or unique angle of vision.

    f. Response to texture, pattern, shape, form.

  18. Include reference to the outside world as an integral part of the photographic process. Suggest that students discuss the photographing of strangers with their potential subjects. This breaks down a very common problem in street shooting, building up confidence. have students take some of their pictures to the public, recording their responses. This prompts analysis of whom the students actually expect to reach and what they are trying to say. The "instant image" can be a useful tool in this final exercise. These pictures can be shown on the spot, provoking immediate feedback from the onlookers.

  It is hoped that this potpourri of ideas will offer insight that easily finds its way into your own situations. Although immersed in my own undaunted subjectivity, most of the suggestions can easily be converted into other personal approaches. Some last bits of advice: try to keep a parallel between what you desire for students and what they want for themselves. Pave whatever path you choose with a low stress, nonjudgmental and noncompetitive atmosphere. Turn mistakes into a learning experience. All of this will eliminate self-discounting and will result in a group of creative, energized human beings.

Encourage lots of shots. Use them for critical selection for printing and for negative exchange.

... climb, and position yourself for interesting angle shots.

CHECKLIST OF EQUIPMENT AND SUPPLIES

Photograms

blueprint papers (rolls and/or strips)
bulbs: sunlamp or photoflood bulb #1 or #2)
color toner
construction paper
developer (Dektol)
gooseneck lamp
3% hydrogen peroxide or Clorox
hypo-fixer
miscellaneous opaque objects
pails or buckets, plastic (5)
photographic papers (contact and enlarging projection)
repro-negative paper
stop bath (acetic acid)
trays, absorbent—large (14" × 18") cardboard, with plastic mylar liner (5)
trays, developing—smaller (8½" × 10") plastic (3)
water

Pinhole Cameras

aluminum or tin foil, heavy duty
black photographic tape (60 yds × ¾")
boxes, cardboard, and cylindricals: shoeboxes, square film boxes, cereal cylindars, juice cans, coffee cans
bulbs: two 15- or 25-watt for contact printing; one 100-watt)
clothesline
clothespins
developer (Dektol)
heavy piece of glass or contact printer
hypo-fixer
needles (sewing needle #10 preferably)
pails
paints (black flat, spray, latex, india ink)
photographic projection paper
safelight
scissors
sticky tape, double-sided
stop bath
trays, absorbent
trays, developing
water

Optical Devices and Variations

aluminum or tinfoil, heavy duty
black construction paper
black photographic tape
black latex paint or spray paint
can opener
cardboard pieces (3¼" × 4½", with one black surface)
colored acetates
flashlights
fruit juice cans
glassene envelopes
glassene paper, or tracing paper, or drafting vellum
glue (epoxy or Elmer's)
hole cutters
magnifying lenses
magnifying mirrors
mirror mylar (optimally with adhesive back)
paint brushes
paper clips
paper punch
paring knives
photographic paper
reflectors
rubber bands

(and, of course, the chemicals and trays for developing, processing)

Slide Making without a Camera

acetate, colored and clear
bleach, household
brushes
carousel projector
carousel slide trays (for 80 slides)
cellophane
chartpak
china markers
clear film leader
cotton swabs
discarded negatives, slides, film
glass stain/paints
glue (epoxy or Elmer's)
grease pencils
hole punches
India ink
India ink pens
iron
iron-together slide mounts
Magic Markers
pins and needles
paper towels
plastic slip-on slide mounts
plexiglass slides and mounts
rubber cement
Scotch tape
snap-shut slide binders (mounts)
stick-ons (instant letters and images, letrasets)
tissue paper
transparent contact paper
turpentine
U-film
write-on slide mounts (Kodak Ektragraphic)
X-acto knives

Camera Photography

blueprint paper
bulbs (photoflood #1)
cameras
changing bags
clothesline or twine
clothespins
cotton swabs
developer (Dektol)
developing tanks
film (color and black-and-white)
glass plates and cardboard bases
gooseneck lamp
grease pencils
hydrogen peroxide or Clorox
hypo-fixer
pails or buckets, plastic (5)
paper towels
photographic papers (projection and contact)
printing-out paper (studio proof)
repro-negative paper
safelight
scissors
sponges
stop bath
tape (masking or duct)
trays, absorbent, 14" × 18" cardboard with mylar lining (5)
trays, developing (3)
tripod
water

Chapter Four

A Photographic Yellow Pages

by Bobbi Carrey

Here Bobbi Carrey has assembled a catalogue of imaginative ideas for photographic projects in your media program, using everything from candle smoke to moonlight. With these ideas to start you off, and the offerings in the preceding and following chapters, you are encouraged to devise and develop photographic experiences that can easily be integrated with classroom teaching. Now let *your* imagination do the walking.

Camera in hand and a world to discover

Provocative photographic activities can come from almost anywhere or anything. The fifty-odd suggestions that follow represent only a few directions in which to probe. The specific topic of any particular probe is less important, I feel, than the more general goal of helping students find a variety of ways to participate actively with the images of their world. What seems important to me are the processes of following one's own curiosity, of studying the photographic visions of others, and of making connections between things.

The ideas below have been gathered from many different sources: from classrooms, workshops, books, magazines, bulletin boards, and from my own head. I have intentionally presented the material in a sketchy and somewhat random fashion, for I merely want to suggest and stimulate, not dictate imperatives.

1. Xerographic or photostatic copies of pages of *The New York Times* from September, 1851, to one month prior to the present date may be ordered from The New

York Times Information Office, 207 West Forty-third Street, New York, N.Y. 10036.

2. Project a slide against a wall and use as a backdrop for improvisational drama. If there are people in the image, have students interact with them, carrying on a conversation.

3. Have students create body silhouettes (either by tracing an outline of their bodies onto a suitably sized paper or else by making a body photogram with photographic paper) and fill in the insides with photographs of themselves.

4. Select a single photograph and reproduce enough copies on a photostat or Xerox machine so that everyone in the class can respond to it and share individual reactions.

5. Explore the image of the photographer in literature and pop culture.

6. Create a giant pinhole camera by using an old, disgarded appliance box from a refrigerator or stove. The pictures become poster size, and the photographer can even stay inside the camera!

7. Have students bring in baby pictures and see if they can guess "who's who."

8. Compile a series of photographs or slides which show an abstraction, rather than an identifiable object. Have students try to guess what the image really is or could be.

9. Have students create a photo history of themselves. Do the photographs stimulate memories about early childhood? Why were each of the photographs taken?

10. In order to locate material in the Prints and Photographs Division of the Library of Congress, order the catalog *Guide to the Special Collections of Prints and Photographs* from the Superintendent of Documents, Government Printing Office, Washington, D.C. 20402.

11. The French Embassy has original photography exhibitions available free to institutions on a two to three week loan basis. Write: J. S. Cartier, Director of Documentary Exhibits, Ambassade de France, 972 Fifth Avenues, New York, N.Y. 10021.

12. Have students keep a photographic diary, taking or collecting one photograph every day.

13. Have students research unusual uses of cameras and film: moon shots, medical photography, underwater photography, time-lapse photography.

14. Explore photographic galleries. What is the environment like? the color of the walls? the seating space? How are the photographs exhibited? Are they at eye level? Can you step back from the prints?

15. Explore ways of distorting photographic images: i.e., curve the paper in a pinhole camera before exposing the image; bend the paper while exposing under an enlarger; cut up old photographs and recombine them to create a new image.

16. Vaseline self-portraits: have students coat one side of their faces with Vaseline before pressing photographic paper to them. Develop normally to create a reversed silhouette (don't forget to do all this in a darkroom, or the entire sheet of paper will turn black).

17. Create double exposures: possibilities include running the same roll of film through the camera more than one time or exposing each single frame twice, carefully selecting the two images.

18. Make automatic collages by photographing areas with mirrors in them (like department store cosmetic counters or cars, which have rear view mirrors). The mirrors will reflect things outside the immediate scene.

19. Have students make long-term self-portraits by photographing themselves in photo booths once a week for several months. Can you see changes, moods, etc.?

20. Make a story entirely out of photographs, using no words. If you eliminate some of the images, does the story change?

21. To explore motion, have students take pictures of moving objects by following with the camera while taking the shot or have them move the camera while taking still objects. Can a sense of motion be captured in a still image?

22. Hold a piece of glass over a candle to blacken it. By drawing on the black surface with a needle, remove the black, making a negative. Contact print it with a piece of photographic paper.

23. Check to see if there are any branches of Xerox, 3-M, or Itek Company near you; ask if you could bring a class for a demonstration of recent photographic products and machines.

24. To show the effective exploration of a topic through photographs, order some of the series available through Documentary Photo Aids, P. O. Box 2620, Sarasota, Florida. Sample titles include: "The Feminist Revolution" (twenty-six 11" X 14" prints), "Crisis Pictures" (twenty-one 11" X 14" prints), "Child Labor" (fifteen 11" X 14" prints).

25. Create photograms to study shape and form.

26. Use photographs to document a project in progress (a science experiment or a set design for a play).

27. Use a still photograph to generate ideas for making a film.

28. Learn how to develop black-and-white slides by using the Kodak Reversal Processing Kits.

29. Have students take pictures of each other at the beginning and end of the school year for a comparison study.

30. Create photographs of "opposites" and "sames" and have students try to match and create relationships.

31. Mount a photograph on a masonite or wood board and cut into pieces with a power saw to create a jigsaw puzzle.

32. To make texture photograms, cover a piece of photographic paper with many small things (translucent buttons, etc.) and expose to a light source. Then remove the objects, place new objects on the paper, and expose again. Then develop the paper.

33. Show and discuss films made from still photographs: narratives (*La Jette*), documentaries (*Night and Fog*), films that use old photographs (*Ballad of Crowfoot*), etc. What is the effect of using stills in a moving narrative?

34. Look at some films which explore the lives of still photographers: the *Daybooks* of Edward Weston, Eugene Atget, Dorothea Lange. Is it possible to discuss and show the work of a still photographer through the medium of film?

35. Drawing with the moon: exciting lines and patterns can be made using the moon or any other bright light source at night (street lights, car tail lights, etc.). Moving the camera in different ways will produce different patterns and streaks on the film, depending on how long the shutter is kept open.

36. Create images of reflections on glass, on water, on metal.

37. Confront a stranger, engage him or her in conversation, and, finally, take a portrait of this subject, using what was learned in conversation to guide the nature of the photograph.

38. With pencil, paper, and camera, choose an outdoor shooting location. List and describe as many visual phenomena as possible by writing about them. Then take a picture of the scene. Compare the abilities of each medium for expressing what was observed, the mood of the scene, etc.

39. Create a three-dimensional photograph by cutting apart one photograph and remounting sections of it at different levels.

40. Using the same negative for all four prints, create four dramatically different photographs.

41. Explore one camera company's advertising campaign and see how an attempt is made to reach the mass market.

42. Have students study a photograph or slide until they are ready to describe the experience it captures. After using "traditional" vocabulary, students should invent new words to describe feelings about the picture. They can exchange these words to see if the meaning is clear to each other.

43. Have students place a piece of blank paper next to a photograph or projected slide image. Have them translate their feelings about the photograph into abstract drawings. Urge them to try using just one symbol, or to try reproducing the photograph with eyes closed.

44. Look carefully at a photograph and try to imagine what the subject is feeling. Try taking the same physical pose as subject. Image the photographer-subject relationship. Have students reconstruct the original "picture-taking" situation.

45. Look at a photograph or projected slide which contains still objects. Imagine feeling the contours of the objects: touch them, feel their weight, hold them, push them. Try to imagine what each object looks like on the side unexposed to the camera. Draw or describe that side.

46. Find the writings of photographers whose works have appeal. Is their "photographic philosophy" compatible with their images? Are the words still applicable to those images which were made, perhaps, years after the words were written?

47. Explore the different ways in which "framing" serves the photographer by examining some prints. Use strips of cardboard to create new "frames" and explore the different effects which result from different "framings."

48. Explore the subject of photographic criticism. Who writes it? What vocabulary is used? Compare two different reviews of the same photographic exhibition.

49. Research different photographic printing techniques as used by different publishing companies: offset printing, halftones, photogravure, stonetone reproduction, etc. Try to find different examples of photographic reproduction techniques.

50. Explore and research the use of machines to create photographic images: computers, television, Xerox machines, auto-photo booths.

51. Explore the relationship between photography and other arts such as ceramics, painting, jewelry making, video, and filmmaking.

52. Have your class visit a local newspaper to see how photographs are used in the paper. How are assignments made? Who selects the photographs that are printed? Are the images most often used full-frame or are they cropped?

53. Send to Polaroid for a free subscription to *Close-up* at 549 Technology Square, Polaroid Corporation, Cambridge, Mass. 02139.

54. Create your own Photographic Yellow Pages.

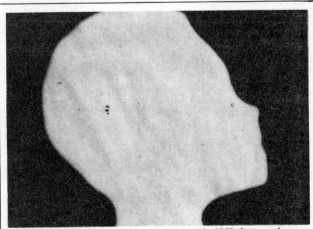

A self-portrait photogram by a Mamaroneck, N.Y. first grader. The silhouette was made by pressing the head against repro-negative paper and shining light on it for about 10 minutes.

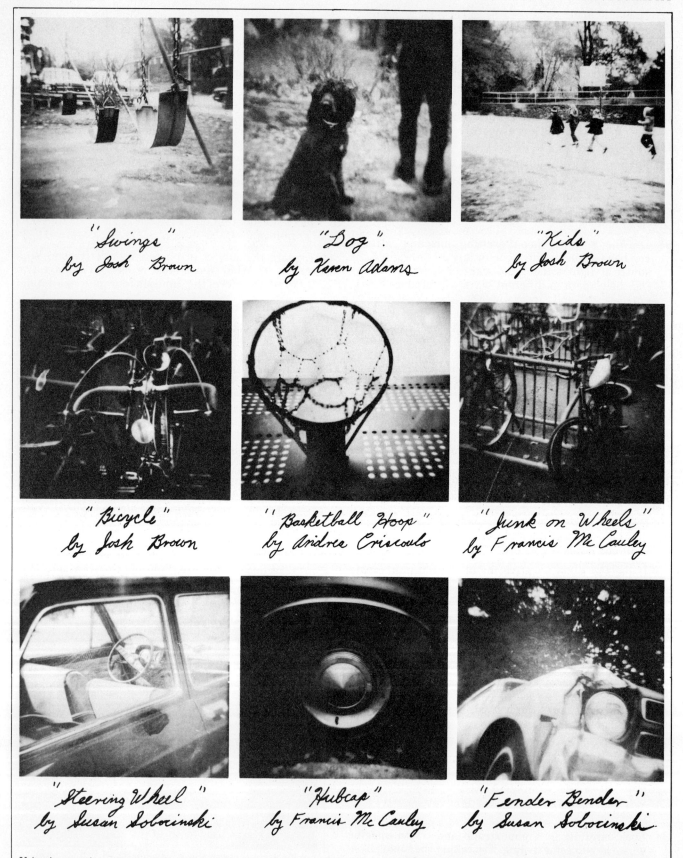

"Swings"
by Josh Brown

"Dog".
by Karen Adams

"Kids"
by Josh Brown

"Bicycle"
by Josh Brown

"Basketball Hoop"
by Andrea Criscoulo

"Junk on Wheels"
by Francis McCauley

"Steering Wheel"
by Susan Sobocinski

"Hubcap"
by Francis McCauley

"Fender Bender"
by Susan Sobocinski

Using inexpensive cameras, sixth graders at Mamaroneck, N.Y., integrated photo study with concepts in science, art, language arts, math, and social studies. Here they composed a photo essay on "Things That Move." Other essays were on "Things That Are Beautiful," "Things That Are Ugly," "Things That Smell," and "Things That Are Round."

A Developmental Perspective

by Ellie Waterston Bartow

Having engaged your students in the educative process of "doing photography," you are invited to involve them in photographic experiences beyond camera activities. In this chapter Ellie Waterson Bartow approaches photography from a number of different directions—historical, personal, aesthetic.

The learning-by-doing theory is particularly adaptable to the study of photography: its history, the concepts that have earned photography a place among the arts, and its role in our lives today.

The following comments seek to orient a teacher to these broad concerns. They also provide some examples of classroom activities through which students can approach photography as a topic in its own right. Both the orientation and the teaching ideas are presented briefly. In the resource section at the end of this book are some suggested readings that are far more comprehensive in covering the historic and aesthetic foundations of photography.

The Historical Perspective

The first camera was the "camera obscura," which, literally translated from Latin, means dark room. During the Renaissance it was discovered that by drilling a hole in the wall of a darkened room, what was outside would be projected on to the opposite wall of a dark chamber as a perfectly detailed, inverted image. People began tracing the image on paper; it was just a matter of time before light-sensitive materials were discovered that captured the image on paper and smaller, portable variations of the camera were invented. The pinhole camera is a rudimentary derivative of the camera obscura and is easily built in the classroom.

Three outstanding pioneers in the development of photography were Louis Jacques Mande Daguerre, William Henry Fox Talbot, and Sir John Herschel. Daguerre discovered that exposing a copper plate coated with a solution of silver halides and developing it in mercury resulted in a positive image. The only drawback to Daguerre's system was the difficulty of reproducing the image from the copper plate. Talbot solved this problem by producing the first negative on paper (also treated with silver halides), which he could then print to get a positive image on another piece of paper. Herschel's invaluable discovery was sodium thiosulfate, "hypo," which permanently fixed the image on paper. The daguerreotype, Talbot's calotype, and the chemicals used by Herschel provided the building blocks of photography.

Men such as these deserve attention in an overview of photographic history. They remind us that it is the individual who solves the problems and creates new art forms, that the medium has an important technical as well as

Chapter Five

Texture and framing make the difference between a mundane shot and a statement.

aesthetic tradition. Older students might wish to replicate some of the old photographic processes of these pioneers. If you ask your students to sort through the family's old photographs, there is a good chance they will discover some examples of these early processes and share them with the class.

This might lead to an assignment in which students create personal photo histories by collecting old pictures of themselves. What do individuals remember about their early childhood? What is it in a photograph that tells you something about the character of the person being pictured and the style of those earlier days in which the picture was taken? What events seem to have merited taking pictures? Can students tell how the camera was generally used? Was the shot posed or candid? formal or informal?

The Technical Perspective

Learning to look, to *really* look, at photographs requires a sensitivity to something beyond what a picture "is of." It requires a feel for the mood, texture, color, shape, and the relation of form to content. It also requires a special vocabulary so that discussion and perception can be specific and thorough. When you've come to the point where your students are particularly engaged with a set of photographs, new or old, you might introduce some of the "formal" analytical tools for photography study. Chapter 3 offered numerous camera activities. What follows is a basic photographic vocabulary of terms and concepts—with some questions and representative activities for exploring them. Once your students have these concepts and

vocabulary under their belts, they will be far better able to analyze the photographs of others as well as those that they create.

Subject. Bring in a variety of photographs. What are the subjects? How do you know? Do different people see different subjects within the same photograph?

Lighting. Bring in photographs of the same thing lit from different angles (or have students take these pictures themselves). Discuss where the light source was for each shot. What effect do the different lighting angles have on the photo?

Angle or point of view. Bring in photographs of the same thing shot from every possible angle (or have your students create the pictures). What is a close-up? a medium shot? a long shot? What effect does angle have on the subject when something is shot head-on? from the side? from underneath? from behind? Does the photographer's literal point of view emotionally "color" what is being said? Can students suggest a point of view that would be more objective, more organically derivative?

Framing or composition. Bring in a series of photographs of the same subject in which the framing changes. How does framing affect the shot? Does it change the interpretation of the image? Make your own frame and experiment with reframing images.

Focus. Bring in examples of in- and out-of-focus shots. Establish a definition for "focus" on the basis of those examples. Experiment with taking shots that are intentionally blurred. With older students, you can explore "depth of field"—what causes it and the effects it produces.

Double exposure. Bring in examples of double exposures. What happens when things are juxtaposed in an unnatural way? Discuss the photographer's ability to manipulate his or her visual environment. What limitations are there?

Candid vs. posed shot. Arrive at a definition of each by looking at examples.

Action vs. still shot. Arrive at a definition of each by looking at examples.

Look alikes. Find photographs of things around you that remind you of other things. Build a composite face out of photographs of inanimate objects: tires for eyes, a steeple for the nose.

Documentary vs. narrative photography. How do documentaries and narratives differ? Bring in examples to illustrate these differences. Can students create definitions that will work in classifying all images they collect?

Texture. How would a photograph feel if you could touch it? What would you take a picture of to illustrate roughness? smoothness? hardness?

Pattern. What is a pattern? Bring in a handful of random photographs and look for natural patterns in them. What is the rhythm of a row of bottles, a picket fence, footprints in the sand, raindrops on water?

Color, line, and shape. Discuss the "formal" elements of color, line, and shape in painting, or photography. Compare different media: photos with graphics, sketches, sculpture, architecture.

Cross-media. Have your students illustrate a poem with photographs or find words that capture the essence of a shot they have taken. Draw a distinction between this sort of photograph-to-words association and the caption. What is the function of a caption? How much information should one give? Bring in examples.

The Photograph as Portrait

Portraiture in earliest times was notorious for three-hour sittings in the glaring sun, which were required by the slow action of the early papers and plates. The pinhole camera is a means of showing how long one had to remain still in order to have a picture that was in focus. Have your students try to do portraits with the pinhole. Look at old photographs carefully and see if you can't spot a hand or a head or one person who is blurred.

As the sophistication of equipment and technique grew, portrait photography was better able to capture the essence of a person. Have your kids take portraits of one another with whatever camera you have decided to use in your class. Start with simple head shots and ask the students to illustrate different emotions in their facial expressions. Have them set up their shots with more background information, reminding them that every bit of information in a photograph can be relevant, that backgrounds make statements and reinforce moods. Once your students feel comfortable taking portraits in the controlled classroom environment, direct them to take shots of people outside the school: old people, children, people shopping, spectators at a sporting event.

For those days when you're not actively engaged in taking or developing pictures, remember that magazines and photography books make good sources for studying photographic portraits. Have the class analyze what they see in the faces of the portrait subjects. Make up biographies for these people. What do their clothes say about them? their postures? their smiles? their eyes? Have your students bring in shots of people they would or wouldn't like to be. What are our preconceptions about certain types of people? How do pictures create stereotypes for us?

The Photograph as Documentary

An historical look at documentary photography will reveal colorful characters like Mathew Brady. A photographer of the Civil War, he surveyed the battlefields in a horse-drawn buggy which he equipped as a darkroom. His work comprises some of the first war reportage and immortalizes a visual record of those days. Compare his works with war reportage today. Have students collect all the war photos they can find to study carefully. Looking at them as a group, do the photographs tend to show one aspect of war more than another? If you didn't know what war was, how might you define it after looking at these shots? Does war mean death? celebration of victory? sitting around a foxhole with your buddies? Choose other broad topics (for examples, human rights, childhood, natural disasters) and find photographs of them throughout history. Become familiar with the work of other great documentary photographers: Jean Eugene Auguste Atget, Margaret Bourke-White, Lewis W. Hine, Dorothea Lange, Walker Evans, and many more.

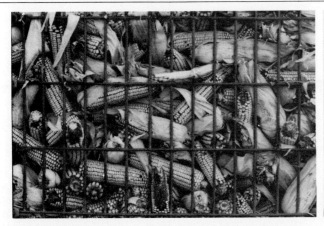

Corn Crib. The same subject, but angle shots and composition capture different patterns, textures.

As you become familiar with these representative photographers, try to discern what qualities in their pictures define their work as "documentary." Have your students look through magazines and newspapers for what they feel are documentary shots. Encourage them to make up a story with the random photographs they have collected. With their cameras, have your students document an event, their neighborhood, an afternoon at the corner drugstore. Can one photograph survive alone as a documentary? Have students think about editing out photographs in a documentary series that restate something said in another shot. Which picture is more forceful? Plan a trip to a newspaper to talk with a staff photographer about his job. Ask how he or she gets to the scene of action on time, how decisions are made about which photographs to use. This interview will contribute heavily to an understanding of documentary photography and the role of the photograph as a source of information.

The Photograph as Art Form

As you and your class trace the development of photography as an art form, spend time studying a few of the masters in this area—people like Alfred Stieglitz, Paul Strand, Diane Arbus, Edward Weston, Imogen Cunningham, and Ansel Adams. Most public and many school libraries have collections of their photographs along with written commentaries in which these artists state their aims, how they arrived at their particular styles, and what they hope to communicate. You can easily find newspaper and magazine articles that discuss new photographers and new concerns within the field. Help your students identify some of the "hot" current trends in the medium. Encourage them to articulate their personal responses to a broad variety of photographic styles and purposes. Check out local photographic exhibits. Perhaps

your students can write reviews of these shows and compare their appraisals with the newspaper reviews. Defining art in any medium is a difficult task, but seeking a definition can be rewarding.

The Commercial Photograph

Avoid confining the class' attention to only those areas that are considered "serious" in the photographic world. There are many types of photography that aren't billed as art, but that illustrate the various ways in which the medium can be effectively and artistically used. Explore photography's applications in advertising, the fashion field, political campaigns. Have your students find copies of old magazines and compare the advertising then with the advertising now. When is color first used? How does the photograph establish to what kind of an audience the product wants to appeal? What different types of photography can you see combined in an ad? As mentioned earlier, any trips that reinforce your study of photography are great: to color labs, to advertising agencies, to magazines, to fashion shootings, to science labs where macrophotography plays an enormously important role (in marketing drugs as well as in noncommercial applications). Have your students select different areas of commercial photography and shoot their own examples of this genre.

These are some of the ways for you and your students to discover the photographic world together. We take many aspects of this world for granted. Photography is enormous in its sphere of influence, and it is time we learn about and put to use the qualities which make the medium an important part of our culture and environment.

High school students make a documentary with photos collected from magazines, books, and newspapers.

P.S. 75, New York, kindergarteners on their first time out with small Diana cameras show that even the youngest have keen powers of observation and can apply basic techniques and principles.

action shots

posed shots with selected backgrounds

through the window

patterns

portrait of teacher

family portrait

a dog's eye-view from a child's eye-level

framing/composition *(left-right)*—roof-top shot, city neighborhood street, park scene.

Part 3
Film

Doing Super 8

by Ellie Waterston Bartow

As chapter 3 explained the beginning steps of still photography, in this chapter Ms. Bartow takes the fear out of filming and provides the basic techniques and principles for starting your filmmaking program, beginning with the easily managed Super 8 camera.

The idea of incorporating Super 8 filmmaking into a school curriculum is intimidating to many in its newness. This article on Super 8 live-action filmmaking in schools aims to "de-new" filmmaking sufficiently to show that it is within the realm of the possible, logistically, and that it is a creative, rewarding, and, above all, educating experience.

Who

Ideally, an entire class will have the opportunity to participate. Just as all learn to read and write, and some become great writers, so should all have the opportunity to make films and possibly become great filmmakers.

If it is necessary to select a group of students for filmmaking, it is important to realize that a student's scholastic standing will have no bearing on the ability to handle equipment efficiently or to express oneself through film. This is not to suggest that everyone will thrive on film—they won't—but the traditional means of academic measure don't apply.

Camera, Meet Student

Fifteen minutes plus a camera and an instruction book should give your students enough time to more or less figure out the nature and function of the different camera parts. A lively way to review this information is to play a "Simon Says" sort of game: "Simon says point to the eyepiece." "Simon says point to the light meter." "Simon says how do you set the focus before a day of shooting?"

"Simon says how do you set the focus before each shot?" Questions of focus ought to be reviewed daily for, when caught up in the momentum of shooting, it's easy to forget to reset unless it has become an almost automatic activity.

Sustaining a relaxed mood about first introductions is a good thing. *Don't touch's* and *be careful's* will stunt if not kill the creative use of the camera. The feeling should be that the camera is a good friend to be treated with respect. It's necessary to know about all the camera's parts and what they do, and the best way to learn this information is for students to find out for themselves. Super 8 cameras are hardy creatures. They won't break, short of hurling them to the floor.

As students examine the camera for the first time, discuss its basic operations. Where does the light come through? What holds the film in place? It's worth sacrificing one roll of cartridge film to reveal what goes on in that otherwise very mysterious box.

Everyone involved should get used to the vocabulary of filmmaking. Suggest each student keep a media dictionary, a collection of terms that the class as a group defines in their own words each time one comes up. Keep the dictionary up to date and refer to it frequently to remind your kids of the importance of having essential terms under control (words like sprockets, f-stop, viewfinder, aperture). Not only technical terms should find their way into the media dictionary but also specific camera motions: pan, tilt, zoom, pull focus.

As teacher, don't feel miffed if one of your students comes up with a technical question about the camera that you can't answer. The wonderful thing about a film project is that it is a process of mutual discovery. Keep reference books on hand (see the resource section for ideas) and look up the answers on the spot, or have your students research the answers outside school and bring them in the next day.

Storyboarding

Familiarity should also be established with storyboarding (see chapter 7 for fuller treatment). Strictly speaking, storyboarding is a sketched outline of a film that indicates each time there is a change of camera position. One needn't be all that rigorous, but do encourage your students to draw in their storyboards no more and no less than what they want to appear on the screen (see figure 1). Have them use their storyboard as a shooting script when they go out filming. Generally all film assignments should begin with storyboarding, even in a documentary when exactly what is going to happen during the course of shooting can't be predicted.

Storyboarding is an organizer. It aids students in defining a story line and improves their ability to sequence and compose shots. In the rudimentary storyboard illustrated in figure 1 there is a line provided to write in what sound will accompany each shot (not essential to the first few films) and a line for the camera action.

What'll I Film

The first film should be fairly simple to encourage free use of the camera. One possibility is to shoot a 50-foot (three-minute) roll on a simple motion. Have each student pick one: throwing a baseball, rocking in a rocking chair, chewing bubble gum. What is the motion made of? What muscles are involved?

The first film is a good time for students to demonstrate their ability to do a pan, a tilt, a zoom, a walking shot, and so on. Tell them that each "take" on any one thing should last about seven seconds. It's always safer to shoot more than less.

Camera motion shouldn't be done sloppily. A pan should lead the eye from one thing to another. It should say: "See this? O.K. Now take a look at this over here."

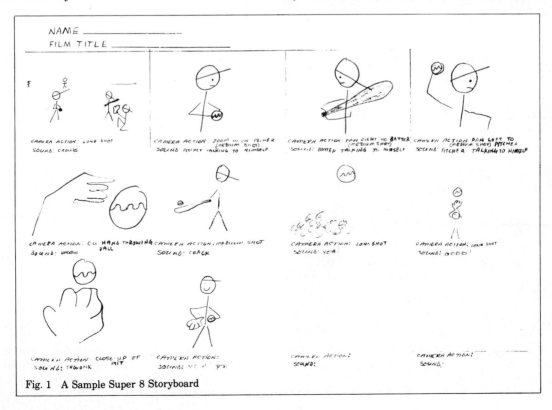

Fig. 1   A Sample Super 8 Storyboard

The first film should be of a fairly simple motion.

Shooting a narrative—an exercise in fiction

A documentary records things as they happen, extracts from reality, and explores aspects of life going on around you.

Discourage "nowhere" pans that provide no information and dilute the effectiveness of the film. Another common ailment is "the zooms," to which kids are very susceptible because it's just so much fun to do. The zoom has the capacity to increase or limit the scope of what the viewer sees, thus directing attention to specifics or generalities. Each camera motion has its own character and is best applied in certain situations for specific effects. Combinations of all these shots are also possible. But for the time being, just run through the list, mastering each type of shot. Experimentation can take place in later films.

Subsequent film topics are up for grabs. The possibilities are limitless. A mood film makes a nice second-go-round in that it deals with only one concept, something that is helpful in the beginning. If you do a mood film, be it inspired by a poem or a song or an ideal such as freedom, ask the class a series of questions to provoke ideas and to further exploration. Ask the class to think of what color this mood reminds them, of what events create this mood. What would freedom mean to a dog, a ball? How can a film show how it feels to be rejected? Explore the mood theme in these ways so that new dimensions in feeling and self-perception are achieved at the same time as new dimensions of self-expression through film.

A narrative film is one that, when storyboarded thoroughly, requires almost no editing. It is an exercise in fiction; something is made up by the student and translated into film. A documentary film, on the other hand, records things as they happen, extracts from reality. What's often confusing is that isolating an event on film somehow separates it from its own reality, rendering it the fiction of the person behind the camera. Students often feel that recording anything on film makes a story of it in the narrative sense, which is why some time needs to be spent arriving at definitions that the whole class understands and accepts for these two types of film.

Documentary films offer the opportunity to make the world your classroom and to expose students to aspects of life going on right around them of which they may not be immediately aware (wealth, poverty, drugs, religion, pollution). A teacher can direct these experiences by making up a list of topics to choose from and encouraging student suggestions. Urge the group to decide what they want to say about their topic. What will their message be? The chances are that this "message" will change during the shooting process, but they will be better able to perceive and analyze this change if they had a position to start with. Bring in books and articles that are pertinent to the documentary film topics. Make the foray as thorough and complete as possible. The more students know about the subject, the more they will know about what to look for in filming. Encourage your kids to involve people in their documentaries. It's too easy to film roll after roll of inanimate stuff, which indicates a hesitancy to approach people. Adding the human element takes practice and a little bit of nerve, but it is well worth the effort.

Editing

Editing is part of the creative process in filmmaking. It can be very tedious working with the tiny frames of Super 8 film. To avoid being bogged down because you can't get the perfect splice, place emphasis initially on the composition and continuity of the film—frame to frame, motion to motion, color to color, theme to theme. Don't worry about

¼" spaces between splices, which result in flashes of light on the screen. With practice those flashes with diminish, and it's not worth hobbling the kids' enthusiasm because of a relatively unimportant detail.

To begin editing, have your students screen the raw footage a number of times until they feel they know it well. Then make a list, shot by shot, numbering each shot as it should appear in the final version. Story line organization is not the only consideration in sequencing the shots. Leading the eye from one frame to the next by motion, color, and overall composition are also factors.

The best way to keep track of a splice is to set up your editor and splicer on a table that is pushed against a wall (see figure 2). Cover the wall with paper. Each time a section is cut out of the film, immediately tape it to the paper and label what it is: "close-up of John eating." If you have numbered the sequence of shots, simply write the corresponding number on the sheet next to the section of film. Place a cardboard box or a brown paper bag beside each chair at the editing table to catch the film as the student pulls it through the editor. This protects the film from touching the floor. Dust and scratches are film's biggest enemies.

Very often the first round of editing is not the last. Students should act as each other's critics, suggesting further editing or the need for additional shots. As the course progresses, student proficiency will lead to more editing within the camera.

Screenings

It is a good idea to screen films in advance that will serve as examples. To avoid leading students to believe that the film being viewed is *the* narrative or *the* documentary that they should imitate, show a wide variety of films. Screenings can be approached by genre, by theme, or by chronological groupings. Students should see films that *they* would be capable of doing, as well as more professional ones. There are many good sources for renting films. Public libraries and state universities may have film collections. There are also many major educational film distribution centers across the country (see the resource section for suggestions). Film rental runs into some money, but it is worth setting aside almost one quarter of your budget for this purpose. Avoid instructional films. They have their place, but it's not here.

Biped or Tripod

Many people feel that a tripod is a must for making films because it produces a steadier camera and more carefully composed shots. But it is a cumbersome item, which, if used at all, shouldn't be introduced until the filmmaking program is well underway. During the first few films, students should feel they can move as freely as possible with the camera. When a tripod becomes necessary, have your students set it up for each shot, making sure the legs are level. There are means of obtaining almost or just as steady a shot without a tripod. Standing with feet about a foot and a half apart, with the camera held securely against the chest, one hand free to operate the focusing ring and zoom, your kids will have little trouble remaining steady. Encourage them to move their entire upper torsos, not just their heads, when changing camera position. The more a student can come to work and move naturally with the camera the better. In this way the

Editing Super 8 film

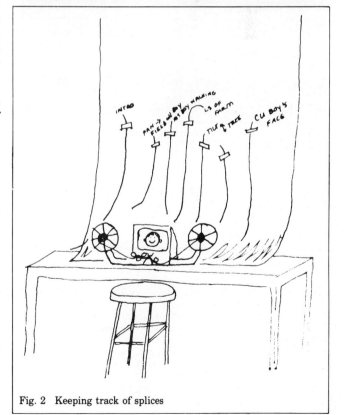
Fig. 2   Keeping track of splices

Stand with feet about a foot apart, camera held securely against chest, one hand free to operate the focusing, and move entire upper torso when changing camera position.

A sixth grader in Omaha, Nebraska, experiments with different shots and views.

camera will become like a third eye, selecting images in unison with the filmmaker's thoughts, actions, and inspirations. There are certain types of films in which the tripod doesn't hinder the filming process: a narrative film, with its sequences prestructured to allow filming within a limited area, often lends itself well to working with a tripod. Documentaries, on the other hand, demand freedom of movement; thus, the tripod would be detrimental.

Critiquing

When a batch of unedited film comes in, the class should look at the new footage, evaluate the framing, the angles, whether the idea that the filmmaker wished to express is clear, and they should suggest how to organize the film to make it better. This group process should continue through the editing, with frequent screenings, in an effort to emphasize that creative expression through film requires self-criticism and that having your friends discuss and criticize your films isn't a criticism of you. There needn't be any grades in filmmaking, so there needn't be that who's-better or what-does-the-teacher-want feeling that tends to squelch experimentation in kids. Take a look at the suggested list of things below to consider when critiquing, and then make up your own.

Sound

Before you start to think about sound tracks and the like, have your students, armed with a few cassette tape recorders, do "sound essays" on topics like mornings at their houses, traffic, soft noises, hard noises, happy nosies, round noises. There truly is a world of sound of which we are unaware. Sit quietly for a moment in your classroom and think about it: there's the heating vent buzzing away in the corner, the fluorescent lights and their low-keyed hum, the creaks of chairs, the breathing of your students. Once you and your kids are tuned in and have begun to perceive the character and relationship of one sound to another, then the time has come to think about adding sound to film.

For early projects, it is easiest to play a record along with the film. If you wish to show a composite reel of different films and put all the sound on one reel of tape, figure out the ratio of tape to leader for a ten-second break between films (about 37½" tape to 15" leader). Splice blank tape and clear leader between each corresponding

---

CRITIQUE BOX

Is the story line or message of the film clear?

Is the film too long?

Are there portions of the film that aren't necessary to the story line?

Is the overall organization of the film appropriate to what the filmmaker is trying to say?

Is the film well composed and organized?

Does the beginning feel like a beginning and the end like an end?

Does the filmmaker look hard for small things that might add strength to the statement? Was there hard thinking about when to come in for a close-up? How imaginative were the fade-ins and -outs, the blur-ins and -outs?

How is the framing? the angle of shots? the camera motion? the focus? the lighting?

Has the editing been done with thought to the relationship of one frame to the next in terms of the story line, composition, color, direction of action, pacing, timing, and rhythm?

film and sound track. The process sounds complicated, but you will be grateful for having done it when the time comes for screening many films. Changing records constantly during a screening can lead to the Excedrin headache of all time. One caution: when you plan to put together a carefully synced tape with a reel of film, make sure that you buy thick, higher-priced tape. The less expensive brands tend to stretch with repeated playing and that throws your timing off. Setting your tape recorder up vertically on the table helps too, for then the heat from the machine doesn't directly touch the tape, stretching it, but rather is distributed through the machine itself.

When your students do narratives, and if you think they can handle the fairly sophisticated slating techniques explained in any technical treatise on film, have them record the sound synchronously. Sound can be synced directly onto the film, but, to do this, tape and film have to be sent to a lab, which does represent additional cost. Otherwise a very effective voice-over-music sound track can be made after the film has been edited. For specifics, read up on the techniques used to do voice-overs, to mark and edit tape (see the Resources section).

When filming documentaries, have your students take cassettes along. It is possible on some Super 8 cameras to plug the cassette in directly so that it will be activated at precisely the same time as the camera motor for lip synchronization. This is where slating comes in. One can also record "wild sound": conversations and random noises recorded before, during, and after shooting that establish, in sound, where you were filming and what was going on. If appropriate to the subject of the film, urge students to buttonhole strangers for their opinions. Interviewing a stranger is harder than filming one. Have your kids practice on their friends at school. What kinds of questions work best? How can you make the subject relax? How direct or personal can you be? Eventually your students will work these questions out and learn tricks for successful interviewing, like reaching into a pocket for something and asking the subject to hang onto the microphone as he or she continues speaking. Once the subject takes the mike, he or she is somehow more comfortable.

Scheduling

In anticipation of the time needed for film processing, be ready with filler activities. Generally, a good schedule is to give a film assignment one day, have students do the storyboarding of the film during the first half of class the next day, and then screen a film or two that illustrates different approaches to that particular topic. The shooting and sound collecting process can take from a couple of days to a week, depending on the film. Then come days of waiting for the film to be developed. This is a good time for delving into the history of film or possibly screening films that aren't related to any assignment but are examples of a genre or period. This is also a good time for field trips. Many universities and other schools have media programs. Take your class to visit and vice versa; share and compare notes. If yours is an elementary class, don't be afraid to take them to a university course in videotaping or film or photography. Wonderful exchanges are possible between such divergent age levels. In-between times are also good for fooling around with editing, for exploring techniques in special effects.

Titling should be done during production, while interest runs high. Here students animate title by adding letters and visuals in stop-action. Setup and technique are same for both Super 8 and 16mm filming.

Titling

Titling is something you can have great fun with. You can scratch the credits for a film in sand or dirt, write them on a sheet, make a mobile, animate the letters, or, more traditionally, write the credits on a piece of cardboard. Instead of a voice-over, titles can be used within the film to establish time lapses or settings. When filming titles, give them seven seconds, just as you give each take when shooting normally. Titling, along with editing and sound, should be done for each film within the production schedule, while interest runs high.

Logistics

The organization of a film room demands flexible work space with tables to put the editors on, bare walls to hang editing paper on, a means to block out light for screenings, lots of chairs, and lots of outlets to accommodate four or five editors, a projector, a tape recorder, and a record player. Have boxes available for students to store their films, film outlines, and storyboards. Make sure students label their films to avoid confusion.

Regarding equipment, with the many models of Super 8 cameras made, it's probably best to suggest those

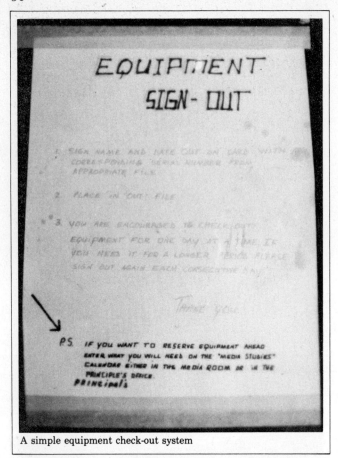

A simple equipment check-out system

and a record player are also needed for sound work.

It's impossible to have enough splicing tape. Some brands are more wieldy than others, and it's worth getting those brands, for students can become very frustrated if the tape is too difficult to handle. Kodak is more expensive than some but easy to work with. A straight edge splicer is preferred to one with wavy edges because it's easier to line up a straight splice. And remember, keep the shiny side up when editing, with sprocket holes on the same side.

In order to determine how much film to stock, estimate before the semester begins approximately how long each film will be, based on the fact that each fifty-foot roll will yield a three-minute film. It's a good idea to do this beforehand because then you can buy in bulk, which often cuts the price. The same strategy applies to all equipment and expendables if you find a dealer with whom you can bargain. Photo stores that do their own processing may offer a better price than those that send their work to a lab.

Once you have all your equipment, take an inventory and get the school to write it into their insurance. And be sure to send in the warranty cards on the equipment so you can make claims if something doesn't function properly.

Establish a sign-out sheet for equipment students use outside of school.

Festival

Staging a festival at the end of a film project is a wonderful culmination. It involves the rest of the school, and it provides a boost to the student filmmakers (and also gives them a deadline to meet). In preparation, put all the sound on one tape synced with the rolls of film so that all you need to do is swtich on the tape and projector at the same time. Prizes and programs are luxuries, but they do make the festival a more official and special occasion.

This article has explored the instruction of Super 8 and the dynamics of self-expression through film for its own sake. Film projects *can* be related to other subject areas: a documentary on the population explosion for social studies, a narrative exploration of melodrama for English, a stop-action film on the growth of a plant, a film on a historical figure. But the ready application of film to enhance other subjects should not become so attractive that the educational benefits of studying film for its own sake are ignored.

Filmmaking has come a long way since its infancy in the schools. It can be used to teach freedom of self-expression, critical skills, organization, the value of sharing opinions with others, and the ability to respond to and make sense out of the world around us. Above all, filmmaking remains an exciting medium through which students and teachers can communicate and learn a lot about themselves and each other.

features the camera *should* have; then you can comparison shop and price hunt on your own. Look for an automatic zoom, an automatic/manual light meter, a single framer (this feature brings the price up, but it is great fun to work with and enables you to make animated films), and a footage counter. The ratio of cameras to students will depend on your budget. The ideal is to have a camera for everyone. But you can economize on the number of cameras by dividing the class in half, with some students filming while others do in-house activities. If you are really strapped for money, divide the class into teams of three: a film person, a sound person, and a director. These roles can be switched for each film. There are advantages to doing at least one film organized as a production team, whether or not you have an abundance of cameras. Group cooperation, and the coordination it demands, is a worthwhile exercise in itself.

Editors are a priority on the equipment list. It's best to have enough machines so that half the class can edit at once. Beware of flimsy, plastic editors. They really don't hold up well.

Cassette tape decks are not quite so important; a couple will suffice. One reel-to-reel tape recorder, patch cords,

MEDIA DICTIONARY

The following terms were assembled and defined by students in grades 4–6, Mamaroneck, N.Y.

ABSTRACT—(adj.) the different point of view of the artist

ANGLE—(n.) a point of view

ANIMATED FILM—(n.) a film made of cartoon characters

APERTURE—(n.) an opening through which light enters

BLUR-OUT, BLUR-IN—(n.) going out of focus on purpose at the end of one scene and slowly coming back into focus as you start the next scene

BLURRED—(adj.) not clear, out of focus

CAPTION—(n.) words written about a photograph which explain something about it

CLOSE-UP or CU—(n.) a shot taken when the subject is very close to the camera

COMPOSITION—(n.) the arrangement of everything within the frame of the image or photograph

CUT—(n.) a sudden change from one shot to another done by splicing (or cutting) your film when you edit it

DOLLY—(n.) something with wheels on it that you can attach the camera to that makes it easy to take smooth shots while you are moving

EDIT—(v.) to collect, arrange and splice various camera shots together in a finished movie

EDIT OUT—(v.) to cut a section out of a film

EDITOR/VIEWER—(n.) machine used to look at film without putting it through a projector. Used when you edit your film

EXTERIOR—(n.) any shot taken of an outdoor scene

F/STOP—(n.) a lightmeter talks to you in f/stops. f/stop 2.8 means there isn't much light so the lens (or the aperture) opens wider to let enough in. f/stop 5.6 or f/stop 8 means there is just the right amount of light, and the lens aperture is opened to a normal size. f/stop 16 means there is lots and lots of light, and the lens aperture is tiny. The f/stops, and the lens aperture react to light just exactly the way your eye and your pupil do.

FADE-OUT, FADE-IN—(n.) when a scene in your film gradually gets light to dark, or dark to light

FRAME—(n.) the outline of the image

INTERIOR—(n.) any shot taken of an indoor scene

LENS—(n.) a piece of glass or plastic which gathers light to make a sharp image

LIGHTMETER—(n.) a device that measures how much light there is

LIVE-ACTION FILM—(n.) "the real thing" not a cartoon

LONG SHOT or LS—(n.) a shot taken when the subject is far away from the camera

MEDIUM SHOT or MS—(n.) a shot that shows just about the full length of a person, taken from not too close or not too far

PAN—(n.) a shot taken by moving the camera from left to right or from right to left (horizontally)

PULL FOCUS—(n.) a pull focus is when you start your scene focused on something in the foreground, with the background out of focus . . . and then, without changing your position or the position of the camera, you adjust the focus ring on the front of the camera so that what was in the foreground goes out of focus, and what was in the background suddenly appears in focus.

SPLICE—(n.) the joining or taping together of film

SPLICER—(n.) the machine used to join or tape film together

TELEPHOTO—(n.) when the camera's lens is set so that you can see as little of the subject as possible, in other words, you seem to very close-up

TILT—(n.) a shot taken by tilting the camera up or down (vertically)

TITLE—(n.) a shot of words that tell important things about the film

TRIPOD—(n.) a three legged device that you can screw a camera on to that will hold the camera absolutely steady

VIEWFINDER—(n.) a window on a camera that shows you what will be in the final picture

WALKING SHOT—(n.) a shot taken while you walk with the camera in your hand

WIDE ANGLE—(n.) when the camera's lens is set so that you can see as much as possible, like a long shot

ZOOM—(v.) this is when you move in on or away from your subject automatically and can only be done with a camera that has a zoom attachment on the lens

A Filmmaking Course

By Jon Dunn and Kit Laybourne

Having mastered the art of holding a camera, pointing it at a subject, and being able to film just what they want, your students are now ready to get into the serious business of filmmaking. In this chapter, Jon Dunn and Kit Laybourne explore the relation between the mind and eye of the artist and the medium of film. Their directions and exercises give a step-by-step approach to the creation of true cinema in a media classroom.

Film is an "all-medium medium" in which time, space, motion, drama, sound, exposition, music, graphics, images, and information exist simultaneously. That the movies are a composite art makes them compelling. But it also makes them very difficult to create.

We have found the best way to teach filmmaking is to break it down into manageable components, a series of structured exercises designed to introduce students to the medium and allow them to practice and master particular facets of it—one at a time. Our building-block mentality seems to work. By means of brief exercises with limited goals, students can develop the cluster of skills required for effective filmmaking.

This filmmaking text has been with us in dog-eared mimeo copies for the past eight years, being taught by us, by teachers we trained, and by friends and colleagues working in kindergarten through college graduate levels. Based on this experience, we can assure you that the thing really did fly, Orville. And the evidence flew in from everywhere. A low-scoring, inner-city first grade spent a year doing most of their work in language skills, math, and social studies within the structure of these filmmaking exercises. Five years later, school officials cited these children as the top students and leaders in the school, with learning styles marked by inventiveness, curiosity, enthusiasm, and self-confidence. An evaluation from an honor graduate of Vanderbilt University said, "This was the only course I ever had where I really learned anything —about the subject or myself." We're proud of such responses and include them here to encourage you to try the filmmaking course with your own students.

The exercises work, we think, because they were formulated as a course of study from one central bias: what students learn and incorporate into themselves in an educational setting is not only the subject matter but the form of instruction itself. How the "what" presented here is translated into instruction thus becomes critical. That people learn to make films in this course—and they do— is virtually a spin-off, for the program is really designed to effect a change in the basic learning styles that characterize many educational environments.

The exercises have been most effective when instructors devoted their time to an analysis of the *process* and its dynamic, not the *products* (the students will attend to

the films without your help), and when the exercises are treated *like exercises:* push-ups, pull-ups, wind-sprints, finger-lifts. A gym instructor wouldn't expect each calisthenic to be performed perfectly every time but would look instead to the overall effect of the exercises. So too film instructors should regard the cumulative effect of these exercises, which include watching films, shooting film, watching one another's exercises, editing, monitoring student progress, and lots of talking.

When students work at these exercises in small groups it helps remove some of the more negative aspects of ego involvement and makes the effort more cooperative. Whatever else the instructor can do to set a noncompetitive tone within and between groups will encourage the students to share, take chances, explore more alternatives, and ultimately learn much more. Small groups also have the practical advantage of allowing you to rotate and recycle minimal amounts of equipment and film stock.

The order of exercises is presented here in a sequence that has been most useful to us when time and resources were available to do it all. But clusters and/or individual exercises can be and have been used in different sequences by teachers with other goals and objectives. We do not perceive the order of exercises as locked in and we encourage you to use whatever is useful and possible for you.

PROLOGUE TO THE COURSE: STORYBOARDING

The natural place to begin is with the storyboard. Storyboarding is a visual notation system for filmmakers, both an exercise in itself and a tool for many of the exercises that follow. The storyboard, and its written partner the *shooting script* or *scenario,* is a technique and an artifact for getting film down on paper.

The basic idea is very simple. For those who like to read definitions, we have teased out these: A film *shot* is what the camera records everytime someone holds the trigger down and film runs through the camera. A *storyboard* is the collected series of single pictures, each of which represents a single *frame* of each shot within a film or film sequence. The usefulness of the storyboard is that it provides the filmmaker with a medium that quickly and easily gives access to almost any technical, conceptual, or aesthetic problem lurking behind his or her untested idea.

If one can say that the basic job of the filmmaker is that of collecting images and ordering them in such a way as to make a statement that others can understand, then the filmmaker has to be familiar with all the possibilities of both choosing and ordering images. Storyboarding activities help young filmmakers discover these possibilities or variables.

Variables in technique: selecting images and shooting
In all storyboarding activities, students explore the different ways that images can be selected. Kids get practice in studying camera location (distance, angle, field of view) and composition (framing, lighting, color, texture). Although it is difficult to use storyboarding as an aid to exploring camera movement, there are ways of getting at this, too.

Variables in conceptualization: developing sequences and editing
A second group of variables has to do with the different ways that images can be brought together. Specifically,

these storyboarding activities develop discovery-based learning about four ways of bringing images into sequence: by narrative progressions (stories), by free associations (dreams), by design connections, and by contextual patternings (documentaries).

Looking back on it, there are many reasons why we found it important to spend time developing filmmaking activities that don't demand either cameras or film. Although no one has questioned the validity of storyboarding as a useful filmmaking tool, we would like to list the sound and pragmatic reasons we've found for doing such activities. Storyboarding is:

- a thing to do before the cameras come
- a means of insuring individual work among many students
- a preventative for film waste
- a means for teachers to check student ideas before production begins
- a framework for a better critical eye
- a vocabulary builder for film terminology
- a promoter of student response to each other's work
- something to do when equipment breaks down or film is at the lab
- a means of developing perceptual skills necessary in making movies
- a kind of homework which doesn't require production gear
- a medium for non-literate students to express their ideas
- an activity with immediate feedback
- a technically easy thing to do
- a low-cost activity

Many of the storyboarding activities in this course involve hunting through magazines for pictures to be used in new ways. We like the whole notion of recycling images.

UNIT ONE: DISCOVERING THE SEEING EYE

Perhaps one of the earliest and most surprising phenomena that a teacher of film (or for that matter any perceptive teacher) discovers is that students do not *see.* The National Perception Test run on TV a few years ago confirmed that Americans, contrary to their assumptions on the matter, do not see what is before their eyes largely because of perceptual laziness and cultural indoctrination.

Our experience in teaching this course and others with people of all ages and backgrounds demonstrates that much of what happens in front of one's eyeballs never registers consciously on the brain behind them. What does register is filtered through that curious maze of intellectual, racial, sexual, experiential, aesthetic, and other biases we generally call "learning."

The purpose of the exercises in this first unit, besides introducing the students to cinematography, is to enable them to begin to see. The exercises also involve the students looking at *what is seen* and *the structure imposed* by people on their vision. These abilities are also directly transferable to every other learning situation.

Exercise 1: Seeing within a Photograph

Idea/Problem
The filmmaker's most basic skill is the ability to see the totality of a thing, its details, its relationships, and (as in the title of the Wallace Stevens poem) "not the ideas

Photo study for storyboard

scene with a Monstrous Mitchell camera which is too heavy to move in any direction but which has a fantastic zoom lens capable of capturing the smallest detail. The students are to study the photograph until each one "sees" something to tell about. Any photograph contains many possible film-worthy situations. Our sample photograph on this page could lead to a film story about the relationship of the two boys, or the three boys, to a documentary on village life, to a nature film, or to a film interested only in the form of wooden structures or the texture of living things, etc.

Having "seen" what he or she wants to "film," keeping with a specific sequence in mind and using a ruler or a movable framer gizmo (see storyboarder's framer, figure 1), the student outlines in pencil five to ten *images* within the photograph that can reveal the film in the student's mind. Each image is numbered in sequence (or if you have multiple copies of the same photo, the student can cut out the images). In marking off each individual shot, the student should try to keep close to a rectangle shape with a ratio of 3 height to 4 width. This 3:4 ratio is the standard *aspect ratio* of motion picture photography. The five or more images in sequence constitute both a *cameraless movie* and a *basic storyboard* (see figures 2 and 3 for two different story treatments for the same photograph).

about the thing, but the thing itself." The filmmaker must next be able to put this vision on film. He or she must select images and put them in such an order that the viewer will see a particular relationship among the selected images.

Often the filmmaker shows us the relationship among images through the convention of a narrative structure. Other times, the filmmaker uses a documentary structure to show us a personal view of what he or she sees. Although these two structures are most prevalent, when a filmmaker is faced with a situation, there is an almost limitless choice of structure and images. No two filmmakers when dealing with the same situation will make the same film.

But first the student filmmakers must begin to see. This exercise helps sharpen their eyes for composing shots and helps them see the multiplicity of alternatives inherent in any situation.

Exercise

Give each student a copy of the same photograph. It should contain lots of *action* or details. You can tell the students that they have been dropped in front of this

Optional exercises

Have each student do a second storyboard that is different from the first one, or have the students rearrange the images originally selected to create a different meaning or emphasis. How is meaning or interpretation changed by a simple rearrangement of the sequence of images?

Have the students label each of their shots in terms of how far the camera would be from the action. Students can also be asked to write captions beneath each frame or to provide a separate written discussion of the *story* or *relationship* that is being examined.

Since this activity is also helpful in showing something about *framing,* select a visual element that many of the students have chosen and have the students compare how the picture was framed by different people. What feelings and effects do the various framings cause?

Be sure to have students compare their own storyboard to those of others in the class. Throughout this and all the other exercises, such comparisons should emphasize the positive.

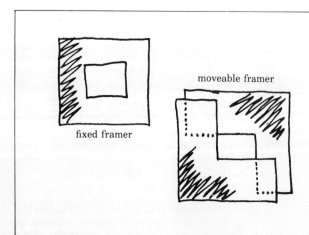

moveable framer

fixed framer

Fig. 1 Storyboarder's Framers

In deciding just what portion of a photograph or drawing to select for a storyboard, a simple framing device can be helpful. One kind is the *fixed framer,* which consists of a piece of cardboard with a frame cut out of it. Remember the 3 to 4 *aspect ratio* of the camera's field of vision. By sliding the framer over a particular visual you can contrast different possible *compositions.* The framer can also be used to make pencil lines that direct subsequent cutting. A variation is the *moveable framer,* made of two "L" shaped pieces of cardboard. By working these two together it is easy to experiment with different sizes of frames when studying a photograph before cutting it up.

Comments

Getting a large number of the same photograph is often difficult. If you are particularly solvent, you can have a commercial printer duplicate copies for you, and he can blow up small photos into large ones. If you have access to a darkroom, you can print many copies from the same negative. A high school photography club will often help. If you have access to a photocopy machine, you can experiment with how well a photograph can be reproduced. Some machines are better than others. If you can find a line drawing with lots of action, this will duplicate well by photocopy. Finally, if you can't find a way to have the same photograph duplicated in quantity, have the kids choose their own photographs from magazines. This is the final resort. The problem with using magazines is that images cannot be repeated, and there is no way to see what the whole photograph was like after it is storyboarded. Also, if the pictures selected are different, the kids cannot compare their own work to that of others in the class.

Exercise 2: A Narrative Storyboard

Idea/problem

It is easy for a filmmaker to lose control of his idea during the process of actually capturing it through the camera. This activity provides students with a good medium for making visual notations of images and sequences of action they want to film. It helps kids sharpen their ideas and spot conceptual weaknesses before time, energy,

and film have been committed. Also, by doing a narrative storyboard, the student provides some basis for the teacher to be of help in offering criticism and guidance. The problem to be solved in this activity might be given in conjunction with a first assignment in filmmaking.

Exercise

Students who will work together on the movie first decide on the basic *action* for a short narrative film. Next, they visit the *scene* or *scenes* of the film and discuss how the shooting might go. Returning to class, the problem is now to *fix* the content of each shot and the order of the shots by making pencil sketches. It is important to stress that the quality of the kids' artwork is not important. Simple drawings, with no detail, are better for storyboarding than finely rendered masterpieces. Have each sketch in the storyboard done on a separate piece of paper (index cards work well).

When all the sketches have been done, students should assemble their full storyboards by pinning individual frames onto a bulletin board. Here everyone can easily study the projected flow of images and the story they seek to tell. Individual frames may be added, or deleted, or the sequence may be changed easily and simply. When the order looks right, the cards are numbered. When the storyboard is disassembled, it is an easy reference which can be used when the filmmakers are *on location*.

An Example

Our protagonist in our narrative (see figure 4) is a comics freak. He reads comics all the time. Even on his way to school. And he dreams about being Superboy. In the

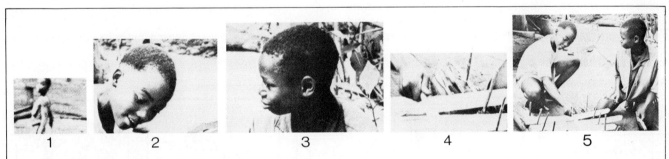

Fig. 2 Example of a Basic Storyboard—First Treatment

The fifth frame in this storyboard is the entire scene as presented in the full photograph. Here the order of images explores the relationship between the three children. Central to this interpretation is the teaching/learning experience of the two boys in the foreground. The first frame arouses a curiosity that the last shot resolves. But if the first and last frames were switched there would be a quite different meaning.

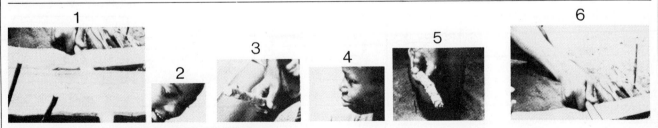

Fig. 3 Example of a Basic Storyboard—Another Treatment

This treatment stresses the rhythm of the musicians and the action that such a scene would really have. All the shots are close-ups. There is no *establishing shot*, such as frame 5 in figure 2 above. Using only close-ups tends to disorient the viewer and emphasize movement above all other variables. Note that the action in frames 1 and 6 is repeated, though framed a little differently.

house next door lives a girl with a thing about dogs. As she walks her dog each morning before school starts, she dreams up stories about herself and her dog—saving lost cats, catching robbers, etc.—they are public avengers with super powers. Our story deals with the inevitable: a collision of fantasies, brought on by a collision of the bodies of the protagonist and the girl next door.

For this narrative, two different approaches can be taken to draw the storyboard frames, but the action covered for both is the same (see figure 4). In the first approach, each frame is a sketch showing part of each shot as it would be seen within the camera's viewfinder. In the second, each frame consists of aerial charts showing the camera setup for each shot. Students should choose whichever style of framing is most easy and helpful for them.

Comment

In order to promote conceptualization in purely visual terms, it is best not to have students put any written descriptions or dialogue information on their storyboards. They can provide this either in written or verbal form when they present their work to the class or to the teacher.

It may be helpful to have the entire class work on the same basic story line, with all individuals developing separate *treatments* of the narrative. This encourages interaction. By studying all the storyboards (with, say, groups working on different sections of the rough story), a class as a whole can choose a final film treatment for a group production.

Optional Exercises

Have students choose partners and swap storyboards. After explaining their entire story to each other, partners must carefully study the storyboard done by the other and make suggestions about possible additions or deletions.

If single frames of the storyboards are done on file cards, have the creator of each storyboard shuffle the cards, give them to someone else, and have the new person put the cards in whatever order makes sense.

Exercise 3: The Camera as Eye (Narrative Filmmaking)

Idea/problem

The eye is a selective "seer," sharply focusing on only a small segment of the area within the field of vision at any given time. The brain, consciously or otherwise, controls this selectivity. The camera, however, works differently. Its eye sees everything within a given range, equally and unselectively.

The significance of these differences is often missed by the beginning filmmaker who considers the camera something to look *through* instead of something to look *with*. Thus he or she continues to use the same selectivity mechanisms normally used when looking at the world. Consequently what the *student sees* while filming often differs from what the film reveals and subsequent *audiences see*.

A prime skill for the young filmmaker to acquire is using the picture frame as *selector* so that the camera sees exactly what the brain is seeing. While all the exercises have the development of this skill as a tacit goal, this exercise concentrates on getting the student to see *with*, not merely through, the camera.

Exercise

While the aim here is to get students to use the frame as the selector of images put before an audience, several other important areas can also be developed: composition of the images within the frame; movement into, out of, and within the frame; screen direction; screen time; continuity.

1. With one cartridge of Super 8 film or its equivalent, shoot a narrative film (one that tells a story) with an identifiable plot, having a beginning, middle, and end; shoot it in that

Fig. 4 Example of a Narrative Storyboard

This example illustrates two different approaches to drawing storyboard frames. The action covered in each is the same. In the first series, each frame is a sketch showing part of each shot as it would be seen within the camera's viewfinder. In the second approach, the frames consist of aerial charts representing the camera setup for each shot. Students should choose whatever style of drawing is most easy and helpful for them.

order (despite Godard) and in correct sequence (so that it can be shown *as shot* without editing). This film will run approximately 3 minutes, 20 seconds.

2. The film is to be made in no less than 12 shots and no more than 15 shots. A shot, in this case, is the length of film exposed during any one time that the camera's shutter is activated. The duration of each shot is decided by the filmmaker; it may last a fraction of a second or several minutes, depending on the effect desired.

3. The camera's eye may not move *during* the shooting (no pans, zooms, focal changes, etc.). Each shot should be carefully composed to show exactly what the filmmaker wants the audience to see.

Films

The films cited here and elsewhere in this chapter are frequently found in school or public library film collections. Almost all of them are well-known "classics." We recommend that you take time to speak with your film librarian about newer or other films that might serve the same purposes as the titles mentioned here. You might also refer to a number of periodicals that review 16mm films. Many libraries will be able to show you the catalogs of 16mm film distributors from whom these films can be purchased or rented. Finally, you can write to film distributors directly and they will happily send you their catalogs of their collections. The Educational Film Library Association (known as EFLA—see the Resources section) has a number of publications that will be helpful in your selection and identification of films for the exercises described herein, and they also are the best source for film distributors' addresses. It should go without saying that it is *absolutely essential* that the teacher preview any film before showing.

The following films show excellent use of the frame or shot as selector: *The Golden Fish* and *Sky* (both use minimal camera movement); *In the Kitchen* and *La Jette* (both use no camera movement); *Occurrence at Owl Creek Bridge* and *Chickamauga* (incredible use of point of view); *Junkyard*, *Peace*, and *Voices in the Wilderness*.

Comment

In developing this exercise, the instructor should encourage an attitude of positive criticism, urging students to talk freely, without undue ego involvement, about effective shots or how shots might have been different. It is better, and also more difficult, to stress talk about how the shots carried the story as opposed to the sheer cleverness of the story itself. The emphasis is on using the camera to see *with*, not on what is seen through the lens. Throughout these exercises, the emphasis during discussion should fall on *form*, on the use of the medium, as opposed to emphasis on *content*, on the choice of subject matter.

Exercise 4: Editing Time and Space

Idea/problem

The Occidental "seer" sees both space and time as continuous and contiguous and time as flowing in one direction. Neither space nor time needs to be continuous or contiguous in film, and time can flow in many directions. Time and space are not constants but variables which a filmmaker uses to create a film. The editor can collapse or stretch time. The editor can connect Bali and Bala, or connect different ages, or make a life flow backwards. All this becomes evident when one first begins to edit.

Exercise

The main purpose is to help the student distinguish between real time and film reel time, but this exercise also allows the student to practice the mechanical and organizing detail necessary in editing.

Take the story told in one cartridge of film (Exercise 3) and retell it in exactly 60 or 90 seconds by editing, but maintain the sequence, continuity, and general story line of the original footage.

Optional Exercises

Take the *outtakes* from the preceding exercise (the leftover 110 to 120 seconds of film) and edit them into another 60-second film that has nothing to do with the story told in the preceding editing assignment. A variation on this is to have students swap their outtakes and then construct the second film.

Films

These films deal with time and space and editing: *Time Is, Time Piece, La Jette, La Poulet, Occurrence at Owl Creek Bridge, The House, Help My Snowman is Burning Down.*

Comment

There are many acceptable film editors for under $30. Get one with these features: a large viewing screen that shows the entire frame, easy access to the frame viewed in the screen (so you can cut precisely at the frame desired), reel locks on the rewind arms, and fluid back and forth movement through the gears. The one sketched in figure 5 is adaptable to both 8mm and Super 8 film.

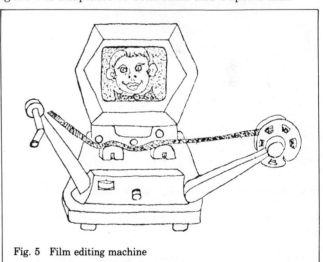

Fig. 5   Film editing machine

There are also several acceptable film cutters and splicers available for under $10. The most important features are immovable pins, so that every cut is the same, and a cutting blade which cuts straight on a frame line as opposed to one which cuts through the frame diagonally.

The splices most often used in 8mm are presstape, Guillotine rolltape (dry), and glue (wet). We have no real preference, but be forewarned that some expensive projectors do not take splices of any kind very well. Basic simple projectors do much better.

Two things which help the editing job become more pleasant are cleanliness and organization. Fingerprints or dust under a splice tape are permanently a part of the

Splicing 16mm film

film. In fact, fingerprints anywhere can etch themselves into the emulsion. Practice handling film by the edges and cleaning dirt off immediately.

Students should develop an index and notation system which enables them to locate any particular shot cut out of the film. Pinning cut film to a cork board under numbers and having a sheet with corresponding numbers and descriptions is a large step toward good organization. A medium size box can also be a good portable editing room. Hang the film into the box (so it stays clean and undamaged) and pin or tape it under numbers written on the rim.

Also important to editing is a grasp of Axiom Eleven from Dunn's Dialectic and Laybourne's Law. Axiom Eleven posits: "One minute of film shot equals one hour of editing." Laybourne's Law states: "Estimate how long the job will take; multiply by six!"

UNIT TWO: EXPLORING ALTERNATIVE EYES

Part of what the teacher will learn from the previous unit of exercises is that students look at the world in conventional and predictably stereotyped ways. Even in the exercise using the camera frame as the selector, most shots will be from similar and familiar angles and with similar camera-to-subject distances.

Not so evident is that talk about films has slipped into conventionalized patterns which may miss the basic experience offered by a particular film. In order to follow a conversation, you must know the language being spoken. Many of the most effective films leave people looking for an appropriate language to express their ideas and feelings about the film experience.

The major purpose of this section is to ask students to discover alternative ways to look at their experiences, both visual and audio, and to use the variables available to express these to others. The ability to explore alternatives and varying modes of explanation are valuable tools in any intellectual or creative pursuit.

Exercise 5: Exploring Camera Variables

Idea/problem

Human perception of the visible environment is generally predetermined by the accident of evolution which endowed a mobile biped platform with a seeing apparatus which, for most adults, is located 4–7 feet above foot level. In the main, humans see the world from within this 3-foot horizontal band. This narrow range of view is not an incorrectable limitation (man can crawl through the bushes or fly to the moon) but one of habit. Predictably, most film is shot by habit from within this 3-foot band. Obviously the camera has no such limitation. It can see from wherever it is placed. It can see at various speeds. It can see events backwards. It can alter colors. It can control focus. And so on.

Exercise

The purpose of this exercise is for the student to discover as many camera variables and classes of variables as possible.

Shoot one cartridge of film. With each shot, explore a different variable of the camera. The kinds of variables should include: camera angle and position, the speed at which frames are shot per second, camera movement (including focal movement), focus, light and light sources, filters and other mediums through which to shoot, and so on. This last variable is incredibly rich, and, in the past, students have used ordinary household items (from colanders to bottles) to achieve some incredible effects.

Optional Exercises

1. Shoot the above exercise with a single object as the subject matter.

2. Begin by treating some object abstractly (dealing with color, form, or fragments of the object) and gradually change your treatment to one which is more concrete, dealing with the object in context.

For example, using a fireplug as a subject, begin with still, close-up shots of the texture of cracking paint or the hexagon patterns of the cap bolts; then shoot down on the circular top, rotating the camera; then pan rapidly around the vertical striations of the body; then move along the chain, holding the camera sideways; and so on, ending with a shot of a firefighter attaching a hose, or a dog sniffing the base.

Films

Suggested films that explore various ways of seeing are: *Up Is Down, Time Is, Omega,* and *Pas De Deux.*

Comment

This exercise could justly be called "The Great Liberator." Over the years it has turned more people on to film and to their own potential as filmmakers than anything else in the course.

Allow this to be a truly discovery-based exercise. You may ask the class to brainstorm on the assignment before they shoot, listing all the variables they can think of and listing all they anticipate discovering while they do the exercise. There is no real learning if the instructor simply gives out a list of variables without student involvement.

A simple gadget to help in "looking" and "seeing" is the director's viewfinder. Your students can make their own with cardboard tubing (see figure 6).

Exercise 6: Sound Experiences

Idea/problem

The importance of sound is usually underestimated by beginning film students, who, after laboring over visual images, often casually pick some record which "goes with" the film. Yet sound, more than pictures, strikes at the very core of the emotional content in film. Its presence is very different from visual presence. Sound surrounds the listener. One cannot turn off the ears in the same way one can close the eyes. Sound enters through the viscera; we are struck by its vibrations like tuning forks. Yet all too frequently, sound is considered secondary.

Exercise

1. Make a sound track of music, effects, and/or narrative voice which strongly supports the visual images of the edited narrative film (Exercise 3).
2. With outtakes from any of your exercises, cut a film to match the tempo of any piece of music.

Optional Exercises

You might wish to anticipate an exploration of mood within film (Unit five) by asking students first to select a sound track that creates a certain mood, then to shoot a film that captures or reinforces that mood.

Another effective exercise is to play records or tapes as the sound track to "professional" 16mm films. In one titled *Moods of Surfing,* the waves seem much less imposing with a Brubeck track than with a Mahler. Other films to play around with include: *Sky, Dream of Wild Horses, Peace, Other Voices in the Wilderness,* and *Frank Film.*

Comment

Here is a short guide to three sound-making skills which students may need to explore in this exercise. Note that there is a chapter in this book on creative work with sound. Apply its comments to student filmmaking.

1. Use the patch cord to get relatively "clean" sound from records, tape, etc., onto a taped sound track. A patch cord is an electric wire, with a jack at both ends, which allows you to transfer sound directly from one source to an audio tape recorder without going through speaker and microphone again. Plug one jack into the socket marked "exterior speaker" or "tape out" on the original source machine; the other jack is plugged into the socket marked "auxiliary input" on the copying machine. You can use the volume control to fade sound in or out and modulate sound through the track. There is not, unfortunately, total standardization among jack sizes, and finding the right adapters is sometimes Kafkaesque. Always record at the fastest speed possible, using 7½ ips., for greater fidelity.
2. Mix sound on stereo tape decks to allow you to overlap two or more sound sources. As you can surmise, after you have put sound on one stereo channel, you can add a different sound to the other channel and thus overlap or *double expose* sound. Further, by using a "Y-jack," so named for its shape, you can re-record the sound from channels A and B onto

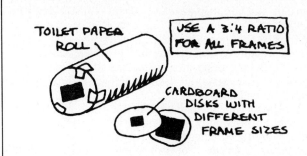

Fig. 6 Director's Viewfinder
A cardboard toilet paper roll or other tubing can make a nice viewfinder. Have kids cut out different "frames" in the disks that they tape to one end of the roll. Different sized frames correspond to different lenses and shots that the filmmaker can use: a big frame equals a "wide-angle" or "establishing" or "long-shot;" a tiny frame equals a "telephoto" or "close-up" shot. Have kids study the effects of different frames by standing in one spot and holding different openings to the other end of the roll. Then have students check out which frame they find most effective in studying a particular object or activity in the classroom.

channel A of another stereo deck, leaving channel B open for yet another sound source. Stereo mixing is a particularly effective and easy way to edit sound.

3. Cutting and splicing sound tape gives the capability for precise sound editing. By applying the "instant stop" button on the tape deck and slowly pulling the tape manually a few times across the recording-playback head, you can hear precisely where a sound begins or ends. On a two-headed machine, head two is the record-playback head; on a three-headed machine, head three plays back. The best cutting block is a simple slotted piece of metal with two slits, one diagonal and the other perpendicular.

On the tape selected, place the spot to be cut directly over the diagonal slit and, with a single-edge safety razor blade, cut the tape. You can then attach it to another diagonally cut tape with an adhesive splicing tape especially made for this purpose. The diagonal cut eliminates "popping" sounds as the cut passes over the head.

A very helpful trick in synchronizing a sound track to a Super 8 film is to cut the tape just before the first sound and splice colored leader or paper leader onto the beginning of the tape. This way you can see where the sound begins and start both the sound and image simultaneously. However, since projectors and tape recorders run at slightly different speeds, do not expect precise sync or lip sync.

Exercise 7: An Interlude with Storyboarding: Comic Relief

Idea/problem

Comic strips are highly sophisticated narrative storyboards. They tell their stories with much visual information and a minimum of verbal data. By studying the ways that comics tell their stories, students can discover much about the selection and ordering of visual images. Comics, as do all mediums, vary widely in their effective exploration of alternatives. Traditional comics have many static and wide-angle graphics, but some comics, notably the super-hero type, use a rich selection of angles, distances, and special effects. From the latter variety, students can find an imaginative use of various angles and viewpoint positions and can also develop a basic film-storyboarding vocabulary.

Exercise

Each student cuts apart the *shots* or *frames* of a comic strip. Next, he groups them according to how much each shot shows of a particular scene. Each grouping should be given a name based on this thought: "If the camera were taking the picture instead of an artist drawing it, how far back would the camera be?" The categories the kids select ought to produce names like these: *extreme close-up, close-up, medium shot, two-shot* (two people), *long shot*, etc. The whole class can work at compiling a master list of the shots and agreeing on a name for each. This activity will produce a shared vocabulary that will help in subsequent work and discussions.

Optional Exercises

Select a short 16mm film (any kind will do) and show it to the class a number of times. During one of the screenings, have kids "shout out" the kind of shots as they appear. Do the shots developed from comic analysis match those used in the real movies?

Have kids rearrange the frames of a given comic book so that it tells a new story. Put dialogue into each shot by writing the words beneath the new sequence of images.

Tally the numbers of close-ups, long shots, etc., in an entire comic book. Are there more of one kind than another? Why?

See if it is possible to cut any single shot out of a comic book without hurting the clarity of the story. Is there any point at which a new frame would make things clearer?

Have the kids study the ways that *time* is conveyed in comics. Search out other graphic symbols that comic books have. For example, what is the difference between symbols for the narrator's voice (third person), dialogue between characters (first person), and thoughts (second person, interior monologue)? What graphic symbols denote dreams, telephone conversations, simultaneous action?

Comment

Either in addition to another project or as a problem itself, you might have your students collect samples of all the different kinds of photographs that they discover as they leaf through magazines. By doing this and compiling lists of all the variables they uncover, students will develop an awareness of the tremendous variety of photographic images that exist. Also, they will develop a respect for the craftsmanship and creativity of professional photographers.

It may be helpful to set parameters in searching out different kinds of photographs. For example: camera angle, lighting, choice of lens, special effects in printing (like double exposure, high contrast, color separation). Or genres of photography: still life, documentary, reportage, portraiture. Or the applied uses of photography: news, science, fashion, commercial art, or art for its own sake.

BOGUS FILMS

The opaque projector can be transformed into a super storyboarding gimmick (see figure 7) that offers students a really neat way to share their storyboarding. The creator mounts his or her work on a long roll of paper and then projects it with the opaque projector. Kids can even make audiotapes of music, dialogue, sound effects, or narration tracks and play these additional creations as they direct

their storyboards through the opaque projector. This activity can be done with visuals that the kids have hand drawn themselves or have gleaned from magazines, comic books, or other sources.

UNIT THREE: SEEING THE ESSENTIAL

A pervasive problem for people today is information overload: a glut of data, opinions, commentaries, rumors, guesses, premonitions—sometimes revealed as such, sometimes masquerading as fact. We are often left apathetic or confused, trying to separate fact from fiction.

The problem for the young filmmaker is to look at an event, decide what is the nature of that event, and select those images which an audience will read to understand the event. The discrimination exercised in the following unit is applicable to any investigation and is particularly apt for any interface with mass or environmental media. We feel that dealing with the problems raised in this unit is central to achieving a semblance of sanity in the modern world.

Exercise 8: A Documentary Storyboard

Idea/problem

When making a documentary film, the filmmaker first gathers images about the topic. Then, from studying the material collected, the documentarist must develop ways of putting those images together so they will relay an *interpretative* or *objective* point of view. During the shooting, the filmmaker usually tries not to "interfere" with the environment or action being filmed, but gathers images while things are happening. The documentarist has no more control during editing than during shooting; for, unlike working in a narrative mode, there is no predetermined structure to aid making decisions about what pieces of film should go where.

Exercise

Each student selects a "topic" for his or her storyboard. The subject should be a broad one so that a wide variety of pictures can be found in newspapers and in magazines. Good topics might include: ecology, cities, war, women, ethnic minorities, school, animals, disasters, sports, children, old people, feet, trees, etc. After finding as many images as possible (at least twice as many as the final storyboard will use), students spread their pictures out

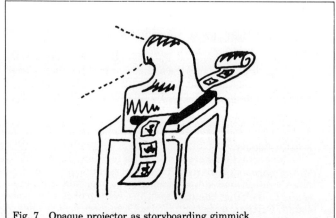

Fig. 7   Opaque projector as storyboarding gimmick

and look for patterns to group the images. If the topic were cities, for example, the kids might be able to discover patterns like the size of buildings, or bridges, or images of old and new, or images without people, or colors, or feelings of loneliness, or expressions of alienation. Discourage students from using any kind of narrative device to connect series of images.

An Example

Let us make a short documentary storyboard about "faces," using cutouts from magazines (see figure 8). Three *patterning* principles will work at the same time, yet the storyboard will try for one overall effect.

The first five frames move progressively from further-out to closer-in. The facial expressions become increasingly more serious and direct, the images more and more abstract as the storyboard proceeds. The overall effect is to lead the viewer to focus on the eyes in the faces of each frame. In the last frame, although the picture is a long shot, the viewer should be led forcefully into the center of the photograph, right into the troubled and averted eyes of the young soldier.

Comment

It is valuable to have some of your students working individually within the same topic categories. This allows them to contrast different approaches to the same subject. It is also helpful for students to write about the organizing patterns they used. They might swap their documentary storyboards and have others see if they can deduce the patterning principles used or (by shuffling the frames) discover new patterns.

Optional Exercise

Students can do a second documentary storyboard, selecting an abstract topic. For example: loneliness, love, joy, fear, friendship.

Exercise 9: Discovering the Thing Itself (Documentary Filmmaking)

Idea/problem

Beyond the aesthetic consideration of using the frame precisely and using the full potential of the camera, the filmmaker is still faced with the problem of what to show an audience. Which images must be collected to capture the essential nature of any event? The filmmaker must also decide which shooting technique best captures the nature of an event. Should a film documenting the excitement of a high school football game differ in format from a film on the school's chess team?

This is a difficult problem which entails a few skills on the filmmaker's part: first, an understanding of what is filmed; second, an ability to select the essential details which reveal the nature of the subject; third, the ability to select an appropriate format for the subject. Given the proposition that chess is more exciting than football, the filmmaker must deal with the philosophical question: Can any film be objective, or is the process inherently subjective?

Exercise

With one cartridge of film have each student document some person, activity, situation, or locale they feel they know well. Have them select those images that capture the essence of the subject and that faithfully communicate the filmmaker's point of view to an audience. The subject should be divided into its important components, and the camera should concentrate on each of these salient features. Further, ask them to make the tone of their shooting match the tone of their subject.

Films

Glass, Law and Order, Imogen Cunningham, Junkyard, City of Gold, Hospital.

Fig. 8 Example of Documentary Storyboard
Three patterns of "Faces" make an impact, and the documentalist a statement.

Comment

This is a good time to immerse your class in questions of emulsion. Decide when it is appropriate to use color film and when black-and-white is better. For example, would shooting Halloween costumes or Mummers or Mardi Gras in black-and-white capture the flavor of those subjects? Does shooting a slum in color brighten the tone of an otherwise bleak existence?

Exercise 10: Editing by Visual Patterning

Idea/problem

Few beginners think beyond content or temporal continuity in their editing, yet there is a more valuable kind of continuity to the filmmaker. This is one in which he or she places images side by side, using, as a criterion, how much each visual adds to the meaning of the visuals on either side of it and how well images add up to a more comprehensive understanding of the subject documented.

An editor should attempt to develop visual patterns in successive cuts. The patterns themselves should add to or develop the filmmaker's meaning. Regardless even of content, an editor attempts to create a visual "meaning" or to pattern the images in such a way that the very order is significant. The example of patterning in the documentary storyboard demonstrates what can be done with even the simplest of images.

Exercise

Edit a documentary film sequence down to 90 or 120 seconds. Edit so that each cut relates strongly to and enhances the audience's understanding of each adjoining cut. Let the cuts in each sequence of shots pile up details so that the cumulative images reveal the nature of your subject more clearly to your audience and give them a better understanding than they would probably get from a first hand viewing of the subject themselves.

Optional Exercise

After the final cut is completed, make a voice-over sound track which is:

1. descriptive, verbally reinforcing the images on the screen
2. additionally informative, including details not shown on the screen
3. as objective as possible, sticking to the facts

Films

Letter from Siberia, Glass, Sky, Leaf, Very Nice-Very Nice, diving sequence from *Olympiad, La Jette, I Think They Call Him John.*

Exercise 11: Exploring Bias

Idea/problem

People tend to believe what they see, mistaking film for reality and equating film images with actual images. Film is an illusory art. Aside from objectivity-subjectivity disputes, it is plain that one can lie with film, manipulate images, or otherwise give false impressions. The purpose of the following exercises is not, however, to teach students to lie but rather to help them to be more critical of films they see and to be more careful of viewpoint in films they make.

Exercise

With one 50-foot cartridge shoot one of the following films:

1. Choose a subject which has a "favorable" reputation and shoot it with a totally unfavorable bias; for example, a film depicting Santa Claus as a greedy, mercenary old miser.

2. Choose a subject which has a fairly unfavorable reputation and shoot it with a totally favorable bias; for example, a film which depicts an urban slum as a vacation paradise.

This objective should be reached through visual images, with careful attention to camera angles, camera movement, and lighting. This is also a good place to attempt optical distortion.

Sound can powerfully complement visual images. Contrasting sound can be even more powerful or more humorous. A sense of irony, using a sound track that counterpoints the visual, can often gain audience attention and involvement more readily than a straightforward presentation. Humor is by its nature incongruous and can be more incisive than the self-serious.

3. For your edited propaganda film, make a sound track supporting your visuals with ironic counterpoint; for example, the Santa Claus-greed images could be emphasized by spiritual Christmas hymns or the voices of little children extolling Santa's virtues.

4. Take your straightforward documentary film (Exercise 9) and make an incongruous sound track, seeing if you can make humorous what was shot seriously.

Films

Unanswered Question, Hat, Toys, The Selling of the Pentagon, Pigs, Chiefs.

Comment

This might be the best place to put the objective-subjective myth to rest. An effective exercise is one requiring three film crews, each of which is to film the same event, place, people, etc. The first group is told to be positive in approach; the second, negative; and the third, perfectly objective. Let the class try to distinguish which is which when viewing the finished films. Can the intentional bias be fortified and extended through the editing process? Can such bias be removed through editing? What happens when you include a sound track? Can a sound track be biased in the same way as the visuals? Is the intended bias evident if the sound track is played without the film?

UNIT FOUR: THE DESIGNING EYE

The exercises in this unit attempt to formalize some of the design components of film. They also work at strengthening the patterning-perception skills developed in the last section. If we consider the current state of knowledge and data gathering, we realize how important it is that students recognize patterns. These patterns do not have to be "content" patterns to be meaningful, useful, or information yielding. The *formal* patterns we are looking for in these exercises can yield fruitful, alternative explanations of events.

Exercise 12: A Design Storyboard

Idea/problem

Besides understanding methods of selecting and ordering images based on *subject* (documentary) and on *story* (narrative), the filmmaker must learn to use *design elements*. A visual design perspective is critical in creating any kind of movie. Moreover, an entire genre of films uses design as content, as subject or story matter, in addition to using the design elements to mediate organization and structure. This storyboarding problem helps kids discover and explore the dimensions of *movie art*.

Exercise

To begin, have each student look through magazines for a single favorite photograph that he or she especially likes and would want to use as the basis for the *design storyboard*. Next, locate a photograph that relates to the first in some way other than through subject matter or story line. Some "other ways" include: 1) composition of the total picture; 2) color; 3) texture; 4) the shape of a central part of the image; 5) contrast; 6) framing; 7) lighting; 8) direction of suggested movement; 9) feeling of movement; or 10) combinations that are strongly *opposite* in the kinds of design relationships listed here. The third picture in the storyboard must relate to the second (but not necessarily to the first) visual. Following this procedure, build a string of ten frames in the storyboard. The fifth photograph, to review the rule, would have a *design connection* with those photographs on either side of it (the fourth and sixth) but not necessarily with any other selected visual. For an example of a *design storyboard*, see figure 9.

Optional Exercises

As students present their design storyboards to the class by means of an opaque projector, have others try to figure out the connecting principles joining each image with those on either side of it. Photographs should be projected two at a time for this activity.

The entire class can compose a master list of the "design elements" by which it is possible to join images. Then, small groups can isolate one facet of these elements, say, *texture*, and make a storyboard that explores just this dimension.

Have each student use the new way of selecting and ordering images by reworking storyboards previously done. Can they find any natural *design connections* their "eye" put together as they worked on narrative or documentary storyboards? Is is possible to reframe old visuals to accentuate the new combining strategies?

Exercise 13: Exploring Motion

Idea/problem

Film art, we believe, is more analogous to music, poetry, and dance than it is to expository prose, novels, short stories, or drama (except to the extent that the latter is musical, poetic, or choreographed). Film is a temporal art and a movement art. Yet most students think of their films in terms of *content* (the story, the plot, etc.) rather than *form*. The medium is the missal, or missile, as the case may be.

Further, film is uniquely equipped to capture the lyric beauty of movement. The next two exercises get students to explore film as *pure form*, so that the *content* of the film is *form*.

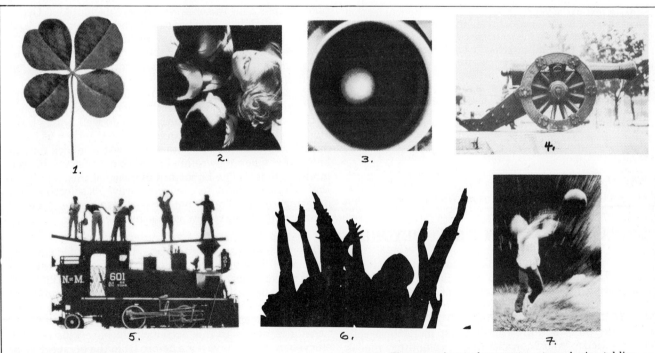

Fig. 9   Example of Design Storyboard

Design connectors used:

#1 to #2—Parallel composition in the four elements of the clover and the group.

#2 to #3—The circular relationship of the group is extended in the shot of a jet engine. In both the balance is slightly left of center.

#3 to #4—Matching shapes of a circle within a circle join these images.

#4 to #5—The cannon's muzzle presents a strong horizontal line that is similar to the structure and framing of the railroad engine.

#5 to #6—The flat texture of both photos and the high contrast of each provides a clear connecting principle. Strong vertical lines add to this connection.

#6 to #7—There is a parallel feeling of movement in both photographs—upward and out. There is also a reversal of basic shapes: dark on light in the first; light on dark in the second.

Exercise

Shoot one cartridge of film on moving objects. In each shot follow the movement with the camera. Select your images carefully so that definite colors, shapes, textures, compositions, motions, and directions of movement occur.

Films

Diving sequence from *Olympiad, Dream of Wild Horses,* bicycle sequence from *Butch Cassidy and the Sundance Kid, Ski the Outer Limit, Headcracker Suite, Capriccio, Ballet Adagio, Pas de Deux.*

Exercise 14: Editing for Design

Idea/problem

So far our editing exercises have dealt with criteria having to do with temporal continuity and "meaning," but film artistry has a strong formal facet that audiences, critics, and young filmmakers may miss. The overall design and sequence design, when done well, is invisible. It is a medium which carries out the filmmaker's intent without calling attention to itself. There are a few simple exercises the students can try to improve their films. These focus on color, shape, line, texture, composition, direction, and motion.

Exercise

1. Edit the motion film to any length. Splice each shot to the next, using dominant, recurring visual elements as the criterion for joining shots together. If a color is strong in one shot, let it recur in the next one. Then pick another criterion: a shape, a texture, a composition, or a similar motion; let that element recur in the next cut. Test student editing skills by having them structure the motions to flow together harmoniously, or have them mismatch cuts for a dissonant effect.

2. From the outtakes of previous exercises, edit a 60-second film using the outtakes from this exercise as formal transitions between sequences.

3. Use discarded 16mm films, old commercials, or the outtakes of earlier exercises, and edit a short film employing the formal design elements outlined above as sole criteria for joining images.

Films

Why Man Creates, Time Is, Omega, Imogen Cunningham, Pas de Deux, Meadows Green, Nine Variations on a Dance Theme, The Desert.

UNIT FIVE: TAKING THE STEP BEYOND

The importance of feelings and emotions is finally being recognized by the educational community. Schools of Humanistic Education and Departments of Affective Education are appearing on campuses and in school districts. Concurrently, and perhaps springing from the same societal source, there is a growing interest in Eastern religions, mysticism, and "nonscientific" explanatory modes for dealing with experience. For a long time, however, film and the other arts have been dealing with emotion and what the Occidental scholar would call nonlogical modes of cognition.

Filmmaking, perhaps more than any other medium, allows for experimentation with alternate ways of constructing reality. The exercises suggested in this section barely scratch the surface of these possibilities, and students and teachers might undertake an additional assignment to develop new exercises exploring the non-rational and nonlogical interior world of emotion, feeling, and imagination.

Exercise 15: A Dream Storyboard

Idea/problem

We spend one-third of our lives sleeping. When we sleep, we dream, and dreaming is the mind's way of talking with itself, an intramural communication that takes place in almost pure imagery. (Ever notice how little talking there is in dreams?) Dreams are important, and dreaming is a special form of communication ordered more by "association" than "logic," more by psychic weight than by force of reason.

Many people concerned with the aesthetics of film consider movies to be the closest thing we have to dreams, and many filmmakers explore the medium from just this perspective. This activity is designed to allow students to attempt the same thing.

Exercise

Have students write down (upon awakening, before the day's activities obscure details and weaken impressions) any notes they can recall about their dream. Try especially hard to isolate a particular sequence that was clear, and make a storyboard of it by drawing or assembling pictures that re-create the specific images remembered. Figure 10 illustrates a student-made *dream storyboard.*

Sometimes it is difficult to remember any dreams. A parallel activity is to have students collect a number of photographs that in some way seem "dreamlike." Order these images into a storyboard and choose a sequence that "feels" right. Do not attempt to follow patterns or sequences previously used. Exclude design connections, story lines, and documentary patterning. Rely solely on intuition and feelings.

Unless familiar with your students and have some insight into dreams and dream theory or a real confidence in this kind of thing, teachers would do well *not* to have students go into long explanations about either of these dream-storyboarding activities. The best feedback for the kids comes when they relate how each other's storyboards made them feel. The important message of this activity is that it gives weight to nonlinear ways of selecting and ordering images. The activity seeks to legitimize modes of expression that have few verbal handles.

Optional Exercises

The teacher may wish to lead a discussion focusing on the "logic" of association (or whatever it is) that seems to bring dream images together. A good way to initiate this talk would be for teachers to describe one of their dreams or to make a *dream storyboard* out of images that were personally moving in some deep way.

An alternative to this activity is to have kids reorder storyboards they have done before from the perspective of dreamlike intuition. This works especially well with documentary storyboards.

Ask students to create a storyboard about an abstract word or phrase (such as love, feeling at home, alone on another planet, sickness). Sometimes a memory from early childhood can be an effective goad to finding pictures and putting them in order (such as being held closely by mother, walking with father, being chased home from school by the class bully).

Exercise 16: Setting Moods

Idea/problem

Like other art forms, film can evoke a wide range of emotions. For many, this affective side of cinematography is its sole reason for being. Thus, a critical skill for the filmmaker is the ability to set a scene that clearly conveys its emotional content as it develops its subject or story line. Earlier, the importance of *sound* in setting a mood or tone was explored. Now we examine the capacity of *images* to express the emotional richness of human life and the heightened experience which results when *both* work harmoniously to stimulate our feelings.

Exercise

Select some piece of art (music, poetry, sculpture, painting) which makes you feel a certain way. Decide what the feeling is and then make a film in which the imagery evokes that same feeling for you.

Optional Exercises

Make a sound track for your film. After running the sound track and film separately (to see if they actually make you feel the same), run them together to see if the feeling is intensified.

Take a short poem or piece of music as a sound track and have separate groups of students make a film to fit the same track. A remarkable variety of films will usually result.

Films

Seven Authors in Search of a Reader, Chickamauga, Dream of Wild Horses, and films by independent filmmakers such as Brakhage, Breer, Van Der Beek, Emschwiller, Snow, Belson, DeWitt, and many more.

Comment

Motion pictures and storyboards are specific mediums of communication. In some ways they are like all other communication arts and plastic arts and language arts and performing arts. In some ways they are different.

The most effective way of helping children appreciate both the essence and uniqueness of various media is by inventing activities to mix different media. Have students choose different art forms and try to see how they can be storyboarded (poetry seems to work especially well). Parts of prose selections can be storyboarded, too. Storyboarding pictures of a piece of sculpture, of a painting, or of a building can reveal important things about these arts. How could a storyboard help a play director to conceptualize ideas to the actors? Are there ways to storyboard favorite pieces of music? Can one mix dance and storyboarding? Is it possible to use storyboarding to create pieces of art in other media? Or vice versa? Can live actors interact with screen situations? Related-arts programs and multimedia programs open exciting possibilities, moving all the arts toward oneness and people toward an integration of experience.

UNIT SIX: COMMENCEMENT

This final part is not meant to be an ending. Unit Six and the exercises it contains, attempts to put the last touches

Fig. 10 Example of a Dream Storyboard

The first image starts a series of free associations. The result is a dream about things coming to an end.

Young filmmakers Cal Lewin and Larry Doff ponder a directional problem during filming of *The Starter*.

Discussing scenes with lighting crew during night shooting of *Mission: Garbanzo*. Lighting equipment was borrowed from a local TV station.

dium to use in creating film ideas and stories. Writing is better. The teacher would do well to separate storyboarding from writing for the screen.

In general, filmmakers use one of three styles for writing formats when they begin to work on a movie. There aren't many filmmakers who rely on "inspiration" alone —most spend hours and hours at the typewriter.

A *screenplay* is straight prose. It reads like a novel or short story. Special emphasis is given to describing locations and pieces of action within the film-to-be. Emphasis is also given to motivation, personality, and stylistic traits of the characters. Most films that aren't adapted from books or other sources originate as screenplays. There is no other way to present the detail of idea, situation, and story that the filmmaker needs.

A *scenario* looks like the written text of a play. Each "scene" is briefly described and the largest portion of writing is dialogue lines for various characters. Scenarios rarely provide details about movement within scenes, camera setups, or musical scores. If a particular style of filmmaking is required for a scene, this is noted briefly. For example, a scenario might describe images needed in a montage sequence: "montage: various newspapers carry banner headlines about robbery." Or a scenario might say something like: "The lighting in this scene should be very dark (low key), with tall shadows cast on the sides of the room as Quasimoto moves about."

A *shooting script* comes closest to a storyboard. A shooting script is usually made by the director, who separates all pieces of action (and dialogue) into small sections that will be filmed at the same time. Using either notes, sketches, diagrams, lists of shots, or a combination of all these, the director determines and analyzes the specific *shots* needed. The shooting script becomes a working document on location. The director needs it to previsualize each scene, to make the technical arrangements for each scene, to explain the desired effect to the crew and other coworkers, and, most important, to serve as a general guideline so that nothing critical will be forgotten during the madness of filming.

Exercise

For the next two exercises, process the making of the films through the steps of screenplay, scenario, and shooting script. Obviously, the value of this approach is dependent upon the writing skills of your students.

on the skills you have been developing in order to allow students to continue to use filmmaking in the process of self-discovery.

Filmmaking should already have made you more aware of your students' perceptions, needs, points of view, and personalities. And your students can continue to use their films as mirrors, as self-reflections in which they can measure change and growth.

This use of film to uncover and explore what is most human in our experience is probably the most valuable contribution film can make and the best reason for including it in the educational environment.

Exercise 17: Screenplays, Scenarios, and Shooting Scripts

Idea/problem

While storyboarding is very helpful for determining specific choices and flows of image, it is not the best me-

Exercise 18: Mini Epics

Idea/problem

So far, the exercises have concentrated on the components of filmmaking in a structured, particularized way. But film art is a union of these many components, as well as others which we have not dealt with (such as acting). One form of film work that synthesizes these skills most succinctly is the best of television advertising. No genre allows a student to test better the acquired cinematic skills, gives freer reign to fertile and imaginative ideas, or displays such a diabolical sense of humor as does the TV commercial or advertisement. It is also an excellent class project to do before turning students loose on EPIC PRODUCTIONS.

Exercise

Shoot, edit, and track an advertisement, either commercial or public service, in 10-, 20-, 30-, 40-, or 60-second formats.

Films

Every year the advertising industry provides awards, known as *Clios,* for the best spots (30- or 60-second film advertisements generally shown on television). A 16mm reel of winning spots is available from American TV Commercials, 30 East 60 Street, New York, N.Y. 10022.

Exercise 19: The Great American Dream

Idea/problem

The GREAT IDEA that each student or team of students has been frustratedly harboring all year is now ready for filming! The reason for holding the EPIC until last is that generally the merit of the idea far exceeds the students' ability to carry it out in film. More budding film interest has been mortally wounded by an unsatisfactory rendering of a good idea. By now, however, the chances for survival have been greatly improved.

Exercise

The obvious—write, storyboard, shoot, edit, track, publicize, and release THE FILM.

Comment

Allow teams and specialization to grow out of stated interest. Do not go "Hollywood" in over-specializing production crews. Some people will naturally gravitate toward editing, sound, etc., but allow that to evolve by generalizing all the tasks and permitting everyone to work at every job. However, it is important that roles and production jobs are clearly defined, and that the crew is explicit about expectations for individual members. Part of these expectations will revolve around scheduling, so it is good policy to have the crew set down a firm (yieldingly firm) production schedule that enables the students to plan without undue frustration.

A further, final note: students often feel that they can only work with original material. In doing so, they are losing a veritable cornucopia of ideas and stories, which they might have adapted into an "original film."

A POSTSCRIPT

Were we to make a case for the inclusion of filmmaking in the curriculum as part of the creative arts or humanities courses, we would have little opposition. In fact, throughout this country—in colleges, secondary schools, elementary schools, and even nursery schools—filmmaking is being taught in art departments, in communications departments, in humanities sections, and as part of English courses. That filmmaking has a legitimate place in those contexts is indisputable.

However, we would go further and state that the skills developed in this course are basic skills for survival in a mediated, technologically rich culture. Among the skills developed in this course are: *sensing*—students heighten their perceptions to sense things that would normally escape their attention in day-to-day living, and they become more aware of persons, things, and conditions in their

Filmmaking puts the learner in the center of the learning process.

environment; *reacting*—students relate to spontaneous thoughts and gut-level feelings aroused in everyday life; *responding*—students put emotions, feelings, ideas, and concepts into more complete frameworks or emerging systems; *reproducing*—students study old forms and content, then copy and rearrange them, understanding and mastering the techniques and appreciating excellence and originality; *creating*—students find activities in which they invent or re-invent new forms. All of these skills are broadly applicable to every pursuit in modern life.

This filmmaking course has other facets to recommend it. First, it deals in basic communications skills; second, it is experiential and, additionally, allows teacher and student to explore new ground and learn together in a context where no "teacher-expert" presumption is built in.

Taken as a communication skill, filmmaking becomes a way, a means—like reading and writing— of doing a discipline. Making a film is a way to study and learn history, sociology, or whatever. It has already been acknowledged as a highly acceptable way of "doing" anthropology.

Taken as experiential learning, filmmaking puts the learner in the center of the process. The spin-offs in terms of student motivation, increased positive self-image, active student participation, and renewed interest in other forms of learning are enormous and well documented. In many schools, filmmaking is a cooperative group project, and its value in teaching ways of accommodating group process is, by itself, justification for including it in the regular curriculum.

However, these exercises also suggest that the logical structure with which we build our rationale may be suspect. So we close with a simple request: "Try it, you'll like it." By trying it, experiencing it, and allowing all the alternatives to bounce around, you may develop into a person who is more open and better able to adapt to the rapid changes in the world today.

Stills from student film *Kung Phooey,* created by classes at Buena Vista School Annex, San Francisco, under the Artists-in-Schools Program, where filmmaker Darryl Savilla worked extensively with elementary and secondary schools in the Bay area.

Doing Animation

by Kit Laybourne; with a segment on
abstract animation by Todd
Flinchbaugh

Chapter Eight

Animation, judging by the quality of a Saturday
morning TV cartoon, may have sunk to an artistic
low in the lives of today's students. Here animator
Kit Laybourne explains how to make budding
Disneys out of all your animated animators.

Animated filmmaking is a technique of extreme simplicity: a stationary motion picture camera takes a few pictures (frames) at a time rather than continuously.

A truly wonderful universe is yours if you keep this simple definition in mind and if you can round up a tripod, some lights, and a camera that can expose single frames. It is a universe where a child's imaginings can be captured and shared, where simple objects can tell stories, and where children's artwork can come to life.

As a classroom technique, there are many things that animation has going for it:

It costs little. Of all the kinds of filmmaking that kids can do, animation costs the least because it uses very little film. Only a few extra filmmaking items are required. These are inexpensive. The materials that are needed for creating the kinds of animated films described here are already available in schools.

It is easy. Once the basic principles of animation are understood, making films is really simple. Due to the high degree of preproduction planning that is possible with animation, once the film has been shot there is generally little need for editing. The materials that kids work with present no unexpected problems such as those you can run into during live-action filmmaking with actors and shooting locations. Finally, it is easy to think of many interesting and diverse subjects, formats, and techniques for animated films.

It has organizational flexibility. You can fit animation into just about any classroom corner. Because animation takes place in one fixed location with fixed equipment setups, it is possible to begin and stop work without supervision once students are familiar with the process. Animation can be done by large or small groups of students, by individuals, and by very young as well as mature or adult students. It can be organized so that little preparation for filmmaking is necessary or so that there is a high ratio of time spent gathering and planning a production to time spend actually shooting. In short, animation can fit almost any combination of time, space, numbers and materials requirements.

It has many applications. Animated filmmaking can also fit just about any instructional objective. Kids can make animated movies that relate to work being done in any discipline. It can be used to create activities that provide "motivational support" or "skills development." But from my point of view, the medium's greatest potential lies in its ability to provide an unparalleled vehicle for

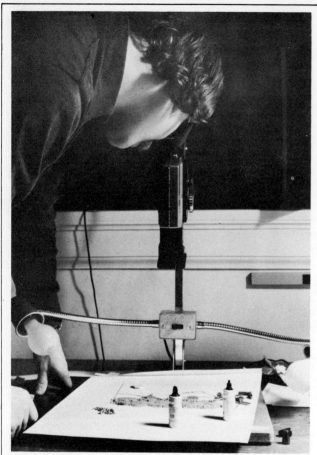

Super 8 animation setup: compact equipment and procedures
uncomplicated enough even for the faint-hearted

Painting on clear leader

personal, creative expression. It is the best medium of all
for giving vent to pure imagination and fantasy.

It has its own "subject." Finally, for those of you who
get hooked on the processes and possibilities of animated
filmmaking, this genre offers itself as something worth
full-scale "study" by your classes. The literature on animation is varied: from historical development of the medium, to studies of particular animators like Disney and
more contemporary artists, to explorations of how animation can extend human perception about scientific phenomena, to animation's unique role within commercial
and public television and *Sesame Street.* There are many
films to study. Animation is all over the television channels and many of the best children's films are animated.

Now with so much going for it, you might wonder if
there are some things going against it. There are. Even
the fastest animation technique turns out to be a slow
process. If you or your students don't have the patience for
meticulous work, it is silly to begin. There are a few technical potholes that one can run into. Each of these has
been marked as clearly as possible in the remarks that
follow. Undoubtedly a few have been missed, for this discussion can only be a cursory introduction and hardly
begins to say all that one could say. Nonetheless there is
enough information for you to get you started in animation. Hopefully there is not too much detail to put a
damper on your own modifying and evaluating, inventing
and discarding, problem solving and creating.

These notes are organized according to five different
genres of animation:

1) Cameraless Animation—Scratch-and-Doodle Movies
2) Storyboarding and Still-Scan Animation
3) Stop-Action Animation
4) Cutout Animation
5) Flip Books

CAMERALESS ANIMATION—
SCRATCH-AND-DOODLE MOVIES

Scratch-and-doodle filmmaking is a Super Gimmick. It
costs almost nothing. It can be done by large or small
groups. It has immediate feedback—you show the movies
the minute they're done. It's easy to do, even with the
littlest children, and it is always successful. It's fun to do
every single time.

In scratch-and-doodle filmmaking, there is no camera
and no developing. Children work directly on the surface
of 16mm film. There are a number of different ways that
they can make a variety of different kinds of movies.

It is in discovering the variations of technique and effect
that scratch and doodle filmmaking can become more
than a Super Gimmick. In addition to all the nice things
kids will feel about themselves, the activities described
here are helpful in leading students to a better understanding of film on many levels. The activities force a

discovery of film technology, they help develop basics in film appreciation and terminology. And, especially important, they introduce kids to animated filmmaking.

Drawing on Clear Leader

For this activity, students draw directly upon clear leader, a piece of clear 16mm film. The materials used to draw with have only one qualification: they must be translucent, that is, permit light to be projected through them. Among the drawing materials that work well are: 1) *Magic Markers*—which must be checked first, for some do not stick to acetate even though they claim to mark on anything; 2) *grease pencils;* 3) some kinds of *paints*—though care must be taken that the paint, upon drying, doesn't crack and fall off the film and thereby clog the projector; 4) some kinds of *inks*. Other kinds of drawing materials will work too, and it is good to have students experiment with the different kinds available.

Before kids play around with the abstract and representational "styles" of doodle movies, they'll need to know two facts: 1) that 16mm film is projected at 24 frames per second, though it is possible to project scratch-and-doodle films at the "silent speed" of 18 frames per second; 2) that the sprocket holes on the clear leader define the frame lines for the individual pictures that make up film's moving images.

Exploring fact one. An activity that can help kids get a feeling for the speed of projection is to have them solidly color a different number of frames. For example, can the eye pick out one frame of color within a series of clear (white when projected) frames? Or within a series of another solid color? What is the effect of coloring three adjacent frames? Or 6? Or 12? Or 24? Sometimes kids can be helped in this experiment by making a measuring standard (denoting lengths of frames and time) upon a clear sheet of paper that they can put under their piece of clear leader (see figure 1):

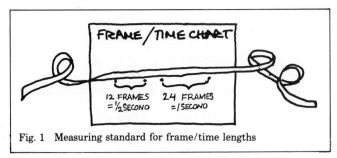

Fig. 1   Measuring standard for frame/time lengths

Exploring fact two. The *frame line* on a piece of clear leader is found by drawing an imaginary line across the film to join adjacent sets of *sprocket holes*. Sometimes you may get clear leader with only one set of sprocket holes. It works the same way. If you have kids look at a "real" piece of 16mm film that has regular images on it, they will see right away how the frame line works (see figure 2).

Abstract technique. The following style or technique for marking on clear leader produces an abstract effect: The kids mark either randomly or in repeated designs upon the film *without* reference to the individual frames. With some experimentation, they will be able to determine what effect is produced by different sorts of drawing and coloring as well as the effects produced by using

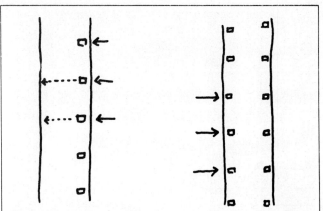

Fig. 2   Clear leader may have one or two sets of sprockets. The frame lines (indicated by arrows) are found by drawing imaginary lines from the sprockets straight across the film.

different drawing materials. It is possible to have kids figure out different "printing" techniques and work over the film that way—for example, using a sponge and ink, or a stamp made from of an eraser (see figure 3).

Representational technique. The second general style of marking on clear leader involves using the frame lines. By carefully modifying the shape of images that are re-

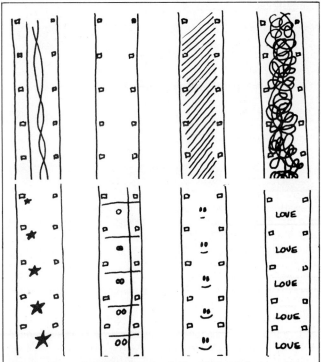

Fig. 3   Abstract designing: 1) simple line design 2) finger prints 3) diagonal lines 4) scribbles
Representational designing: 5) A star moves across the screen and gets bigger. 6) A dot divides, but two lines stay in place. 7) A smile grows (or it could be a simple or a more complicated design). 8) The "love" sign; here it lasts about 1/4 second.

Children will discover that variations in drawings must be very gradual to get the effect of smooth movement. It is a good suggestion to repeat each doodle 2 times before making a small change.

In working with large groups, unroll 16mm film without cutting the film into pieces and avoid need to splice later. Besides, kids like to rub shoulders with friends.

peated on a number of adjacent frames, you can create the illusion of motion when the film runs through the projector. One thing to remember about drawing on film in this way is that the frames are awfully small. The success of making an image move generally depends upon 1) its simplicity of design; 2) the character of the drawing material (such as a Magic Marker with a fine point); and 3) the artistic control of the students, a factor often related to their age and motor control (see figure 3).

Scratching on Opaque Leader

Using the same techniques and knowing the same facts, kids can get a different effect by using opaque (it's usually colored black) leader instead of clear leader. Warning: be sure to get opaque leader that is made of clear celluloid with dark emulsion covering it. In the past couple of years, a new kind of black leader has been produced that is made of darkened celluloid throughout—no good for what you want to do. Scissors, straight pins, any pointed, sharp objects are good for scraping the emulsion off the opaque leader. The best tool is a silk screen line cutter. This stylus consists of a metal loop, with sharp edges, that is attached to a plastic handle like that of inexpensive paint brushes. The first time you try scratch drawing, be sure to have the students test both sides of the leader to find the emulsion coated side that they will be working with. Otherwise they will scrape and scratch without producing any clear space, or until they scratch right through the celluloid itself.

As with all scratch-and-doodle movies, after the film is completed, it can be shown without further processing. In projection the screen will be dark except where light comes through the scraped areas. Using Magic Markers, kids can color in their scratched-on images. In this way, for example, a thin line of light can change color. Or each of two dancing dots can have a different hue.

An Important Aside About Projection

If you are working with a large group of kids, have them sit close to each other (the floor is good) when they are scratching or doodling. It's nice to rub shoulders with friends but, more important, this way the teacher can unroll the 16mm film throughout the class *without* cutting it into pieces which would have to be spliced together for projection.

Here are three techniques for screening cameraless animations:

1. Splice both ends together. Do this *after* you've threaded the film if you have an automatic leading projector. The loop you've created can keep going round and round. It helps to have someone standing near the front of the projector and feeding the machine.

2. Run the projector at silent speed. (There is usually a switch on the projector reading "sound" and "silent.") What this does is make the film pass through the projection gate at 18 frames per second instead of 24. You get more for your money.

3. If the projector has a reverse control, simply project the film until it is almost done, stop the machine, put it into reverse mode, then show the movie backwards.

Always play sound with your scratch-and-doodle films. It's a weird thing to discover that no matter what kind or tempo of music you select to play, it somehow seems to work. Try different records with the films or, better, have the kids create their own sound tracks by using a tape recorder. Some ideas: an audio collage of "found sounds," a percussion ensemble, singing and humming and boop-booping, recording things at one speed and playing them back at another.

There is no way to avoid splicing if kids are to take lengths of leader home to work on. So get a 16mm splicer (tape or cement) from the school's media center. Remember to leave about four feet of blank leader on the beginning of the film to accomodate threading the projector.

Creating a Sound Track

This activity is a dismal failure in terms of our aesthetic sensibilities. But it is great fun and absolutely fascinating. To do it you should have a piece of clear leader that has sprocket holes along one side of the film only. Look at a regular 16mm film that has a sound track (see figure 4). Along the edge of the film opposite the sprocket holes, you will see a thin strip of lines, a little less than ¼-inch wide, that parallels the length of the movie. This is the film's *optical sound track*. The ever changing "lines" that run along the edge of the film are "read" by the 16mm projector's excitor lamp as the film passes through the projector. You can find the *excitor lamp* on the projector by looking beneath the projection *gate* (see figure 5).

The way to make a sound track by hand is to try to duplicate along the unsprocketed side of the leader some patterns that are vaguely similar to those delicate ones you see on a "real" 16mm film. This is done by drawing a sound track with either a fine-pointed Magic Marker or with pen and ink. You can also use a piece of black leader for this exercise. Here you have students scratch a series of marks along the edge in the space normally filled by the optical sound track (see figure 6).

It is great fun, and often more successful, to create the sound track first and then to scratch or doodle the images to go with the audio portion of the film. In order to synchronize this effectively you must be aware of how the visuals and the sound track are actually projected. In projecting the film, while the visuals and the sound track are "read" by the projector *at the same time*, they are nonetheless "read" within the machine *at different places*. Look at the projector and you will see that the images are projected in the gate, and that the sound is projected by the excitor lamp, which is located further toward the beginning of the film. All this translates to the fact that the sound for a given frame is *advanced exactly 26 frames ahead* of its image (see figure 7).

Norman McLaren

The primary developer and popularizer of hand-drawn films is the Canadian filmmaker Norman McLaren. For over 30 years he worked at the National Film Board of Canada, producing a sizable body of short films (lasting 3–9 minutes), all using scratch-and-doodle and animation techniques. McLaren's wonderful movies are commercially available in this country, and prints of them can be found in most school and public library film collections. I strongly urge you to show some of McLaren's movies to your students while they are exploring cameraless animation. Two titles are specifically recommended: *Begone Dull Care* (7 min. 48 sec. Color) is a beautiful example of abstract drawn-on and scratched-on filmmaking, and a lively visual interpretation of jazz music played by the famed Oscar Peterson Trio, *Pen Point Percussion* (8 min. 41 sec. Color) is a demonstration and explanation by McLaren himself of making synthetic sound on film. The Resources section of this book lists other McLaren films, and a filmography of his films is also available from the

Fig. 4   Magnification of a piece of 16mm film. Arrow points to optical sound track.

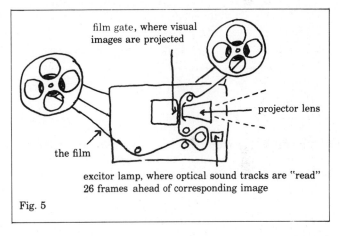

film gate, where visual images are projected

projector lens

the film

excitor lamp, where optical sound tracks are "read" 26 frames ahead of corresponding image

Fig. 5

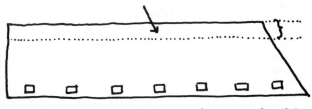

Fig. 6   On a piece of opaque leader, scratch out a sound track in the column marked by arrow.

Fig. 7   If you have a "sound" scratched in at point **A,** to get an image to appear at the same time you hear the sound you must scratch a design on the frame at point **B.**

National Film Board (Suite 819, 680 Fifth Avenue, New York, N.Y. 10019), as is a set of print materials describing his career and technique.

Working from Discarded 16mm Movies: Assemblage

All the skills that students can develop through the preceding activities can also be applied to experimentation with old or discarded exposed films.

Using a 16mm viewer (or just holding strips of film up to a window), students select a piece of film that interests them. Here are some examples of the things they might do:

1. If the film is black-and-white, they can color the images and do various tinting effects.

2. They can superimpose representation or abstract image patterns by either coloring on the film or by scraping away the emulsion.

3. Using a solution of peroxide, or another similar cleaning solvent, students can bleach off the visual portion of the film, leaving the original sound track. They can then create their own images. Conversely, they can bleach off just the sound track and create a new one in its place.

4. Interesting distortion effects can be achieved with either color or black-and-white film by bleaching off only portions of the sound track emulsion.

STORYBOARDING AND STILL-SCAN ANIMATION

There is a lot of information about the techniques of storyboarding in the chapter 7 which deals with live-action filmmaking. You may wish to review those earlier notes in the context of the ideas that follow, because the still-scan genre of animation involves making films out of storyboards. If storyboarding is a helpful element in exploring live-action filmmaking, it is an essential part of working in animation.

Storyboarding (A Recapitulation)

The storyboard is a device that was originally developed in conjunction with animated film. The reasons for its development remain important as a technique for conceptualizing.

The storyboard as a notation system. The use of small sketches gives the animator a way to work-out the style, continuity and visual approach of the film. Unlike live-action filmmaking, in animation one doesn't want to risk creating a few scenes "on speculation," to be used or discarded in the editing process. So the storyboard gives the filmmaker an extremely concrete and specific outline for his or her labors. It eliminates wasted hours of drawing and shooting.

The amount of detail within each frame or panel depends on the individual animator's desire to work out the specifics beforehand. The number of drawings can vary widely. Some scenes can be adequately previewed by one or two sketches; more complicated sequences may require many drawings. The important thing to remember is that *animation is about movement.* Although the storyboard is made up of static images, use it to figure out and describe things in motion.

The storyboard as communicator. It is really difficult to explain the visual flow and texture of an animated movie, especially when the image making tends toward the abstract and fantastic. A storyboard can help here. Not only is it useful in explaining a concept to the others in the class but a storyboard is just about the only way a teacher can gain access to student ideas and be of help in the conceptualization process.

Still-Scan Animation

Still-Scan filmmaking bears a close operational relationship to storyboarding. Each of the storyboards outlined in the filmmaking chapter can be easily turned into still-scan movies. To do this, two new variables are introduced: camera effects and the duration of the shots.

There are many kinds of camera effects: pans, zooms, tracking shots; fast, slow, jerky, or no movement of the camera; change of focus while the camera is running; addition of filters and other lighting effects; fading-in, fading-out, superimposition, dissolves. Duration can range from one or two frames per image to many seconds per image. In filming storyboards, one can use the camera to frame a particular portion or a number of parts of the same photograph or drawing. In effect, this multiplies infinitely the available number of images. Further, one can choose to repeat a given still image at different places within the film (as well as for different durations).

Image sources. Magazine photographs are an excellent source of still images to use in still-scan films. Collect photographic magazines in particular. Many art books have excellent reproductions of photographs. Original artwork is a great source—oil paintings, water colors, pencil drawings, and charcoal sketches all work fine. Or choose other mediums. Your students' own still photographs can be used to make still-scan movies: black-and-white prints, old family snap shots, and 35mm slides—anything that can be projected onto a screen and then rephotographed with a motion picture camera.

Camera and setups. In either Super 8mm or 16mm formats, the camera to be used in still-scan filmmaking must have two capabilities: 1) macro or *close-up* focus, and 2) reflex or *through-the-lens* focus. In addition, certain features make the work easier and enlarge the technical possibilities: automatic exposure control, single-frame capability, zoom lens, and dissolve-fade controls.

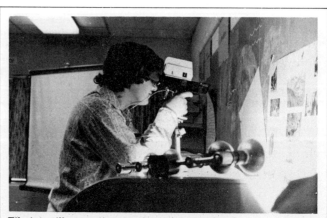

Filming still-scan animation from photographs

The sketches in figures 8 and 9 suggest two very common camera setups for still-scan filmmaking. As in all animated filmmaking, the camera must be kept absolutely stationary between exposures. Hence you must have a very sturdy tripod or copystand or another apparatus. Artificial lighting is almost always necessary.

Production sheets. In making still-scan films, it is important to devise a notation system which can be used in planning the film and, more important, while filming. The storyboard will often be the basis for developing your *production sheet.* Notes about shooting can often be added to the sheet of paper on which still images are mounted. My own bias is toward a kind of production sheet that lists (in order and in one place) each shot within the film. An example of the way I like to do it and would recommend for student use is shown in figure 10. You can develop your own formula and format for a production sheet. It will have to contain information about:

1. *sequence of still images*—by order of filming and not necessarily order of storyboard.
2. *framing*—one still image may comprise a number of different camera shots.
3. *camera movement*—which should be rehearsed before the actual filming.
4. *shot duration*—a cable release is needed if you are planning to shoot in fractions of seconds; for longer duration shots, and shots with camera movement, live-action filming is suggested rather than single-framing.
5. *special effects*—lighting, filters, fades, super-impositions, whatever.
6. *sound track information*—if you are to work closely with a sound track, then the track should be recorded, analyzed, timed, and noted on the production sheets prior to planning the visual sequence.

Setup for still-scan animation. Note improvised lighting from opaque projector.

STOP-ACTION ANIMATION

Under the not-so-apt rubric of *stop-action,* this section introduces six different techniques for animation. All have two common characteristics: they all must be *prepared* under the camera; and the nature of the specific technique is characterized strongly by the *materials* used in the technique. Under actual conditions and practices in making an animated film, each of these stop-action techniques can be mixed with one or more of the others.

The importance of materials merits special comment. An awareness of the texture, the shape, the maleability, and the impact of various materials often leads to good ideas in animation. Materials themselves seem to generate experimentation. As the animator gets to know what he can do with certain materials, he or she uncovers and creates different effects. Experimentation frees the animator from a self-imposed tyranny of "stories" and

Fig. 8   Tripod arrangement for filming animation

Fig. 9   Copy stand arrangement for filming animation

FRAME #	SHOT #	CAMERA COMPOSITION	CAMERA MOVEMENT	DURATION	EFFECTS
#1	#1	full shot	zoom & pan	15	fade in
#2	2	close-up		4	
#2	3	close-up		4	out of focus
#2	4	very close-up		8	into focus
#3	5	close-up	pan	7	
#3	6	medium shot		5	
#4	7	close-up		8	
#3	8	full shot		3	
#4	9	full shot		2	shake
#3	10	close-up		1	

Shot #
1. full shot - fade-in - pan and zoom left for close up of end of tracks 15 sec.

2. Close-up of bandit on left - 4 sec.
3. Close-up of bandit with binoculars - 4 sec.
4. Extreme close-up of train and zoom back for full shot - 8 sec.
5. Close-up "Old #9" and pan back to face of engi-neer - 7 sec.

6. Medium shot of wheels - go out of focus - 5 sec.
7. Close-up - pull into focus on Pauline's face. 8 sec.
8. full shot of frame #3 3 sec.

9. full shot #4 - shake camera. 2 sec.
10. Close-up "Cowcatcher" in frame #3. 1 sec.

Fig. 10   Example of a student-made storyboard production sheet

"messages." Exploring the nature and capabilities for motion within various materials often brings out a sensibility for working in pure design and rhythm.

Below is a brief summary of the six basic stop-action techniques.

Time-Lapse Animation

Most people are familiar with the photographic effect of filming a natural phenomenon one frame at a time in various stages of growth and then compressing the time frame to demonstrate growth. The classic examples are films of flowers bursting forth in bloom and of the setting of the sun. Those films are done by *time-lapse* photography. The most common extension of this technique by the animator is to use the fixed camera to record the organic development of paintings, drawings, or such three-dimensional objects as wood sculpture and other constructed pieces. An awareness of materials will generate many imaginative ideas: a blackboard can be used to have an

Stop-action filming of small objects. *Left,* a student uses her dollhouse as a set; *right,* a still from her movie.

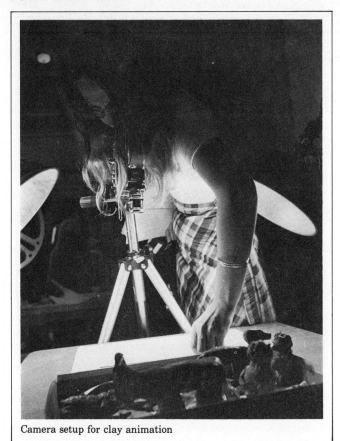

Camera setup for clay animation

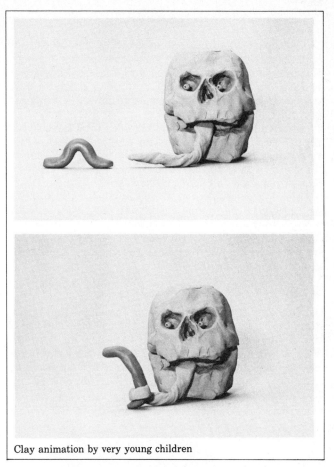

Clay animation by very young children

entire classroom work together quickly in creating a nice animated film; the slowly yielded contours of a linoleum block can make an interesting film; working with sand on a rear-lighted glass surface can lead to some very beautiful animations.

Collage Animation

Using either found or created fragments of images, the process (and relationships) of two dimensional collages can be explored in stop-action fashion. Portions of a collage can continue to move under the animation camera; lines can be added or subtracted and images can be altered in other graphic ways. This technique has been effectively used to explore the special logic of dreams and the subliminal impact of media images in their never-ending bombardment of our sensoriums.

Animation of Small Objects

The most ubiquitous objects can be used to create interesting films: pipe cleaners, pencils, pennies, pop-tops, pajamas, plates, penknives, pansies, parabolas, peas, pills, pistols and pyramids. In working with multiple sets of small objects, design patterns can become the focus of the film, or one can explore themes or topics.

Puppet Animation

Puppetry technique has been used often and effectively in animation. The materials from which puppets are made both limit and isolate possibilities for these kinds of movies. The size of the puppets is another important factor.

Clay Animation

Clay animation might be viewed as a hybrid technique, combining time-lapse and puppet animation. But clay animations have been done so effectively that they seem to demand their own category. The material is easy to work with, and figures can move and undergo transformations or transmutations with ease. Colored plasticine is the best material to use. The camera, fixed on its tripod, is focused on a table top surface. The animation can begin with a lump of clay and slowly, a frame at a time, record its growth to, say, a man. The metamorphosis can continue —the man turns into a flower, into a snake, into a ball that rolls away. Remember to keep the camera absolutely stationary during any given scene. If students want to attempt a camera "pan" or "zoom," have them make very tiny movements between exposures.

Pixillation

Through convention rather than any particular logic in the term, the animation of people has taken on a special name: pixillation. The technique is fun and workable with relatively large groups. Your students can make their classmates do all manner of wonderful things: skate without skates, jump over great distances, pop in and out of a scene, change clothing in an instant, be chased around the room by a refrigerator. The technique is achieved in much the same way as in the preceding ones: the camera remains stationary; the "actors" make small movements between exposures (usually taken two frames at a time).

CUTOUT ANIMATION

The cutout genre of animation provides the easiest and quickest way of creating cartoons—films with a dramatic storyline and characters. This kind of filmmaking is particularly well suited for young children, yet adults seem to enjoy it much too. Making cutout animated films has been developed to a fine science and a fine art form by Yvonne Andersen, Director of the Yellowball Workshop in Lexington, Massachusetts. Her film *Let's Make a Film* (16 min. Color. Yellow Ball Workshop, 62 Tarbell Avenue, Lexington, Mass. 02173) and her two books, *Teaching Film Animation to Children* (New York: Van Nostrand, 1971) and *Make Your Own Animated Movies* (Boston: Little, Brown, 1970) provide everything one needs to know about cutout animation. The summary that follows provides a very skimpy overview for doing cutout animation. For more details and technical information, Andersen's works are essential reading.

Setup

Using a copy-stand, a tripod, or a homemade animation stand of some sort, firmly mount the camera (Super 8 or 16mm) above a flat surface. Move the cutout figures a little at a time on this flat surface, between two-frame exposures. Camera operation, choice of film stock, light-

ing, editing and soundwork are all similar to other genres of animation.

Materials

The backgrounds. The sheet of paper upon which the characters will move should be a little larger than the field of exposure for which the camera has been positioned. Backgrounds can be painted, done with Magic Markers, created by collage from found images, or just about anything you can think of.

The figures. Bodies and other figures are cut out of medium-weight posterboard and colored or painted. Limbs that are to "move" in the action are hinged to the torso —Yvonne Andersen accomplished this easily with a piece of thread that is taped to the respective pieces. A close-up visual of one or more characters can be done in a larger size on a separate piece of paper if it is difficult to move the camera around. If you have a good zoom lens, separate close-up shots can be achieved by re-framing the camera.

Overlays. These are often used to create the illusion of movement within the faces of the characters. For example, four or five different mouths can be laid over a character's "standard" mouth to simulate talking; or an eye can be painted without the eyeball, and during filming a black pupil can be moved to show eye movement.

Variations

There are two well known variations of the cutout genre that should be mentioned here. In both cases, the under-the-camera technique is similar to paper cutouts outlined above.

Silhouette animation. This technique has been developed to its current high state by animator Lotte Reiniger. In this technique, the silhouettes are made from black cutouts that are lit from behind. The high contrast masks the "joints" of the characters. Colored lights can be used beneath the art work.

Felt animation. This form of animation is much like paper cutouts. The texture and "feel" of felt, along with its more limited tolerance for cutting and color, force the animator into a more stylized treatment.

FLIP BOOKS

Remember those serialized drawings you did as a kid on the dog-eared edges of your textbook? By flipping through the pages you would make the drawn character or design "move." Or sometimes you could buy a small flip book in a store, or you'd discover one in a comic book, or get a miniature one as a Cracker Jack prize.

Flip books provide an experiential definition for *cel animation,* the process of drawing on clear acetate or celluloid sheets by which the most "realistic" and "sophisticated" animated films are made. The following notes will only introduce cel animation. While you can do cel animation with children, it is a fairly complicated procedure that imposes far more rigorous techniques than are normally undertaken by younger children. Cel animation also requires more sophisticated and expensive production tools than are normally available in elementary schools. Flip books, on the other hand, are both inexpensive and manageable. They provide an effective introduction to the principles and scope of cel animation.

Camera setup for close-up of cutout animation by Bill Fuchs, 11, for his film *The Idol.* Note the separate hands, mouths, and eyelids on the table. Mouths and eyes open, hands move upward. (Courtesy of Yvonne Andersen, from her *Teaching Film Animation to Children*)

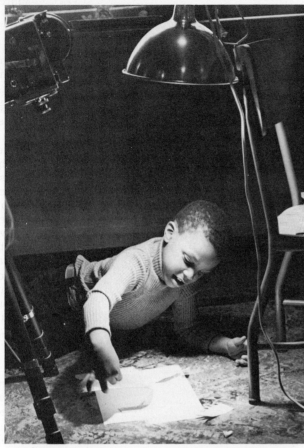

Tripod setup and teamwork in the kindergarten, P.S.75, New York. The artist moves her cutout, and her partner prepares to shoot the next 16mm frames.

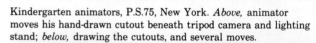

Kindergarten animators, P.S.75, New York. *Above*, animator moves his hand-drawn cutout beneath tripod camera and lighting stand; *below*, drawing the cutouts, and several moves.

In *Al Kaseltzer Strikes Again*, the gangster reaches into the scene with his hand and lights a cigarette with a burning match. He blows out the match. Smoke floats up from the cigarette, which is burning shorter. The gangster wiggles his eyebrows, looks from one side to the other, blinks, and says, "They will probably have a double guard at the bank!"

This scene is longer and more complex. More things happen. The arm, which is a cutout, must be moved slowly upward into the scene, one-quarter inch for every 2 frames taken. The match flame burns continually. The flickering effect of fire is made by changing the flame every 2 frames. The end of the cigarette is painted red when it is lit, and is cut shorter and shorter during filming. Other movements are those of the eyes, eyebrows, and smoke.

Cutout figures and other stop-action forms can be animated by using overlays, as demonstrated by *Al Kaselzer Strikes Again*. (Courtesy of Yvonne Andersen, from her *Make Your Own Animated Movies*)

Begin by giving each student his or her own small pad of unlined paper. Check to be sure that the dimensions of the pad are such that you can subsequently film it with your movie camera. A 6" × 4" pad is about the smallest that can be recommended. Remember, too, that the camera will frame a rectangle with the proportions 4" × 3", so have the students confine their drawing to an area within the flip book that conforms to these dimensions. Be sure the paper is such that you can see through one sheet to the sheet below it.

The first doodle is drawn on the last page of the flip book. The doodle should be a simple image, for it will have to be repeated, with modifications, many times. The page directly preceding the last one is dropped down—you should just be able to make out the earlier image. This image is retraced, with slight variation, following the overall movement that the student animator plans on developing. The next page is lowered, and the process continues for the duration of the book. The process can extend to a second and a third book. Periodically the artist should "flip" through the pages to see how work is progressing.

When all the artwork has been completed, the flip book is placed under the camera. The pages are exposed individually under the camera, usually with two "frames" per page. The binding of the pad itself provides an accurate registration system. The parallel between doing flip book animation and full cel animation is now complete: as the paper (cels) are "flipped," the camera works like the human eye, and the image has the illusion of moving. The finished movies can be dazzling.

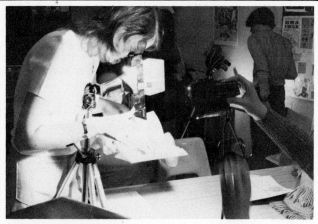

Animating with flip book

Cel animation by students at Wichita High School

Silhouette animation using rear screen projection. Pictures here demonstrate the different moves.

ABSTRACT ANIMATION

[*Editor's note:* Simple abstract animation was introduced earlier in our discussion of cameraless animation. Two forms of abstract animation—animation with small objects and kinestasis film—are more sophisticated and apply elements of camera animation. This segment presents two exercises on these abstract animation forms. It was prepared by Todd Flinchbaugh, a San Francisco film artist who served as filmmaker-in-residence with the Wichita Public School System, and appeared originally in *Medialog,* an occassional journal of the Center for Understanding Media, under the title, "Artists-in-Schools: Two Exercises in Abstract Animation" (January, 1974).]

Through variations of design, motion, rhythm, and art color, a film can produce a strong emotional reaction without representational designs or a story. Student experiments in abstract filmmaking increase their awareness of these basic film elements. This awareness leads to a better appreciation of the works of well-known makers of abstract films as well as increased sensitivity as to how the basic elements are used to create an emotional involvement in live action, dramatic films.

It is common for students to experiment in abstract filmmaking through drawing on clear leader. Although this offers some fine possibilities, the format size is a great limitation. The following animation exercises provide an opportunity for further exploration of the basic film elements in a more workable format.

The Exercises

Each student is asked to create a short (approximately 15-second) film using either of two basic techniques and materials of his or her choice. The film is not to be a story film. It is to use patterns, rhythms, movement, and timing to achieve its effect. The film may contain wholly abstract patterns or may include some representational images if the student so desires.

Artist-in-residence, filmmaker Todd Flinchbaugh, with students at Wichita High School doing abstract film animation with small objects

Math readiness: these kindergarteners become familiar with cuisiniere measuring rods as they use them to create abstract animations.

Exercise 1: small objects films

The student films this project under an animation camera (any camera which can single frame). The set up is that used for a cutout animation. The student creates patterns with a series of small objects, following these patterns with other patterns, until a film is built up. The patterns may slowly evolve or may spring out quickly. It is usually best to create an entire film with one type of object. For example, a film with fifty pennies will work well. A great many materials lend themselves to this process. Try aspirin tablets on a black background, colored marbles on felt, pieces of sparkle, colored tooth-picks, pipe cleaners, or even patterns made by sprinkling baby powder and pushing it around with the fingers.

Exercise 2: Kinestasis Films

TYPE 1. Make a random pattern of dots, lines, or punched holes on a piece of paper or a 4 × 6 index card. Make a series of these random patterns, one pattern on each card. Don't try to animate the patterns as in a flip book. Be random. (If the cards are punched for registration, the filming process is easier.) Then, make an abstract film by filming these cards under the camera, a few frames each. Vary the time from one frame to about a second to create rhythm and pacing.

The patterns may be shot randomly, or the student may look at them and attempt to create an organization from them. Perhaps some intentional effects will be created by making more cards. In addition to dots, line patterns, or punched holes, this process can be used with ink blots or paint smears. Several films can be made from the same collection of cards.

TYPE 2. Instead of using patterns created on paper, use a series of brightly colored shirts, towels, or cloth remnants. A friendly neighborhood pattern center may donate some remnants for an eye-boggling op art film. Usually colors are the key to a fabric kinestasis, but sometimes the patterns can be used for themes. The filming process is the same as for drawn-on-paper kinestasis films.

Teaching Suggestions

These exercises may prove to be especially exciting to students who are unsure of their drawing ability. Some students have a natural feeling for the time and rhythm elements of film, but have difficulty with stories or representational drawings. These students have a chance to show their imagination with these exercises.

One does not have to introduce these techniques through a dry analysis of the process. A presentation of two sample films may be a good beginner. The students are then encouraged to find any variation which seems exciting. Students usually can deduce the general process from the specific without too much trouble. It's more rewarding that way. For the small objects section, a variation is just to make some materials available and see what happens with them. One can easily build outward on the possibility of finding other materials for such films.

These exercises are also valuable for the student who is stuck without a "good idea." Since it is almost impossible to sit back and think up a film with these materials, the student has no choice but to jump in. Good themes usually present themselves as the student interacts with the materials.

Most students do some planning of patterns or timing before starting to film, but usually leave a good bit of space for improvisation. Perhaps a few basic patterns are a good foundation for starting. Better ideas often come during the filming process itself. Some students plan out the overall pace of the film, fast parts and slow parts, but leave the patterns to the inspiration of the moment. Others plan patterns, but time by improvising. It is important to keep an open mind on these projects. Too rigid planning is detrimental.

For the "Small Objects Films" the choice of material is an important creative decision in itself. The type of film is affected by the materials to be used. Pennies suggest a different type of film than does baby powder. Discovering different materials is usually a good deal of fun for the students.

In addition to exploration of materials, timing is the key undercurrent of this project. Students usually grasp quite rapidly that the variations of timing are what makes a film succeed or fail. In the abstract kinestasis films, rhythm is the key element. Often a discussion of a drum beat will clarify this principle. A steady beat becomes monotonous and therefore is boring. A beat which starts slow, speeds up, slows down, pauses, and ends with a flourish is interesting. Tension is built and released through variety. Surprise is a valuable ally.

In the small object films, the variety of the patterns is the key element. A series of similar patterns followed by a different pattern provides pleasant surprise. Rhythm may be non-existent, but the flow of the motion provides opportunity for variation.

In addition to these elements, the abstract kinestasis films often have the viewer's eye jumping all around. The eye searches for a key point in each design, even if it is only on the screen a short time. The attention shifts from design to design. Students often pick up on this process and make it work for them by attempting to get the viewer going in a circle or in a back and forth ping-pong motion.

Variations and Follow-up

These exercises can be designed for a group or for an individual. They can be a formal assignment to the entire class or introduced to certain individuals when appropriate. Some students will be able to do endless varieties of films with these processes.

The exercises can be used to introduce the films of Oskar Fischinger, Rene Jodoin, Robert Breer, Norman McLaren, the Whitney brothers, or Jordan Belson. The importance of timing suggests obvious comparisons to music. The films can lead to a discussion of abstract painting. The action painters like Jackson Pollack and the op-art painters like Frank Stella seem especially appropriate. In addition, many live-action directors apply these design/motion principles to their films. The cutting of a powerful sequence may be analyzed in these purely visual terms. A chase sequence offers an appropriate form for such discussion. More sophisticated classes may relate these principles of design/motion to the theories of Sergei Eisenstein or Slavko Vorkapitch.

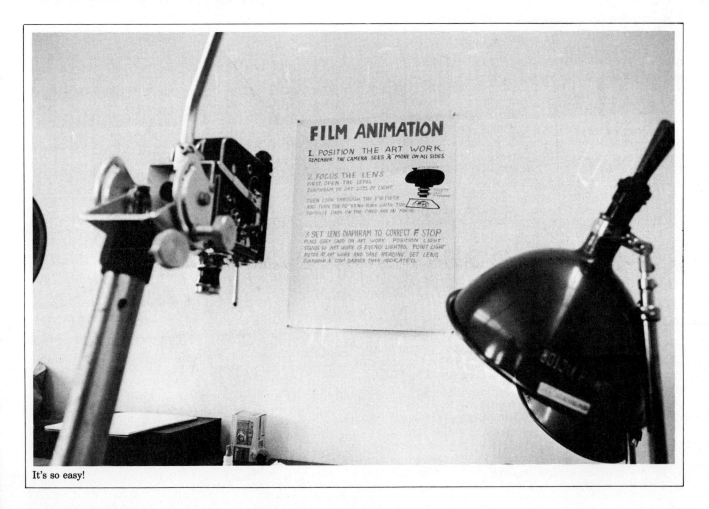

It's so easy!

Talking about Movies: Subverting The Old School Game

by Richard A. Lacey

Did you ever come out of a film with a group of friends and find that nobody had anything to say, even though the film may have moved all deeply, or perhaps, conversely, failed to move you? In the media classroom, where group communication is so vital, silence can be a real problem. Worse yet is "the old school game"—empty discussion and busy work. In this chapter Richard A. Lacey offers some tested suggestions for bringing meaningful dialogue to the media classroom.

One of the thorniest problems of film study is how to talk about movies. Classroom discussion is a medium altogether different from film, requiring a major shift in state of mind. The vivid dreamlike experience of film evaporates when the lights go on, and rigorous, linear talk can be a rude awakening.

A freewheeling discussion among high schoolers can easily disintegrate amid unproductive interaction patterns: talkative students dominate; some students keep quiet no matter what; some guess what the teacher wants to hear; some can't think of anything that won't sound dumb. While it is true that many conventional schoolroom constraints will kill a film discussion, students want and need a structure for talking about movies.

The lesson format—sequential questions and topics about values, social issues, themes, characterization, etc. —provides a comfortable framework for group investigation of film content in a way that reminds students of discussions about books. It's familiar turf, and the talk can be lively. An alert teacher can relate the film to other materials the class has studied, especially when it was selected to reinforce particular ideas in a curriculum unit. A few companies have packaged short films and excerpts from feature films around topics like violence, making choices, and justice, saving schools the trouble of showing a whole feature film simply to illustrate s single concept.

Unfortunately much of this business-as-usual distracts students from the concrete film experience; it isn't film study. Discussion geared to lessons exploits film primarily for references to support general ideas. The film becomes merely incidental. For the sake of economy, lessons neglect details of composition, settings, rhythm, music, texture. They also ignore feelings except to illustrate a prescribed idea.

By contrast, when young elementary-schoolers talk about a movie they say what is naturally on their minds —how they felt, what an image or sound reminded them of, how they liked this or that, how they reacted differently from someone else. Unless directed otherwise, they generally concentrate on images, sounds, and feelings, and their short discussions have spark and spontaneity.

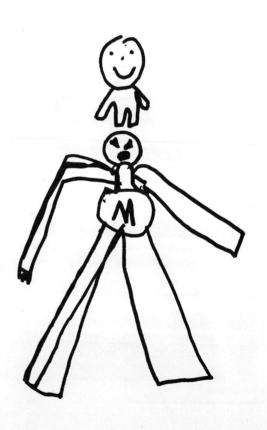

Chapter Nine

Such discussions live because they probe how films work and the ways that images and sounds evoke feelings and ideas. The talk is personally significant: children learn about themselves and each other. Although all see the same movie, each sees it in a distinctly personal way and eagerly compares notes. Energy comes from the excitement of discovering through a shared intense film experience how alike and how different we are.

We lose sight of this process with older students when abstract ideas about meaning so dominate discussion that the sensuous experience that gives substance to film study fades away. Yet a student can explore a movie only as deeply as he can see into it. Rich insights spring only from rich perceptions.

In order to discuss film productively with any group of students, we can talk specifically about two groups of topics: 1) what we saw and heard—the concrete substance of the movie; and 2) what we thought and how we felt—the perceived content of the movie. The following twenty-five discussion devices are designed frankly to undermine the weighty edifice of abstractions that older students assiduously construct—The Old School Game—and to provide variety and specificity to younger students' discussions. These schemes are by no means guaranteed to work, but some will periodically alert students to substance and content in movies as they explore meaning. Several of the devices are games, simple diversions that take only moments to do. However, while they may sometimes seem to be distractions, they are actually ways to return to the important subject at hand—the movie itself.

This brief catalogue of devices extends ideas developed in Richard L. Lacey's *Seeing with Feeling: Film in the Classroom* (Philadelphia: W. B. Saunders Company, 1972). The theory and practice of the image-sound skim, the first device listed, occupies a full chapter in that book because it can be expanded to a full approach to exploring a movie in depth. Similarly, many of the tactics and suggestions summarized below can be developed and consolidated into strategies for film study. As you develop your repertoire, these approaches gradually become less contrived. Over time you can invent refinements and fresh tactics to subvert The Old School Game.

1. *Image-sound skimming.* Have each student state at least one image or sound from the film—anything at all—that pops into mind. Have everyone contribute several times, even if they repeat what someone else has said. Keep the talk moving

Young children respond to film experiences very personally.

rapidly and randomly. This device can be used for longer periods after students become accustomed to it; they can easily learn to do it themselves in small groups.

The secret of the exercise is to keep comments as short as possible so that everyone contributes rapid-fire comments. Interruptions are okay; in fact, they often help. Image-sound skimming can be fun, and it is surprising how much raw information a whole group can mine that individuals—including you—have nearly forgotten or missed entirely during the screening.

Later, examine a few specific images and sounds, exploring how they functioned and what effects they had, how they contributed to the students' sense of meaning in the film.

2. *Bolstering vague, incoherent opinions.* Let a discussion drift once in a while, but instead of worrying that vague opinions and unfocused comments in a loose discussion may be unproductive, use them to advantage. In relaxed bull sessions students are groping for unpretentious ways to express significant hunches and reactions.

List or tape-record students' comments. Then help the group expand and refine one or two ideas as if they may be the key to understanding the film. This attitude is not so far-fetched, incidentally, for hunches can often lead to important insights. Concentrate with the group on building a coherent, cogent viewpoint, whether or not everyone originally agreed with it; find every possible specific instance in the film that will support the position. When the interpretation is reasonably clear, test its consistency on randomly selected scenes and sequences.

I like the Light house and the ship. Becauce I like the eyes on the house and on the ship.

Vito

When the lights go on the teacher leads but doesn't dominate film discussion.

This device has two purposes: 1) it helps students realize that unfocused ideas may be worth pursuing, and 2) it mobilizes students to search their collective memory for evidence to nurture promising notions into strong ideas.

3. *Brainstorming.* When a discussion bogs down, a good directive question may not help because no one feels spontaneous —there's no energy. Brainstorming is a non-directive way to get a discussion unstuck. After checking whether the students also sense that momentum has halted, brainstorm the group for ideas about what can be done about the problem and for random ideas about the film. Stress that no suggestion or impression is out of line; there are no "right answers."
If the session produces a useful idea, the students will have made a genuine contribution. If not, you may still have accomplished your purpose by releasing energy, encouraging spontaneity, and sharing your problem with the students. At that point the good directive question you kept in reserve may work.

4. *Force-fitting a film to the here-and-now.* Sometimes a discussion moves along reasonable paths but seems unimportant: you sense that the film is worth caring about, but neither your questions nor students' comments forge significant personal links with the film.

Search the film for prominent images or themes that might be force-fitted with a concern that is evident in the present situation. For example, a dull session about a film in which clothes were important came alive when I asked volunteers to discuss the messages that they conveyed through what they were wearing—and how—at that moment.

This general technique is risky in three ways: 1) students may feel that you are manipulating them for the sake of livelier discussion, and they may be right; 2) the force-fit may be so arbitrary that there is no honest way to make the discussion personally significant—the links to the film experience are simply not present; 3) you may divert the students so successfully to some topic they care strongly about that you neglect the film. Remember to direct the group's attention back to the film so that they can relate their intense concerns to a common experience with forms and focus.

5. *Using videotape to observe discussion process.* Part of the unacknowledged content of a discussion about movies is the interaction process. Studying videotaped portions of discussion can provide information for improving the process. Usually the feedback is used to review whether people are building upon one another's ideas, dominating discussion, holding back, subtly undermining other views, etc. Because a

distinctively important aspect of film study involves recalling and using specific references to the movie, it is useful to review the videotape with that in mind: how much of the conversation deals specifically with the movie?

6. *Using a fishbowl.* This feedback device is useful when a group is too large for fruitful discussion and when a video camera is unavailable. One group of students sits in a circle around another circle of students and observes silently. At an appropriate time they offer their observations—not their judgments—about process. Subsequently, the group can offer suggestions and expand on ideas raised in the inner circle discussion.

Another technique is to ask the outside circle to concentrate not on group process but on all the specific information they can recall to provide substance to a general discussion by the inside circle.

7. *Imitating film characters on videotape.* Often we identify with characters in movies; sometimes we wish we could be like the characters. Film critic Pauline Kael reported that both John F. Kennedy and Lucky Luciano had wanted Gary Grant to play their role in a biographical movie. Even Cary Grant has said that he wishes he could be Cary Grant! One of the strongest appeals of movies is the way they stimulate our fantasies.

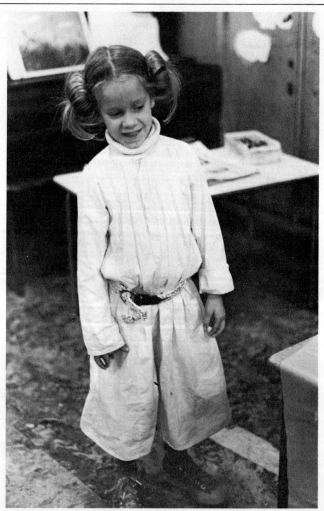

Children and adults alike are stimulated by their film fantasies. This little girl saw herself as Princess Leia in *Star Wars*.

Exploit this appeal with a videotape exercise. A volunteer tries to adopt some of the characteristics of the person he or she fantasizes being, practicing imitations on videotape. Have the student exaggerate prominent characteristics and subtle details or highlight them by imitating the opposite characteristics.

8. *Playing "in the manner of the character."* This game is related to the exercise above and is appropriate for a small group familiar with many films. The person who is "It" leaves the room while the group decides on a movie character that "It" must guess. "It" asks each person in the group to do something in the manner of the character—for example, to ask a question or complain or walk into the room in the manner of the character—until "It" guesses the character.

In discussions, occasionally have students practice role-playing a few characters in the film at hand in order to develop a repertoire for the game. The closer attention they pay to the details of gesture, expression, stance, voice inflection, etc., the better they will be able to play.

9. *Role-playing.* When discussions tend consistently to stray from visual details and resemble literary discussions instead of film study, role-playing can refresh students about the critical differences between the two disciplines. Have one group of students role-play characters from a piece of written fiction while others role-play characters from a film; assign student directors. Present the two short scenes to the class and discuss the cues that the players and directors relied upon in order to interpret the roles. If the film from which the characters were drawn is available, show an excerpt and concentrate on distinctly cinematic effects.

10. *Preconditioning.* Either before or directly after a sizeable group watches a movie, distribute a viewing and discussion guide containing a list of general questions or statements that each individual should study. However, do not inform the group that you have randomly distributed two versions of the guide, each suggesting very different viewpoints based on the same specific parts of the movie. After some discussion, reveal your game and ask the students to divide into two groups according to the differences they detected in the ways they behaved in discussion.

If you conduct this exercise in various forms several times, the group will catch on to a sure-fire way to beat your game —explore details with care.

11. *Turning a listening exercise into a seeing exercise.* A remarkably effective short exercise to improve listening skills is temporarily to impose a rule that participants in discussion must repeat in their own words, if possible, what the last person said to that person's satisfaction before stating their own view. A modification of this exercise can be applied uniquely to film discussions. Temporarily impose a rule that anyone who wants to talk about a scene in a film must first summarize it, then state what immediately preceded and followed it.

12. *Stopping a film.* Perhaps you have already stopped movies in mid-reel in order to review or anticipate developments with the class. A way to use this device in order later to focus attention on particular parts of the film without unduly annoying the students is the following procedure. Tell the students before screening the film that you will occasionally stop the projector to signal briefly a scene the group will be asked to discuss. Gently warn the audience before stopping the film, then quickly switch to reverse for a few seconds before resuming the picture so that the scene will appear again as the reel continues; the transition will be smoother.

13. *Frame, scene, and sequence analysis.* This exercise can be paired with the one above. Analyze with the group a particularly interesting scene or sequence after a general discussion. Then resume the original discussion, perhaps showing the film again if it is short. Probe to find how much more closely students observed details, composition, etc.

14. *Watching movies through different glasses.* Shift a discussion by having students respond to the movie from someone else's perspective. For instance, a Marxist may see differently than a Freudian psychologist. In Studs Terkel's *Working* a dentist says that whenever he saw a movie or play he paid most attention to the actors' teeth—bridgework, chips, cracks, fillings—he couldn't help it!

Using different glasses in discussions, students often exaggerate their adopted views and resort to haranguing one another (e.g., feminists yell "Male chauvinist pig!" and political conservatives peer in closets for communists). Let gross exaggeration continue for a time; it will provide lots of material for examining stereotyped behavior and prejudice. However the exercise can become ridiculous unless you take care to help students express viewpoints consistent with how a responsible and sensitive person might respond.

This device helps students to expand the range of views available to them as they interpret a movie. In addition it disciplines them to attend to details in a movie as they concentrate on seeing in new ways.

15. *Clarifying values.* Values education is growing in many schools, some of which are using short films and feature film excerpts organized around value issues. If you use movies for values education, focus occasionally upon specific images, especially on ways the camera treats various subjects. Editing

or camera techniques, details of setting, etc., are often subtly value-laden.

When values education sessions based on a movie take the form of the general question, "What would you do in this situation and why?" it is important to consider all that is implied in the specific situation that the *movie* has developed over time. The more general the hypothetical situation is, the less meaning the question has. In short, use the movie as more than a discussion-starter; use it for all it's worth.

16. *Scripting.* To examine a sequence freshly, have students develop alternative scripts of scenes. Usually a variety of possible treatments can challenge the version produced. The exercise becomes especially valid to students when they consider screenwriters' accounts of the amazing amount of rewriting, wheeling and dealing, hustling, and so forth that lies behind the version of the film that the audience finally sees. The student's suggested version may improve the produced version. Indeed, it may even resemble what the first screenwriter originally had in mind! In discussing the different versions of given scenes, concentrate not on whether one version is "better" than another. Rather, focus on the differences of intended effect among the various versions.

17. *Editing.* After screening a film present this hypothetical situation: The producer has stated that the film just shown is still unfinished. Two minutes (or whatever) must be edited from this version to make a final print. How can we determine what to cut?

18. *Dating a movie.* If the group has studied film history, show an unfamiliar movie "from the archives" and challenge the group to figure out when it was produced. No offhand guessing; students must support all tentative conclusions with specific evidence from the film.

19. *Focusing on settings.* Discuss an entire film by examining *only* the different ways that setting and props function in the film. Allow other elements such as character or plot to enter the discussion only if absolutely necessary. This device is useful for a group which has difficulty understanding how to examine concrete details when central action consumes all their attention.

20. *Discussing a movie without mentioning opinions or general ideas.* This exercise, which becomes unduly frustrating for some people if it continues for long, demonstrates how difficult it is for some of us to dwell simply on concrete details and feelings rather than on abstract ideas and opinions. The exercise is useful when you need a way to emphasize dramatically the importance of bringing rarified discussions down to earth.

21. *Discussing critical reviews before seeing a movie.* Many people read reviews to decide whether they will bother seeing a particular movie. Rarely do moviegoers collect reviews to study *after* seeing a movie in order to compare and contrast the critics' insights with their own.

Have the group study and discuss a set of reviews about an unfamiliar movie as if they have actually seen the movie. Then show the movie and conduct another discussion. Finally, discuss whether seeing the movie significantly influenced the quality of discussion.

22. *Tricking the group.* Play a stunt on the group—overt or subtle, funny or not funny depending on your mood, intuition, and willingness to risk incurring a bit of student resentment. Discuss the feelings of the group and of individuals about having been manipulated; share your own mixed feelings about having manipulated the class, especially your thoughts about having done so for a useful "higher" purpose. Then show a film, perhaps a commercial that the students enjoy, which employs several manipulative devices and again discuss feelings and opinions about manipulation, focusing on the many subtle methods that were employed. In later discussions, when students stray from the specific film experience to talk about high-flown ideas that a film "made them feel," shift attention immediately to how the film manipulated the students' feelings.

A natural though considerably more sophisticated step from that point is to consider the extent to which films actually make us feel anything and whether, by being aware or manipulative techniques, we can be both immune to deception yet sensitive to the illusions which illuminate meaning.

23. *Running a film backwards.* Although this device may seem like plain foolishness, it can be an effective, often humorous way for students to concentrate on details of editing and direction. As they try to anticipate what's coming next, they are usually surprised at how much they missed the first time.

This device is especially interesting with reels of commercials, which are packed with cinematic tricks. Sometimes you can run a single commercial back and forth many times and students will continue to discover fresh details and editorial nuances.

24. *Role-playing a director.* Have a student role-play the director of a film the class has studied. The "director" is weary of promotional appearances. Although he has heard that the class is particularly well-acquainted with his film and might ask perceptive questions, he's skeptical. The group must convince him it is serious about his work, or he will keep his answers superficial.

This exercise will work best if the role-player rehearses, and if he studies the film thoroughly before facing the class. He should prepare several ways to steer questions and responses into vague channels, irrelevant anecdotes about famous actors, interesting stories about incidents on the set, etc. After the interview, discuss whether it was difficult to keep the conversation superficial and whether the role-player ever felt he really had to be sharp.

25. *Analyzing a verbal sequence.* One National Training Laboratory study of interpersonal communication estimated that the messages in a typical discussion consist of 7 percent verbal content, 23 percent voice inflection, and 70 percent nonverbal cues. Have the group view a sequence or scene containing plenty of conversation. Then, considering every possible detail of movement or expression that could influence communication, identify all the messages that occur throughout the conversation. How do the results compare with the figures from the National Training Laboratory?

There—twenty-five devices.

Finally, here's an extra suggestion to start you on your next twenty-five ways to disrupt The Old School Game, a discussion-starter for a group of relative strangers to your film study sessions, a new class. Before having the class members introduce themselves, show a short film and ask everyone to identify with a particular image in the film that appeals to oneself for any reason at all. Then play a simple get-acquainted game with a wrinkle: each person states his or her name plus the image or detail he or she has just identified with, repeating in sequence the name and personal image of each preceding person in the game. In this way you can announce and put immediately into practice four central elements of film study: seeing, feeling, identifying, and perceiving oneself and others in fresh ways.

Children's Film Theater:
An Eye for an I

By Susan Rice

Are American films for children as good as foreign ones? Should you introduce the films you show your children? Do films make children violent? Should you stop the film if the audience gets too noisey? In this chapter Susan Rice reports the results of a two year research project which provided answers to these and other questions regarding children's film theater.

Chapter Ten

> **Adult:** *"Would you like to see one long movie or a lot of short ones?"*
> **Children:** *"A lot of long ones!"*

In 1970 the Center for Understanding Media embarked on a program involving children and movies. We valued both and thought they could help each other. We didn't conceive of the Children's Film Theater project as a particularly revolutionary or complex experiment; it wasn't regulated by the varia of scientific calibration. We did not seek to prove that children's reading levels would increase proportionally to their exposure to film through the administration of reading readiness tests, nor did we wire their brains to electrodes to establish a link between heightened psycho-motor responses and flickering wall stimuli. What we did do was simply to undertake a *documented* program involving regularly scheduled screenings and evaluation of children's films. We did this because no extensive or reasonably current listing of children's films—not to mention one based on the observed responses and feelings of children *themselves*—was available. Anyone interested in using films with children was forced to rely on the catalog descriptions of the distribution companies (hardly a reliable source) or on the repeated use of well-known children's film "classics" (like *The Red Balloon* and *The Golden Fish*) with which many of the children were already familiar. Those impartial listings that did exist generally sprang from the fevered imaginations of adults whose experience with the films was restricted to the sanctity of preview screening rooms, whose evaluations were for the most part arrived at on the basis of what children *should* like rather than what they *do* like.

When we initiated the Children's Film Theater, we took as "given" the principle that children can develop good taste by tasting good things, that entertaining movies were always—directly or indirectly—"education" (while the inverse did not always hold true), and that short films were a more appropriate medium for small people than features.

The project itself extended for two years and involved over 4000 children from public, private, and parochial schools, after school programs, community groups, and nurseries. The film programs were generally 40 to 60

Confident, articulate, film-wise

minutes long. The size of the audience varied from eight to 200, though we came to prefer much smaller groups (30 to 40) for the kinds of activities we like to do after the films. The groups were economically and racially mixed and, in some cases, polylingual; some of the children spoke no English at all. Ages ranged from three-and-a-half to ten. We did not often combine age groups at single screenings, although we did use most of the films with all age groups. *Films Kids Like* (Chicago: American Library Association, 1973), an annotated catalog of 225 short films for children, was selectively compiled from the screenings of the Children's Film Theater project. My purpose here is not to reiterate or capsulize the information that can be found in that book. I do commend it to your attention, however, for it is an invaluable aid to anyone interested in children, children's films, and how to show films to kids. The philosophy and the nuts and bolts information are set forth economically in the book's introduction. The book is richly illustrated with stills from the films tested in the project and, equally valuable, with shots of youngsters engaged in film activities and reproductions of the young viewers' own artistic responses to their film experiences. A second volume, *More Films Kids Like* (Chicago: American Library Association, 1977) is also recommended.

Upon compiling *Films Kids Like,* I found myself one of a common contemporary phenomenon: the instant expert. I was invited to give speeches and lead seminars. I found myself lecturing people who had given more of themselves to children and children's media than I could ever hope to do. Some of them asked for more specific information, PROOF! Others wanted to know what could

possibly be educational about a film that didn't use words to convey its meaning. Generally the response to our project was interested and enthusiastic, and I, in turn, learned a great deal from the audiences I spoke to.

What follows is a little true or false quiz developed to assess your understanding and notions about using films with kids.

A LITTLE TRUE OR FALSE QUIZ

1. *American films for children fall far below the level of foreign films for children.*   T ☐   F ☐
False. Sort of. American animation generally falls below the level of animation done in countries like Czechoslovakia, Bulgaria, Hungary, and Canada, but people like Eli Noyes, Jr. and Bruce Cayard are fast closing the gap. Americans tend to restrict themselves to line animation, clay animation, and pixillation, while middle European animators seem to move just about anything they can work their hands on—glass, wool, wood, photographs, things you can't identify. This may be explained by the generosity of the governments who put their money behind the ideology that childhood is the most vital and influential time of our lives, whereas children's filmmaking in the U.S.A. falls into the arena of free enterprise. And we are just beginning to realize what a firm investment (literally) children are, even as consumers of animation. This has meant a boom for cartoons—mostly the television variety which involve little more than the animation of mouths and occasional hands or eyelids. But it also means that film distributors are beginning to recognize a real market for children's films. And some of those distributors would as soon spend their money on imaginative animation and imagination as they would on the predictable talking sticks. In the area of live-action filmmaking for children, this country is faring far better than even the largest producers of children's films, India and Japan. This subject is an apt one for much closer examination, so suffice it to say that (unlike almost anything else) things are looking better for American short films for children.

2. *Silence is Golden.*   T ☐   F ☐
False. Kids talk for a number of reasons: because they're bored (though they tend to move more than talk when that is the case), because they're interested, because they're frightened, because they're involved. When you use films with kids you become fairly sensitive to what the talk means. We found out as much about the children's feelings and reactions from what they said *during* the films as anything else. This is the TV generation; they have been reared to concentrate on small moving images and vague sounds while all kinds of hell are breaking loose around them. Think what a pleasure it is to have a *big* image and high fidelity sound to lose yourself in with all kinds of hell breaking loose around you. Kids do not seem to be terribly distracted by the talking of other kids; sometimes they are comforted by it.

3. *If a group gets too raucous, stop the projector.*
          T ☐   F ☐
True. Let the punishment fit the crime.

4. *Movies for children should always be properly introduced.*   T ☐   F ☐
False. Movies for children should always be judiciously screened prior to showing to see if any introduction is required. Ushers in movie houses don't tell us anything about what we are going to see, so why breed the expectation in children? Dwight MacDonald, one of the most revered American film critics, when he attempted to introduce classics of the screen for his course in film at Santa Cruz, was implored by his students to "shut up and show the movie!" Children who can't read like to know the name of a movie. It's only fair that

Still from short film, *The Babysitter*

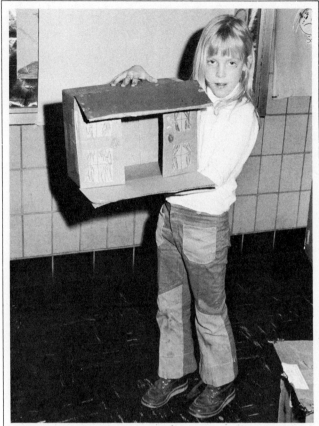

Motivated and proud to go beyond the immediate film experience

they should know. Unless you think that you can do a better rendering of the subject matter than the filmmaker, that information should suffice, along with the number of films on the program. Kids like to know how much they're in for, and they like to count down. I guess it makes them feel a part of things.

5. *Quality films work in every situation for audiences large and small.*   T ☐   F ☐

False. Some films that work wonderfully in small groups (up to forty) fail miserably in large (one hundred or more) screening situations. Some that work well in large situations are flat in more intimate settings. Age, of course, of both the film and the audience is a major variable, as well. To find out which films work in what situations, you can either toy with disaster or acquire a copy of *Films Kids Like*. We are currently looking more deeply into the matter of small and large audiences for children's films and will include a special section on this subject in the supplement to *FKL*.

6. *Kids like animated cartoons best.*   T ☐   F ☐

False. Kids are most familiar with animated cartoons, and the recognition factor is a source of delight for them, a feeling of power. Kids also like live-action movies with kids in them with whom they can identify. They like story films of books they have read (recognition again). And they also like straightforward, slow-moving, narrated, linear portraits that do not bear the slightest resemblance to their usual TV fare. Kids like movies that respect them and that allow them to respond (even if unconsciously) to a sensuous surface. Of course kids like some animated cartoons, but not a whole program of them. A whole program of one genre is suicide. Mix it up—live-action, animation, narrated, non-narrated, fairy tales, music films, story films, sports films. You know.

7. *Movies make children violent.*   T ☐   F ☐

True. Not all movies by any means. But some. First, the bad news: I have actually seen children begin to hit one another upon viewing one of those sportsthrillclimax films. Now, the good news: There was no hitting or violence when the same film was shown with a warning prior to screening. Occasionally one must invoke Rice's Rule of Order: Use threats before some films ("No more movies if I see anybody so much as move."). You'll recognize the films that require the invocation of this rule the moment you prescreen them. You have one other option in desperate situations: make the primary offenders light captains or projector watchers. If this seems like rewarding vice, it is. But it is far from punishing virtue which is what happens to the rest of the audience when a couple of chronically loud or aggressively angry kids begin to cut up.

8. *Movies work miracles.*   T ☐   F ☐

False. Movies cannot work miracles. They are a medium; they are affected by those who generate them and those who receive them. In this respect, perhaps, movies are no more than a book, a painting, or a piece of chalk. But they are also magic. I know of no other medium that so thoroughly widens the eyes, engages the senses, and plunges us so intensely into a waking dream conjoining conscious and unconscious states. And movies do even more for children. At their best, they provide feelings of identity, affiliation, and power in most dramatic form. And these experiences can resonate for a lifetime.

Still from short film, *The Mole and the Lollipop*

Is What You See All You Get?

by Kay Weidemann, Gerry Laybourne,
and Maureen Gaffney

Media, like all subjects in a child's education, is not taught as an end in itself. Rather, it is an important component in the process of growth. Media education should aid in a child's self-growth, in coping with demands of a changing world, and in reaching specific curricular objectives. Here the authors describe three tested programs which grew out of children's film experiences. It is a provocative introduction to what to do when the lights go on.

The film ends. The projector is turned off. What kind of experience was it? The kids seemed attentive, even absorbed, and, as the lights come on, faces turn toward you in expectation. There is some confusion, some excitement, and some questioning. What's next?

Unfortunately, in many classrooms the lights signify an end to the film experience. But why shortchange the kids? No matter how good the film, seeing it is only a partial experience if it isn't used to stimulate discussion and act as a catalyst for related activities. If there is no exploration or feedback on the experience, how can we raise this new generation to be critical viewers of the various and all-pervasive media?

When the lights go on, why not continue the experience? In continuing the work of the Children's Film Theater, we looked for quality films that ignited a special response in kids and developed programs of films that worked together to realize particular educational objectives.

To give you an idea of our approach and to encourage you to develop your own programs and activities "when the lights go on," we offer three sample programs that we tested and found successful for classroom use: Exotic Menus, Point of View, and Pulling Together.

EXOTIC MENUS

Aimed at six- to ten-year-olds, this program can stimulate creative writing, encourage imagination "what if . . ." situations, or lay the groundwork for a unit on cooking.

Films

Chow Fun. Serious Business Company (4 min.) A short animated film full of colorful nonsense. A fantasy about the dreams that come from overindulging in exotic food.

Green Eggs and Ham. BFA Educational Media (9 min.) A film version of the Dr. Seuss classic whose outlandish characters and rhyme reveal that.you can't judge a taste by its color.

Dragon Stew. BFA Educational Media (14 min.) A young man with a prize-winning but untestable recipe for dragon stew is faced with a dilemma when, much to his chagrin, the main ingredient (a dragon) is caught.

People Soup. Learning Corporation of America (13 min.) Two young boys have fun experimenting with the food they find in their kitchen; such experimentation leads to a bizarre ending.

What to Do When the Lights Go On

Recipe Rip-off. Taking off on *Dragon Stew,* ask kids to invent their own free form recipes for "Dinosaur Delight" and other exotic dishes, using the strangest and most imaginative ingredients they can think of.

The Semi-Annual (Name of Your) School Cook-Off. The title obviously comes from the Pillsbury Bake-Off, but you can get the kids into some serious cooking by having them bring in their favorite recipes from home. This can lead into activities on nutrition, measurement, shopping locally for food, making cookbooks, learning how to read recipes and menus, and discussing different ethnic cultures and cuisines.

Culinary Graphics. The kids can draw, construct collages, paper sculptures, or clay figures to represent particular foods or their associations with particular foods or different ethnic cuisines. Ask them to create graphics or constructions of dreams that come from overeating, of stomachs after ingesting "Dinosaur Delight," etc.

What If. . . . Have the kids invent "what if . . ." situations and write or discuss the results. Examples: What if you were the food reviewer for your local paper; how would you describe the food in the school cafeteria (or the food your classmates bring from home)? What if the main ingredients in a recipe were missing; what could you substitute? What if you are what you eat; what do certain foods or meals make you become?

POINT OF VIEW

The objectives of the Point of View program, best done with a humorous slant, are to develop an awareness that there are many different points of view, and to explore this idea through creative writing or filmmaking. This program seems to be most successful with older kids, ten to twelve.

Bad Dog. Eccentric Circle Cinema Workshop (6½ min.) From a dog's eye-view, we see Central Park (New York City) during a winter frolic.

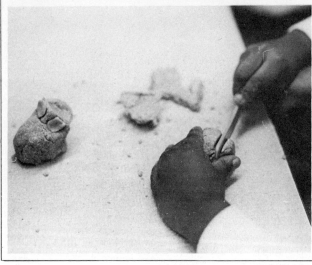

have the kids explore their environment from a bird's-eye-view, a dog's-eye-view, or any other point of view they can think of.

Time Study. Choose an immobile, inanimate object (fire hydrant, mailbox, waste basket, water fountain, park bench) and have kids keep a written log, every fifteen minutes over a period of two hours, for what happens around or to the object. Vary the exercise by sketching, filming, or tape-recording. Kids enjoy using simple observation techniques like this.

Trying On Points of View. Have kids imagine the function of an object (lunch box, TV set, egg beaters, radiator, bicycle) as if they had never seen it used. Ask them to describe it from three different points of view, such as a Martian's, an animal's, and a toddler's. Encourage inventive descriptions and new ways of looking at common objects and their uses.

Machines That Change The Way We See. Explore visual distortion by gathering as many "machines" that alter vision as you can find. Use crystal balls, discarded eyeglasses, various lenses, prisms, cameras, microscopes, telescopes, periscopes, kaleidoscopes, colored cellophane, etc. Ask the kids to discuss what each "machine" does and how it could affect their view of the world if they always saw things the way they did through the "machine."

PULLING TOGETHER

This program of animated films is geared to three- to five-year-olds. Its objectives are to promote discussion of cooperation and develop simple group interaction skills through dramatic play.

Films

Zebras. Texture Films (10 min.) A drawing animation with a lively sound track about a zebra with a problem. Another animal helps the zebra find a solution.

Frederick. Connecticut Films, Inc. (6 min.) Mice preparing for winter discover that cooperation can take place on different levels and that poets also have something to contribute. The film itself is animated from the collages and text of Leo Leonni's popular picture book (Pantheon, 1967; available in trade, library and paper editions).

Mole and the Chewing Gum. Phoenix Films (9 min.). The mole, a Czechoslovakian Mickey Mouse, picks up chewing gum and literally gets attached to it. Cooperative animals help him as he humorously and frustratedly attempts to get unstuck.

Six Penguins. Contemporary/McGraw-Hill Films (5 min.) The slapstick routines of penguin puppets enhance this classic fable format of the Golden Rule.

What To Do When the Lights Go On

Cooperation is an important theme in the preschool curriculum. Films provide an easy format for discussing essential social values. The fable format seems to make it easier for this age group.

Tug-of-War. The basic game of Tug-of-War teaches a lot about the mechanics of cooperation. Winning requires pulling together. Activities involving body movement are effective with this age group, and you can use many other simple team games to show how cooperation works.

Cockaboody. Pyramid (6 min.) Using the sound track of an actual play situation, the Hubleys have animated a "sketch" of toddler's play that combines reality and fantasy.

Overture Nyitany. Contemporary/McGraw-Hill Films (9 min.) Time-lapse micro-photography and synchronized editing to the classical music score make this nonverbal film of the embrionic development and birth of a chick literally pulsate with the force of life. The microscopic view both alters and reveals the process in a unique, exciting way.

Marble. Films, Inc. (7 min.) When he loses his special marble, a young boy dreams/acts out an elaborate nonverbal recovery episode. He is saved from a potential threat by seeing the situation from the marble's point of view.

What to Do When the Lights Go On

It's important to discuss the idea of Point of View before showing the films. Kids will need this focus in order to get the most from the follow-up activities.

Low Ball, High Ball—Where Is My Eyeball? Have kids crawl around the room and discuss what they see from belly level. If you have access to video or Super 8 cameras,

Playacting. Using the basic plots from the films in this program, ask groups of five or six kids each to produce their own version of one of the stories. To make the selection process easier, have each group pull a title from a hat. The groups will need adult assistance to organize their "play" and to help keep them from getting frustrated. Not only will they be acting out plots that deal with cooperation, they will also actively discover what cooperation means in the process of presenting their version of the film.

Jigsaw Mix-Up. Take two relatively simple jigsaw puzzles that have about the same number of pieces and divide each one in half, randomly, so that each "half" contains the same number of pieces, or so one group has only one piece more than the other. Do not be as concerned with symmetry as with the number of pieces per pile. Ask for volunteers and form two teams of three or four kids each. Give each team half of puzzle A and half of puzzle B. Ask each team to complete one whole puzzle. Since the only

way to do this is by trading pieces (which they must do one at a time), the players will have to cooperate. The process of trading pieces and trying to figure out the puzzle can become very complicated, but it is fascinating. It might be helpful to have adult assistance in the form of question-asking about where a piece might fit or if a piece belongs. Or have the remaining kids act as kibitzers as they roam from one team's table to another. Be sure to have the "observers" talk with the team members afterward about what happened. Since the object of this exercise is to learn about cooperation, winning is not important, and, in fact, the exercise can be stopped before either puzzle is completed if interest wanes.

Taffy Pull. A sticky but wonderfully engrossing follow-up, especially to the Mole film. (Most recipe books have taffy recipes—but avoid molasses taffy, which is particularly messy and can produce negative side-effects if kids eat too much of it.)

Part 4
Video

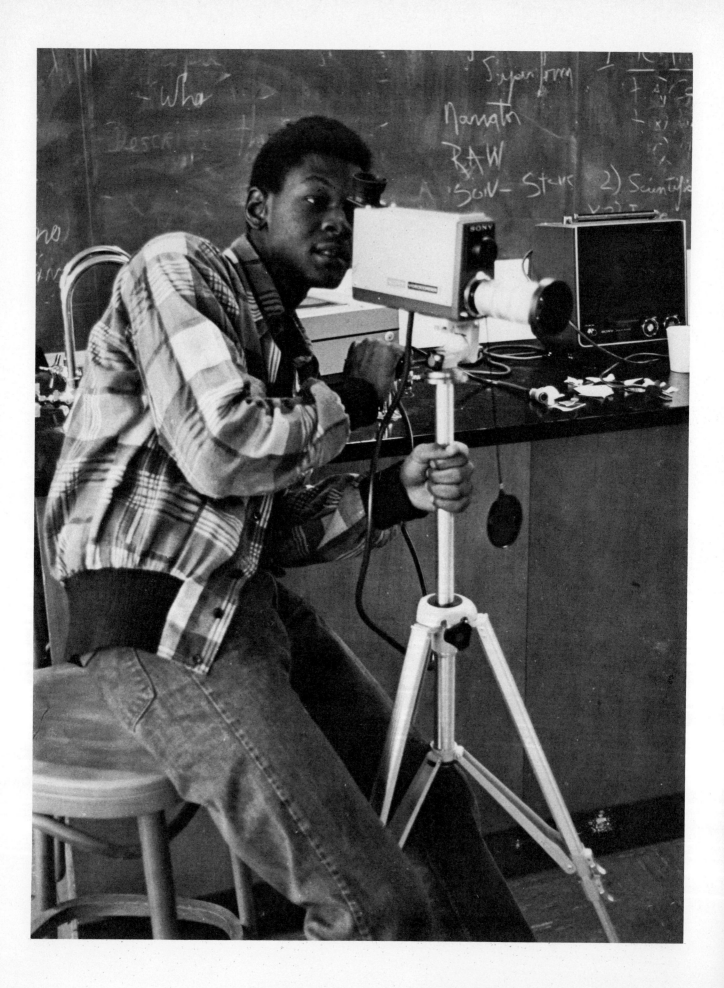

Doing Videotape

by Kit Laybourne

Only a few short years ago it would have been impossible to imagine doing the kinds of activities described in this chapter. There was nothing to do them with. But a new kind of machine—VTR—has been making its way into the classroom. Focusing on the "software" (*what* to do with the equipment) rather than with the "hardware" (*how* to operate the equipment), Kit Laybourne offers some twenty-five activities to demonstrate the almost endless potential of videotape.

"Mommy, are we live or on tape?"

Behind that question is today's television experience, made possible by videotape. The machine that has introduced it to the classroom and has caused such great excitement among teachers and students alike is a portable, half-inch videotape recorder—VTR. The camera weighs a mere six pounds, and the recording/playback deck, to which the camera is attached by a cable, weighs only nineteen pounds. With a special attachment, the tape can be replayed through any TV set. Once the basic equipment has been acquired, day-to-day operating costs are minimal because video tapes can be reused. The system is readily available through numerous manufacturers.

But the most revolutionary feature of these new video systems is not their size or economy but their ease of operation, their accessibility. The tyranny of audiovisual technicians has ended. What little there is to know about the equipment and its operating procedures has already been fully detailed in a number of publications designed especially for classroom teachers (see the Resources section for a selective list of good titles). My concern here is about what educators might do with videotape, and why.

Videotape making can be a primary experience by which young people can understand and experience the symbolic code system of television, the medium that so thoroughly dominates their lives. But video is not television. Not quite. Although students will understandably first approach classroom video tools in terms of the one-way medium that they have spent their lifetimes watching, their own video making can be used to expand that limited vision. The activities described below try to show how.

Every activity can be done with a single camera VTR system: a portapak or a less mobile setup of camera, recording deck, and playback monitor. For these activities, multi-camera studies and/or video editing setups are *not* required. Furthermore, the gear does not need to be absolutely portable. Almost all the activities here can also be done in any classroom with any video camera and recording deck, including those one-inch monsters that many schools already have. So no matter what kind of videotape equipment you've seen in your school's closets, if you can get the gear into your classroom, you can try the ideas that follow.

The lightweight, easy-to-operate VTR has revolutionized media use in the classroom and the library media center.

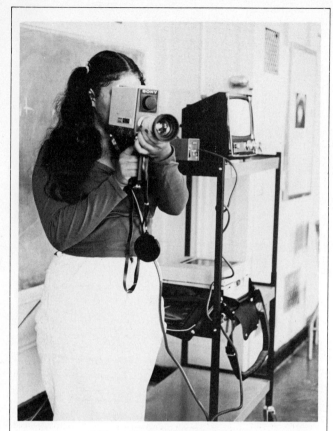

Single camera VTR system: portapak camera, playback monitor, and recording deck

DRAMATIC/IMPROVISATIONAL MODES

Nonverbal gaming is a nice way to begin working in videotape. The games provide an easy and nonthreatening way to explore the new video environment. They help students learn to concentrate on what they are doing, not on the camera. The exercises also help develop an individual's awareness of the other people he or she is working with, a sensibility analogous to peripheral vision. Each game is self-contained, an activity that can be done again and again. As kids repeat various exercises they will easily see themselves getting better and better in their performance. Finally, because of their emphasis on body movement, these improvisations are visually rich. They provide a beautiful and exciting "subject matter" on which kids can develop their shooting techniques.

The first five activities are adapted from Viola Spolin's marvelous collection of "theater games" to teach dramatic skills, *Improvisations for the Theater* (Evanston, Ill.: Northwestern University Pr., 1963). My particular modification of Spolin's approach leaves out much of her philosophy and technique, but you are urged to refer to her book for further reading.

Theater Games

Circle mimes and introduction. The teacher asks the class to sit in a circle. A basic ground rule of this activity is that no one can make any noise. Using pantomime, someone in the circle creates an object (blows up a balloon, sharpens a pencil, makes an ice cream sundae) which is then passed along to the person to the right. How the person accepts the created object (pops the balloon, writes a note, eats the sundae) signifies an understanding of what was created. The receiver then creates another object which is passed along as the game continues. The tape is played back immediately.

Mirroring. Students pair off while the teacher or a student uses the portable VTR. Facing each other, one of the partners moves his or her arms and body slowly. The other partner becomes a "mirror" that exactly reproduces the movements of its "object." Periodically, the teacher claps hands to signifify that the roles of the pairs should change. A variation of mirroring can help students perceive how our faces often mask rather than express our feelings. In this mirroring improvisation the pairs stand close, and one partner mirrors the slowly changing expressions on the other's face. Again, no verbal communications are allowed during this activity. As a follow-up, ask students which kind of mirroring activity was more difficult. Explore why. Initiate immediate playback.

Making a machine. Someone in the class is asked to go to the center of the room. By using his or her body to create a repetitive set of motions (say, lifting one arm and stamping the other foot), the student begins to suggest a machine. As other students see a way that they can "hook up" with the machine, they enter the center and become part of the mechanical action. This continues until all the students take part. During this activity, have students concentrate on maintaining a constant rhythm among all the "parts" of the machine. After everyone has joined in, you can have each participant add a sound for his or her particular piece of motion. After this, you can ask the person who initiated the activity to either slow down or speed up the entire machine. To insure that everyone is paying attention to the overall machine, you might arbitrarily switch the single person within the machine who serves as its "timer" or, to use a machine term, its servomechanism.

Long-distance touching. One of the points of this activity is to help students extend their abilities to maintain an intensive concentration with another student. An even number of students go to the center of the room and touch their hands in the middle of a circle (eight to twelve students is a good size for this activity). Each person identi-

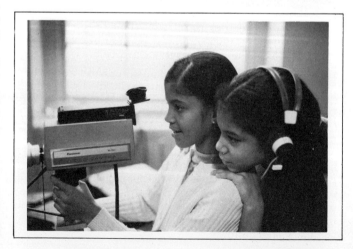

fies a "partner" who is facing them across the circle. They
touch fingertips. The teacher asks each person to take a
step backward. For as long as it is physically possible, the
pairs should continue to actually touch fingertips. Continue to ask all members to take another step backward
until the originally compact group is spread out to all
corners of the room. Even when they can no longer physically touch, ask the students to lean toward their partners
and struggle as hard as possible to remain touching. During playback, ask students to recall the distance at which
it was impossible to continue maintaining the illusion of
touching their partners.

Tug-of-war. This is another activity that asks students
to do a pantomime. This time it's a group activity. Select
two students to demonstrate a tug-of-war. Throw them an
imaginary rope and have the class watch the tension between the two. Then split the class and have them join the
action. The game should be played for "real" except for
the fact that everyone will be tugging on an imaginary
rope. Remind participants to "feel" the rope's thickness
and texture. The activity should be taped from a distance
so that the camera sees the entire event—both teams. You
might ask students to continue the tug-of-war until one
team is successfully pulled across the center line. Have
students discuss how each side worked as a "group." Have
them reflect upon how difficult it is to let oneself and one's
team "lose" in this kind of competitive game situation.

Dramatic Productions

An important kind of videotape making involves acting
out a story. Younger children, especially, seem to have a
natural affinity for this kind of activity. Fantasy play is
a central component of every child's development. Video
fortifies and extends these dramatic impulses and
capabilities. The instant playback of VTR systems can
heighten the experience of performing, and it can help
students perceive and actively manipulate various elements of dramatic structure.

An improvisation becomes a teleplay. This activity begins with an ordinary improvisational situation that the
kids act out with very little planning. After a "situation"
has been chosen, students quickly assign themselves the
various "characters" that the scene calls for. (Two examples: 1) a movie theater with various comic stereotypes—
the lady with the hat, the man who gives away the plot,
the popcorn eater; 2) a locker room, where the action
develops between members and the coach of a team that
has just lost a national championship because two of the
stars broke training the evening before.) The first run-
through of the improvisation your students choose should
be done fast and then played back immediately. While
viewing the tape, kids naturally come up with ways to
improve the improvisation. The focus of the discussions at
this point should be on having each participant identify
their character in the improvisation and describe carefully what their particular character "desires" within the
conflict of the improvisation. The class does the improvisation for a second time. During this playback the group
begins to "fix" action and characterization. Sometimes it
is helpful to outline the developing "teleplay" on the
blackboard. Usually, a director is appointed at this time.
When everyone feels they are ready, the drama is taped
for a final time in its more formal and scripted form. This
means that the director and the cameraperson can inter-

Second graders improvise a theater game, "being trees," and
enjoy immediate playback/feedback.

rupt a straight run-through in order to change angles, get
a close-up, and the like. This places new demands on the
actors. If the students feel their teleplay is pretty good,
they might ask another class to see it and give their responses.

Dramatic readings. Whether in a classroom, on a stage,
or "on location" outdoors and elsewhere, the portable
VTR equipment can be used to tape almost any sort of
student drama. On a more informal basis, students can
make effective tapes of dramatic readings. In this activity
the video image constantly remains close-in on the faces
of the students reading parts in a play. The camera can
be stopped between each reader to avoid panning movements. Because one never really sees background, cos-
tume, movement, or the spatial relationships between
characters, and because the "headshots" of students deliv-
ering their lines follow each other immediately, this format is very easy to do and requires little preparation.
Taping of dramatic readings focuses on the verbal and
facial expression of those participating and somehow asks
the viewer to use his imagination in a highly participatory
and effective way.

Plays. Once students have rehearsed a play, it is easy
and fun to video-record it. If a production is being conducted on a school stage, the portable equipment can
record the drama in different ways and usually without

Playback of a street interview

any additional lighting. Naturally, the simplest way to do this is by positioning the camera on a tripod at the front center of the stage and then shooting the play continuously. A somewhat more complicated (and more effective) technique is to have the camera move around on the stage to cover different pieces of action from different positions. Taping a play in this way, the actors will have to stop the action from time to time as the camera and sound people choose a good location for the next scene or piece of stage "business." It will help if a student video director works with the players to develop a "shooting script" that delineates camera coverage. If you decide to break up the shooting of a play in "real time," remember that you can also break up the locations of the shooting. Abandon the stage and its sets for more realistic and varied sets. Also remember that with a single camera you cannot edit your tapes. Hence things have to be shot in their final order with as much continuity joining the various shots as possible. Always have your students try a sample scene first. They will soon discover both the difficulties and the rewards of this kind of videotaping.

TV Shows. Kids really enjoy producing and videotaping their own versions of quiz shows, game shows, and talk shows. By having them do these in the classroom, a teacher can provide the children with experiences against which they can begin to develop a critical and creative framework for judging TV's largest amount of fare. The teacher may want to use these situations for something "educationally significant"—a spelling bee, a quiz show on a recent history unit, a game of charades, or a panel discussion (simulation) of a social studies topic. The content of the program is a less significant learning experience than the process of preparing, producing, presenting, and evaluating a videotape. A nice variation on these sorts of productions is to have older children prepare shows for younger children: story readings, puppet shows, discussions of school rules, etc.

DOCUMENTARY/JOURNALISTIC MODES

A journalistic approach to the use of video centers upon the role of the news reporter. The reporter's effectiveness, in turn, depends on his or her interviewing skills. These three activities are designed to reveal the formal compo-

nents of interviewing and the responsibilities that go along with the "power" a student receives when pointing a camera or a microphone at someone.

Using Portable Format Equipment

Street Shooting. A group of three students leaves the environment of the school to interview someone. One student carries the portapak, one uses the camera, and the third handles a microphone that is plugged into the video deck. Their task is to interview someone—a shopkeeper, an old person in a park, a man on the street. But the job doesn't end here as it would in a filmmaking or print journalism assignment. The students immediately rewind their tape and play it back (through the camera, on-the-spot) for the person they have been interviewing. After the entire interview has been replayed, the kids can continue to ask questions of the subject. The process repeats itself. When playing back such street interviews in class, have the children compare the first interview with the second one. Have them compare the way in which one gets to know the subject in this process as opposed to the technique and format used on commercial TV. Are there particular portions of the interview which, if used alone, would make quite different comments about the person they interviewed? What kind of responsibility does the video maker have to a person or group being taped?

Portraits. The class divides into pairs. The idea is for the students to collect no more than five minutes of material on their partners. This visual material should be "unrehearsed;" that is, the students should video-record each other in what they feel are "natural" situations. The tape is not edited. The video maker next creates a sound track. This audio material is dubbed in over the visual material (an easy process that the directions for your portable VTR will explain). The audio track can be made by having the video maker "interview" the subject or by having the subject simply do an extemporaneous autobiographical monologue. The audio track can be transferred to the videotape from an audio tape recorder or "dubbed live" by the pairs during playback. When the completed tapes are played for the class, the "subject" or a friend might be asked to comment on how close the portrait came to "real" life. When I use this approach, I find that children get a lot out of reflecting on the demands placed on them as both the video maker and the subject of the videotape portrait.

Student-made "news studio"

The Objectivity Myth. The idea behind this activity is to help kids see how much the video maker's point of view (and related camera and interviewing techniques) color his documentation of a place or event. The class is divided into three groups. An appropriate subject is chosen for making three ten-minute tapes. (A student lunchroom, a "MacDonald's" hamburger stand, and a school athletic event all provide good topics for this activity.) The first group is sent to the site and asked to make an "objective," "impartial" record of what is taking place. This should include both some interviews of those involved and some footage that records the activity and environment of the selected topic. When the first group returns, a second group is given the same assignment, except that they are asked to use the camera and conduct their interviews so as to effect a "bad" or "negative" interpretation of the setting. Finally, the third group approaches the situation with the bias of making it seem as "good" and "positive" as they can. The tapes are viewed with an emphasis on talking about how a video maker can manage to be "objective" and about what techniques can be used to "load" the presentation. Three groups covering the same subject inevitably come up with quite different things. The children can discuss what aspects makes one treatment better than the other.

Using Non-Portable Format Equipment

For the most part, television today uses the forms that were developed for earlier drama, radio, motion picture, and newspaper mediums. In using portable and simple-to-operate videotape systems, most of us will tend to explore the medium from the perspective of these older, known mediums. To a certain extent, this is fine; kids ought to be provided with experiences that can promote their critical and creative competence with regard to current television forms. At the same time, we need to be particularly sensitive to the unrevealed potentials of this new medium. It is clear that portable video systems can do things that no other medium can do. We need to create opportunities for our students (and ourselves) to explore and chart the full domain of videotape.

The next two activities try to place the preceding concerns into concrete experiences for children.

Newscasting. To begin, the class lists all the constituents of a typical TV news program: interviews, advertisements, editorials, weather forecasts, sports coverage, commentary, "on-the-spot" reports. Then class members select roles for their own news show about the school. Two students are named "director" and "assistant director." It is their jobs, respectively, to coordinate the allocation, time length, and sequence of news items and to direct the cameraperson during the actual taping. A "news studio" can be built complete with station logo, credit sheets, and news desks. Everyone is given a few minutes to prepare for their presentations. And everyone must know precisely how long (in seconds) their presentation should be. Those students who are doing "hard news" can collect stories from PTA bulletins or information gleaned from other teachers, kids, or administrators. Students who are assigned advertisements can use magazine ads for ideas and copy during their "spots." Other students may wish to prepare props (a weather map, a mock list of baseball scores, etc.). People doing live interviews can plan the "role" one person will adopt during the interview and

Shooting a head shot for a dramatic reading or report. Note rear projection on screen used for background.

Improvising a dolly shot, using school's trash cart for mobility.

prepare a list of questions that the "interviewer" will ask. When it is time to tape, as little time as possible should be taken between various parts of the show. One of the most important things for kids to experience is the pressure that live newscasting places on all participants. Naturally, the program should be played back a number of times so that individual students can check their performances, discuss the difficulties of this kind of production, and relate what they have experienced to that which they see at home.

In-depth Interviews. I recommend this for older students, particularly if they have recently completed some short "man-on-the-street" interviews. The activity is deceptively simple. A cameraperson and an interviewer make a one-hour appointment with someone neither of them knows too well—perhaps another student, or better, a teacher, administrator, or other non-teaching adult in the school community. The only rule in this activity is that the interview *must* last 30 minutes. As with the preceding activity, you may wish to require students to replay the videotape immediately for the person who has been interviewed. It will surprise you, I think, to observe how interesting and compelling such interviews are for the whole class to see. They reveal the two-dimensional quality of most TV interviews—especially the "talk"

Portable video on documentary location—*Foxfire* Director Eliot Wigginton (*left*) and video artist Chuck Anderson (*second*) and students with a local resident of Rabun Gap, Georgia

shows. These in-depth interviewing activities really test the interviewer's ability to listen carefully and to draw out new material for comments made during the session.

There are two distinct steps in making a television message: first, one must gather "telling" images and sounds; second, one must order or sequence those pieces of audio and visual information. The single camera VTR system is almost unequalled in the first task. It gathers sounds and images easily, cheaply, and enables you to see them right away. But in the task of ordering pieces of tape—in the task of editing—the single camera VTR is far less facile. Without two video recorders, it is impossible to edit what has previously been gathered.

The documentary mode of VTR making is the one most affected by the limitations of editing. As you have seen in preceding activities, the video maker is sometimes forced to edit in his head—to put things onto tape in their final order on the first try. An alternative is to "edit live" by means of a simple *switcher* or a more complicated *special effects generator*. Some of the preceding activities (especially *Extemporaneous Newscasting*) are assisted by such live-editing capabilities. In some of the activities described in the next section, the task of physically resequencing videotape is not really needed: the viewer can create meaning from previously taped materials through discussion and re-viewing. (VTR playback is switched forward and backward with speed, ease, and effect.) Throughout all these documentary/journalistic activities, however, you will consciously have to minimize the need for editing. It's possible. They've all been done with a single camera VTR system.

SELF-REFLECTIVE MODES

Video gives children immediate access to their own behavior. Unlike anything that came along before it, the videotape recorder allows the teacher to help kids discover who they are and how they relate to others.

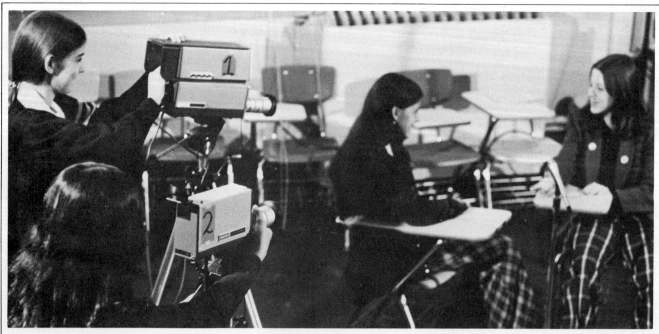

Highschoolers taping in-school interview

Monitoring Self

The first four activities try to subvert our culture's vanity taboos. While "taking pride" in one's appearance is acceptable practice within our society, too much fascination with how one looks is strongly put down. The myth of Narcissus is alive and well in our classrooms. But I suggest you work hard at letting kids freely inspect their own images and actions as they show up on videotape.

There is little need for formal discussions during the immediate playback of tapes. Instead, try to establish a quiet, reflective atmosphere. Occasionally interject a positive comment about what we're watching. It is only over a long period of time that kids will make the kinds of important observations about themselves that these activities seek to engender. Don't push for epiphanies. Let them happen in their own time and on the kids' own level.

Dictionary of feelings. The class spreads out while one student or the teacher begins taping. The teacher asks the children to close their eyes and to use their entire bodies in expressing a series of emotions. The teacher might begin with something relatively concrete for students to "try on": "Imagine that you are an old tree on a cold winter day; change this tree into a young willow on a balmy spring morning; now become a tree that sits on the top of a high hill and can 'see' for miles." These concrete referents can be followed by a series of more abstract emotions for the children to experience: "Imagine that you are lonely; now that you are angry at a friend who has hurt your feelings; imagine that you feel guilty about hurting the feelings of your best friend because you've done something stupid, something that you didn't really mean; finally, change this emotion into the one you feel when you have done something more terrific than you have ever done before—you are really feeling pleased with yourself.

Tapping and towing. There are two parts to this activity. First, the class is divided into pairs that form two rows, with one of the students in each pair facing the video camera and the other standing behind the first, also facing the camera. The person in front closes his eyes as his partner begins gently to pat his shoulders and head. After a minute of this the roles change. In the second part of this activity one student in each pair closes his eyes while his partner tows him slowly through the classroom, being careful to avoid bumping into objects or other wandering pairs. The roles change after a few minutes. The tape is replayed immediately.

Isolation booth. The camera is mounted on a tripod and left in a room where students can use the equipment alone. Naturally, the class is given operating instructions. One at a time, students enter the isolation booth. They turn on the machine and stand in front of it for as long as they want, doing whatever they wish. After an individual has finished, he or she stops the recorder and rewinds the tape. The student then watches the taped playback in the small screen of the camera and listens to the sound through an earphone that comes with the machine. Students should erase the tape before the next participant uses the equipment; it is important that no one sees the "performance" other than the creator.

Self-portraits. In this activity each video maker creates an indirect self-portrait by collecting images and sounds of people, places, and events that subjectively seem to

Video can be used at any age to provide students immediate access to their own behavior.

Director, players, and script (Courtesy of WNVT/Channel 53, Loudoun County, Va.)

capture his or her world. This kind of production might require a student to have access to the VTR while at home (optimal but often impractical). Or a student might use the VTR during free periods to interview friends or to tape favorite recreational moments within the school day. A class trip can provide an easy situation in which to collect self-portrait materials. The basic thrust behind this activity is to have students try to amplify their interests and fascinations so that others can experience and know more about them. Young people often like to make "running comments" while taping. The built-in microphone of the portapak VTR camera easily picks up these self-dialogues. When self-portrait tapes are viewed for the class (with the individual's permission, always), it is fun to discuss how this kind of taping really lets you "into someone else's head."

Group Monitoring

The next three activities switch the focus from self-reflection to reflecting upon the group in which one operates. Two activities, *role-playing* and *examining values* ask the individual to try out a particular behavior within the context of an "invented" situation. The other activity calls upon the individual to study his or her part in a real situation—the classroom.

Role-playing. Begin with an improvised situation based on a possible student experience: a confrontation among members of a team, a meeting between parents and a principal, a situation in which one student has been mistreated by friends. During playback, the emphasis should fall on developing the ability to "unpack" the situation in terms of "feelings," "needs," and "actions" that either impede or promote helpful interaction among the "characters" of the improvisation. Generally, a good role-playing situation is one in which students adopt the roles of persons about whom they know and with whom they have experienced difficulty in communicating. The pay-off in this activity comes when students look back over their taped "encounters." Individuals can be asked to re-analyze both their own and other character's feelings and needs in the situation. The class can try to spot "actions" that were crucial in determining the outcome of the improvisations. Once the students have sorted out the situation, they can try to determine behavior that would lead to the resolution of various conflicts. Then, using the same situation or one closely parallel, they can reenact the encounter, using their new insights to produce a more positive outcome.

Time-lapse ethnography. The teacher asks the class to work out a schedule for documenting the sorts of "environments" that exist within the classroom over the course of a typical day's activities. The camera is mounted on a tripod in one corner of the room. At predetermined intervals (perhaps every ten minutes), one student goes to the camera and records thirty seconds of class activity by slowly panning the camera across the room. Three minutes of tape are accumulated per class hour. During playback at the end of the day, ask the students to make notes about 1) the kinds of groupings that took place; 2) their own activity within each setting; and 3) their own abilities and preferences for each of the determined "environments."

Examining values. A volume that is loaded with terrific exercises aimed at helping students identify and develop their own sets of values is *Values Clarification: A Handbook of Practical Strategies for Teachers & Students,* by Sidney Simon et al (New York: Hart, 1972), and available in both paperbound and casebound editions. It contains 79 interrelated "strategies" that aid students in examining, developing, and prizing their own values, ideals, and goals. There is probably no single resource that can be more helpful in exploring the self self-reflective modes.

VIDEO ART

These following activities attempt to set students on an open-ended course. There is no predetermined destination. Few students will have seen on broadcast television anything similar to the kinds of tapes these activities yield. This makes it very important for the teacher to work at increasing tolerances for just "playing around"— the *process* becomes the *product* in a very concrete sense. And that particular notion is central in charting the unexplored domain of video—what is called Video Art.

The first activity, *Video collages,* has students "recycling" images from broadcast television. Even the most arbitrary and accidental selection will have surprising impact. The effect of the collage is to alter the normal context in which students perceive television. The result is much like what the traveler experiences when returning home from an overseas holiday: one sees things differently. Developing a new perspective for looking at television is a requisite in exploring new alternatives for video-making. The last activity, *Video feedback cycle,* can be viewed as a metaphor for all work in the medium. The *process* of making a non-figurative, video feedback tape requires the student to become "partners" with the machine in generating images. It is only by seeing what one is doing in the TV monitor that the student video artist is able to create something that is "alive" and "interesting." An interactive relationship must be developed between what the student is doing, what he is seeing on the tape, and what he goes on to do.

Video collages. Here is an activity that is found to be nicely open-ended. Working either individually or in small groups, students are asked to use the videotape system to create 60-second collages. Each collage should consist of no less than ten different shots derived from either or both of two possble sources: 1) the taping of commercial broadcasting; 2) original, student-produced taping. Tell the students to try any effect they wish. Encourage failure—pushing ideas until they somehow collapse from going too far. It is often effective to require the older students to write about what the experimental collage tries to say or show, what the expected response of the viewers will be, and what new, experimental production was suggested by the one just completed. Not only do they find it fun to compare the creator's intentions with the audience's reaction, but this sort of self-evaluation/feedback cycle can be used itself as a definition for what the videotape medium is all about.

Sound ideas. The bias of most video makers is to create the visuals first and then add sound to the images. This activity urges you to reverse this process. Some possibilities are: 1) Students choose a short piece of music and play it aloud during a taping session while the camera explores abstract drawings or the classroom in ways that "fit" the music and often fortify and extend the music's beat. 2) Students can audio-record a familiar announcer or advertisement from either television or radio and subsequently use this audio as sound track for a parody of the original media message—for example, a third-grader can open his or her mouth and say, in Walter Cronkite's voice, "And that's the way it is . . ." 3) A reverse of the preceding: students record a favorite television personality and then dub their own voices. The following pages will provide additional ideas for using sound as an initial source for video activities.

Inter-media environments. Explore the use of video, both original and prerecorded, with other art forms. Following are some suggested activities to start you on creating your own exciting inter-media environments:

1. Initiate a game in which a student sits in front of a TV monitor and watches a prerecorded interview into which he must cast himself.
2. Student-made or commercial films can be rephotographed during screening by holding the video camera at a sharp angle to the screen or by taping only part of the overall image on the movie screen.
3. Students' photographs or drawings can be taped with voice-over commentaries by the artists; this presentation is particularly effective at parent "open-house" events.
4. Two video machines and two monitors can be used to create dialogues between two TV sets, or to combine the head of one person with the torso of another, or for any number of interrelated sculptures.

Video feedback cycle. Using a portapak or other single camera VTR system, there is a way to hook up the recording deck to a monitor so that what the camera is taping and recording is seen concurrently on the TV set. This setup is helpful for many of the activities outlined above. It enables the entire class to witness what the camera operator is seeing and doing with the camera. However this video feedback activity can be used for a different purpose and in a different way. Point the camera directly at the monitor with the monitor adjusted so that it has high contrast—bright whites and deep blacks. What happens is that the monitor and camera feed back upon each other so as to create weird abstract patterns. Sometimes the patterns (actually a picture of a picture of a picture an infinite number of times) work best if the camera is held on its side or upside-down. By slowly moving the zoom lens

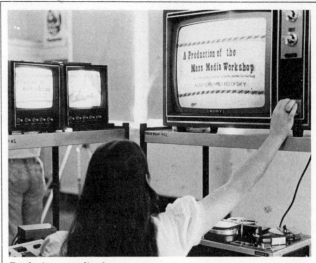

Producing a media show.

Video feedback. Camera points at its own monitor and the artist manipulates contrast and zoom controls.

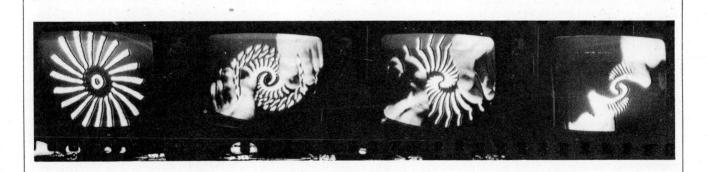

Videoart: feedback from camera alone, then a more sophisticated image when the video artist exposes own foot to the camera at the same time camera focuses on the monitor.

Behind the camera—young children, teacher, and media specialist all working together.

and changing the f-stop or diaphragm opening, the abstract patterns seem to organically grow and change. Once children have tried this a few times, they become very facile at making the patterns move in whatever ways and with whatever rhythms they desire. When music is added to the experiment, the results are even more fun and more effective. One eleven-year-old described the process as "far out." I wondered how much further out he and his generation could take the half-inch technology.

A POSTCRIPT: VIDEO VIEWING AND DISCUSSIONS

Long before they reach high school, students are conditioned to a special set of listening and participating skills associated with "class discussions." Often this behavior syndrome works fine—it *is* possible to listen to discussions with "one ear," to do other things at the same time, to let one's mind wander in and out of the conversation. But such forms of inattention are *not* appropriate when you are playing back a piece of videotape that deals with the genuine feelings and behavior of people in the classroom.

Because the most innocuous, casual comment can resonate deeply within a child, what you and your students say to each other during playback and discussion becomes terribly important. Everyone in the room must strive for a level of keen attention and maintain it throughout the playback sessions.

An informed approach to video discussions requires some rules. Here are three that I developed with Dr. An-

dreas Steinmetz, who specializes in affective learning and research. Consider using these rules especially if you will be exploring video as a tool for self-reflection.

Rule 1: Separating Fact from Fantasy

When dealing with issues of consequence to the individuals in your classroom, discussion cannot be clear and helpful unless there is a separation of fact from opinion, empirical observation from observation. Comments should go like this: "I saw you . . . (the fact or observation), and that makes me feel that . . . (the opinion or interpretation)." This first rule is cumbersome only at first; it quickly becomes an accustomed pattern of speech which enables the person you are speaking about to understand your comment and react appropriately to it. The rule avoids both the mind-reading syndrome and the tendency to ascribe unwarranted motives. The tape itself becomes the "final authority" in verifying the *fact*. The person or group appearing in the tape becomes the "final authority" in verifying the *interpretation* or *opinion*. This distinction between facts and fantasies gives everyone a helpful handle for processing his or her classmates' verbal information.

Rule 2: Verbal Feedback Cycles

Conversation is the only convenient and effective medium for dealing with videotapes. Not often—but often enough—I have found that conversation is dangerously subject to distortion. People don't listen very well for very long. The second rule is an exercise in learning how to listen better. Once or twice during each discussion session, the teacher or anyone else in the group cries out, "Rule 2," and points to someone who has been listening. The invocation of Rule 2 is only appropriate at that moment immediately following the conclusion of someone's comment about a piece of tape. Before the conversation continues, the person indicated must restate or paraphrase exactly what the previous speaker has been saying. The discussion is not allowed to proceed until the person "feeding back" what he or she has heard has been told by the person being paraphrased that the feedback perceptions are accurate.

Rule 3: Strength Training

There is something wonderful in the human species that causes us to worry about our weaknesses and focus energy on making ourselves better. It is an endearing quality, but not necessarily a helpful one. For it is usually much more effective to identify and amplify one's strengths than to deal exclusively with one's liabilities. Rule 3 may smack of a Pollyanna attitude but it works. I like to devote the last ten minutes of each viewing and discussion session to "strength training." The procedure is simple. Everyone in the class gets the chance to say something nice about everyone else. Only positive comments are permitted. Each person gets his or her share. Now although the generated feedback is hardly spontaneous or unsolicited, it is nonetheless genuine and successful in making everyone else feel good. Rule 3 provides a regular reminder that the group's overall intent is to work positively, that there is concern for everyone, and that the purpose is to help people perceive, evaluate, and strengthen their powers of personal expression and perception.

Chapter Thirteen

Studio Television

by Jean Baity

For more than five years Jean Baity had worked as a full-time volunteer in various elementary schools in her town, Mamaroneck. Professionally trained and experienced in TV and radio, she not only recruited, coordinated, and trained other volunteers but she also taught teachers much about studio television. In the following article, she shares some of the expertise she accumulated in her work with kids and teachers.

THE PLACE OF STUDIO TELEVISION IN AN ELEMENTARY SCHOOL

"Pan more to the right, Camera 2."
"I can't. I'll fall off my chair."

This dialog is part of the reality of a closed circuit television studio in an elementary school. Children can be actively involved in the business of television. They can operate industrial type cameras, videotape recorders, sound systems, and special effects generators.

But why bother with a TV studio, especially at the elementary level? Why not do simple projects in the classroom and school, or use a video-rover and go outside? Being a participant in a studio situation requires discipline and structure. Children develop a strong sense of responsibility when they are part of the reality of a television "crew." They learn to follow directions and to direct others. Open-ended television activities are valuable, but they are quite different from the experiences children get from participating in "real communication." When very young they begin to understand and evaluate the medium which may dominate their lives.

What are the pre-requisites for setting up a TV studio? Assuming that a simulated studio would be considered a valuable project in an elementary school, I would say the following:

1. *Joint enthusiasm* for the project by administration and faculty. Without enthusiastic support from both it cannot succeed.
2. *A room of its own.* A joint setup in a multi-media room is as conducive to television production as televising on railroad tracks would be.
3. *Simple, dependable equipment with adequate service.* New EJIA half-inch videotape recorders have proved far less troublesome than the old one-inch recorders. Equipment is now less expensive and cameras require less lighting than they did just a few years ago.
4. *Wiring by a qualified technician.*

The Studio Room

With a little ingenuity, a simple classroom or storage room that has adequate ventilation—and preferably in a quiet area of the school—can be converted into a TV Studio. One wall can be painted in a pastel color (yellow or

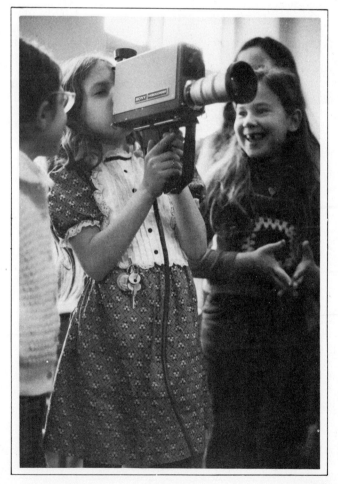

light blue) to use as a backdrop. Two pieces of inexpensive panelling hinged together at an angle make a versatile corner, which simulates a pannelled room. Flats used in stage plays can be effective. Draperies can be tacked to the wall with a power stapler. A carpet or an area rug on the floor will keep the noise level down and help baffle the sound.

Equipment

Cameras. At least one vidicon camera is needed, but two would be better, and these should be equipped with viewfinder and rear zoom and focus. (Small people have trouble reaching around to the front of the camera for controls.)

Monitor (to see what is going out over the air).

Videotape recorder (the more trouble-free half-inch system). The recorder is the key element. It is a tremendous asset to see oneself and then to be able to try again and watch the improvement.

Sound system. A sound mixer is often available in the school. One desk microphone and two lavalier microphones are minimum equipment. Children's voices are soft and are picked up much better on chest mikes. A boom microphone is a luxury and can be substituted with a desk mike (for example, place desk mike on the floor in front of a group).

Audiotape recorder. The recorder (reel-to-reel has better sound quality than cassette) and record player are essential for "finished productions." The use of music for openings, closings, and transitions adds interest.

Special effects generator. Although television equipment companies urge a SEG with a two-camera system, a simple switching device is adequate. Special effects such as split screens are rarely used. A SEG must have an extra preview monitor besides the two camera monitors.

Control room. In a two-camera setup the director must have some way to talk to the cameramen and to set up shots without having his or her voice picked up on the mikes. The director and the camera monitors could be in a closet or a refrigerator box. The director and the camera operators will all need headsets.

Lighting

If lighting is done professionally, grids will probably be installed in the studio. However, two or three floodlights

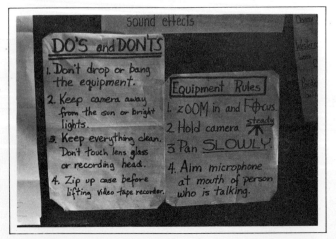

on stands and one or two spotlights could suffice. For the simplest setup, two lights could be mounted above the camera at either end of a four-foot horizontal board.

Props

Minimum props would be a table, podium, some chairs, and two music stands. Miscellaneous items such as a book case, flannel board, fireplace, or other state props are useful.

Graphics

Visuals greatly enhance any program. Black Magic Marker on yellow construction paper can produce a simple title card. Commercial paste-on letters are helpful. Black matte finish cardboard is good for mounting pictures and can be used repeatedly. Moving signs (often borrowed from or disposed of by liquor stores) can be transformed into professional looking visuals. A rear screen projection setup can be built with a few dollars worth of Mylar purchased from a windowglass shop. Movie, slide, and overhead projections can be used on the rear screen. Transparencies made from pictures in newspapers and magazines are especially effective and readily available. A scroll can be made with two dowel sticks, a cardboard box with one side cut out, and yellow shelf paper.

The Crew

Children can be taught (during lunch hour, after school) how to operate all equipment. Volunteer parents can be most helpful in training children and in running equipment. In a sophisticated two-camera setup fifth graders have proved to be competent directors, doing switching, calling shots, and coordinating the entire program. Three to twelve people can be used as a technical crew. Suggested jobs are: Producer, Director, Technical Director, Floor Manager, Camera One, Camera Two, Audio, Record Player, Tape Recorder, Videotape Recorder, Rear Screen Operator, Productions Assistant.

TIPS FOR PREPARING A TELEVISION PROGRAM: A GUIDE FOR ELEMENTARY SCHOOL STUDENTS

The Script

Typed copy. The script should be typed, with a copy for each performer and two copies for the technical crew. A 3-inch margin should be left on the RIGHT side of the page for technical crew's notes.

Information program. 1) Greet the audience. Say "Hello" or "Hi," not "Good Morning" or "Good Afternoon," for the program may be played any time of day. 2) Introduce yourself: "I am Mary Smith and this is Bob Jones." 3) Explain what you will talk about: "Today we will talk about oak trees—the pin oak, red oak, and post oak." 4) Summarize at end of program. Restate what you have talked about and say goodbye to the audience.

Interview program. 1) Greet the audience. 2) Introduce yourself. 3) Tell the audience who your guest is, and give some background information about him or her. 4) Welcome guest to the school or program. 5) Ask the guest questions, which you will have prepared in advance.

A small studio setup

6) Thank guest at close of program, and say goodbye to the audience.

Title Card

Any of the following forms can be used for making a title card:

Standard title card. On a sheet of yellow construction paper the size of a music stand or slightly larger, write the title with black Magic Marker (crayon does not show up well). Make letters at least 1–1½ inches high. Leave a margin of at least 3 inches around all four sides of the sign. Space words so the sign is easy to read. Add some pictures or cartoon drawings to make sign more interesting; make these images larger than the letters and keep them within the margins.

3-D title card. Make a sign with objects on or near it. Example: for a pet shop program, use a toy lion holding the sign, and place a background card or cloth behind the entire setting.

Moving title card. Make a sign that moves in some way, or use moving signs or objects discarded or borrowed from local merchants. Examples: for news, travel or current events program, use a globe that turns; for a program on space, use a rocket that pulls through cardboard; for a program on sailing, use a fish tank that is filled with water and has a toy boat floating on the water, and shoot

through the side of the glass. Any of these signs need overall background also.

Opening Music

Select any one of the following ways to produce music to open show:

Available recorded music (disc or tape). Select a song that goes with your subject, such as "How Much Is That Doggie in the Window" for a pet shop program. Use differ-

Simple title graphics and rear screen projection

ent speeds for various effects. "Peter and the Wolf" music, for example, is very eerie when played at slow speed.

Special taped recorded music. Tape music at home from theme music on radio or TV shows. For example: tape the "Dragnet" theme for play of "The Plot to Abolish November."

Live music. Fellow students are often good musicians. Get a friend to play guitar, flute, recorder, piano, or any other instrument.

Visuals

Set decorations. Have some ideas of where talent should be placed—sitting at a table, standing at a lectern, etc. Decide on background: the studio has black velvet draperies, plain walls, and panelling on which signs and pictures can be pinned. Objects can also be placed on a table for interest. If you have old drapery at home with interesting patterns or textures, try it on camera.

Visuals during the program. Plan things to look at. Use transparencies projected overhead. For a pet program, show a live animal. For an author or literary program, project the author's book with an opaque projector. Use pictures found in magazines or in books the same way; pictures should be at least 8" X 6" in size to project well. Show models, such as automobiles, rockets, trains. Project slides or films. Take portapak and videotape on location outside the studio.

Performers' Clothes

Never wear white—it glares. Pale colors are best.

Pep up the show with *interesting costumes.* Examples: a space helmet for a space show, a cowboy hat for a program on horses, athletic gear for various sports programs.

SUGGESTED USES FOR VIDEO SYSTEMS IN ELEMENTARY SCHOOLS

Student Involved Programs

Language arts development. 1) Videotape child for self awareness. For example, use the traditional "show-and-tell" situations, book reports, poetry readings. Let the child view the tape privately after the first TV experience. 2) Book reports: use original pictures made by the children, or show pictures from the book; dramatize the book

with costumes; make a four-part cartoon of the book. 3) Drama: present traditional dramatic programs, using costumes, scenery, props; or use pantomime; create original drama by freezing scene on videotape, play back tape and analyze how to create next action; create small vignettes from class or teacher suggestions. 4) Choral reading. 5) Reading the classics: an older child could read aloud (tape) a more difficult story (such as *Tom Sawyer* or *Treasure Island*) in continued installments for younger children. 6) Puppet shows. 7) Original storywriting: read and illustrated by the author or classmates.

Social studies. 1) Current events: Earth Day, Moratoriums, elections, memorial programs for deceased public or famous persons, new developments in space technology, telethons. 2) Group discussions: view on tape later to analyze as an observer rather than as a participant. 3) Role playing: tape situation such as foreign visitor trying to make himself understood, then analyze roles via video playback.

Science. 1) Tape especially good student demonstrations or exhibits. 2) Produce a program on current scientific problems or advances, such as ecology.

Spelling. Televise class contests and inter-class competitions.

Interviews. 1) Parents with interesting occupations or hobbies or activities, such as an author, doctor, veterinarian, race car driver, mechanic. 2) Local residents who might be of special interest to the students by virtue of their occupations, or relationship to some unit or subject under study, or closeness to the school ground or activity, *e.g.*, pet shop owner, supermarket manager, policeman, school cross-guard, fireman. 3) Visitors, such as politicians, ex-drug addict, a war veteran, a famous or near-famous alumnus.

Trip reports. 1) Class field trip to concert: for example, have kids do finger puppet show of *Firebird Suite,* using recorded music. 2) Personal student trip: for example, have student describe a visit to the Amish country, showing mementos, pictures or slides, and describing or explaining folklore, dress, customs.

Special individual study. In-depth study of an interest field (space, optical illusions).

Hobbies. Describe and demonstrate a hobby, emphasizing how student viewer might begin.

Talent. Plan a program with student talent (artist, guitarist, magician, dancer).

Videotaping a play in a studio setup

A young child reads the script for children's own puppet video show.

Special holiday programs, including historical backgrounds. 1) Religious: Rosh Hashanah, Yom Kippur, Christmas, Easter. 2) National: Columbus Day, Lincoln's Birthday, Martin Luther King's Birthday, Memorial Day. 3) Other: Arbor Day, Halloween, Mardi Gras, St. Patrick's Day, Chinese New Year.

On location. To bring back material for a program on any subject, use portapak, or use an instamatic or polaroid camera to take still or slide pictures, and tape record for added sound.

Special education. Videotape child in simple situations, such as show-and-tell. Do this in low key way for specific purpose, such as self-image or sentence development.

Physical education. Videotape beginners or underachievers to show them graphically where the problem areas are, and the successes.

Daily news program. Use "Today Show" format, or make official school announcements.

Teacher Produced Programs

Teacher evaluation. Videotape teacher in classroom situation. Let teacher view self privately and erase tape if desired.

Mathematics. Videotape single concept ideas for math lab.

Science. Tape well-planned and concise demonstration, explanation, or review.

Art. Tape simple art projects usable in classroom when part of class is occupied in another activity. Examples: paper bag puppets, pull-out clay construction.

Nurse/Teacher. Videotape programs on drugs, safety, first aid, audiometer, dental health, anti-smoking, sex education.

Physical education. Videotape demonstrated lessons in bicycle safety, or any other activities that might require special demonstrations and explanations.

Music. 1) Sing-alongs: these can be videotaped, but there is not enough time in a short classroom period to include the time the children are learning the music. 2) Music appreciation. 3) Recorder series: make short tapes to reinforce half-hour teaching sessions.

System-wide faculty workshops. Videotape especially good demonstrations.

Parent conferences. Show videotape of particularly difficult student problems. Use to elicit support for school program or further ideas from parents for resolving.

Public relations. Videotape school programs for parents, other faculty, school board, or community.

Behind the cameras with a student production crew. The director puts the documentary together. Here she cues an on-camera reporter to the prompt sheets held by another crew member.

CUE SHEET FOR TELEVISION WORKSHOP

To cameras

freeze: do not move

pan up, pan down, pan left, pan right: rotate the camera on its axis—the camera turns from one direction to another

frame: center the picture so that the subject is well located

focus: get the picture into the sharpest focus

head room: more space wanted above the actor (pan up)

single shot: a shot of one person

two-shot: a shot of two people

group shot: a shot of a group of people

wide shot or *long shot* or *cover shot:* whole scene of action

medium shot: a shot of the person from the waist up

closeup: a head and shoulders shot

tighten or *loosen:* get a shot closer or further away from the subject

dolly in, push in: move the camera toward the set

dolly back, pull back: move the camera away from the set

crankup, tilt down: move the camera head up, or down

zoom: use zoom lens to move image in or out

To the technical director of switcher

standby or *ready:* get ready—instructions will follow immediately

take: switch immediately to camera indicated

fade in: turn up the grain so that the picture slowly appears out of a black screen (used for special effects)

fade down: turn down the grain so that the picture slowly disappears into a black screen (used for special effects)

go to black: same as fade out

dissolve: fade one camera out and another in, so that images overlap for a moment on screen

super (superimpose): add the picture from one camera to that of another already on the air, so that the two cameras are on the air at the same time

lose or *go through* or *take out:* remove one of the two cameras that are on the air at the same time and leave on just one camera

To audio

open mike: turn on the mike

standby with the music: audio person starts turntable and holds the record until he or she gets the cue

hit the music: come in strong, full volume at the opening of the music

sneak in the music: let the start of the music be imperceptible

cut the music: make an abrupt stop of music

fade out music, sneak out music: imperceptibly and slowly turn down and off

music down, music down and under: hold music behind speech or other sound, but do not turn out entirely

music up: raise volume of music

cross fade: fade out one audio's source as another is faded in, so that they overlap for a moment

sequence: follow one number immediately after the preceding one without a pause

To projectionist

hit film, roll film: start the projection running

dissolve to film, take film: go to film from previous source

Highschoolers making-up for their TV show

Television Studies

by Kit Laybourne

Educators and parents alike bemoan the supposed effects that television is having on children and young people and their learning. But what is being done about it? Television is here to stay. Rather than run away from it, Kit Laybourne lays out a strategy for making the consumption and creation of the televised product a part of the media curriculum.

"Fish don't know they live in water."

John Culkin was talking about kids and television. Unpacking the aphorism is easy, and it has far-reaching implications for our schools.

The primacy of television in the lives of today's kids is undeniable. The average American youngster spends more time watching TV than he spends in the classroom. TV weans our kids, baby-sits for them, and, in its own definite way, TV schools them, too.

New media technologies shape and reshape our lives and our views in ways that we don't perceive. While we've all accumulated many years' worth of television viewing, few of us really "see" what the medium is about. Most of us are unaware of the role TV plays in affecting our relationships, in providing us with information and opinions about the world, in molding our values and aspirations, or in touching us in countless other ways. So we are like the fish, swimming in an environment that we don't perceive because the environment has become part of the way we are.

The worst aspect of TV viewing has nothing to do with the content of most programs—as bad as that often is. The final condemnation of television's influence on children is the trance-like passivity that kids adopt while watching the tube.

Certainly the easiest way of dealing with this dilemma is to throw out the TV set. This is a drastic option for parents. Yet, it is an option that, in essence, most educa-

The technological reality. *Left*, a well equipped multi-camera system in a high school; *right*, a child manipulates a smaller but still sophisticated system with special effects generator (SEG), sync generator, and several preview monitors.

tors have embraced. Judging from what goes on in most classrooms today, it is as if there were no such thing as television. After school is out, TV is the most important input in the lives of most children, but inside the classroom little is done with that resource. Rarely is there any effort to equip students with skills that can help them cope with the tremendous amount of information beamed at them over the airwaves.

Teachers should be helping students develop ways of participating with television. All activities listed here work toward this basic goal. They are presented in three groupings. *Creating Video Profiles*, the first set of activities, seeks to help children discover the role that TV watching plays in their own lives. Students need to become aware of the habits and dependencies each individual unconsciously develops while watching television in order to discover all the possibilities for information, interaction, and entertainment that the medium holds out for them. The second batch of activities are grouped under the rubric *Opening New Channels*. The goal here is to provide students with frameworks for analyzing and experiencing the content of today's broadcast TV. In this grouping there is particular emphasis on studying local TV programming and institutions. *Testing the Modern World* is my title for the last group of activities. It is a tag taken from a quote by E. B. White: "Television is going to be the test of the modern world." You may find that these activities are suited for older students. The goal is to help kids define the larger patterns and concerns which tie the medium of television to our society as a whole.

CREATING VIDEO PROFILES

A chart of viewing habits. Students estimate how much TV they watch in a day, a week, a year. Then they begin to keep a detailed record of all viewing in the course of a full week. These television diaries include: name of program; time it was seen; where and with whom it was watched; a precis of program content; an evaluation (good, bad, mediocre); reason for viewing (entertainment, to learn something, boredom, etc.); who selected the program (student, sibling, parent). After the study has been made, students analyze their own records in order to create a "Viewing Profile" and to total weekly hours of viewing (checking to see how close they came in their original

estimates). The teacher can help the class create graphs and charts for various components of the raw data. For example, the information on hours spent a week in front of TV can be totalled and a class average derived. To find the yearly average multiply by 52. Estimate a lifetime projection. Other time charts can show peak viewing hours on weekdays and weekends. An "audience" graph can be developed to process information about who chooses and who attends TV watching. A "rating" chart can be made that measures the amount of "good" programming seen against the amount of "bad" programming. A final phase of this activity is to have the students compile a "Classroom-TV-Watching Profile" against which each child can compare his or her personal profile.

Switching profiles. Using information gathered in the preceding activity, kids might swap profiles with someone else in the classroom and spend a week watching TV "through the other's eyes." What does what someone else watches tell you about the person? Or the class might want to schedule everyone to watch a particular list of programs during one week. There should be a discussion period each day to review experiences of the preceding day. "Switching profiles" can yield other levels of information when exchanges are made out of the peer group (with an older or younger member of the family or with the teacher). Here again, the exercise centers on studying others' viewing diets to see what that reveals about them and, by comparison, about one's own viewing habits. Such activities will give the teacher much insight into class viewing patterns and preferences and can lead to interdisciplinary work.

The perfect viewing environment. Because much of the meaning of television resides in the way it is seen, it is worth designing activities to help students study what has become their unperceived viewing environment. Have students write or describe their favorite place to watch TV and their favorite activities to do during TV watching. Make an assignment sheet for students to use in trying out and evaluating various options in viewing environment: distance (3 feet, 10 feet, 30 feet); position (lying on the floor, sitting up straight, moving around, upside down); lighting (dark, one light on, daylight); combining activities (try reading while watching TV, playing a game, doing a puzzle, eating); groupings (watching alone, with friends, with family). Forbid watching for a few days or a weekend. Ask students to keep track of what happens. How was time spent that was usually devoted to the TV? Have kids ask their parents (or grandparents) what they did in their pre-TV childhoods. Referring to their survey of options and their experiences when not watching TV, have the kids design a "perfect environment"—a "video space." What would be the arrangement of furniture and lighting? Would students allow non-watching activities to accompany viewing? Would their video spaces be different for different sorts of programming? Would their spaces differ from a movie theater? The goal here would be to have kids reflect upon the *way* they watch or don't watch TV as opposed to *what* they watch.

Interviewing eyewitnesses. The aim of this activity is to develop questioning skills, to get kids interested in what others watch, and to let them know that what they watch is important to someone else. The class should work together to develop questions before breaking into pairs. Have children find the child they know least in the class-

room to interview. We've found these questions helpful: Name a program you learned something from. Name a program that you did not learn anything from. Which TV character would you like to be? Who on TV is most like your mother? Most like your father? Which TV character would you like for a best friend? The class can make up another set of questions to ask parents: What are your favorite programs? How is TV different today from when you started watching it? Do you think the news is fair? How much television should little children watch? What do you think are the best children's programs? How much TV do you watch in a week?

OPENING NEW CHANNELS

Family white papers. Students view and then discuss a particular program with their parents. Everyone is fascinated to know what other people's folks said and thought about a familiar show. If you choose to begin a series of Family White Papers, it may be helpful to send the kids home with a note that explains to parents what you are trying to do. Most parents are terribly anxiety-ridden about the Pied Piper in their livingrooms. They are eager to participate with their children's TV watching and, unlike "academic" areas, feel they have plenty of expertise to share with their kids.

Getting inside the tube. There is no need for videotape equipment in order to simulate television production in the classroom. Place a big cardboard box on top of a table so that students can stand behind the box; cut out the rounded rectangle shape of the TV screen. Add dials and knobs and a coat of paint. Individuals or pairs of students can use the "TV set" as a stage for many kinds of improvised TV shows: talk show formats (a student is interviewed about a hobby); news show formats (an "eyewitness" report or an "editorial" about some facet of school life); game shows; situation comedies; advertisements; a Sesame Street puppet show. Not only are such simulations lots of fun and not only do they provide kids with "public speaking" experiences, but, through an explicit or implied comparison with common broadcasting, these activities provide students with an experienced set of references for judging the value and artistry of what they see at home. Their viewing will be less catatonic because they have new ways of participation.

Indexing television. Television programs can easily be divided into groups. A child flips to a program he has never seen before, but the serious tone, the man seated at a table, and the map behind him cue the child, and he immediately knows it is a news program. This activity aims at improving classification skills, at learning about similarities and differences, and at being able to group similar things.

Have a class make a master list of all programs that the children remember. Decide which programs are similar in kind and then try to devise labels for these general groups (cop show, quiz show, western, news program, educational program, sports program, cartoon, soap opera, variety show, situation comedy). Talk about the conventions used in each type that tell you what kind of program it is.

Later, bring a television set into the classroom. Every hour throughout the day quickly flip through the channels, asking kids to classify the programs. Have students tally the amount of show categories aired. Is the balance acceptable to the children? Appropriate for community needs?

Video budgeting. For thirty cents you can get a Yellow Pages for television—*TV Guide.* It is a first-rate resource book which can be used to help kids gain greater discrimination in their viewing patterns. The first thing Monday morning, have the class decide on a fixed number of hours for the following week's TV viewing. With *TV Guide* for program suggestions and the principle of majority rule, a schedule can be established that everyone must follow. Such an "experimental" week will provide shared experiments for discussions. And it will be an exercise in conscious control over what is to be seen and when. A similar experiment can be designed for one or two days when they all will watch only programs that they have never seen before. As TV becomes a habit, few children seek out new things to watch. There is often very little knowledge of the breadth of programming that is available. Over-allocation of time for a TV budget also makes a point. Have everyone (teacher too) devote Saturday morning, 8:00 A.M. to 12 noon, watching TV. No other activity allowed; no games, conversations, or snacks allowed.

Group talk. Television is a great subject for getting kids to talk to each other in a way that happens so seldom in classrooms oriented to individual expression and achievement. Care should be taken in setting up "Group Talk" so that children learn about sticking to the subject, listening to their peers, and gathering facts. Divide the class into groups of five or six. This could be an on-going group that meets every day to talk about TV. The teacher plays the role of facilitator and is allowed to call a point of order. If the facilitator thinks that Willy has not heard Eliza, he may ask Willy to repeat what was said. If someone strays from the subject, the facilitator calls a point of order. The facilitator may not, however, voice an opinion on the topic. Children may call a point of order if this occurs. That is the setup. Here are some suggestions for discussions: Have the class choose a program for everyone to watch and discuss it the following day. Have the teacher assign a program for class viewing and discussion. Bring a TV into the classroom, watch a program, and break into discussion groups immediately following it.

And now a word from our sponsors. The volume, the effect, and the reason for commercials on television comprise another example of something that everyone is familiar with but few have thought about. Have students

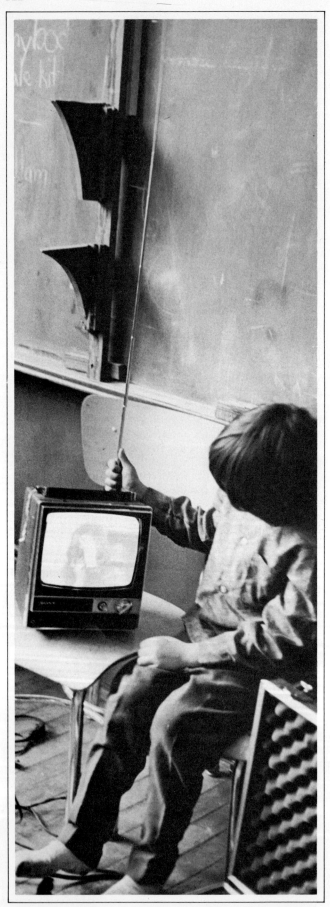

time commercials and figure out about how many they see during a week, a month, a year, etc. What commercials can the class remember? Are there favorite ones? Disliked ones? Do commercials actually help sell things? Do you buy products advertised on television? Do television commercials fairly represent the products they attempt to sell? How are long commercials (60-second) different from short (10–30-second) ones? Are various commercials aimed at different people? Does the time of day influence what is being advertised? Why aren't there any commercials on public TV stations? It is possible to rent 16mm films that compile "the best" commercials of every year as judged by ad agencies. Show these to your classes and conduct further analyses of the "art" of TV ads, how they sell, what they do to a society that sees them so often.

TESTING THE MODERN WORLD

Visiting a local station. A class trip to a local TV or CATV station can provide a good fulcrum to help students understand the role that television plays in their community and, by extension, within the fabric of American life. A number of independent or small group "research projects" might prepare the class if the findings of each group were shared prior to the visit. Possible research topics are:

a survey of programs that originate at the local station
a list of community resources that have been (or have not been) taped in the station's programming
a list of "issues" covered on the local station's news programs
a profile of the station's editorial stance
a study of studio production techniques
career opportunities in local television—including job training programs
cost of advertising per minute and the percentage of time devoted to commercials during different parts of the day
station ownership and its "public access file" (as required by FCC station licensing procedures)
FCC regulations governing local broadcasting
amount and significance of "network" programming on the local station(s)

Preparing such background studies will lead to a list of specific questions. During the trip itself, students might be asked to take notes, tape interviews, and shoot videotape of what they discover. Finally, there could be important follow-up activities: a taped and verbal report for other classes, a list of recommendations submitted to the television station, the local government, or other groups.

Creating a channel. For older students, here is a good hypothetical problem. (With the advent of CATV systems in many communities, the problem is not all that hypothetical.) The class will pretend that it has been given a channel of its own and is responsible for programming at least five hours of TV daily. The problem is two-fold. First, kids will have to decide what programming would be appropriate for their community. Here the teacher should stress the obligation of this new channel (what is its name?) to serve the needs of local residents. The class can imagine that it can either select "canned" programs from networks or create its own "live" programming. There are no limits to what is possible. The second problem in creating a channel has to do with building an imaginary organization. What jobs will there be, and who in the class will fill them? What is the station's policy for "equal representation" among various parts of the community? Will there be an editorial policy?

The business of broadcasting: a simulation. The future of broadcasting will depend upon the citizenry's understanding that the medium belongs, in fact if not in practice, to the people. A simulation activity can help sensitize students to the complexities that are a part of what TV is like today and what is necessary to change it. The class is divided into six groups for a debate arising out of this event:

THE SITUATION: A network-owned station in a particular city is seeking to have its broadcast license renewed by the Federal Communications Commission (FCC). Their petition will be contested before the FCC commissioners.

THE GROUPS: 1) An independent group with substantial financial backing will seek to persuade the FCC that it can and will do better programming for the community and, hence, should be granted the license. 2) The current representatives of the network-affiliated station will argue, naturally, that what they have done merits approval of their application to renew the license. 3) Also involved in the situation are representatives of the local government. Their job is to protect the interest of the city and also to avoid any criticism of local officials. 4) Participating in the issue is a well-organized coalition of the community's poor. Their position is that neither those presently operating the station nor those seeking the license are adequately addressing the needs of the community. 5) At the same time, the local cable operators are trying to get the city to grant them a franchise. They seek to align themselves with whatever group will most help their goal. 6) The final group in this simulation are the FCC commissioners themselves. They must hear the arguments and make the decision.

PROCEDURE: The first five groups will prepare twenty-minute presentations before the mock-FCC panel. After due consideration of the arguments, the FCC members must present and justify their decision. A reading of FCC Commissioner Nicholas Johnson's "How To Talk Back to Your Television Set," or other pertinent materials, can provide each group with information about its goals and with suggestions for other groups it may need to contact for support. The issues involved in the two groups seeking the same FCC license provide one dramatic situation. The role of the community will be critical in swinging the opinion of the FCC. All groups will have a vested interest or social concern in the status and future of all other groups and the class should be asked to study just what these interests are. This will be particularly true for the cable operators and the representatives of city government.

FOLLOW-UP: After research has been done and each group has defined its interests, after the presentation of arguments has been made and decisions reached by those who would, in fact, have the power to make them (the FCC and the local government), each member of the class should try to divest himself of his role and, working as a group, lay out entirely new legislative and philosophical foundations for directing the future character and growth of television.

Part 5
Sound

Sound Study

by Louis Giansante

God gave man two ears, but only one mouth, that he might hear twice as much as he speaks
Epictetus the Stoic

In this chapter Louis Giansante explores our acoustic environment. Recogning the electronic bias of today's young people, he capitalizes on the ubiquitousness of sound machines and offers a pack of activities to develop sound awareness and aural communication. Starting with simple activities involving sounds found around us, he leads into variations and extensions of sounds, and introduces transmission and effects through mechanical means, ways to extend the ear, sound communication systems, and media mixes.

This chapter and the next, "Doing Audiotape," are meant to be used together. Both chapters owe a great deal to the work and ideas of Tony Schwartz. Others whose ideas have contributed are: Susan Rice, Dolores and David Linton, Lenny Lipton, Robert Samples, David Booth, Robert Barton, Douglas Young, Gary Cuminale, Tom Proietti, and Dennis O'Brien.

LET US BUILD A CASE FOR THE EAR

Media studies, on all grade levels, have a very strong bias toward the visual—film, photography, video—while the aural is often given a back seat, if not ignored entirely. The monopoly of the eye is certainly understandable, given the centuries that sight has dominated our perceptions of reality. (When the most sophisticated technologists on earth, space experts, continue to employ such terms as "How do you *read* me?" that domination again becomes apparent.) But all the media and all the senses should be explored, studied, and played with. The study of our acoustic sound environment could potentially be the most important.

If McLuhan is right, our senses are being reprogrammed by the electronic environment in which we live. The total supremacy of the eye is giving way to the ear—to an oral/aural world similar to the tribal or "acoustic" environment of preliterate peoples. Simply by being surrounded by this environment from birth, our children are most likely to have an acoustic bias.

There are not many sources to consult for those interested in exploring their acoustic environment or in helping kids to do so. Thanks to our visual bias, "visual" thinkers, theoreticians and producers abound. But for anyone working thoughtfully in sound, the best source of support and inspiration is Tony Schwartz. His *The Responsive Chord* (New York: Anchor Press/Doubleday, 1973) is essential reading. Run—do not walk—to get a copy. Schwartz's thoughts often bring to mind activities

and projects that teachers can use and expand upon themselves. *The Responsive Chord* incorporates the study of sound into a theoretical model of communication for our electronically configured world. The book is very readable and just filled with ideas and examples. A chapter to note especially is "Education in the Global Village," which is devoted to education.

Sound study can mean many things: radio, live music, recordings (especially the "rock" phenomenon), film sound tracks, sound in advertising, electronic or "new" music, "environmental" record albums—just to name some obvious ones.

Except for some very basic physiological data, we know little about how our brain processes information—how it gets in, how it is stored, how we recall it to get it out again. We do know that sound is very much connected to the emotional and intuitive parts of man. Sounds often bypass the rational, conscious processes of our brains and engage us directly, immediately, and strongly. The right sounds in the right contexts can trigger feelings, emotions, and past experiences in a way that no visual cue can.

SOUND ACTIVITIES

In trying to decide how best to teach something, it is always a good idea to begin with your students. Where are they in relation to the area you would like to explore?

Begin by surveying the class. How many students own their own cassette tape recorders? In the late 50s and into the 60s many children had transistor radios near their ears, in their pockets, or under their pillows. But technology marches on. You'll be surprised to discover the number of students who own cassettes today. Ask how many have homes with stereo record or tape systems. Remember, you are dealing with an audience that has a great deal of listening experience—possibly more than your own.

Continue your home survey by having students note how many radios there are in the house. Are they AM or FM? Clock radios? Which rooms are they in? Ask the students which station(s) they listen to and why. Do their parents listen to the same stations? Why or why not? Explore the radio band to see how many different kinds of stations you can find—AM "Top 40," FM "Easy Listening," all news stations, all weather, etc.

A digression on quality: "There is an absolute contradiction between the sound perception and media orientation children are developing at home and the perception fostered by the school environment." This strong statement by Tony Schwartz refers not only to the terrible acoustic properties of most classrooms, but also to the discrepancy between sound heard at home over high quality stereo systems and sound heard over school AV equipment. Students immediately sense the great difference because their bias is not toward the *content*, as yours is. And often they resent the discrepancy, sometimes openly and vocally and often times unconsciously by simply tuning out.

Certainly money is always tight. But if you are ever in the position of influencing the purchase of sound equipment, remember: there is a direct relationship between the student's development of *perception* and the *sound quality* of equipment used!

Just Listening Vs. Really Hearing

Exploring and developing sound perception should include a lot of listening. We are constantly surrounded by sounds, but it is impossible and useless to listen to all of them. Sometimes it helps to focus our listening so that we really *hear* sounds around us. Here are a few activities aimed at sensitizing children to the sounds they make and to the sounds in the environment.

Conversations with sounds but no words. This exercise helps children to use their voices as they use their bodies. It might help things along to suggest dramatic roles for these wordless conversations—mother and baby, teacher and student, boyfriend and girlfriend, coach and player. Tape these "conversations," noting how well various emotions were expressed (anger, love, fear, excitement). At the very least, this activity will suggest that a lot can be "said" without words.

A variation on conversation. Play out scenes in which the dialogue consists of the repetition of just one word or phrase. See if it's possible to convey intention with tone of voice.

Footsteps. Listen to the sounds of footsteps passing in the hall or outside the window. Whose are they? Where is the person going? What is he or she thinking? Stretch your hearing by listening to moving sounds until they disappear.

What others hear. Listen to sounds as you think others might hear them. A dog's bark means one thing to its owner and another thing to you, and certainly something else to another dog!

Sound effects. Read a story "straight." Assign children to portray various sound effects appropriate to the story (eg., cows mooing, cars honking, water splashing, feet walking, etc.). Read the story again with the children's sound effects. Tape record the exercise and play it back for the participants.

Telephone. This mechanical device probably plays a big part in your students' lives. Start them exploring the role it plays and how they use it. If possible present them with a phone, but refer to it only as a new invention, nameless as yet, which can send and receive sound through wires. It will soon be available on the market. How many possible uses can they think of for this wonderful new invention? Make a list as a class or have groups compete. Be prepared to accept funny as well as futuristic answers. Discuss how telephones are used in our culture today.

Turn Up the Music—It's Too Noisy in Here

An increased awareness of sound in the environment may lead to some discussion of what is "noise" and the present concern for "noise pollution." Except for sounds that are so loud that they physically damage hearing, you should find that the differences between "sound" and "noise" are relative. The specific context and your relation to the sound are most important. As Tony Schwartz observed, "A sound is not noise because it is loud. It is noise because it disturbs us or interferes with our activity. Noise is *unwanted sound.*"

Sound vs. noise. Have students try to define "sound" and "noise" and list or tape examples of each. Noise could turn out to be "my kid brother or sister" while blaring rock music might be "good sound."

The Tape Recorder as an Extension of the Ear

Probably the best way to sharpen your students' sound perceptions is to involve them in the process of tape recording. Again to quote Tony Schwartz, "When a student is given the task of using sound to communicate, he must learn all the elements that affect his own listening. In coming to grips with this problem, he will become a more perceptive and attentive listener." Here are some simple recording activities that can be done with cassette recorders and that do not have to involve editing.

Sound close-ups. Tape the sounds of things you do not necessarily consider aural experiences (eg., a person swallowing or a cat eating). This exercise is analogous to photographing an extreme close-up of something.

School sounds. Have some students record sounds from around school. Play back the tape in class the next day for the other students and ask them if they can identify the sounds. Besides obvious sounds that everyone will recognize, encourage students to listen for more subtle sounds that don't usually catch their attention. Examples: Do all closing doors sound the same? Can you tell where you are in the school from the sound of a door closing?

Mysterious environment. Divide the class into groups, each of which is to go to an undefined location to record the sounds of that environment. Then have each group plays its tape for the rest of the class, who in turn try to identify the location and elements of the taped sounds.

Sound map. Direct some students to take a tour with a cassette recorder and record sounds heard along the way. Have the other students then listen to the tape and ask them if they can literally retrace the route.

Sound story. With some preplanning to eliminate editing, it is possible to tell a story using sound only. The sounds must be arranged in sequence so that the progression of the story is clear. "Story" can be loosely translated to include anything from fictional dramatic situations to accounts of real-life events, such as "How I Spend My Lunch Period" and "A Trip to the Supermarket." The important thing is not to use narration to explain what is being heard.

Re-creating an environment. This exercise is for older students and multiple recorders. Have a group select an environment such as a shopping mall, cafeteria, or street. They are to observe the physical surroundings and the people and record the different sounds of the environment on the various recorders. Back in class, they should, as a group, re-create the scene using the recorded sound. This will involve positioning the recorders around the room to make the rest of the class feel as if they are actually in the recorded environment. Have everyone listen with eyes closed.

Sound Editing

The ability to edit—to eliminate, to rearrange, to juxtapose—is an important skill for refining audiotape projects and can be easily mastered by many children. Here are a few activities that are not only fun but also easily teach what editing is all about.

New questions. Interview someone using a prepared list of questions. Then edit out your original questions and record new questions to insert in their places. One corny example: to the question, "What is usually in your family's garbage cans?" a student may answer, "Oh, rotten fruits and vegetables, tin cans, old newspapers, chewed bubble gum, and some broken glass." Replace the original question with something like, "What did you have for supper last night?"

New answers. This activity requires more editing skill. Interview someone using a prepared list of random questions, some funny, some serious: "What's your favorite color?" "What do you think of the President?" "How high is up?" "What is your nickname?" "What do you like about summer?" Then edit out the questions and attempt to rearrange words and phrases from the answers to create new thoughts. (Attempts at humor are usually successful here.)

Same sounds—new thoughts. Give each person (or group) the same tape of sounds—for example, sixty seconds of music, ten sound effects, and some dialogue recorded from radio or TV. The assignment is to edit and rearrange the sounds to some purpose and with a specific length, for example, sixty seconds. It's fascinating to hear how many different tapes were created from the same sounds.

Hear/Say Vs. Read/Write

One important distinction that can be explored with older children is the difference between spoken and written language. As Tony Schwartz states, "Words sound different from the way they look, and therefore must be considered in different terms." The following experiments will help your students study the difference between oral and printed communication.

Personal impressions. Tape one person talking about some subject. Play back the tape for another person or for the class. The listener must guess the speaker's age, sex, occupation, etc.

Sound of speech. Casually tape someone talking normally. Then write the words down and, on another occasion, have that person *read* his or her own words *aloud.* It is often difficult for people to read aloud the text of spoken language, even their own. The way we speak and the way we write are so different.

Different media—different impressions. Find an important but somewhat open-ended statement (maybe part of a political speech). Working with two groups, have one group *read* a printed version of the text and then react to it and its writer. Have the other group *hear* a recording of the statement and react to it and its speaker. Compare reactions. The point is that we can receive different impressions from words that we hear and words that we read.

Tape trade. This is an excellent project that has as one of its benefits a greater understanding of the differences between written and spoken messages. Set yourself and your class the problem of trying to communicate regularly *by tape only* with a comparable class in another part of the country—or even in another English-speaking country. Tapes that the entire class helps to prepared can lead to a much clearer understanding of the characteristics of aural communication and of the advantages and disadvantages of the tape medium.

People-to-People Sound

There is often a strong, direct relationship between sound and emotions. The sound of other human beings talking and revealing their feelings can be a powerful experience. As Tony Schwartz observes, "The real value of radio (and tape recording) is in the people-to-people aspects of it. One human being can sense another human being." Interviewing people is important if your students are to explore this aspect of sound.

Interview. Given a defined topic, interview a number of people. As a beginning activity this is good for learning (by doing) basic technical skills about recording, using a microphone, etc., as well as how to ask questions, how people respond to being interviewed and recorded, and how you personally respond to the people you question.

Sound portraits. Interview someone with the purpose of editing his or her words into a sound portrait of that person. The interview can easily involve a half-hour or more of tape, but the edited tape should be limited to five minutes or less. By carefully selecting and arranging, it is possible to give a strong sense of the person being interviewed in only a few minutes. Often students are fascinated by doing portraits of older adults, possibly grandparents. A tape recorder can sometimes add a new dimension to a personal relationship. Note: many students will need help learning how to ask questions that call for more than "yes or no" answers. The preceding activity, "Interview," should be explored fully before attempting "Sound Portraits."

Audiobiography. If students can have access to recorders away from school, have each one record an autobiography in sound. This can include many different approaches, from interviewing parents and friends who know you to recording the sounds of music or things or places that are important to you. This activity can lead students to recognize the importance of using a tape recorder to express something about themselves and about other people.

"Quick, Hand Me That Babbling Brook"

Recently there has been a renewed interest in the live radio dramas recorded in the 30's and 40's. A number of these old radio shows, both dramas and comedies, have been reissued as phonodiscs.

B.T.V. (Before television). Play some of these shows for your students. Discuss what *they think* it was like to listen to them on the radio thirty years ago. Then ask them to interview their parents or grandparents who may remember the original broadcasts. What was it like listening to those shows? Did they listen alone or with the whole family? Did they have a favorite show? Did people listen to radio shows then the way we watch television today?

Radio/TV dialogue. Listen closely to the dialogue in those old-time radio dramas. Tape a scene of dialogue from a current television drama. Compare dialogue in the two media. How explicit is each? How much information about the time of day and location of the scene does each provide? Is music used in the same places and for the same reasons (e.g., to create suspense or excitement)?

Create your own radio show. Listen closely to old radio shows noting the various sound effects. Today you can buy

People-to-people sound

sound effects records, but back then all the sounds were created "live" in the studio. Recreate one of those shows or, better still, write your own script as a class. This is a thoroughly involving activity. Along with writing dialogue and selecting music, students will need to experiment in creating realistic sound effects. (For examples: crinkled cellophane can create bacon frying or a variety of fire effects; a babbling brook can be simulated by gently blowing through a straw into a glass of water.) This activity will work best if you can use at least two microphones, as with a stereo tape recorder or a small microphone mixer. One mike can record the narrator and actors, and the other can record the music and effects.

MEDIA MIX—SIGHT AND SOUND

Sound is very often found in some relation to visuals—films, still photography slideshows, television, etc. So take it where you find it! Try exploring the relationships that can exist in aural/visual communications.

Stills

Bring a picture to life. Start by selecting one visually interesting picture and have students prepare a sound track that will bring it to life. The sound track might include narration, dramatized dialogue, music, real or created sound effects. It may be helpful to limit the length of the sound track, say, to thirty seconds.

Stills and sound. A variation of the above activity would be to select several pictures on the same topic, such as pictures of wrecked cars from traffic accidents. Students should then create a sound track to accompany the pictures as if they were to complete a television Public Service Announcement on safe driving. A subject such as this one is good because there are many possible approaches to the sound track. For example, one student may "hear" terrible crashes and screams while another may "hear" only the descriptions of eyewitnesses or of a mother whose child had been killed in the accident.

Working with sound and a few still pictures is the start of learning how to produce sound/slide show, or as it is equally awkwardly described, the slide/tape show. Any efforts at producing more elaborate combinations of sound

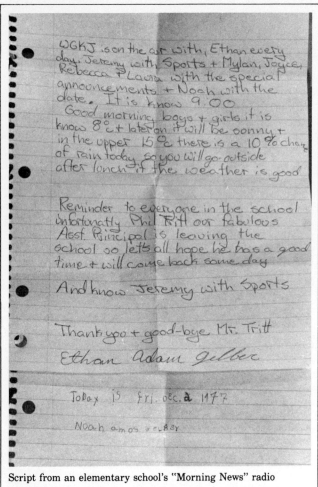

Script from an elementary school's "Morning News" radio
program

are commercial sound experts who have been given a
product and visuals. They are to complete the commercial
by creating a sound track. Students can attempt to be
imitative of real commercials, though the best sound
tracks are usually in ironic contrast to the visuals.

Film

Sound films made from still pictures. A real media-mix!
Explore the way sound has been combined with still pictures in such diverse films as Charles Braverman's *American Time Capsule* and Bernice Abbot's *Eugene Atget.*
Though each film is composed entirely of still pictures
they differ greatly in subject matter, pace, and type of
sound chosen. How appropriate is each sound track for its
visuals? Can you imagine switching sound tracks, or can
you suggest a better sound track for either?

Do movies need sound?. Instead of playing the movie
with its sound, play the sound track alone. (A short, "nonverbal" film is best, like *Pigs, Leaf, Dream of the Wild
Horses, Orange and Blue.*) You may find it convenient to
tape record it beforehand. Talk about what kind of film it
might be, based on the sound. Then project the film with
its sound. This is a good way to demonstrate the difference
between a narrated and non-narrated film, and to investi-
gate the uses of sound in film. Is the image most important? Does the sound have to "say" what the picture is
"saying"? Can it say something different? Do movies need
sound?

Music and mood. This is a common film study exercise.
Again find a short, "nonverbal" film and this time create
a new sound track (maybe simply find new music) to
change the *mood* of the film. Or simply experiment freely
with different pieces of music to see what different soundtracks would "feel" like, what they do to the total experience of the film.

Silent film score. Try adding a sound track to an existing silent film. Chaplin shorts are excellent for this exercise. Try adding a rock score to a silent Chaplin film. Then
try a piece of classical music. Play the film as a silent.
What works best?

Audience sound. Record responses of an audience to a
movie while it is being shown. It is generally best that the
audience does not know about this. Play back the tape as
you show the movie again, with the sound track lowered.
It is a totally new experience. Use a comedy, and the
principle of the laugh track will be demonstrated. Use the
audience recording made during one movie for a totally
different movie.

"Frank Film." We have all heard film sound tracks
with more than one sound occurring simultaneously—
mixtures of music, dialogue or narration, sound effects,
etc. But a totally new concept in film sound can be experienced by viewing *Frank Film,* the 1974 Academy Award
winning short film by Frank Mouris with sound by Tony
Schwartz. The visuals are so compelling that children of
all ages (and adults too, for that matter) will watch with
eyes riveted to the screen. However, the sound track may
be uncomfortable and disconcerting to many (you are, in
fact, hearing two soundtracks played simultaneously). It
is well worth showing if you and your class are interested
in exploring and extending your limits of aural perception.

and stills must start with an understanding of what is
possible and what is effective when joining the two media.
These activities provide a start.

Self-portraits. Have each child collect photographs of
himself or herself from infancy to the present. Tape these
consecutively on roll paper, so they can appear smoothly
on the opaque projector. Ask each child to compose a
sound track to accompany these images, using sound
effects, music, and/or narrative.

Sound collages. The technique described above will
work with other subjects too. Pick a topic—either something concrete like "Dogs and Cats" or "People in Uni-
form," or an abstract idea like "Friendship" or "Fear."
Find the pictures to tape on the roll of paper in magazines
or else have students draw their own. Then make a collection of sounds to be played with the collection of pictures.

Television

Audio without video. Have students try listening to the
audio on television without the video. How well can they
identify the action? What can music add to commercials,
action dramas, soap operas?

Commercial sound. Record a television commercial
onto videotape (for a product that can be brought into
class, if possible). Have the class or a group pretend they

Doing Audiotape

by Louis Giansante

Here, for the fledgling audiophile, Louis Giansante presents a mini-course in basic sound equipment and technical skills, from portable cassettes and reel-to-reel recorders to editing and transferring tapes.

Chapter Sixteen

Children often come up with fascinating tape projects because they feel so technically "competent" in the medium. Compared to filmmaking and video making, creating audiotapes is surprisingly easy. The operation of basic recording equipment and the use of simple editing gear can be learned quickly. Refining the basic skills of recording and editing (as well as listening and observing) takes time and practice, but the almost instant feedback can be an exciting, motivating experience for many children.

The following notes will deal with basic pieces of equipment, technical skills, and operating methods that can be used to complete the activities suggested in "Sound Study."

We are not comparing brand names or quoting prices of equipment. Models and prices vary greatly and are constantly updated and modified. Such information should be gathered from local representatives who keep up with the latest equipment on the market. Another way to follow the market is to make use of the Reader Service Info Cards often found in magazines like *Media & Methods* and *Audio Visual Instruction.* For more specific information on desirable characteristics in classroom tape recorders, record players, recording tape, and stereo compenents, as well as valuable tips on "liberating" your equipment for best use, I refer to Dolores and David Linton's *Practical Guide to Classroom Media,* chapters 7 and 8. The best guide for using any piece of equipment is the manual or booklet accompanying it at purchase. Read it carefully, follow the instructions, and remember to save the manual for reference in the future.

Cassettes

Most portable cassette recorders manufactured in the past few years have a number of common features.

Power. Portable recorders run on batteries, though most come supplied with an AC power cord. Use it when near an outlet to save batteries.

Built-in condenser microphone. These small mikes are actually built right into the body of the recorder. They are omni-directional (receive sound equally well from all points within a 360-degree plane) and are surprisingly sensitive. They work best when recording group discussions or activities or when the sound of the entire environment is desired. Because they record *every* sound in the immediate area, they are not good for interviewing or for selective recording of particular sounds.

External microphone. In addition to a condenser mike, most cassettes have an external microphone with a manu-

Kindergarteners learning to use sound controls

An older student creating a sound collage

Cassette tape. Cassette tape can be used again and again if you are not interested in saving the original program. You can buy cassettes in various lengths of recording time with the 60-minute cassette most often used (30 minutes on a side). Though you can purchase cassettes up to 120 minutes in length, experience has shown that these long tapes sometimes jam and snarl. If a cassette tape breaks, it is possible to splice the two ends together. Cassette splicing kits are available for this purpose. Do not attempt to use the kits for more than repairing breaks, however. It is virtually impossible and not worth the trouble to edit cassette tape.

Reel-to-Reel Recorders

For most in-class activities or when portability is not a requirement, you can use a reel-to-reel recorder. These recorders need ¼" reel tape. There are two kinds of reel-to-reel recorders—mono and stereo. "Mono" means that as the tape passes through the recorder once, information is being recorded on *one track* of the tape. "Stereo" means that two separate sources of information can be recorded on *two tracks* of the tape as the tape passes through the recorder.

Recording tracks. Don't let this talk of "tracks" or "channels" throw you. All it means is that the surface of ¼" recording tape can be subdivided so that more than one channel of information may be carried on the tape. This subdivision is determined by the type of recorder you have and the kind of "heads" it has. *Professional machines* designed for monaural recording usually have a head the full width of the tape (¼" wide). *Dual track* or *half track* machines have heads which can record a signal on half the width of the tape. When you come to the end of the tape, you flip the reel over, put it on the feed spindle of the recorder and record on the other half of the tape. *Four track* or *quarter track* machines use heads that "quarter" the input or output. The only point of confusion here may be that four track machines can be either mono or stereo. In either case, when you have finished recording two tracks on the tape in one direction, you can flip the reel over and record on the other two tracks. More specific instructions should be found in the instruction manual accompanying your recorder.

The reason for this whole explanation is to point out that the amount of actual recording time on a reel of tape can differ depending on the kind of machine you have. If you are forced to record a lot of information on a limited tape supply, a quarter track mono recorder will give you twice as much recording time as a half track recorder, given that the "speeds" are identical.

Standard speeds. Most recorders (mono or stereo) have three standard running speeds—7½, 3¾, or 1⅞ ips (inches per second). These speeds refer to how fast the tape is passing across the recording head. The higher the speed, the better the quality of the recording. For most recording, either of the higher speeds is fine. The 1⅞ speed (the speed of cassette recorders) is used mostly for recording speech. Music does not record satisfactorily at this low speed on a reel-to-reel recorder.

Automatic or manual record level. Many recorders offer you a choice of recording or "gain" controls. You can either let the machine set the correct recording level automatically or you can do it manually. Automatic would work best with your younger children, but making a qual-

ally operated on/off switch, allowing the operator to move away from the recorder and still maintain control of the tape. External mikes are usually *cardioid,* that is, they pick up sound best in a somewhat heart-shaped pattern, extending out from the face of the mike. They should be used whenever interviewing because they de-emphasize background noise, which is a special problem in most "on location" situations.

AGC or ARL (Automatic Gain Control or Automatic Record Level). This feature means that you do not have to adjust the volume of the recording you are making to be sure it is correct. The recorder automatically maintains the incoming sound at the proper level.

Jacks. These are sockets, both "inputs" and "outputs," for various plugs and patch cords that can be used with the recorder. Jacks are found on most pieces of audio equipment. On most cassette recorders one jack will simply be marked MIC. for plugging in the external microphone. Other common jacks on cassettes are the auxiliary Input and the External Speaker jacks. The Auxiliary Input jack (AUX. IN or LINE IN) is used for recording *from* an external source, such as a radio, phonograph, receiver, another recorder, etc. Sound will be traveling *into* the recorder. The External Speaker jack (EXT. SP.) is used to connect a larger speaker to the recorder or for connecting an earphone or headphones for private listening. Sound will be traveling *out of* the recorder.

ity recording manually is not difficult. All you really must know is how a VU meter works.

VU Meter. This gadget is a gauge that monitors the volume of recorded sound. By using the volume control knob, the idea is to keep the pointer or needle in the window from peaking into the danger or red zone. Experiment with yours to see how difficult it is to keep the needle where you want it. To illustrate this point try recording something with the needle "buried" in the red zone. Your students will quickly learn what "distortion" means. Some recorders use one or two neon glow lamps to help you set the level. You can get good results with this level setting system, but the VU meter is both more accurate and more fun to use.

Jacks. The number and exact designation of jacks can vary, depending on your machine. It is certain, however, that some will be inputs for recording sound onto the recorder and others will be outputs, either for transferring sound to another recorder or through headphones or to an additional speaker. Some common designations for inputs are MIC. (microphone), AUX. IN. (auxiliary input), LINE IN (can be used the same as AUX. IN.). Some common output designations are LINE OUT (for connection to another recorder), EXT. SP. (external speaker), MON. (to connect headphones for monitoring sound privately). Again, check your manual for more specifics.

Patch Cords. When any two pieces of audio equipment are connected for the purpose of transferring sound, the connection is called a "patch" and the cable used a "patch cord." One example: to record a piece of music from a record, one end of a patch cord would be connected to an *output* on a phonograph and the other end to an *input* on the tape recorder. Patch cords come in different lengths and with any combination of plugs on the ends so that virtually any two pieces of equipment can be connected. The three most common types of audio plugs are: 1) phone plug, 2) RCA phono plug, and 3) mini plug. If necessary, you can buy plug *adaptors* to change one plug to another.

Heads. The heads, the most important part of the recorder, are where the sound is recorded onto and played back from the tape. Most less expensive recorders use two heads—an *erase* head for "cleaning" the tape before it passes to the *record/playback* head. In many recorders this latter head performs the two functions of recording and of playing back. More expensive recorders separate these functions and thus have three separate heads. Find

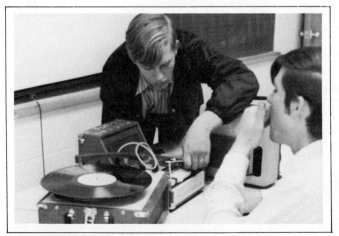

Young student editing videotape. The monitor at her right enables her to screen playback as she edits.

the heads on your machine and know the function of each, for such information is necessary when learning how to manually splice tape. You should know where the heads are also in order to clean them regularly (after around every ten hours of use). Keeping the heads clean is very important, and students can easily learn how and should assume that responsibility. Some Q-tips and denatured alcohol will do the trick.

Erasing. From the preceding description it should be obvious that one way to *erase* a tape so that it can be reused is to simply place the recorder in the *record* position, with the volume control set at zero. The tape will be erased as it passes the erase head. Of course, this is a tedious process and *bulk erasers* are available which can "clean" a whole roll in only seconds.

Editing

Many of the activities and assignments suggested earlier can be completed without any editing. However some require it, and even fairly young students can master the few mechanical fundamentals. Editing can involve anything from simply removing extraneous noises or awkward pauses on the tape to creatively rearranging and juxtaposing various sections of tape to some purpose. Audiotape can be edited either electronically or physically.

Electronic editing. The tape is never physically cut. You need two recorders patched together to edit electronically since, in effect, you are re-recording sections of sound you want to keep onto a new tape. To achieve clean, tight edits this way you must have a recorder with an "instant pause" or "cue" control that permits you to start and stop recording precisely without an annoying wind-up sound or an audible click from the on/off switch. During this editing process you do use more tape, but once your edited tape is completed, the tape with your "raw" sound can be erased and reused.

Physical editing. The tape is actually cut into pieces and physically handled and rearranged. Sections of tape are joined, end to end, by covering the base (shiny) side of both sections with a special splicing tape (for most recording tapes, the oxide coating which comes in contact with the head is dull). Do not use ordinary cellophane tape because the adhesive will tend to "bleed" or spread from under the edges of the tape. This can cause damage to your recorder heads if they get gummed up with adhesive as splices pass by.

Physical editing can be done with one real recorder and some type of splicing device. These devices are basically of two types. *Splicing blocks* (either plastic or metal) simply hold the tape in place while it is cut (according to guide marks on the block) with a razor blade or x-acto knife. The block provides for alignment of the adhesive tape as well. For younger children, or if the use of razor blades makes you nervous, there are splicing devices that look similar to film splicers. They have a cutting blade built-in for cutting the tape and trimming the splice, and they keep the splicing tape stored conveniently on a roll. These are usually more expensive than simple splicing blocks.

All methods of making tape splices involve cutting the tape *diagonally* rather than on a perpendicular plane. The diagonal splice passes by the head more easily and is perfectly inaudible. Remember this if your tape breaks and the only splicing device you have is a pair of scissors. Overlap the two ends of tape slightly and cut on the diagonal across both tapes before applying a piece of splicing tape.

It is very important (for editing purposes) to know which head is which on your recorder. All methods of physical splicing involve marking the tape while it is on the recorder at exactly the point at which you want to make your splice. To do this you must know which head of your recorder is your playback head. On most two-headed recorders, where the tape passes from left to right, the first head is the erase head, and the second is the record/playback head. But to be sure, consult your instruction manual. Instructions accompanying splicing devices will provide you with information on how to locate your playback head and how to mark the tape for splicing.

One final note on physical editing. Remember that though it is possible to record from one to four tracks on a piece of tape (depending on your recorder), once you cut the tape you have severed *all* the tracks. Since you can only hear one track at a time on a mono recorder, it makes sense to record only one track when doing assignments that will be physically edited.

A valuable booklet providing a more detailed approach to tape splicing and editing is *Tape Editing* by Joel Tall. Copies are available for one dollar to cover handling and shipping from ELPA Marketing Industries, Inc., either New Hyde Park, N.Y. 11040, or Scottsdale, Ariz. 85253.

Transferring Tapes

There is one particular combination of equipment and technique that you'll probably want to know about.

Many of you may be in the position of having only cassette recorders for "on location" recording away from school, though you also have reel-to-reel recorders available in the classroom. It is not advisable to attempt to edit cassette tape. Therefore, if you wish to edit sound recorded on cassette, it must first be *transferred* to ¼" tape. You are, in effect, making a ¼" tape copy of either all or parts of your cassette recording so that you can edit. To do this, you need a patch cord with the proper plugs on the ends to connect the output of your cassette recorder to the auxiliary input of your reel-to-reel recorder. Place the reel-to-reel recorder in *record* position and then place the cassette in *playback* position. If you have an automatic recording level device on your reel-to-reel recorder you don't even have to worry about that. If your original cassette recording is of very low volume, you can boost it up somewhat by controlling the recording level *manually*.

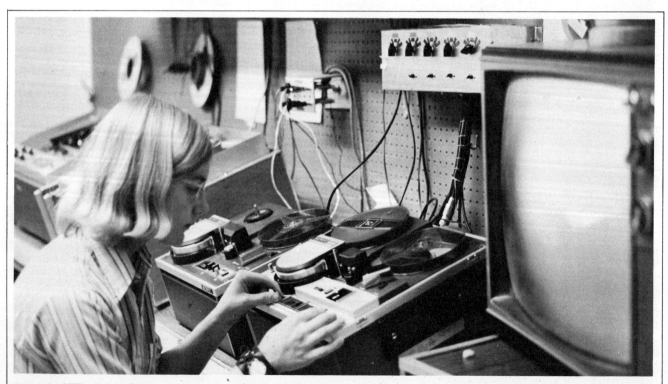

Using the VTR editing system

Chapter Seventeen

Emancipating Noise

by Don Kaplan

Don Kaplan holds that beauty is in the ear of the beholder. The cornicopia of emancipated noise exercises in this chapter will lead you and your students to think more about sounds, to relate sound and image to each other, and to explore their uses and their reuses. Join in the fun, but be sure to shut the door when Mrs. Grundy passes by.

The eminent music historian David Ewen, writing on music and musicians in his *Composers of Tomorrow's Music* (New York: Dodd, 1971), noted that the avant-composers hold that noises have a definite and important place in the musical arts. They believe that there is music in noise and that noise is as basic to contemporary musical writing as it is to contemporary life.

Actually, noise and word and vocal sounds have always had a place in music. As used here, "noise sounds" are sounds of indeterminate pitch or sounds produced by objects ordinarily used for nonmusical purposes; "word and vocal sounds" refer to words, syllables, letters, sentence fragments, and vocal sounds of indeterminate pitch used for their auditory quality rather than content (although words may be used in a dramatic manner that conveys their content). Primitive peoples used both the objects and sounds natural to their environment and the anatomy of their own bodies as percussive and vocal instruments. This precedent for using sounds musically has been further developed in modern times. The contemporary composer Olivier Messiaen, for example, has written many compositions based on the rhythms and melodies of bird songs. Others have incorporated sleighbells and wind machines, have imitated natural effects such as storms and the sea (especially in operas, in tone-poems, and in other program music), and have given percussive instruments (themselves "noise" sounds) a fundamental role in music.

Meaningless texts—that is, word and vocal sounds—appear in the songs of primitive tribes, in American Indian chants, in East Indian literature, in Buddhist canons, and in Berlioz's opera of *The Damnation of Faust*. Even the contemporary method of graphic notation (which represents aural qualities visually) has its ancestry in Medieval manuscripts (where letters assumed the shapes of objects and people), in the pictorial vocal writing of Monteverdi's lyrics in Renaissance madrigals, which often reflected their content through auditory effects, and in Bach's musical settings of words (notated in shapes corresponding to their content). In the late nineteenth century impressionistic music dispensed with words in favor of meaningless sounds. And in this century F. B. Pratella (in *The Technical Manifesto of Futurist Music*, March 11, 1911) called for the "songs of factories, warships, motorcars, and aeroplanes" (man-made accoustical effects). Another Futurist, F.T. Marinetti, in his poem "Zing-Tumb-Tumb" (1917), used syllables, vowels, and consonants depicting the sounds of weapons. The develop-

ment of jazz introduced "scatting" as a vocal style, and audiotape enabled composers to manipulate vocal and found sounds electronically (musique concrete).

Just as people have experimented with found sounds throughout history, your students can examine familiar sounds as new musical resources and thereby gain a heightened awareness of themselves and their environment. The following explorations, like those in "Sound Study," develop student capacity for abstract thinking and can be used to generate more complex exercises in creating sound textures, in conducting a group of players, and in composing for media, dance, and theater. The exercise in word composition can be integrated into language arts curricula to aid visual, oral, and auditory discrimination, word comprehension, creative writing, the study of poetry, and to facilitate reading and writing through aural/visual awareness.

Putting aside the ready application of these exercises to other subject matter as a secondary gain, the primary focus of this chapter is on creating sound compositions and translating sound into pictorial representations or images. These composing and notating activities develop the ability to relate sound to image and image to sound. As your students become more comfortable with the close relationship between sound and image, their media-making activities, such as composing a sound track for a film, doing an animated film to go with a particular musical piece or sound track, and adding sound to slide shows, will benefit.

Content

1. The entire group sits in a semicircle. Each person, in turn, says "hello" to the student next to him. No substitutions are permitted ("hi," "hiya," "how-ja-do"), and each person must say the word in a different manner.

There are many ways to say "hello" by changing quality and expression without altering the word itself. Ask the class to suggest other words (e.g., "now," "blueberry").

Variation. Say a word or phrase, giving it one quality verbally but a different attitude physically ("Glad to see you!"—but your body expresses disinterest). We often meet people who say one thing through their mouths but tell us otherwise with their bodies.

2. Choose a word with emotional content and repeat it, intensifying the expression with each repetition (see figure 1). Permit your body to help the vocal expression.

3. Choose a word that sounds like its meaning (onomatopoetic) and explore its content by intensifying the way you say it—make it sound more like its meaning.

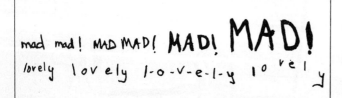

Fig. 1   Word notation of increasing emotional intensity

4. Reinvent words that do not sound like their meaning or words that could be made more effective; for example, write a new word for "raucous" or "bubble."

5. Invent words that sound:

hairy	cozy
slippery	machine-like
sticky	like insects

6. Notate words according to their meaning (See figure 2).

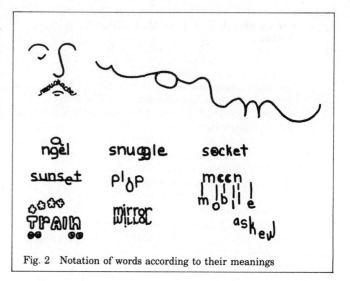

Fig. 2   Notation of words according to their meanings

RESOURCES

R. Murray Schafer, *When Words Sing* (New York: Associated Music publishers, Inc., 1970). Contains many exercises using words for musical purposes.

Transformation

1. Repeat a word and determine its rhythmic content. Compare the rhythms of several words. Then separate into small groups, each group with a single word and one person within each group acting as conductor. The conductor leads the "chorus" by indicating tempo, entrances, phrasing, and dynamics (volume, accents). Try incorporating words with different qualities or emotional content.

2. Write out words, short phrases, or lines from a poem and indicate accents and pulses. This exercise can easily (and painlessly!) evolve into traditional rhythmic notation by transforming pulses into whole, half, quarter, and eighth notes and rests. More complex rhythmic notations can then be build based upon this information.

3. Before class, prepare a tape consisting of one word (three or more syllables) repeated continuously for five or ten minutes. Play the tape in class and ask students what they heard. They will probably "hear" several different words or phrases. The effect is similar to the game of "Telephone" in which a message is "transformed" as it passes from one person to the next, with the final message ending up quite differently from the original one.

4. With the whole class, choose one word and repeat it rapidly until it transforms into a second word, then a

third, and so on. Try not to plan ahead or decide what the word might lead to. Try to evolve words as a group rather than by allowing individuals to force the group to follow them. If this occurs ask students to do the exercise on their own.

5. This exercise is done individually. Give students the following instructions: Repeat your first name aloud until it becomes a meaningless sound, disassociated from yourself. Use this sound and say it:

- in a middle register
- as high as you can; as low as you can
- as quickly as you can; as slowly as you can
- as loud as you can; then in a whisper
- as an explosion; as an implosion
- percussively (staccato); smoothly (legato)
- say it and swallow it
- in the funniest way you can; in the saddest
- sliding from a low to high register; from a high to low register
- repeating it rhythmically; without rhythm (no accents)
- getting louder (crescendo); getting softer (decrescendo)
- emphasizing the vowels; emphasizing the consonants
- without vowels; without consonants
- jumping back and forth among syllables, vowels, and consonants
- with your mouth wide open; through your teeth
- backwards

6. With the entire group, begin by exploring the sounds in your own name. Eventually become aware of the other sounds around you and try to "relate" your sounds to the others. The director may stop this improvisation, or the group may evolve an ending by itself. Discuss the ways you have discovered for relating sounds.

RESOURCES

Ernst Toch, *Geographical Fugue* (New York: Mills Music, 1950).

————. *Valse* (New York: Mills Music, 1962). Both works are for mixed chorus and are entirely spoken, with rhythmic indications.

Composition

1. Choose a single word and write a composition for three or four voices. Use the word itself for notation; indicate dynamics and relationships among parts through the graphics (see figure 3).

Working in small groups, rehearse the compositions and perform them for the rest of the class. *Note:* different performers should be able to perform the composition in a similar manner.

2. Combine words, phrases, and sentences into a composition in which the performers interpret, through graphic notation, what sounds to produce, in which order, and with what quality to produce them (see figure 4). Different performers may interpret the composition in different ways.

Found Sounds

Have each individual find several objects in the environment which would not ordinarily be considered musical instruments but can be made to produce sounds. Choose at least four of these objects (found sounds) and write a piece for them, using a minimum of eight measures. Give the composition a pulse of three or four, with each set of three or four pulses (beats) comprising a measure. Eight

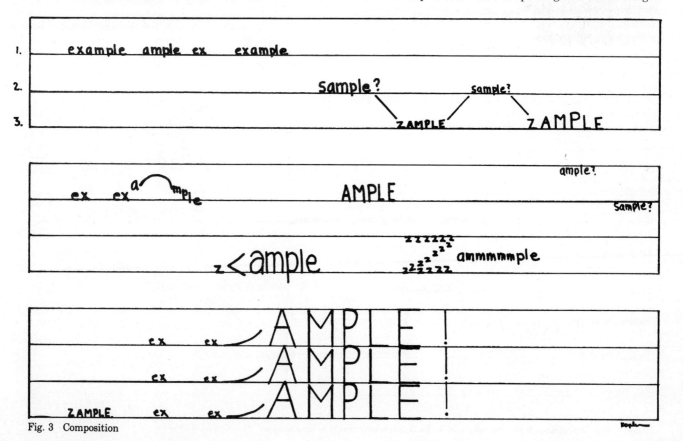

Fig. 3   Composition

measures is a convenient length to begin with, because the composition can be easily divided into two phrases—statement/response or theme/variation. Invent symbols for each instrument and notate the composition. Divide the class into groups of five or more, depending upon the number of sounds, with the composer acting as conductor and with one person on each part. If the group is small, the composer may play an instrument as well as conduct. After rehearsing from the score, the group then tapes its performance of the composition. When all the groups have been taped, the entire class listens to the playback.

This procedure is similar to that of composing for a string quartet, mixed chorus, or any other combination of instruments or voices—except that the instruments are unconventional. This is not an improvised composition but one that is developed by choosing specific combinations of sounds.

Discourage using a drawing of the object for notation; represent the *quality* of the sound, rather than what the instrument looks like (see figure 5).

The problems encountered in notating these compositions are the same ones that led to the evolution of standardized musical notation. Since there may be solos, overlappings, and combinations of sounds at different times, these must be clearly indicated. To aid you in writing clear and comprehensive notations, use the following questions as a guide: Are players able to follow their parts easily, particularly in relation to other parts? Are dynamics (intensities) indicated, and is it clear when to enter and when to stop? Is the score explicit enough so that the piece can be played again identically? Can the score be performed by another group without having the composer present? Try exchanging compositions and find out.

During playback, composers should try to identify their own compositions (this may not be easy!), discover what they like or dislike, and compare the quality of the live performance with that of the tape. Have each group identify the objects used by the other groups. Encourage your students to express any images that the music suggests.

FOUND SOUNDS DISCOGRAPHY

Henry Bryant, *Kingdom Come,* 1970 (Desto Records, DC–7108). Whistles, sirens, klaxons, buzzers, electric bells, ratchets, air-compressors.

John Cage, *Fontana Mix,* 1958 (Mainstream, 5005). Sounds amplified on tape—cigarette ashes falling into astrays, putting on and taking off glasses, swallowing, smoking cigarette, grunting, coughing, scraping microphones over glass. His unrecorded composition 4"33" is four minutes and thirty-three seconds of silence.

Jean Dubuffet, *Musical Experiences,* 1960 (Finnader, SR–9002). A wide variety of found and tape-manipulated sounds by the artist.

Mauricio Kagel, *"Acustica," for Experimental Sound Generator and Loudspeaker,* 1968–1970 (Deutsche Grammophon, DG–2707059). A wide variety, with photographs of the instruments.

Erik Satie, *Parade,* 1917 (Vanguard, C10037/38). Sirens, airplane motors, typewriters, roulette wheels.

Edgard Varese, *Ionisation,* 1931 (Columbia, MS–6146). Two sirens and percussion instruments of the composer's own invention.

There are other composers who have incorporated found sounds in their music, and recordings of those are readily available under several labels: George Gershwin, in his *An American in Paris* (taxi horns); Gustav Mahler, in his *Symphony No. 4* (sleigh bells); Maurice Ravel, in *L'Enfant et Les Sortileges* (cheese grater); Ralph Vaughan Williams, in *Sinfonia Antartica* (wind machine); and Richard Strauss, in *Don Quixote* (wind machine). For recordings that deal primarily with vocal sounds, listen to *Extended Voices* (Odyssey, 32160156), for various sounds; and Arnold Schoenberg's *Pierrot Linaire,* 1912 (many recordings available), for use of "sprechstimme" (speech-song).

RESOURCES

The graphic poetry of Marinetti and the Futurists.

David Ewen, *Composers of Tomorrow's Music* (New York: Dodd, 1971). A non-technical introduction to the avant-garde movement, centering on Ives, Schoenberg, Webern, Bouley, Varese, Stockhausen, Xenakis.

Notations (New York: Something Else Press, 1969). Graphic notations for browsing; included are found and word sounds.

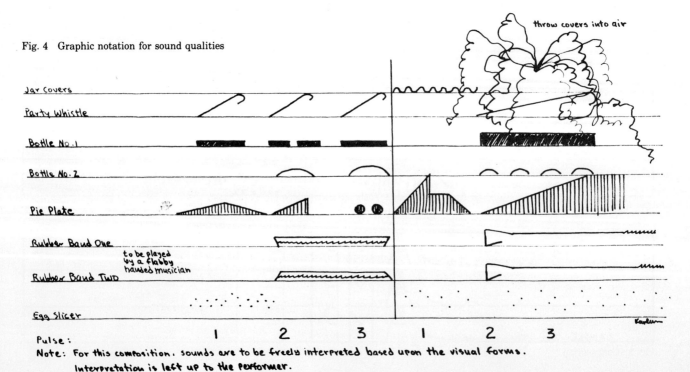

Fig. 4   Graphic notation for sound qualities

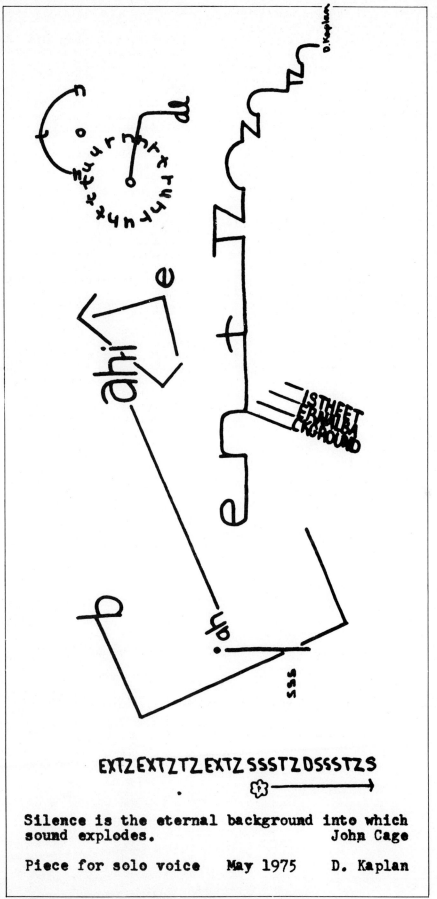

Fig. 5 Found sound score (from *Composition #One*, Don Kaplan, 1968)

Part 6
Other Media

Animating the Overhead

by Georgeanna Spencer

It's time to recycle that dinosaur of audiovisual machinery, the overhead projector. In the past it either took up valuable storage space when not in use, or put the kids to sleep when brought out of the closet. Here Georgeanna Spencer offers a variety of uses and activities for all ages, revealing there is a lot of life left in that old machine and making it a truly lively component of today's media classroom.

The overhead projector is a great piece of hardware for creative media activities. Most schools have several, and yet it is probably the most overlooked and underutilized piece of audiovisual equipment they own. It is simple to operate, offers an almost infinite number of uses, and can project an image on any surface under any light condition.

Instead of letting these projectors collect dust in the various classrooms throughout your school, collect a set of them in one room. Set up the projectors—two or three if possible—in the middle of the room, a good distance from the wall or screen you will be projecting on. Have a variety of items available for screening. Put aside an hour or so on a number of consecutive days and, with the students, explore the creative, as opposed to the didactic, potential of this familiar tool.

MATERIALS

Just about any material can be used. Here is a checklist for a start, but be sure to have both translucent and transparent materials as well as some interesting opaque forms that can make intriguing silhouettes:

loosely woven fabrics	tissue paper
straw table mats	paper towels
screens	Saran wrap
strainers	crystalline paints
mesh materials	sewing awl
laces	cellophane
feathers	glass containers of water
sand	Scotch tape
Magic Markers/inks	clear acetate sheets or rolls
scissors	clear x-ray film
clear marbles	colored theater gel
leaves and ferns	vegetable oil
pine needles	liquid shampoo
paper clips/fasteners	food coloring
cut paper	paste/glue

Opaque objects or materials become black silhouettes when placed on overhead. Colored cellophane, food coloring in water, food coloring in vegetable oil, Magic Markers and inks, and crystalline paints provide colorful accents to various creations.

Projecting a simple cutout silhouette puppet

ACTIVITIES

Framing

Make frames of various sizes by folding a piece of construction paper or cardboard in half and cutting a rectangle through the fold. With the two pieces of "L" shaped board, students can experiment with framing different portions of a projected picture. Placing the frame or frames on the lighted surface of the overhead projector also creates a stage for various other experiments. The opaque projector may also be used for learning framing: project images from magazines, books and other sources for the entire class.

Shadow Silhouettes and Pantomime

Beginning exercises in animating the overhead for very young children can be simple shadow puppetry, starting with projections of the children's own hands. If the children show interest, more complicated hand-shadow figures and pantomime activities can be practiced and invented. First have the children place their hands on the lighted surface of the overhead, and then let them place their entire bodies in the path of the light so their silhouettes are projected. Introduce pantomime to express various actions and emotions. Images of near and far, large and small, are also easily created—use the projections to develop an understanding of such abstractions.

Shadow Hand Puppets

Again, start with simple forms. On a piece of paper draw a profile of a head and the form of a hand, with a "collar" for each (figure 1). Cut out the head and the hand. Form the "collar" into a ring and fasten it with glue or tape (figure 2). Make a "cape" of cloth that will cover the operating hand. Sew or staple the top edge into two finger-sized openings. Attach the cape to the cut-out head and hand, or slip it over the operating fingers (figure 3). As a background or set for puppet action, make a colorful collage of cellophane, gels, or tissue.

Still Life

Create a still life picture. Arrange pebbles at the base of the projector's picture plane. Lay a clump of grasses at the edge of the picture with stems projecting down and out of view. Play a Haiku or simple nature poem on a cassette, or have the children read simple nature poetry. Move the weeds or grasses gently as though a soft breeze were stirring. If a softer image is desired, use translucent tissue or frosted acetate under the still life.

Collage. To make a collage, assemble a variety of materials on the projector surface and use different textures, densities, shapes, and colors. Recycle and mix media in free form, abstract designs, or still life: cut strips of acetate, old filmstrips, old negatives, tissue papers, etc. Wet paper towels or tissue paper become exciting textural shapes when peeled off layer by layer. The still life can be created freely, or children can follow simple line drawings that guide their compositions.

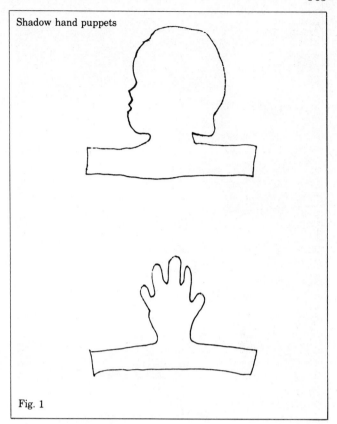

Shadow hand puppets

Fig. 1

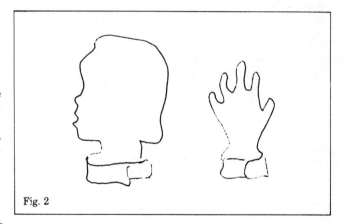

Fig. 2

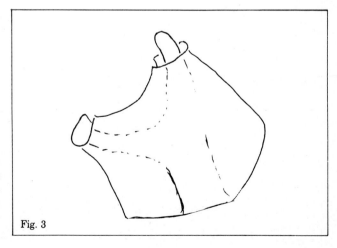

Fig. 3

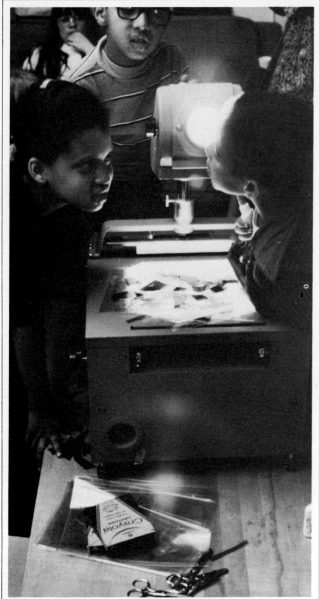

Recycling and mixing media with the overhead. Strips of acetate, old filmstrips, tissues make a projected collage.

Animations

Clear acetate strips and strips cut from clear x-ray film work well as tabs for activating puppets of all kinds. Because the tabs are clear, they hardly show during "performance." Puppets can be hinged with commercial paper fasteners that come in many sizes, including ones that are only about a quarter of an inch wide at the "button" part. If commercial fasterers are not available, fine wire can be bent into a figure-8, the ends dropped together through the puppet pieces and then opened to make the attachment. A sewing awl or compass point works well in making the hole through which either the wire or paper fasteners are fitted.

Human figures. Ancient shadow puppets were made using a torso silhouette.The lower jaw and the arms were operated with hinges. This simple puppet can talk and gesture with great effect. Because the legs are not shown, a number of figures can be moved forward and back to simulate movement.

Talking Face (Figure 4). On a clear acetate sheet draw a partial face with hair, brows, nose, and upper lip. On a separate acetate tab that slides back and forth, draw the eyeballs; and on another hinged acetate tab that moves up and down, draw the lower lip, chin, and jawlines. Manipulate the tabs to animate a talking face.

Chewing face (Figure 5). To make the same face chew, simply add cheeks. Draw each cheek on a separate hinged acetate tab and fasten the tabs so they move closer or further apart. As with the moving face, the mouth for the chewing face is fastened to move up and down.

Walking animal puppets. The simplest animal puppets are made of one-piece silhouettes that simulate movement through being jogged up and down, forward and back. For an animated walk, an animal silhouette can be hinged in the middle so that the front and back halves move. Adding a hinged head to the figure will naturally give greater versatility, and the multiple-hinged joints for the legs, neck, tail, etc., make more complex movement possible.

Cartoon vegetable garden. The motion in this cartoon will simulate seed packets growing as the gardener waters, as the illustration in figure 6 shows. A three-part visual is required to create the effect. First, the armless silhouette of the gardener and the silhouette of the ground are attached to a clear acetate. Then the arm and

Fig. 4   Talking face

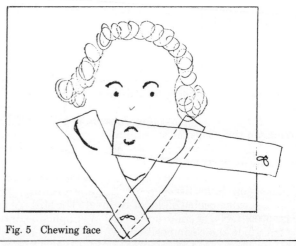

Fig. 5   Chewing face

the watering can are pivoted on the shoulder. The arm and can are actually made of opaque paper but are placed on a transparent acetate tab, and the tab also has water drops drawn on it with Magic Marker ink. As the arm moves, so does the water across the garden. And the seed packets are drawn directly on a separate acetate sheet with the tab at the bottom to allow them to "grow" into the garden.

Fig. 6   Cartoon vegetable garden

Oscillations

The Sun. Younger students can make these next two simple transparencies (figure 7). The first is a sun with one set of rays; the second is a sun with another set of rays, different in style and possibly using a second color. The two are placed on the overhead at the same time, and the top one is moved slightly to make the rays dance.

 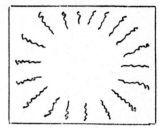

Fig. 7   The Sun

Abstract wheel. To make another oscillation, draw concentric circles on each of two separate transparencies. Move the top transparency slightly in various directions to create an illusion of circular motion. Screens or woven mats moved over each other on the surface plane of the overhead will also create startling optical effects.

Profile Puzzle Game

On an acetate sheet draw an opaque figure of hair. Attach a simple chain at the forehead and jawline (figure 8). To change the profile as the person speaks, shake or manipulate the chain with a pencil eraser. For some variations try the following: 1) Attach the chain to clear acetate and place different hair silhouettes down as the profile and character changes. 2) Have two heads facing each other, with but only one chain between. Alternate the profile for the head that is speaking. 3) Attach the chain at either edge of an acetate sheet and loop the chain to form and reform simple figures. The students can continuously change the shapes as a story is told by someone else in the room. If you use several projectors and profiles at the same time, all projecting at the same screen, you can represent several characters concurrently. 4) Have the children jiggle the acetate to change the shape randomly. Call for continuous use of the imagination in identifying each new shape. Make a brief, spontaneous story to go with a particularly pleasing shape.

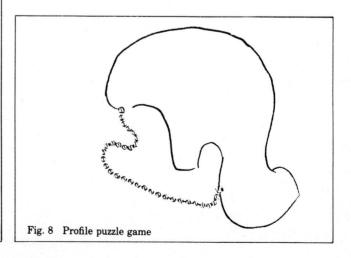

Fig. 8   Profile puzzle game

Jelly-Jiggle Envelope

Make a sensual squeezable out of a clear vinyl pack that is sealed on three sides. These envelopes are commercially available and come in many sizes, or you can make an envelope from a strip of vinyl or X-ray film. Paritally fill the pocket with liquid shampoo or vegetable oil, and add food coloring. Add some small flat objects, such as cut paper, paper clips, or cut vinyl shapes. Seal the open end with tape. Lay the envelope on the overhead surface. With the slightest touch of your fingers you can reorganize the contents and change the picture, creating unpredictable projections.

Extravaganzas and Effects

Light shows. Use two clear concave clock faces or shallow bowls. Put oil, water, and food coloring in the lower one. Place the second bowl on top. Play rhythmic music and tap the filled bowls to the beat. The changing pressure will change the color play on the screen.

Alternate screens. Cover rug tubes and cardboard cartons with white butcher paper. Have the children assemble the covered cartons as a multi-faceted screening area and use it for a projection environment.

Moving backgrounds. Movie makers used to film "action" against a moving backdrop to simulate travelling past a landscape. In the same way, puppets can be jogged along in front of a moving background drawn on acetate roll. Gel or sheets of cellophane can be used to color larger areas, and linear detail can be drawn with the ink markers.

Rear screen projection. Suspend a bed sheet between the audience and the performers. Project from the overhead onto the sheet, with the audience watching from the other side.

Music interpretation. Students can select music and illustrate it with a story and with pictures projected on the overhead. The interpretations can be made through a series of pictures/puppets that tell a narrative or through a series of abstract color and pattern designs which explore emotions and moods.

Multiple screens and projections. As you and your students continue to build and create color, form, and textures through your experiments, you might find it desirable to combine images from two or more overheads. That's just the beginning. Try juxtaposing slide and movie projectors. For those who have the equipment, these activities involving the overhead projector can be videotaped, and where color is important, the projections can be filmed with Super 8 or with 16mm equipment. The light source from the overhead is more than sufficient to do this filming.

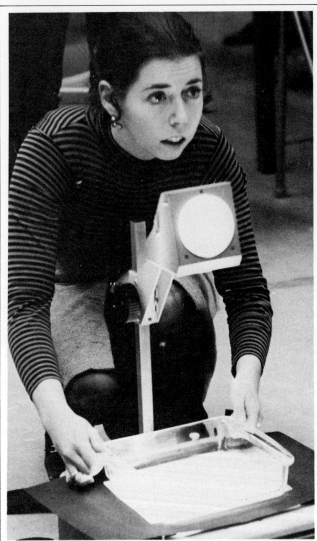

The overhead, a great piece of media hardware. Here a teacher animates with a glass full of moving liquids.

Media Bag

By Milo Dalbey

You don't need complex electronic equipment to enter the world of media. If you are short on equipment but long on desire, start doing the media with "familiar hardware" that is readily and inexpensively available. Here Milo Dalbey packs a bag full of activities that the very youngest child can do, and that even the most "sophisticated" older student will grab for too.

For one reason or another, "using media" has come to signify the employment of electronic devices—film, audiotape, and videotape specifically—for self-expression. By restricting our focus to these relatively complex media, we may limit the exploration of spontaneous creativity with simple, more accessible materials that can be put to use in dramatic ways. Here follow some models and suggested approaches to new experiences involving "familiar hardware."

Communication Cubes

Remember the cigar or shoe box filled with those treasured posessions of string, marbles, jacks, rubber bands, clothespins, nails, washers, Dixie cup covers with pictures of Sunset Carson or Deanna Durbin on the back, a jackknife, some pebbles, and Captain Midnight's Secret Decoding Ring? The box containing these objects revealed the child's world of fantasy.

Photos, textures, string, cellophane, scissors, paste, and a child's imagination are the ingredients that can transform a cardboard box into a unique sensory montage.

The project can be developed for any grade level with a degree of sophistication appropriate to the child's ability. Have each child bring in a box of any shape or size and constructed of cardboard or similar material. The child, through various treatments of the box, then communicates something about his or her own world.

The essential structure of the box should not be changed. However, slots, folds, hinged sides, or lids may

Chapter Nineteen

Communication cubes

be incorporated in the design to beckon the viewer to touch, feel, and examine the contents. Some enterprising children will place a portable cassette tape recorder within the box to add the dimension of sound. The activity entails working with a three-dimensional structure and therefore demands consideration for all possible sides, both exterior and interior. Some children may choose to work exclusively with photographs from magazines, pasting them on the box's surface. These images portray current perceptions about the state of the child's environment. Other projects may show nonobjective designs that require the viewer to peer through a tiny opening in a black box, to press a button that activates a small battery and bulb, or to experience an environment which suggests the surface of another planet.

"Feelies"—the elimination of sight as the primary sensory decision maker—is a variation on the communication cube that calls for a box to be altered in any fashion to respond to sensations and explorations by all the senses except sight. Students will concentrate on how things feel, taste, and sound by discovering a variety of materials, including those which are usually discarded because of visual bias.

Lifted Slides

Any clear, wide, transparent tape as well as clear "contact" paper can be used to remove images intact from most magazines, including newspapers and most comic books. If the ink will come off when a moistened finger is rubbed on the image, the image is ready to be transferred to the tape. The process is as follows:

Place the tape over the desired image and burnish with a fingernail or blunt scissors. Cut around the image which is now stuck to the tape and then immerse it in a pan of warm water. After about a minute, students can peel the paper from the tape and discover a transparent image which is permanently fixed to the tape. Make sure to rinse the new transparency thoroughly in order to remove any minor residue of glue. Finally, the transparency can be trimmed to the appropriate size and placed in a slide mount, which, in turn, can be projected in normal fashion using a slide projector. This process is a marvelous way to obtain instant enlarged images which can subsequently be turned into storyboards within the context of a larger experiment or presentation.

Slide Recycling and Multi-Media Projects

"My pictures didn't come out!" need not be a cry of despair. Learn to recycle. Reuse 35mm slides by having your students bleach them, burn them, scratch them, poke holes in them. Add stick-on letters, cellophane, tissue paper, rubber cement, ink. Tape two together or mask them to create differently shaped images. Darken your room as much as possible and project them on the wall, ceiling, floor, on boxes, closets, or on other students. Focus in and out, zoom in and out. Have students move their hands quickly in front of the lens to create strobe effects. Add several projectors, overlap images, introduce sound that has a definite strong beat. Above all, don't let the students sit back passively and just look. Let them become involved in the creation and presentation of images.

Additional Tips

1. Seamless, white art paper (9' X 10') costs about $10 and makes an inexpensive, fairly durable, large screen.
2. Try bending images by using cardboard boxes covered with white paper as a movable modular projection surface.
3. Distort images by projecting them through a glass or a plastic container filled with colored water.
4. Choreograph your image making with well-known movements in symphonies or popular pieces.
5. Have students nonverbally react to and interpret images projected on them and around them.
6. Introduce other types of hardware, such as movie projectors and overhead projectors.
7. Using two movie projectors, one behind the other, thread the first one with film. Do not attach the end to a take-up reel but thread the same film through the second projector. Turn the projectors on at the same time and see what happens.

Pleasure Domes

Pleasure domes can be constructed inexpensively and with relative ease. It's difficult to describe but easy to do. The essential material for this inflatable environment is polyurethane plastic, which can be purchased from most building material supply houses or plastic supply companies.

You can experiment (and should) with all sizes and shapes of pleasure domes. Here is just one possibility:

A 40' X 50' sheet of polyurethane plastic folded in half horizontally creates a 40' X 25' rectangle. Seal the edges of the three open sides by folding them over two inches

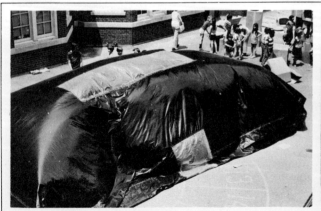

The indescribable pleasure dome

and reinforcing them with Monsanto all-purpose plastic tape. The plastic rectangle is now thoroughly sealed off. Set this plastic envelope aside.

Cut a separate piece of polyurethane into a strip 5' wide by 15' – 20' long. Fold this strip in half lengthwise. Make a 2" seam along the long side and seal with plastic tape. You now have a flat rectangle that will become a cylinder when it is filled with air. Attach one end of this tube with plastic tape to a hole which is cut into the plastic envelope you have set aside. You can cut this round hole in the envelope with a scissors or a razor blade, and it should be about 18" in diameter. The tube is then attached with plastic tape to what will become the base of the inflated dome.

The other end of the tube is attached to an ordinary rectangular portable floor fan, which is the power source for this bubble environment. Cut a piece of cardboard to fit flush over the grating of the fan. Cut a hole 18" in diameter to allow air flow. Attach the cardboard to the fan with masking tape. Attach the tube to the opening in the cardboard with plastic tape.

This is not a prototype. Use your imagination in shaping your own pleasure dome. Crazy shapes are much more exciting than the conventional one described above. It will take eight to ten minutes to inflate the bubble. When it

has assumed inflated form, make a 5' slit in the front or side with a razor knife, or scissors. This slit is your entrance and exit. It also provides the necessary exhaust for the intake of air from the fan, which must be left on at all times. The sides, top, bottom of the incision should be reinforced with plastic tape to prevent a giant tear from forming.

Children who experiment with the pleasure dome will find it an exciting sensory environment. There are endless things they can do with it, especially if they use other light sources. Flood lamps placed on the inside of the bubble or on the outside allow the creation of three-dimensional shadow images. If you use an overhead projector to throw images on the bubble, you promote an extraordinary experience for the people inside. A slide projector can be used inside or outside to throw color and images on or through the pleasure dome.

One of the most stimulating experiences is the use of sound within this environment. The acoustical effect is almost stereophonic. Equally important, the inflatable structure tolerates movement on the inside, and this encourages children to create their own kinetic forms, dances, and shadowplays. The dome is as much fun for spectators as it is for participants.

Pleasure inside the dome

Part 7
Curriculum Design

Taming King Kong: Lessons of the Recent Past

by Richard A. Lacey

If the title of this chapter sounds fanciful, Richard A. Lacey's intentions are anything but. Here is a chary description of the pitfalls which exist in setting up a media program in a school. As you read them, you will probably be reminded of your own situation, for the obstacles are universal. Lacey gives some good, practical advice on how to tame your own "King Kongs."

Teachers have been "doing the media" for over a decade, and their creative energies in this field have given rise to projects of great variety and ingenuity. Exemplary media presentations are easy to cite: a videotaped interview with elderly members of a community, conducted and produced entirely by students; a discussion of film in which students, parents, and teachers shared feelings and ideas so openly that they agreed to meet regularly for more discussions. In some schools a porta-pack has become as familiar a tool for learning as a book or a pencil.

These examples may not be typical, but they do illustrate what can be done, often with resources available in most schools or school districts. Once you are convinced of the possibilities a media arts program holds for richer, more responsive learning, you are ready to plan and initiate the atmosphere necessary for such a program to flourish.

Setting up the Larger Environment

Turning possibility into reality requires four qualities that most teachers have and one that they need to develop. Energy, knowledge, patience, and ingenuity are hallmarks of the good teacher; in addition, a media teacher must have a strategy for school change. Doing the media also means doing politics.

Many school people can be persuaded that doing the media in schools is important as long as it's done well, doesn't detract from regular business, and produces the results that have sometimes astonished us all: pride in accomplishment, specific products to which school people can point, improved student attitudes toward school and classmates, and more confidence and greater precision in various forms of expression. But there is no documented format available, no guarantee that doing the media will consistently produce these extraordinary results. And there are new unsympathetic forces to contend with: skepticism toward innovation; concern that traditional academic standards, "basic skills," and important social values are being neglected; concern about accountability and cost. Then, too, early enthusiasm for media studies among some teachers and schools has waned. There are many reasons: too few committed, energetic people to fol-

Graphic of King Kong created by Marlene Hazzikostas, teacher in P.S. 24, Riverdale, N.Y., for school sweat shirt

low through on ideas; poor administrative support; scheduling and curricular conflicts; criticism inside and outside of school; lack of information; equipment problems.

Some of these difficulties, such as project costs in the face of drastic budget cuts, plague all educational programs. But the most typical problems can be avoided by using a strategy based on three hard-earned lessons designed for self-preservation. These basic principles are essential for planning and developing new programs that can survive past infancy and make a lasting difference in the life of a school.

Be clear about your purposes—to yourself as well as to others. Be able to state simply, confidently, and without jargon the sound arguments for doing the media to a variety of interested as well as skeptical audiences: school board members and administrators, parents, students, teachers. If you can't do this or if you sense that you are merely parroting the experts, examine your motives and goals and put off until tomorrow the media project you could start today.

Although the ideas and approaches in this book grow out of successful experience and sound theory, they will surely raise questions that deserve lucid, thoughtful answers, not slogans. Among the many popular and professional books and articles on media that have flooded the educational market there is a fair balance of cheerleading, utopian fancy, practical hints, sound but complex theory, horse sense, and claptrap. Countless notions about media studies are floating around. Before starting any project, then, decide what ideas make the most sense to you and express them in your own words.

There are reasons why clearly stated, easy-to-understand objectives are crucial. Reports on such innovative movements as humanistic and open education continually note how often teachers can't explain the reasons for what they are doing to administrators. As a result, many opportunities to extend learning are missed. Moreover, the success of a program often depends on the understanding, support, and collaboration of co-workers. Unless others comprehend your intentions, they may work at cross-purposes rather than in harmony with you.

Involve as many influential people as you can in your early plans for doing the media, especially parents, influential colleagues, and school administrators. Do not forget custodians. Be certain that no one who could significantly affect the program is excluded or uninformed of developments. There are bound to be problems along the way, and, when they arise, you will need all the friends you can get. Maintain communication after the project is well established, for these informal consultants often see things that those who are more immediately involved may miss. Be sure that the invitation to participate is genuine. For example, a parent's concerns that a child may have nightmares about King Kong or that learning to use a videotape machine may steal time from reading are by no means trivial, nor can they be convincingly addressed with vague references to the TV generation or the global village. You may have to compromise by scrapping some pet schemes, but the sacrifice will be worth making.

Establish a mutual support group to help you think about and build your program. Effective use of film, videotape, and other media can become complicated and usually requires careful organization and regular periods for reflection about what has been happening, why it has

been happening, and what can be learned from the experience. The best way to maintain perspective and unearth new possibilities is to meet regularly with a small, problem-solving support group who share ideas and resources and plan and assess a range of approaches.

The assumption underlying these suggestions is this: when programs run smoothly in a direction that is clear and generally desirable to everyone, film, videotape, and other media *can* be integrated into classrooms and whole schools sufficiently to support and extend learning. Exactly how these media can accomplish these purposes will become clear in other chapters, but if you accept the premise, you will agree that there is more to effective media study than good teaching and equipment. There must also be strong organization, support from the top and the bottom of the school structure, and wide understanding of purposes, methods, and problems. While the strategy is neither easy nor problem free, it focuses attention on shared problem solving and broad understanding of classroom goals, essential factors for building educational programs that can last and grow.

Manageable choices, with a media library specialist for guidance and assistnace

Setting up the Classroom Environment

The major purpose of doing the media is to create a richer, more diverse, and more responsive atmosphere within the classroom, a setting where students can learn actively. Teachers have discovered that such settings help them learn too. When they find ways to learn by doing on the job, they stay vital professionally and make their working lives interesting.

Integrating media into the total curriculum is an advanced step—a goal, in fact. While moving gradually toward that goal, allowing ample time to reflect and plan, you will find it useful to keep in mind some general characteristics of the environment you would like to develop. To some they may seem immediately feasible, to others hopelessly ambitious. However these characteristics are usually found to some degree in every classroom where teachers use different ways to reach individual students. Here are just a few:

Manageable choices. Students would regularly select among a range of alternative activities without feeling overwhelmed or confused. The teacher would be available for guidance, especially to make sure each student can give reasons for a particular choice and can articulate the

characteristics—or none—depending on the teacher's goals beyond "doing media." Using media will not necessarily enrich the environment significantly or help a teacher and students explore experiences in depth unless the teacher keeps larger aims in view and shares and assesses them openly.

Learning by doing the media is challenging because the field is still an open-ended enterprise. Books and experts notwithstanding, we are all still beginners, and practically anyone can make a contribution.

Just one "but": The field of education is cluttered with fallen structures because their adherents neglected to build foundations of trust, understanding, and collaboration within the total school community to support such promising ventures. In the 1960s a great deal of money, time, hope, and effort was spent discovering some simple but demanding lessons about process, planning, and continuing dialogue about purposes. Those of us who helped spend those resources like to think that if educators of the 1970s will have used the lessons well, then the 1980s shall prove all will have been worthwhile.

Now's your chance to do the media.

projects's method and objective. There would be variety in the scale, duration, and organization of activities. For students who seem most comfortable learning under firm direction and supervision, appropriate settings and tasks would be available, but the activities would be designed to relate to the work pursued by more independent students.

Opportunities for self-initiated learning. Students would regularly define new problems and methods for solving them, using the teacher as one among several resources available for consultation and assistance. By gradually increasing in degrees of difficulty, these opportunities would be designed around and nourishing for student confidence.

Cumulative learning. There would be long-range projects as well as short-term activities, often involving groups of students or individuals who would be engaged only periodically in the project. In the classroom there would be visible evidence of steady development over time so that students and adults would experience a sustained, continuing effort.

Activities outside the classroom. The relationship between classroom activities and the world outside would become apparent through media projects which would integrate the two settings.

Plentiful chances to reflect and plan. Both time and space would be provided for this critical aspect of learning. It is important that students be aware of what they are doing, why, with what results, with what options in mind, that they assume responsibility for taking initiatives. This activity would also provide important information for the teacher's planning, for diagnosing the needs of individual students, and for helping groups of students cooperate effectively. Videotape could be a valuable tool for teacher and students to assess how well they are solving problems together.

While these few characteristics are stated in general terms, they are not idealistic, nor do they mean that the only valid direction is to move toward an "open classroom." In fact, any teacher can begin to achieve one or more of these characteristics without drastically changing curriculum, classroom structure, or teaching methods.

The simplest student motion picture film, still photograph, or videotape project could exhibit all of the above

An effective teacher is an invaluable resource.

Approaches to
Curriculum Design

by Kit Laybourne

Chances are that as you create a media program in your school, you will be embarking on a perilous journey with skeptics from the more established departments or factions ready to challenge you at every turn. It is up to you, the exponent of media education to secure your place in the overall school program. To do this you must build a curriculum that is educationally valid, vital, and well fitted to your particular circumstances. In this chapter Kit Laybourne offers some very sound advice to all media curriculum designers.

It is not easy to plan media teaching, and for good reason. In such a new field few teachers have had much formal training. It is difficult to design learning activities without being able to draw on one's own learning experiences. The presence of media equipment is often intimidating too, and for the same reason: it is unfamiliar.

The most frustrating source of difficulty comes from the vast range of material to be covered in media studies. Each of the media forms discussed in this book can be an entire *subject to learn about*. Each has its own history, technical foundations, social dimensions, and implications for the future. These media are also *new modes of learning*. Each media form has a unique code system and requires its own set of skills for successful expression.

The following items are intended to help you design your own media studies curriculum. They are loosely presented as an overall process that can help locate priorities, set goals, determine logistics, invent activities, develop an overall program, and offer ways of evaluating it.

First, there is an outline of a general *methodology* for curriculum design. Its particular value is in reviewing all the steps that are required in planning what you will teach and in providing a sequential process for developing ideas thoroughly and rigorously.

A questionnaire is next. It tries to make you define all the instructional givens with which you will be working. As such, the questions provide a self-diagnostic tool to analyze your overall *teaching environment*.

The third item is a simple checklist aimed at reminding you of all the sorts of *classroom activities* that can be programmed into media studies. The list is a brainstorming device and urges you to select a broad variety of learning processes for your curriculum.

Finally, *reportorial format* is described for use in putting your curriculum into written form. It is provided because schools and school systems often require curriculum statements—particularly in a new area such as media studies.

Team planning for media teaching

In short, these notes seek to help you fashion a curriculum that will work for *your* interests, *your* students, *your* resources, and *your* school. At the same time, however, not one of the four approaches is intended as a sure-fire prescription for success in deciding what to teach or how to teach.

In the final analysis, coming up with just the right selection of activities and ideas is a creative challenge you will face all by yourself. It is the critical challenge. Usually the most difficult aspect of designing a curriculum is the lonely process of molding an overall plan that unifies separate ideas, topics, and activities into a single, purposeful entity.

Being able to state concisely the overall purpose and orientation of your curriculum is not just an academic exercise. It has real utility. A firm conceptual groundwork enables a teacher to see and cut out peripheral materials and topics. It acts as a source for designing learning experiences. A conceptual frame helps students see the value of what they are doing—it helps them see the forest as well as the trees. Not least of all, a strong conceptual base is a necessity in convincing administrators and others that you know what you are doing and that what you are doing is important.

METHODOLOGY FOR CURRICULUM DEVELOPMENT IN MEDIA STUDIES

Designing a curriculum is like doing a puzzle. There are a number of pieces that must fit together for the thing to work as a whole. Furthermore, the pieces need to fall into place in just the right sequence. See if the following outline can be useful in providing a step-by-step process for designing your curriculum. At the very least, you ought to check that, in one way or another, you've considered and dealt with each of the fifteen basic tasks.

Diagnosis

1. *Yourself:* interests, experiences, teaching styles, learning styles, professional goals, time availability, media experience.
2. *Your students:* size of groups, ages, backgrounds, interests, academic skills, social skills, time available for outside work, learning styles, remedial needs, media experiences.
3. *Your school:* space, available resources (hardware and software), budget, administrative receptiveness, class sizes, access to community resources, class schedules, other media teaching and teachers.
4. *Media environment:* do a thorough study of existing media within the community; evaluate relative significance; judge role of such media in lives of your students; pick priorities.

Content

5. *Theoretical base for understanding media:* place specific curriculum possibilities and goals within the context of media study, *per se*. Be able to express the philosophical dimensions and consequences of understanding media in terms of your curriculum.
6. *Defining content and objectives:* identify requisite or assumed knowledge; determine most appropriate modes of inquiry; select major topics and minor ones; develop behavioral objectives; determine what is *not* to be included.
7. *Checking other models and resources:* review ways in which others have defined a similar selection of content; locate print and non-print resources to be used within the curriculum; establish and maintain a familiarity with the literature of the field(s).

8. *Organizing content:* determine sequence of ideas and processes (the content) of your curriculum; locate interdisciplinary links.

Experiences

9. *Pedagogical base:* determine general teaching/learning principles you are after; identify specific learning options to be incorporated into your curriculum; develop a strategy that will provide individual students with access to the unexplored structures and values of your classroom.
10. *Inventing activities:* incorporate a broad variety of learning modes; cross-check the realistic use of resources at your disposal (people, space, hardware, software); collect and review ideas from others.
11. *Organizing experiences:* sequence activities to match the content structure and flow; develop mechanisms for student input and feedback; schedule available time; use different instructional formats and materials.
12. *Preparing materials:* design and produce materials for your own use and materials for student use; order items from outside the classroom.

Evaluation

13. *What to evaluate:* criteria should include your interest, your ability to provide students with specific feedback on their performance and capabilities, political necessity within the school, your interest in mapping individual needs of students, your desire to determine the overall success of the curriculum and the relative value of specific units.
14. *How to evaluate:* review methodological options; select and prepare evaluation strategies that fit with your time, ability, and interest; prepare resulting materials.
15. *Integrating feedback:* structure curriculum into stages which lend themselves to evaluation and provide flexibility in reordering the curriculum in terms of evolving student interest and your estimation of need; devise activities that create within the classroom a climate for evaluation both between you and your students and between one student and another.

DIAGNOSIS OF TEACHING ENVIRONMENT

The following questionnaire is designed to help you conduct a thorough diagnosis of your teaching environment. Taking stock of what you've got to work with is a necessary first step in building an effective curriculum. If you are able to answer each of the 25 questions, you'll be well-anchored in the realities of your particular classroom and you will have established the parameters of the curriculum to be developed.

Your Students

1. What experiences, if any, have your students had in media studies?
2. What media forms are most important in their lives?
3. What topics or approaches to media will be most interesting to them as a starting point?
4. What areas of the traditional basic skills is your class, as a whole, best at doing? Where are their weaknesses?
5. Does their socio-economic background suggest topics or learning processes that should be emphasized?
6. What is the quality of interpersonal skills/needs among your students? Are there areas needing special attention?

Yourself

7. What areas or topics of media studies most interest you?
8. Does your own teaching style suggest things that ought or ought not be undertaken?

9. How much time will planning and carrying out a media studies unit require? Are you able to make the commitment?

10. What area or areas of media studies are you most familiar with?

Logistics

11. How many students are in your class? (Or, if appropriate, how many students are in a course and how many sections of the course are given?)

12. What kind of space will you be using? Consider possible learning environments within the entire school building and within the community.

13. What kinds of equipment will be available for your teaching?

14. Is there a specified budget you can work within? Where will you get the expendable items required for your course or unit?

15. What resources will be available for your use (including texts, library facilities, films, etc.).

Administrative/Academic

16. What team teaching, departmental, or other academic affiliation will you be working within for the development and teaching of your curriculum?

17. Are there other media courses or teachers working in media with whom you can cooperate? Will there be any duplication of emphasis?

18. Is there a particular interdisciplinary context in which you wish or will be urged to develop your curriculum?

19. What kind of administrative support can you expect, and what levels of administrative support will you need?

Curricular Givens

20. Can you write down in one sentence what it is you wish to do in your media teaching?

21. What is the duration, in weeks, of your course or unit?

22. How many class sessions will there be per week?

23. What is the length of each class session or amount of time you wish, daily, to devote to media teaching?

24. What experiences have you had previously in teaching elements of the new curriculum you plan on creating?

25. What traditional basic skills do you wish to stress within your media course or unit?

CHECKLIST OF ACTIVITIES

The more kinds of learning options you can build into your curriculum, the better it may be. It will be better because your chances are greater for letting each student experience a particular learning style that is appropriate for that student. And the curriculum will be stronger yet if you can help each student gauge his or her particular aptitudes and interests within the broad spectrum of ways to learn.

In this context, the following list can be useful in selecting experiences that will help kids understand media. Its purpose is to give you something to bounce your own ideas off of, not to provide a comprehensive listing of all possible options in creating specific learning activities. The list shows my own bias toward inductive learning.

This checklist of generalized things-to-do can be applied to many areas of media studies. The list does *not* include the huge variety of media-based activities that many of your own curricula will include. Elsewhere in this volume you'll find plenty of guidance with those.

Verbal activities
    small group discussions
    large group discussions
    brainstorming
    "content" analysis
    "feelings" analysis
    games
    interviews (including telephone)
    oral reports (individuals and groups)
Written activities
    workbooks (commercially produced or teacher produced)
    journals (for personal reflections)
    notebooks (compilations of all class work)
    short reports (on books, film, television, etc.)
    research papers
    tear-files (collections of articles, photographs, quotes)
Reading activities
    newspapers
    mimeographed materials (teacher produced)
    reprints
    library research
    magazines
    textbooks
    classroom libraries
Groupings/duration
    individual
    small groups (three to six)
    large groups (ten to fifteen)
    full class
    short-term activities (done within a single class)
    long-term activities (done over part or duration of a course)
Community interface
    guests
    field trips
    festivals (student run)
    festivals (by outside organizations)
    workshops for younger students
    school assembly programs
    PTA/community group presentations
    parent/kid evenings
    community media outlets (newspapers, cable, school newsletters)
Student choice
    totally assigned by teacher
    students select among specific options
    students create own problems and "contract" for them
    use of free time
    "earned" free time
    students create activities for others in class (curriculum planning)
Group skills
    listening to others (feedback loops)
    selecting a leader
    annotating a group discussion
    identification of "feelings" and "agendas"
    sticking to topics
    selecting an outcome
Quantitative activities
    surveys and polls
    questionnaires
    measurement, statistical analysis
    projections
    cost analysis
Evaluative activities
    self-analysis of learning profiles and performances (all items here)
    multiple choice (cognitive items)
    feedback discussions on curriculum/class participation
    behavioral objectives known to students
    questionnaires (anonymous)
    explicit "grading" policies (many options here)

Graphic activities
    charts, posters
    maps, diagrams
    instruction booklets
    class "anthologies" of student work, written and graphic
    magazines, newspapers, newsletters—including
        photography
Teacher-centered activities
    lectures
    presentations (commercially produced films,
        tapes, records)
    presentations (teacher-prepared materials)
    demonstrations
    individual "consultations"
    sharing "personal concerns"

FORMAT FOR ARTICULATING CURRICULUM

While it may not happen very often, it *is* possible to share curricular ideas with other teachers. I know this because I've experienced it. In the help I've gotten from others, I've noticed a pattern: the best ideas have always come through discussions with other teachers or artists, not through formally articulated curriculum models. This may be due to two problems that written curricula seldom solve.

The first is a problem of *tone.* Most curricular works tend to be "teacher proof." They are lock-step prescriptions that leave little room for the teacher to modify the materials to suit his or her particular interests and strengths. When something is written it tends to become canonized and rigid. I prefer a tone that is descriptive, not prescriptive.

The second problem has to do with *detail.* Curriculum writers seem to have great difficulty in providing enough concrete detail so that their ideas can be replicated without overdoing the detail. As a result they tend to bore you to sleep trying to get through all of the detail.

It is all a matter of balance and of time. A written curriculum guide that will be of use to someone ought to mirror the kind of dialogue that one teacher shares with another: it should be informal, anecdotal, practical, and conceptually true. Above all, a curriculum guide that will be useful should be accessible and digestible, requiring an economic use of time and effort to locate the guide and interpret the material within.

All these goals are being sought in the following format for articulating the curriculum that you design. There is a real danger that the liveliness of one's ideas can get squashed when using a standard reportorial tool. So if you decide to use it, follow the format loosely. Try to get your enthusiasms into it. Write it as if you were informally swapping ideas with a friend.

Title

Give a break to people who may not be interested in what interests you—tell them right out front what your course is about.

Context

A quick summary about the level, duration, and environment for which you have designed the curriculum: the kinds of people it's planned for; the interdisciplinary tie-in you are pursuing (if any); the number of kids involved; its relationship to other curricula (if that is important). The purpose of this section is to help readers identify immediately the milieu your curriculum addresses.

Content

First, provide a short narrative that outlines the basic elements of subject matter—the ones of special importance to you. This should be, in effect, a brief *rationale.* It shows your general analysis of the problem and links your curriculum to the real world: to students, learning processes, cultural demands, and particular facets of the discipline(s) involved.

Next, provide a more specific analysis of content by separating the concepts to be learned (including attitudes, sensibilities, and feelings you want to develop) from the processes of the curriculum (ways of thinking and working to be reinforced, or initiated, and habits or skills to be mastered). This second level of content analysis can take the form of "behavioral objectives."

Experiences

You can save a lot of energy, space, and words by proceeding directly with descriptions of the things-to-do or activities through which your course is structured. This way the hidden structures of your curriculum are accessible and the sharp teacher can see immediately the "heavier" pedagogic concerns that are manifest in any activity.

It is not necessary to describe all of the activities in a course curriculum. Usually you can give the drift of what you are doing—and give a lot of pragmatic information—by describing 1) *openers:* initial activities that get things moving; 2) *builders:* activities that break apart into discrete manageable form the major content items of the course; and 3) *culminators:* activities marking the conclusion and synthesis of the course content.

Resources

Depending on the sort of curriculum you are outlining, provide a straightforward list of good books, films, organizations, and equipment requirements of your curriculum. The idea is to help readers by annotating only those resources that are really central to the curriculum you have designed. Keep the list as short as possible—this is not the place to impress people with your amazing grasp of the literature of an entire field.

Evaluation

You should describe here only what you think is helpful. Depending on how you feel about evaluation and upon your specific curriculum, I generally recommend three varieties of comments: 1) warnings about particularly tricky or volatile phases or activities; 2) pragmatic descriptions of special tools that you found helpful in figuring out how things were going; and 3) analysis of broad strategies for evaluation or feedback that you have experienced as being helpful in the context of your curriculum.

Postscript

Pay attention to the visual impact of what you write. As best you can, make it compelling and fun to read.

An Integrated Media Arts Curriculum

by Milo Dalbey

Noting the gap between the culture of media and school culture, and the resulting dissonance in the experience of school-age children and young people, the various chapters in this book have set out to bring media into the schools. The guiding principle has been to allow students to be intelligent participators and appreciative, selective consumers of our media culture. In advancing this principle, the authors urged you to develop your own media skills and then to impart them to your students. In this final chapter, Milo Dalbey offers a model curriculum of media studies applicable to any school. It is fitting that he sould end on an uncertain note, puzzling over the place of media in curriculum and reminding us that there are many issues yet to be settled in our media-filled future.

The broad aim of a language arts curriculum is to promote students' proficiency in the use of language—in listening, speaking, writing, and reading. The art education curriculum has a basic aim of providing activities which increase sensory perceptions.

In the traditional school structure it is the rule to separate these two avenues of learning. In most elementary schools, classes in reading and writing skills are often confined to the morning, while art activities are generally left for the afternoon. Thus schools, like other institutions in our culture, arrange things in a linear, categorized fashion, and, as a result, the very structure of the school's curricula impedes a fundamental goal of learning—the ability to make connections, to see, hear, smell, taste, and touch the relationships of all things past and present.

To limit language arts to the spoken and written word is clearly archaic in today's society. Similarly, not to provide students with an opportunity to work with and understand contemporary forms of image-making keeps both art and language education in the nineteenth century. But things being what they are in today's schools, the processes by which learning can be a truly comprehensive experience (not a specialized compilation of unrelated facts) depends upon the individual teacher's ability to provide opportunities where all aspects of the child's environment are explored and examined.

It is not my purpose here to suggest that a media arts curriculum can become a super-structure that neatly packages existing curricula into a new unity. However, if media studies can be explored as one of these *connectors* that are usually missing, a helpful bridge can be constructed that allows students to move freely and with

Chapter Twenty-two

159

A Model K-6 Media Arts Curriculum
TEACHING LEVELS

Activity Groupings	K-2	3-4	5-6
PHOTOGRAPHY MAKING	- CAMERALESS SLIDE-MAKING - SIMPLE PHOTOGRAMS - POLAROID ACTIVITIES	- PINHOLE CAMERAS - OPTICAL DEVICES - PHOTOGRAMS - FILM STRIP (WITH AND WITHOUT CAMERAS) - INSTAMATICS (SLIDES) - SLIDE-TAPES - PLASTIC CAMERAS (NON-DARKROOM DEVELOPING AND PRINTING)	
PHOTOGRAPHY STUDY		- HISTORY OF MEDIUM - CRITICAL VOCABULARY - PHOTO GENRES - PHOTOGRAPHERS	
STILL IMAGE TECHNOLOGY		- STILL CAMERA TECHNOLOGY - LIGHT SENSITIVE MATERIALS AND EMULSIONS - OPTICS AND LIGHT - PHOTOGRAPHY IN THE SCIENCES	
STORYBOARDING	- DRAWING A STORY IN PANELS - ORDERING PHOTO STORIES		- COMIC STRIP ANALYSIS AND MAKING - PHOTO STORYBOARD ACTIVITIES - DEVELOPING SCENARIOS AND SHOOTING SCRIPTS
SCRATCH AND DOODLE FILMMAKING	- FILMING OF SEQUENCED DRAWINGS		- CLEAR LEADER - BLACK LEADER - SOUND TRACKS - OLD FILMS
ANIMATION			- PHOTO MONTAGE FILMS - COMIC STRIP SHOOTING - PIXILLATION - CUT-OUTS - FLIP BOOKS - TITLING
LIVE-ACTION FILMMAKING			- EXPLORING THE CAMERA - NARRATIVE - DOCUMENTARY - DESIGN/EXPERIMENTAL - GROUP AND INDIVIDUAL PROJECTS
FILM	- SCREENING OF SHORT FILMS WITH NON-VERBAL ACTIVITIES	- SCREENINGS WITH VERBAL ACTIVITIES	- TERMINOLOGY (CRITICAL VOCABULARY) - FILM HISTORY

STUDY

FILM TECHNOLOGY		– GROUP PROCESSING GAMES	– GENRES – FILMMAKERS – PERSISTENCE OF VISION – CAMERA/PROJECTION TECHNOLOGY
SOUND MAKING	– NOISE IDENTIFICATION – LISTENING TO OWN VOICE – TELLING A STORY – LISTENING TO RECORDS	– COLLECTING SOUNDS – INTERVIEWING SKILLS – SOUND SCULPTURE – RADIO PROGRAMS – SIMPLE ELECTRONIC EDITING	– LABORATORY PROCESS – EDITING AUDIO TAPE – SOUND DOCUMENTARIES – SOUND MIXING – MAKING FILM SOUND TRACKS
SOUND STUDY	– SOUND EFFECTS IDENTIFICATION	– RADIO SHOWS – LOCAL RADIO BROADCASTING	– ANALYSIS OF FILM SOUND TRACKS
SOUND TECHNOLOGY		– MICROPHONES – SOUND WAVES – HEARING – TAPE RECORDERS	
VIDEO MAKING (½" AND 1" SYSTEMS)	– NON-VERBAL ACTIVITIES – SELF-REFLECTION/FEEDBACK	– SINGLE CAMERA SYSTEM – ROLE PLAYING – CLASSROOM REPORTS – STREET INTERVIEWS – NEWS CASTING – TAPE EXPERIMENTS – GROUP PROCESSING ACTIVITIES	– MULTIPLE CAMERA SYSTEM (STUDIO) – IMPROVISATIONAL DRAMA – VIDEODRAMAS – DOCUMENTARIES/NEWSCASTING – INTERVIEWS – VIDEO COLLAGE – GROUP PROCESSING ACTIVITIES – DEVELOP SCHOOL TV SYSTEM
VIDEO STUDY	– DISCUSSION OF TV PROGRAMS	– DISCUSSION OF TV PROGRAMS	– VIDEO LOG – LOCAL TV BROADCASTING – MASS COMMUNICATIONS – TV AS "BUSINESS" – VIEWING HABITS – TV REGULATION
VIDEO TECHNOLOGY			– VTR TECHNOLOGY – FUTURE SYSTEMS (CABLE, CASSETTE, SATELLITE) – TV/BROADCASTING
MULTI-MEDIA ENVIRONMENTS	– BLURBLE – MULTIPLE FILM PROJECTION – OVERHEADS/SHADOWS AND SILHOUETTE – MIRRORS – MAGNIFICATION	– MULTIPLE PROJECTION/SLIDES, FILMS – VIEWING ENVIRONMENTS – SOUND MIX – PANTOMIME, CHARADES, PUPPETS – OVERHEAD/SHAPE, COMPOSITION	– MULTI-MEDIA SHOWS – DESIGN AND ANALYSIS OF VIEWING SPACE – FUTURE MEDIA ENVIRONMENTS – BOGUS MOVIES/OPAQUE

confidence through an understandable interdisciplinary framework.

To demonstrate my point, let me give you an example: A sixth grade class, after listening to a recording of the Orson Welles' radio broadcast of *War of the Worlds,* was motivated to find out how, why, and in what ways this particular story was changed over the years by the various media that treated it. They read H. G. Wells' original novel and studied its original setting in Edwardian England. They discovered that Howard Koch's radio play for Orson Welles premiered on the eve of World War II, and that in this appearance the setting was New York City *now* (that is, 1938, the time of the broadcast). Finally, the students saw the 1954 Hollywood cinematic version of *War of the Worlds* and noted new changes, including its relocation to the atomic age of suburban California.

The class analyzed how each rendition employed and stressed particular aspects of the story as determined by the particular capabilities of the medium in which it was presented and the social or historical environment in which it made its appearance. Some students researched newspaper accounts of the famous 1938 radio broadcast and the panic that ensured. Amazed at the power of the radio medium, these students were inspired to listen to other old radio programs, which, in turn, led to projects in which they taped stories of their own creation. Other students in the class created *War of the Worlds* story-boards and comic strips. Their interpretations of the drama stressed the impact of visuals and the power of graphic language. Still others used video to create present-day formats of TV reportage on the invastion. And for still others, Super 8 animation became a favorite medium for creative outer space imagery and stories.

A Model K–6 Media Arts Curriculum

The preceding account illustrates the kind of media arts curriculum I value. A single event arouses student curiosity—in this case, hearing the Welles radio program. After that the curriculum follows its own momentum as central questions are articulated and the teacher encourages student explorations. The learning process goes where it goes, crossing and re-crossing many interdisciplinary lines. In this particular example, the students followed one dramatic idea through a historical development that encompassed a broad spectrum of disciplines within the humanities and communications arts. It demonstrates how media should be introduced into the general curriculum, not as yet another discrete subject or discipline which must, somehow, be jammed into the curriculum, but rather as various activities used *when* and *where* they are appropriate within the total context of children's learning.

The accompanying chart of *A Model K–6 Media Arts Curriculum* exemplifies one school's approach to provide a framework for specific activities and skills over the entire k–6 learning continuum. It is not suggested here that there are necessarily specific ages or "grades" for learning skills or for doing certain activities, nor that this is all that should or might be covered. Certainly there are degrees of skills and comprehensions which may require more sophistication, maturity and motor coordination than others, and many subjects need to be reenforced with repetition and progressively more difficult tasks. A curriculum for k–8, say, or another for 9–12 might include many of the same basic activities, though performed and enriched according to the students' capacities and interests. Our k–6 model is offered only to demonstrate how to create a media arts curriculum. It also suggests which kinds of activities one can start with and which others call for greater motor or intellectual skills or more technical experience and information.

"Where should I begin with Kindergarteners?"

"Should photography precede filmmaking?"

"Can a six-year-old make an animated movie?"

"My sixth-graders have taken pictures the last six years and are turned off now!"

"Is it important to teach the scientific principles of a medium?"

"How does watching yourself on videotape relate to the basic skills I am supposed to teach?"

"Do I fit these media activities into Language Arts, Social Studies, Science, or Art?"

"Which comes first, film study or filmmaking?"

"Why can't you include newspapers in your Media Studies course?"

"What qualifications and credentials do you need to teach media?"

"Is everyone going to have to teach this stuff?"

Questions and comments like these are tough because they mix issues—conceptual, pedagogical, logistical, personal, political. But in one way or another, and at one time or another, all these questions beg another question: "What is the *right curriculum* for Media Studies?" And that begs a deeper and more important question yet: "Do we need a *right curriculum*?"

Some reasons for an integrated curriculum:

1. If there were a media curriculum that covered many grade levels, teachers might avoid repeating activities and information that students may have already covered. A curriculum would allow teachers to know what materials and skills the children had covered earlier.

2. An integrated curriculum for media studies could coordinate with important instructional elements within existing curriculum at specific grade levels.

3. Not only would such a curriculum synchronize media skills with the "basic skills," but it would focus attention on the core concepts in understanding media. An integrated curriculum would define and specify a developmental progression of requisite skills common to all activities. This would aid in establishing precise instructional objectives.

4. A curriculum that prescribed teaching from level to level would be an effective strategic tool in establishing media making and media studies within a school system. Media would gain an equal footing with areas like math, science, art, language arts. The field would then get the administrative, personnel, financial, and political support that it deserves.

Some reasons against an integrated curriculum:

1. By delineating a lock-step, formally approved and sanctioned curriculum for all media activities on all levels, teachers might be robbed of their present roles as innovators, researchers, curriculum developers, and media disciples. With a required or semi-required progression of activities and concerns, individual teachers would necessarily end up teaching something that they themselves weren't especially excited about. We have too much of this already.

2. The very act of creating a curriculum alters the nature of the material covered. The medium is the message —in this case, the structure of a formal curriculum brings with itself a linear, cognitive focus that is not altogether good. The learning process for children is different when, on the one hand, kids are simply immersing themselves in a series of relatively isolated and self-contained projects and when, on the other hand, what is being done is part of an interrelated progression of mutually dependent activities. There is a parallel difference for the teacher: when a specific activity is part of a series of activities, one approaches that activity and monitors it differently than if its outcome were not anticipated.

3. An integrated media arts curriculum would limit the field no matter how inclusive the definition. Something would always be left out because it seemed peripheral. After all, you've got to draw the line somewhere. People would be left out too. If media became a sanctioned department or speciality area, it would lose the interdiscipli-

nary nature that it now possesses. One of the most exciting things about the present field is that it brings together people with radically different backgrounds and interests.

4. Although a curriculum might win administrative support in the short-run, it might atrophy growth and vitality in the long-run. Experimentation may diminish as canonized, teacher-proof curricula become mass produced. Furthermore, there is danger that instead of remaining open and constantly taking on new dimensions, the media curriculum staffs become just another group with vested interests. Finally, were a fixed curriculum developed for the "popular" communications media, we might get the feeling that we were "au courant." We'd stop thinking about and watching for the new things that kids need. Right now, all the apparently new technologies and effects of media on society's consciousness are eagerly included in our open, organic, non-defined grab bag of curricular bits and pieces.

Early education in the media arts

Resources

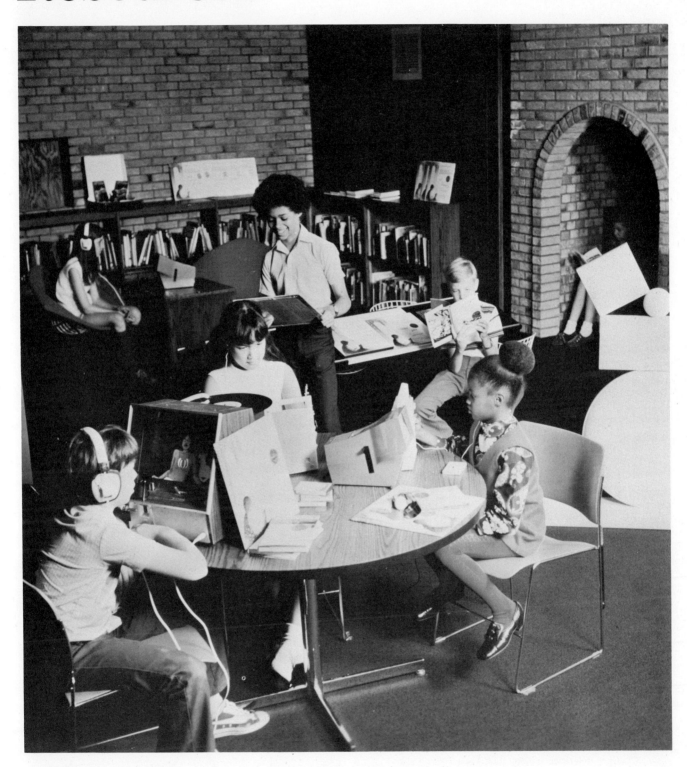

Resources

Compiled by Louis Giansante, Deirdre Boyle, and Pauline Cianciolo

The following listing of books, films, recordings, periodicals, organizations, and media distributors is selective. It includes only those resources which we believe will be of direct value to practicing teachers, librarians, school administrators, media people, and, of course, students. Most of these materials will be suitable for both elementary and high school situations. Because we have detected the need for guidance to be more acute in elementary schools, we have stressed their needs and have included many materials designed specifically for them; we have also indicated in the annotations of other works features which may be useful for elementary programs.

The range and reading interests and media capacities of high school students are generally greater than those of elementary school students, and we know this collection is far from complete to meet their needs. We hope that you will add to this collection valuable resources from your own experience. Often what is good for one teacher or school or classroom does not work for another. Use whatever works for you. And also, be sure to consult with your own librarian or media staff for help in finding new and other materials.

In keeping with the purpose and texts of this book, the emphasis is on materials about *doing* media. So you will find lots of titles here on techniques but little on technology or hardware. We have retained those resources listed in the first (report) edition of *Doing the Media* which have proven to be most helpful, and we have updated and amplified this collection with new and additional titles. In compiling the list we have occasionally drawn upon the words and experiences of participants in courses conducted by the Center for Understanding Media as part of the graduate program in Media Studies at The New School for Social Research.

Arrangement. The collection is arranged in broad groups keyed to the major sections of *Doing the Media:*

Books and Nonprint Materials
>Media Studies
>>General Theory
>>Creativity and Visual Thinking
>>Educational Theory and Practice
>Photography
>Film
>>Films on Filmmaking
>Television and Video
>Sound
>>Recordings
>Other Media
>Curriculum Design
>>Curriculum and Media
>>Library Reference and Selection Tools

Periodicals
Organizations
Media Distributors
>Film Distributors
>Videotape Recordings Distributors/Publishers
>Audiotape Distributors

BOOKS AND NONPRINT MATERIALS

MEDIA STUDIES

General Theory

Carpenter, Edmund. *Oh! What a Blow That Phantom Gave Me.* Bantam, 1974.

Many media scholars believe that a media teacher must become a kind of anthropologist, for it is the anthropologist's task to observe media and the impact of media on the environment in which media exist. The noted anthropologist Carpenter acknowledges this relationship. This book is his personal, multi-cultural look at how media change people and people change media.

Carpenter, Edmund, and McLuhan, Marshall, eds. *Explorations in Communication.* Beacon, 1960.

This collection of essays, originally published in the journal *Explorations,* is an attempt to define a new approach to the study of human communication. Contributing scholars, artists, and media personalities offer their views on both the historical and present impact of various media, from cave painting through the printing press to television. Probably ranks as the single most important collection of essays available in this field.

Ellul, Jacques. *The Technological Society.* Knopf, 1964; Vintage, 1967, pa.

This book is a major philosophical work on the history and sociology of what Ellul calls "la technique," his term for the driving force which has plunged us into the dark ages of technological overkill. While the writing style is difficult and the thesis ultimately pessimistic, this study has been a major influence on media theory.

Kuhns, William. *The Post-Industrial Prophets.* Weybright, 1971; Harper, 1971, pa.

A brief, well-written series of essays describing and analyzing the theoretical perspectives of such media pundits as Marshall McLuhan, Jacques Ellul, Lewis Mumford, Buckminister Fuller, and others. The book serves as both an excellent companion to those authors' writings and a good introduction to various theoretical approaches.

McLuhan, Marshall. *Understanding Media: The Extensions of Man.* McGraw-Hill, 1964; New Amer. Lib., 1973, pa.

The classic! Considered the seminal work of the writer once called "the oracle of the electronic age," this work has already proven itself one of the most influential and controversial books of this century. As a discipline, Media Studies began with this book, first as a revolutionary perception and now as a field of inquiry and learning.

Mumford, Lewis. *Technics & Civilization.* Harcourt, 1963.

A major historical study into how technological change has affected all society, this classic (originally written in 1934) still ranks as the work which influenced succeeding generations and their analyses of media and culture. Excellent bibliographic material for additional study.

Olson, David R., ed. *Media and Symbols.* University of Chicago Press, 1974.

A collection of essays prepared under the auspices of the National Society for the Study of Education. Such noted researchers as Jerome Bruner, Rudolf Arnheim, George Gerbner, and others present their current ideas on the possible and probable impact that media have on both students and the structure of educational institutions. Particularly relevant for administrators, curriculum planners, and media specialists.

Pirsig, Robert M. *Zen and the Art of Motorcycle Maintenance.* Bantam, 1976, pa.

May be fact, may be fiction, in any case, an engrossing, if sometimes rambling, account of one man's confrontation with self, family, friends, technology, and his quest for sanity and a sense of quality in contemporary society.

Postman, Neil. *Crazy Talk, Stupid Talk.* Dial/Delacorte, 1976.

This latest work by a recognized leader in educational reform analyzes our use and misuse of language and how we often fail to communicate. While not specifically written for teachers, this book contains valuable insight into the environments created and perpetuated by the mass media, and it offers sound advice on what we can do to avoid communication dilemmas.

Creativity and Visual Thinking

Arnheim, Rudolf. *Art & Visual Perception: A Psychology of the Creative Eye.* University of California Press, 1954; 1967 pa; The New Version, 1974.

Arnheim, Rudolf. *Film as Art.* University of California Press, 1957; 1967 pa.

Arnheim, Rudolf. *Toward a Psychology of Art.* University of California Press, 1966.

Arnheim, Rudolf. *Visual Thinking.* University of California Press, 1969.

Arnheim, the major authority in visual language and visual thinking, contends that verbal bias hinders creative thought. His works are vivid arguments for integrated arts in education, and essential reading for understanding the relationships between Gestalt psychology and art.

deBono, Edward. *Lateral Thinking: Creativity Step by Step.* Harper, 1970.

This is a resource that presents a philosophy and a system for creative problem solving. The author's brain twisters have direct application in the process of design regardless of the medium in which one works. A bit long-winded, he nonetheless presents an excellent understanding of creative thinking and how it differs from our normally used processes.

Fabun, Don. *You and Creativity.* Glencoe Press, 1968.
A good introduction to creativity. Well laid-out and enjoyable reading.

McKim, Robert. *Experiences in Visual Thinking.* Cole/Brooks Publishing, 1972.
One of the most exciting books ever done on visual communication. Full of exercises and resources.

Sontag, Susan. *On Photography.* Farrar, 1977.
The elegantly written essays in this brief but brilliant book represent a major investigation of the American consumer society's increasing dependence upon images. Sontag examines photography in the mundane context of the family snapshot as well as in its more esoteric context, the latest art craze. These essays first appeared in a somewhat different form in the *New York Review of Books.* An appendix of quotations from such divergent thinkers as Thoreau, Moholy-Nagy, and Agatha Christie concludes this provocative and stimulating study of the social, political, and aesthetic implications of photography in our time.

Brakhage, Stan. *The Brakhage Lectures.* Goodlion, 1972, pa.

Brakhage, Stan. *A Moving Picture Giving & Taking Book.* Frontier Press, 1971, pa.
Brakhage is an innovative, influential film artist who has radicalized and personalized the art of vision for filmmakers and film viewers. His essays, lectures and films confirm his belief that "there is a pursuit of knowledge foreign to language and founded upon visual communication, demanding a development of the optical mind, and dependent upon perception in the original and deepest sense of the world."

Educational Theory and Practice

Leonard, George B. *Education & Ecstasy.* Delacorte, 1968; Dell, 1968, pa.
Highly acclaimed when first published and still valid for its vision of the future of education—a future in which the joy and unity of learning and living are exalted. Leonard offers practical suggestions on how schools can make this vision a reality today. Based on the work of innovative schools, brain research laboratories, and experimental communities, this is a sensitive and thought provoking work.

Liepmann, Lise. *Your Child's Sensory World.* Dial, 1973; Penguin, 1974, pa.
An excellent synthesis of various principles of nonverbal communication and sensory awareness written for parents, teachers, and anyone interested in child development. Valuable insights from such fields as psychology, anthropology, physiology, and general educational theory are presented in a highly readable format. Includes some excellent recommendations for fully developing sensory awareness of young children.

Lopate, Philip. *Being With Children.* Bantam, 1976, pa.
An affectionate, well-written account of a working poet-novelist's experiences as a writer and later as media-maker-in-residence in a New York public school. Lopate's approach to teaching and learning may be considered by some to be outlandish at times, yet his observations and perceptions into the educational process are often brilliant. The book is also an excellent resource for those setting up their own film and video programs in elementary schools, providing numerous successful activities and citing some failures as well.

Piaget, Jean. *The Language and Thought of the Child.* 3rd ed. Atlantic Highlands, N.J.: Humanities Press, 1962; New American Library, 1965, pa.
This now classic study of how children develop intellectually should be required reading for anyone working with young people. Ranks along with such thinkers as John Dewey, Jerome Bruner, A. S. Neill, and Robert Hutchins as a major influence on contemporary theories of child development.

Quinn, Thomas, and Hanks, Cheryl, eds. *Coming to Our Senses: The Significance of the Arts for American Education.* McGraw-Hill, 1977, cloth & pa.
The most comprehensive study ever published on the role of the arts in general education, this is a report by a panel of eminent citizens chaired by David Rockefeller, Jr. The purpose of the study, undertaken for the American Council for the Arts in Education, was to assess the state of all the arts in a variety of educational environments. The report calls for a dramatic reordering of our national priorities, and lists 97 recommendations, designed to give the arts educational parity with traditional disciplines in math and science. Valuable also for its historical perspective and its extensive bibliography of selected materials, list of research reports prepared for the project, notes, and list of resource persons.

Read, Herbert. *Education through Art.* Pantheon, 1958; 1974, pa.
Read's belief that art should be the basis of education has become a manifesto for educational reforms. In his pioneering work, Read discusses the purpose of education, the psychology of perception and imagination, and children's art. The text is illustrated with many reproductions of children's art.

Simon, Sidney et al. *Values Clarification: A Handbook of Practical Strategies for Teachers & Students.* Hart, 1972.
Contains 79 evaluated strategies for examining, developing, and prizing one's own values, ideals, and goals.

PHOTOGRAPHY

Adams, Ansel. *Camera and Lens*. Morgan & Morgan, 1971.

Adams, Ansel. *The Negative*. Morgan & Morgan, 1968.

Adams, Ansel. *The Print*. Morgan & Morgan, 1968.

These classics are just three of the many excellent books by Adams on phototechnique. They are a must for anyone with slightly more than passing interest in the medium.

Berner, Jeff. *The Photographic Experience*. Doubleday-/Anchor, 1975, pa.

Berner approaches visual education historically, technically, and personally. His explorations lead to "stopping the world" and turn "looking" into "seeing" through the art of visual meditation, with and without the lens.

Braundet, Pierre. *Photograms*. Watson-Guptill, 1974.

This book describes making photographs without a camera, from simple processes like contact prints to more complex techniques like halftones and polarization. Full of illustrations and diagrams.

Cooke, Robert W. *Designing with Light on Paper and Film*. Davis, 1969.

A very complete "how-to" description. Gives all sorts of useful information about papers, films, chemicals, light sources, and objects which could be used to make photograms. The appendix, glossary, and bibliography make the book particularly useful.

Davis, Phil. *Photography*. Wm. C. Brown, 1972.

A simple yet very complete introductory photo book. It covers all aspects of the medium, ranging from technical processes to historical trends, and it supplements its in-depth explanations with concise margin summaries. These serve to focus on key points of information and are easily adaptable to most photographic curricula.

Eastman Kodak Company. *Classroom Projects Using Photography. Part I: For the Elementary School Level; Part II: For the Secondary School Level*. Amphoto, 1975, pa.

Kodak generates a constant flow of practical publications ranging from leaflets to books, from the basic to the highly sophisticated, and available in many bookstores and camera stores, and direct (343 State St., Rochester, N.Y., 14650). These two volumes are issued from Kodak's long line of Visual Literacy programs. Each contains projects representing typical classroom activities enhanced by photography.

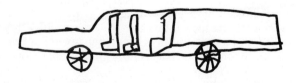

Eastman Kodak Company. *The Here's How Book of Photography*. Eastman Kodak, 1977.

In 39 profusely illustrated articles, color photographs are explained with easy-to-follow directions. Included are such techniques as how to achieve good results from color film under difficult conditions, how to take still life pictures, building a blind for nature photography, taking pictures under water, photographing a night sky, how to photograph children naturally, producing a slide program, and more.

Eastman Kodak Company. *How to Make and Use a Cartridge Pinhole Camera*. Eastman Kodak, n.d.

This two-page, illustrated handout is an almost foolproof guide. Its instructions are easy to follow, and its suggested materials cost next to nothing. Because of the exact measurements and precise cutting required, however, it is suggested that the cardboard pieces be precut for younger children so they can assemble the camera with good results.

Elam, Jane A. Photography: *Simple and Creative*. Van Nostrand Reinhold, 1975, pa.

This book contains experimental work that even beginners can do, though most of it requires a darkroom. Taking photography beyond the snapshot stage, it covers pictures made with and without a camera.

Feininger, Andreas. *Light and Lighting*. Amphoto, 1976.

An excellent reference book on lighting, by a former staff photographer for *Life* magazine. All methods of the craft of lighting are explored and analyzed—proper use of light meters, spot meters, exposures, controlling effects of early morning or late evening light, how to use infra-red light, and much more.

Frye, R. A. *Photographic Tools for Teachers*. Mapleville, R. I.: Roadrunner Press, 1976.

No single book could possibly cover all aspects of classroom photography, but this valuable resource provides a great deal of information for teachers, librarians, and school media specialists. A manual and reference book, it contains a large number of drawings and photographs which provide some historical background, some knowledge of camera types and formats, and some basic information about lenses, exposures, and composition.

Holland, Vicki. *How to Photograph Your World*. Scribner's, 1974.

One of the few photography books intended for students as well as teachers. Easy reading, filled with photographs —a book that can be used as a student text in grades 2–6.

Jacobs, Mark and Kokrda, Ken. *Photography in Focus: A Basic Text*. Skokie, Ill.: National Textbook Co., 1977.

This book and its companion volume, *Curriculum Guide for Photographers*, meant for teachers, develop a complete and practical photography course for high schools.

Lampsan, Nancy, Levinson, Ralph and Feller, Alan. *Photography in the Classroom*. Chicago, Ill., Rohner Printing, 1975.

This step-by-step, "how we did it" manual introduces photography for a school situation with limited funds and space. Its emphasis is on photography as a tool for increased self-awareness and creativity, but its methods and general message can be incorporated into photo programs of all intents. This workbook will strike many familiar chords for it realistically includes the inevitable frustrations along with the potential for accomplishment and delight.

The Leica Manual: The Complete Book of 35mm Photography. Morgan & Morgan, 1977.

Not only for Leica owners, but an encyclopedic reference volume for amateurs and professionals alike. With 36 articles by experts, hundreds of illustrations, and excellent fine photographs, the reader gets tremendous help on how to achieve the best quality from small negatives —how to take pictures in total darkness, how to master all light conditions, how to eliminate unwanted backgrounds, how to do closeup and copywork, photo-journalism, color printing, telephotography, and much much more.

Lyons, Nathan, ed. *Photographers on Photography.* Prentice-Hall, 1966.

An anthology which includes points of view from the turn of the century to the (almost) present. Some of the photographers represented are Ansel Adams, Henri Cartier-Bresson, Dorothea Lange, Aaron Siskind, Edward Weston, and Minor White. Very interesting and certainly one of its kind.

Meiselas, Susan, ed. *Learn to See: A Sourcebook of 101 Photography Projects by Teachers and Students.* Polaroid, 1974, pa.

This is a resource book containing annotated illustrations of 101 classroom-tested projects with Polaroids. Included are excerpts from five points of view of teaching attitudes or strategies and an appendix complete with technical information, reproduction and mounting techniques, and simple book-binding directions. A bibliography rounds out the work, with references on Polaroid, general background, photography for kids, and photographic books for kids. If you can't find this book at your local Polaroid dealer's, write directly to the company (549 Technology Sq., Cambridge, Mass. 02139).

Newhall, Beaumont. *The History of Photography: 1839 to the Present Day.* Museum of Modern Art, 1964, cloth and pa.

A fine treatment of photography's history in a beautifully illustrated book. A useful reference as well as a delightful book to own.

Nibbelink, Don. *Picturing People.* Amphoto, 1975.

A special reference book, but invaluable if you really want to get into this specialty—how to take pictures of every kind of situation involving people. Besides explaining these aspects, the author explains various kinds of light (including painting with light), and also discusses such things as lenses and diffusers, special attachments for special effects, choosing film, and shooting techniques.

Nibbelink, Don, and Anderson, Rex. *Bigger and Better Enlarging.* Amphoto, 1974.

Another specialized reference book for your technical collection, for both color and black-and-white photography. The step-by-step directions cover simple and advanced skills—cropping, sandwiching negatives for special effects, correcting perspective in the enlarger, using texture screens, etc.

O'Brien, James F. *Design by Accident.* Dover, 1968.

Here are lots of ways to create designs and patterns by "accidental effects." They are fun to do and many can be applied to the slidemaking activities described in the photography section of this book.

Picker, Fred. *The Fine Print.* Amphoto, 1975.

A reference tool for the advanced student who wants to get into fine print-making, this beautiful book provides the author's own 70 black-and-white photographs, one to a page, with facing page detailing how the scene was metered, the kind of film used, kind of enlarging paper used, etc., all demonstrating the practicality and usefulness of his system.

Scholastic's Concerned Photographers Program. *Images of Man.* Scholastic.

A series of two sets, which can be ordered in either sound filmstrip form or 35mm slide/tape form, and which include reproductions of some of the greatest photographs ever taken. The series is an excellent supplement to the study of photography, as well as a moving documentation of universal human values and concern.

Shull, Jim. *The Hole Thing: A Manual of Pinhole Fotography.* Morgan & Morgan, 1974.

An incredibly complete and charming source for pinhole camera making—and then some. This quick, inexpensive experience with picture making carries an element of mystique inherent in its simplicity. The author takes the basics a step farther and embellishes the 1-2-3 approach with advanced activities for those who wish to make the pinhole adventure an art in itself.

Snyder, Norman. *The Photography Catalog.* Harper, 1976, pa.

Here are 256 pages packed with lots of know-how and illustrations. Includes such hard-to-find information as descriptions of specialized accessories; printing on wood, cloth and metal (standard printing methods, too); making color prints from black-and-white negatives; antique camera collecting; careers and schools on photography; and oh, so much more. A delightful potpourri of photography miscellany.

Suid, Murray. *Painting with the Sun: A First Book of Photography.* Boston, Mass. (60 Commercial Wharf): CSCS, Inc., 1970, pa.

This small workbook (52 pages), which comes with a teacher's manual (25 pages), is useful as a source of ideas for starting a course in photography at the elementary level. It gives kids pages to paste things in and provides a brief glossary of terms at the end. The teacher's manual goes a little deeper into each of the activities recommended and points up ways of further involving the student in the different aspects of the photographic medium.

Szarkowski, John. *Looking at Photographs.* Museum of Modern Art, 1973.

An anthology of 100 photographs from the collection of the Museum of Modern Art. It offers rich images which span the history of this young medium. Each photo is presented with an essay that concisely points up the photograph's specialness and its maker's personal approach. Within this format, the author also shows how the study of photography closely relates to the broader worlds of art and sociology.

Time-Life Books Editors. *Life Library of Photography.* Time-Life Books, 1970–

A superbly illustrated and well written 17-volume series of technical books. These are a luxury for many schools with limited budgets, but if you can get your library to buy the books they will be used often for their technical information and incredible images. Volumes can be purchased separately ($9.95 each), so if you can only buy a few, you might start with the following two:

Caring for Photographs: Display, Storage, & Restoration (1972) is devoted to archival processing, restoring damaged photos, taking the curl out of a print and checking other damages to paper, framing for exhibitions, and more.

Frontiers of Photography (1972) offers a fascinating view of current experimental developments in photography and future applications, such as holograms, nuclear optics, and computer linkage to photographic processes.

Vestal, David. *The Craft of Photography.* Harper, 1974.

The author covers all aspects of photography in one of the best basic books on the subject available. Drawing on his own 25 years of experience as photographer and instructor, he provides many examples to show why prints turn muddy, or the lighting doesn't work, or exposures go wrong. With tips and illustrations of both good and bad results, the reader gets lots of help for correcting or improving his or her own work.

Workshop for Learning Things. *Camera Cookbook.* The Workshop, n.d., pa.

The Workshop for Learning (see listing in "Organizations" section) is a wonderfully helpful and creative source of books, materials and supplies for elementary and middle schools. This, and the following two titles, relate specifically to photography. It is an inexpensive "how-to" book, with all the instructions, formulas, and basic information you need to go, from the simple plastic camera to finished pictures.

Workshop for Learning Things. *It's So Simple, Click and Print.* The Workshop, n.d., pa.

A students' guide to classroom photography, written from the point of view of sixth graders. Filled with drawings and photographs, it's a real help for getting started.

Workshop for Learning Things. *"Most of the Pictures Came Out Real Well."* The Workshop, n.d., pa.

Pictures and stories by kids in grades 5, 6, 7, and 8. Most of the pictures really did turn out well! This inexpensive booklet is an excellent example of how photography spurs language development.

Zakia, Richard D. *Perception and Photography.* Prentice-Hall, 1974.

Although addressed to photographers and graphic designers, this book will be valued by anyone seriously concerned with the making of visual messages and environments. It is filled with easy-to-follow illustrated

examples of how psychological principles, based on Gestalt laws, can be used in all visual communication.

Zakia, Richard D., and Hollis, N. Todd. *101 Experiments in Photography.* Morgan & Morgan, 1969.

The title says it all—with suggestions and explanations ranging from "Make Your Own Filters" to "Photographs Without Cameras."

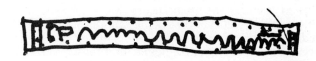

FILM

Amelio, Ralph J. *Film in the Classroom: Why Use It—How to Use It.* Pflaum/Standard (now CEBCO/), 1971, pa.

The author outlines a complete film screening program, tried and found true at the high school level. Incorporated into the program are readings relevant to the wide variety of film genres treated. A helpful book for setting up a film study course.

Amelio, Ralph J. *Hal in the Classroom: Science Fiction Film.* Pflaum/Standard (now CEBCO/), 1974, pa.

This book is intended as a resource tool primarily for teachers in the following areas: future studies, science fiction, film, literature, and English. The films and books referred to (whether called science fiction, fantasy, fantastic or speculative) deal with man and his humanistic concerns, especially with regard to the future.

Amelio, Ralph J. *The Filmic Moment: Teaching American Genre Film through Extracts.* Pflaum/Standard (now CEBCO/), 1975, pa.

A rationale for film study in general and the use of extracts from feature films in particular. Most of the book presents ideas and techniques for the study of various film genres, such as The Western, Science Fiction, etc. Each chapter concludes with a valuable bibliography. A list of film distributors is appended.

Andersen, Yvonne. *Make Your Own Animated Movies.* Little, Brown, 1970, pa.

A "how-to" book for children. With large print and simple illustrations, this is an easy book for kids to read and master. Included are all the little hints that help children avoid frustrations in undertaking the complicated processes of making movies.

Andersen, Yvonne. *Teaching Film Animation to Children.* Van Nostrand Reinhold, 1971.

Here is a very sound sense for working with children and young people in an animation workshop, based on the author's own experiences at the Yellow Ball Workshop, where she is Director and teaches film animation to kids and runs workshops for teachers. The book is very complete and invaluable for anyone wanting to start a workshop. In most cases the equipment must be translated down from 16mm to Super 8. A 13-minute documentary film, *Let's Make a Film,* which shows how animated films are made at the Workshop, can also be purchased or rented from the Yellow Ball Workshop, 62 Tarbell Ave., Lexington, Mass. 02173.

Barton, C. H. *How to Animate Cut-outs.* Amphoto, 1965.
Originally published in England in the 1950s, this book contains some still sound advice and ideas on this technique, aimed at the amateur filmmaker.

Blair, Preston. *Animation: Learn How to Draw Animated Cartoons.* Walter Foster Art Series, Number 26.
Blair is one of the great Disney, MGM animators, and this book is directed to that Disney approach, which is not really practical for amateurs. The walking charts, however, make this book invaluable, and most professional animators do use it. For the serious student who wants to understand animation better.

Burder, John. *The Technique of Editing 16mm Films.* Hastings House, 1968.
A specialized book for those who want more help in the mechanics of film editing.

Byrne-Daniel, J. *Grafilm: An Approach to a New Medium.* Van Nostrand Reinhold, 1970, pa.
A spiffy little book (96 pages) about the combination of graphic and illustrative techniques on film stock. Contents: making a film on paper; making a film without a camera; making a film with one piece of artwork; making a film with pieces of artwork; and making things move.

Cauntier, Julien. *How to Do Tricks in Amateur Films.* Focal Press, 1964.
A brief book with basic information on optical and speed tricks, and an excellent section on stop-action. For both 8mm and 16mm filmmaking.

Eastman Kodak Company. *Movies with a Purpose; A Teacher's Guide to Planning and Producing Super 8 Movies for Classroom Use.* Eastman Kodak, n.d., pa.
Introduces the single concept film as a tool for instruction and one that teachers of any subject can produce and use. Covers all stages of production and makes clear the basic language of filmmaking. This booklet, as numerous other similarly helpful Kodak publications designed for educators, is available from the Motion Picture and Education Markets Division, 343 State St., Rochester, N.Y. 14650. Write for the catalog of complete listings.

Englander, David A. and Gaskill, Arthur L. *How to Shoot a Movie Story: The Technique of Pictorial Continuity.* Morgan & Morgan, 1969, pa.
This little book (135 pages) is by two old-timers and is filled with corny examples. BUT it does present clearly and simply "The Rules" for achieving continuity in filmmaking. The techniques described apply equally to features, documentaries, commercials, or home movies and are essential to achieving professional looking results. You've got to know the rules before you can break them.

Finch, Christopher. *The Art of Walt Disney; from Mickey Mouse to the Magic Kingdom.* With a special essay by Peter Blake. Abrams, 1973. New American Library, 1975 pa.
Certainly the best book on Disney, and in the cloth edition a beautiful example of book art. Lavishly illustrated and well executed, it traces the career of the cartoonist while exploring the diverse artistic and cinematographic techniques he (i.e., Walt Disney Productions) used to make his animated and live action films. Includes a bibliography. The cloth edition is perhaps too expensive for most people, but the trade paperback seems adequate for school use.

Gessner, Robert. *The Moving Image.* Dutton, 1968, cloth and pa.
This work is unique among film books—a pioneer exploration of what is fundamental to the cinema as a storytelling art form. Gessner has created a complete introduction to cinema, distilling his 35 years of experience as teacher, critic, and screen writer into a basic and brilliantly illuminating approach.

Hoos, Gunther and Mikolas, Mark. *Handbook of Super 8 Production.* United Business Publications, 1976, pa.
A standard reference book for one who wants to know what Super 8 can do and how to do it. From budgeting to evaluating equipment systems to mixing a sound track, the authors share their experiences and discoveries as pioneers in the use of Super 8 as a professional medium. In addition to many diagrams and photographs, scattered throughout the book are essays by other Super 8 filmmakers, who offer their insights and present their views on the future of the medium.

Howard, Margaret, ed. *Movies: The Magic of Film.* Scholastic, 1974, pa.
One of a series of thematic units in Scholastic's Contact Program, this unit creatively helps students question why they go to movies, how movies are made, what "Hollywood" is, how a book is made into a film script, and how the rating system works. It was created mainly for junior and senior high school students who read at a fourth–sixth grade level and are poorly motivated by conventional classroom texts and teaching techniques. It can be effective with all kinds of students if teachers would make use of the wide range of activities suggested in the Teaching Guide. (The text, Teaching Guide and Student Logbook are available separately, or a package of materials for an entire class for $99.50).

Johnson, Ron and Bone, Jan. *Understanding the Film.* Amphoto, 1976, pa.
Useful as a junior high school text for film study, this work comprehensively covers filmmaking, including history, technique, criticism, famous films, and film personalities. A special chapter is devoted to a unique case study that takes a scene from *The Sting* from script writing through editing to finished film. The book is lavishly illustrated with film stills and publicity shots. It could be most valuable with "reluctant" learners.

Kuhns, William and Giardino, Thomas. *Behind the Camera.* Pflaum/Standard (now CEBCO/), 1970, pa.
A clear presentation of how cameras work, what kinds of film and camera are best for what application, how to handle light, sound, script writing, acting, editing, titling. In addition, it includes a diary of what went into the making of the student film *Sparrow,* a ten-minute 16mm film also available from the publisher.

Kuhns, William and Stanley, Robert. *Exploring the Film.* Pflaum/Standard (now CEBCO/), 1968, pa.

Regarded as the best introductory text for film study at the secondary school level, this is interesting reading and has terrific graphics and stills too. The emphasis is on the need for seeing and knowing good films. Also available is a companion manual for teachers, *Teaching Program.*

Kuhns, William; assisted by Raymond Groetsch and Joe McJimsey. *The Moving Picture Book.* Pflaum/Standard (now CEBCO/), 1975, pa.

Intended as an introductory text for the high school and early college student, this volume uses films as the central resource of film study. It is designed and written in a way that the films communicate something of themselves directly from the printed page (although the printing and paper do not really meet the standards of author and designer). Taking off from *Citizen Kane* it then covers history and production, filmmaking techniques and vocabulary, editing, sound, animation, criticism, film notes. In all, more thorough and exhaustive than Kuhn's earlier text, it is considered by some the definitive high school film study text.

Kuhns, William. *Themes Two: One Hundred Short Films for Discussion.* Pflaum/Standard (now CEBCO/), 1974.

This loose leaf binder full of film synopses and discussion guidelines is an updated version of the author's 1969 *Short Films for Discussion.* Valuable as an aid in deciding what to screen as well as how to approach the analysis of each film.

Lacey, Richard. *Seeing with Feeling.* W. B. Saunders, 1972, pa.

A practical guide to classroom discussion. Lacey stresses the importance of feeling while seeing, and of open-ended rather than prestructured discussion of films. The book deals mainly with junior high and older classes, but the author has worked extensively with elementary level children and suggests that the principles can be applied successfully with any age group.

Larson, Roger, Jr. *Young Filmmakers.* Dutton, 1971, pa.

Describes some of the films teenagers are making, and suggests what is needed to make 8mm and 16mm films.

Laybourne, Kit. *The Animation Book.* Crown, 1978.

Designed for those who want to use animated filmmaking for personal expression, this will be a valuable tool for animation teachers. Fifteen different techniques are explored and explained, with emphasis on "low technology" and limited budget approaches in both Super 8 and 16mm formats. Also included are contextual analysis through frame enlargements of a variety of recent films, a series of exercises (many of which can be executed within the book itself), a comprehensive catalog of animation tools with cost information, guidance in undertaking a major project, and a thorough resource guide.

Lidstone, John and McIntosh, Don. *Children as Film Makers.* Van Nostrand Reinhold, 1970.

An excellent organizational guide for setting up cinematic shop in lower schools. Included are many useful hints on every aspect of film production, and detailed descriptions of the production of an animated film by a six-year-old and a live-action film by an entire sixth grade.

Lipton, Lenny. *Independent Filmmaking.* Rev. ed. Straight Arrow Books, 1975, pa.

Here is a work to bridge the gap between simplistic how-to-shoot books and highly technical if-you-know-all-about-shooting books. It presents an overview of Super 8 and 16mm filmmaking through all phases of production. Highly readable, it is useful as a reference book for technical information, for diagrams which enlighten rather than confuse, and for problem-solving ideas on a creative level.

Lipton, Lenny. *The Super 8 Book.* Straight Arrow Books, 1975, pa.

Not to be compared to the definitive handbook and reference above, this is nonetheless a highly readable book on the subject, valuable for demystifying the complexities of the process of filmmaking and for the enthusiasm of the author.

Lowndes, Douglas. *Filmmaking in Schools.* Watson-Guptill, 1968.

Lavish in illustrations though thin in text, this has marginal value, but it has excellent ideas for exercises in various aspects of filmmaking.

MacCann, Richard D. *Film: A Montage of Theories.* Dutton, 1970, pa.

An anthology with a rather extensive selection of writings. Some selections are good, some are not presented very clearly (these are excerpts from longer works), some are repetitive, some are merely inconsequential. But the book gives a good overview of what's gone on in film study and so offers a base for further reading.

Madsen, Roy P. *Animated Film: Concepts, Methods, Uses* (Interland Book Ser.). Pitman, 1969.

Animation is introduced at the level of the novice, leading the reader progressively from the simplest concepts to the most sophisticated. The text is illustrated with helpful charts, diagrams, and artwork. Historical background of the genre is also covered.

Manchell, Frank. *Movies and How They Are Made.* Prentice-Hall, 1968.

One of the few halfway decent, without-a-doubt-for-kids books around. It deals with the movie industry and division of labor therein—producer, director, actor, etc.—and illustrates specific points. It's somewhat dull, but short, clear, and readable for grades 3–7.

Manchell, Frank. *When Pictures Began to Move.* Prentice Hall, 1969.

Again, a book for kids. A good history of silent cinema, it deals with not only the usual data on American films of that early time but also foreign movements, and it discusses cinema prehistory and the ways films were first shown. Clearly written and well illustrated, it is interesting enough for the teacher too.

Maynard, Richard. *Classroom Cinema.* Teachers' College, Columbia University, 1977, pa.

This sequel to Maynard's *Celluloid Curriculum: How to Use Movies in the Classroom* (Hayden, 1971) is a combination of a teaching memoir and a guide on film use within standard curricula in English, social studies, values education, and communications.

Maynard, Richard, ed. *Film Attitudes and Issues Series.* Hayden, 1971 ff., pa.

Titles include: *Africa on Film: Myth and Reality; Black Men on Film: Racial Stereotyping; The American West on Film: Myth and Reality; Propaganda on Film: A Nation at War.* The four volumes are sourcebooks of readings on issues of American social history and include sociological essays, contemporary reviews, promotions and advertisements, excerpts from screenplays. For grades 9–12.

Maynard, Richard, ed. *Literature of the Screen Series.* Scholastic, 1974, pa.

This series of four volumes of thematically linked screenplays is also for grades 9–12. *Identity* contains "That's Me," "Loneliness of a Long Distance Runner," "Cool Hand Luke," and "Up the Down Staircase;" *Power* contains "Mr. Smith Goes to Washington," "Face in the Crowd," "The Candidate;" *Men and Women* includes "Splendor in the Grass," "Family Way," and "Nothing But a Man;" and *Values in Conflict* holds "High Noon," "Hustle," and "Savage Innocents."

Monaco, James. *How to Read a Film.* Oxford University Press, 1977.

For the serious student of film this work is invaluable for its broad understanding of the medium. Monaco explores the "language" of film, its syntax, structure, rhetorical devices, and its "vocabulary," demonstrating how a film is carefully tailored to work on both psychological and physiological levels. Included are a brief history of movies as an art; a list .of current equipment and filmstocks; examination of such schools of cinematic art as Realism, Neorealism, Expressionism, and New Wave; the implications of television on motion pictures; and an excellent, thorough glossary of film and media terms. This could be a useful volume for a visual literacy program.

Morrow, James, and Suid, Murray. *Moviemaking Illustrated.* Hayden, 1973.

Available in both a text and a paper edition, this unique book is especially useful if your film rental budget is limited. It demonstrates the basic concepts of filmmaking by exploring the similarity between comic strips and film. Selected panels from comics are used to illustrate techniques of shotmaking, cutting, ground control, direction, and scripting. Also useful is a chapter of exercises to help analyze film techniques by studying visuals on television or in feature films.

Pincus, Edward. *Guide to Filmmaking.* New American Library/Signet, 1969, pa.

A classic in its own right, and inexpensive too. The emphasis is technical and coverage is complete for 16mm filmmaking, with frequent comparisons made to 8 mm. If you can afford only one book on filmmaking, this is the one to get.

Privett, B., and Halas, J. *Cartooning for Amateur Films.* Focal Press, o.p.

Another British import with sound ideas for the amateur animator.

Reisz, Karel, comp. *The Technique of Film Editing.* Hastings House, 1967, pa.

Considered by many *the* classic treatment of film editing, this is an excellent work for the film technique collection.

Rynew, Arden. *Filmmaking for Children.* Rev. ed. CEBCO/ Standard, 1975, pa.

This fiarly unimaginative text details how to set up a school film studio for making live action films—with little or no mention of the great outdoors! Nonetheless, it is a carefully executed and useful book on basic studio techniques. (A teacher's edition and a student handbook are also available from the publisher.)

Smallman, Kirk. *Creative Film Making.* Macmillan, 1969. Bantam, 1972, pa.

Readable and concise, this book establishes a knowledgeable foundation for the serious student filmmaker. Its sound treatment of techniques and its provocative examples make this a must-have book for advanced students. Where it has been used as a basic text in high school cinematography courses it was enthusiastically endorsed by students.

Sohn, David A. *Film: The Creative Eye.* CEBCO/Standard, 1970, pa.

Useful on many levels, this book is especially helpful for setting up a film screening program. Seventeen films are discussed from the point of view of learning to observe accurately and to interpret imaginatively what is seen.

Starr, Cecile. *Discovering the Movies: An Illustrated Introduction to the Motion Pictures.* Van Nostrand Reinhold, 1972.

A unique and fascinating history of movies is presented, not as a backward glance from today's vantage point, but as an evolution of artistic achievements. This primer is richly illustrated with sequences of film stills, and it can be read and enjoyed by students in junior high and up.

Stephenson, Ralph and Debrix, J. R. *The Cinema as Art.* Penguin, 1965, pa.

A very thoughtful treatment of the properties of movies and their artistic potential (and realization, in specific cases). Through a discussion of the various techniques and their implications, the book deals primarily with the different possibilities of space and time in cinema. A fine book for beginners, grades 9 and up.

Talbot, Daniel. *Film: An Anthology.* 2nd ed. University of California Press, 1966, pa.

A more complete anthology than MacCann's, but with fewer and more selective contributions. As the subtitle aptly puts it: "a diverse collection of outstanding writing on film."

Trojanski, John and Rockwood, Louis. *Making It Move.* Pflaum/Standard (now CEBCO/), 1973, pa. Teacher manual; and 16mm film (4 mins.)

This package of teaching materials has some good and some not so good aspects, altogether representing one way to teach animation to elementary students. The film illustrates each of the animation techniques considered in the student handbook: puppet-doll animation, cel animation, kinestatis, pixillation, cut-out animation. The handbook has the added fun of a flip book, and it also contains information on cameras, light meters, film, lighting equipment, tripods, projectors. The teacher's manual offers a helpful bibliography of print and film resources.

Wentz, Bud. *Paper Movie Machines.* San Francisco, Cal.: Troubador Press, 1975., pa.

This is a workbook for making simply outrageous movie machines. It presents a step-by-step, do-it-yourself format requiring easily found materials. As an interesting introduction to early film history, it explains contraptions such as zoetropes and phenakistoscopes, which led to present day animated films.

Films on Filmmaking

Bank Street College of Education. *Child's Eye View.* New York, N.Y. 10001: Bank Street Film Library.

This 16mm color film will not show you how to make films but it demonstrates how the camera and filmmaking are effective tools for learning. The film documents a project of the College of Education Early Childhood Center's After-School Program wherein children, ranging in ages 5–11, each given a Super 8 camera and packs of cartridge film, made films of anything that interested them. The camera proved to be a means to positive self-perception as well as a way to observe and clarify their world. The film is also useful in giving its viewers a better perception of childhood.

Disney, Walt. *Behind the Scenes at the Walt Disney Studio.* Walt Disney Studio, 1940. Distributed (rental only) by Walt Disney Educational Media Co. (16mm 25 min. color and b/w)

This is an excerpt of most of the Robert Benchly studio tour that originally appeared in Disney's capital-raising 1941 feature release *The Reluctant Dragon.* As entertaining as it is instructive, it brings not only a great deal of information about the Disney techniques in animation but also glimpses of some of today's top animators, designers, and directors when they were young Disney art students. Not least of all it offers students an experience with an American original, the humorist's "ordinary man" caricature. Besides its historical value and behind-the-scenes and instructional footage, this film is also valuable as a career-insight film.

McLaren, Norman. *An Interview with Norman McLaren.* International Film Bureau. (16mm 30 min. b/w)

Canadian film artist McLaren, who invented scratch-and-doodle movies, is interviewed by noted movie critic Clyde Gilmour. They discuss and demonstrate the various experimental animation techniques with which McLaren worked during his long, productive career with the National Film Board of Canada. Excerpts from selected McLaren films illustrate his methods and animation techniques.

McLaren, Norman. *Pen Point Percussion.* International Film Bureau. (16mm 8 min. 41 sec. color)

In this film McLaren explains how he makes synthetic sound on film. With an oscilloscope he first demonstrates what familiar sounds look like on the screen; next, how sound shapes up on a film's soundtrack; and then what synthetic sounds sound like when drawn directly on film. This technique is then seen in the film *Loops,* an experimental film in which both sound and visuals were created entirely by the artist drawing directly on the film with ordinary pen and ink. *Loops* (2 min. 43 sec. color) is available from the National Film Board of Canada (see distributors listing), which also has available a descriptive catalog of McLaren's short, color films. A few of the titles which you might want to consider first are: *Begone Dull Care:* painting directly on film, Evelyn Lambart and McLaren create a gay visual expression of jazz music; *Boogie-Doodle:* animation made without using a camera —a brightly colored film experiment in which "boogie" is played by Albert Ammons and "doodle" is drawn by McLaren; *Dots:* an experimental film, in which both sound and visuals were created by drawing directly on film with ordinary pen and ink; *Hoppity Pop:* animation in which the colored visuals are drawn directly on film with pen and ink, and the simple forms dance about the screen to the discordant strains of an old-time circus calliope; *Lines Horizontal:* in a highly recommended example of simple abstract forms, the horizontal lines, drawn on film and moving to Peter Seeger music against a background of beautiful, changing colors, are transformed into an exciting visual experience; *Lines Vertical:* a companion color film, made of vertical lines moving to electronic piano music; *Lines—Vertical and Horizontal,* a 13-minute version of both these films; *Serenal:* McLaren's gay fantasia of patterned sound, made by painting the spirit of fiesta on 16mm film to the lively beat of an island tune of Trinidad's Grand Curcucaya Orchestra; and *Stars and Stripes,* in which the artist experiments by drawing directly on film so that the stars and stripes perform acrobatics to a sprightly march tune.

MOVE, by Vilma Berarducci. (For rental, address inquiries to the author at: 430 M Street, S.W., #303, Washington, D.C. 20034)

This is a 16mm 15 min. color film that documents the experiences of the author and fourth-graders doing Super 8 animated films and flipbooks at the Amidon School in Washington, D.C. The film illustrates the process of making flipbooks and presents some finished films with sound effects added.

UNTITLED. Distributed by Young Directors' Center.

This is a camera-less film made by art students at Newton High School, Newton, Massachusetts. The film is rich in handmaking techniques with materials used with imagination and creativity. It was made for the most part by working directly on clear leader with pens, brushes, stamp markers, opaque and transparent materials. It is recommended that anyone interested in making films should begin with this basic handmaking activity in order to learn directly the meaning of film time and sequences.

The Yellow Ball Cache. The Yellow Ball Workshop. (16mm 18 min. color)

This animated film is a collection of short animated films made by children at the Yellow Ball Workshop using the techniques and programs developed and under the supervision of Yvonne Andersen. Kids aren't as crazy about this film as teachers, but you are urged to view it because it does show what kids can do, and when shown to children it is an effective film for eliciting from them what they think about these films.

Note: To supplement this list, do consider other films on cinematic arts and also those retrospective looks at various periods and artists in film history. For example (and this is only an example, not to select out from all the others), *The Art of Film* series, available from Perspective Films, is a Janus Films series consisting of six 22-minute color films on screenwriting, the camera, performance, music and sound, the edited image, and the director. Preview films before selecting and using to suit your students' needs.

TELEVISION AND VIDEO

Anderson, Chuck. *The Electronic Journalist: An Introduction to Video.* Praeger, 1973.

Based on the author's experiences teaching video to high school students, this book has basic technical information and some video project ideas. It can be used as a handbook by high school students, and it is especially useful to social studies and English teachers interested in the news media.

Anderson, Chuck. *Video Power: Grass Roots Television.* Praeger, 1975.

This book describes uses of video in a variety of communities around the country. It also offers advice on how to prepare your own televised material, how to get it on cable or public television, and how to get community and financial support for your projects.

Barnouw, Eric. *Tube of Plenty: The Evolution of American Television.* Oxford University Press, 1975, pa.

A synthesis and revision of historian Barnouw's classic three-volume *A History of Broadcasting in the United States (A Tower in Babel: To 1933.* 1966; *The Golden Web: 1933 to 1953.* 1968; and *The Image Empire from 1953.*

1970). Excellent resource for both its in-depth research and general historical overview. Helpful specifically for the classroom teacher seeking historical material for curriculum development.

Bensinger, Charles, and Photographic Magazine Editors. *Guide to Videotape Recording.* Petersen, 1973, pa.

This slim paperback contains lots of information for a small price ($2) and can be purchased at newstands. The information is clearly presented and there are numerous helpful diagrams.

Brown, Les. *The New York Times Encyclopedia of Television.* Times Books, 1977.

An A-Z reference book with over 3000 entries covering TV as entertainment (actors, directors, writers, producers) and as an industry (production procedures, spots, ratings, advertising policies and psychology of). Not an essential book, but useful for its handy information.

Brown, Les. *Television: The Business Behind the Box.* Harcourt, 1971; pa., 1973.

A practical, useful and most readable tour through the inner sanctum of network television, written by a *New York Times* reporter-columnist. Provides a comprehensive view of those aspects of commercial television production and management which most of us never get the opportunity to witness first hand. Particularly helpful for those looking for background information and for an understanding of the hard facts of the TV business.

Claro, Joseph, ed. *TV: Behind the Tube.* Scholastic, 1974, pa. Teaching Guide, pa. Student Logbook, pa.

One of a series of thematic units in Scholastic's Contact Program, this package is designed to help students explore television. The four main sections are: How Important is TV in Our Lives?; The TV Business; The Effects of TV; and Making TV Better. The program was created mainly for junior and senior high school students who read at fourth–sixth grade level or who are poorly motivated by conventional classroom texts and teaching techniques. It can be effective with all kinds of students, especially if teachers will make use of the wide range of activities suggested in the teaching guide.

The Electronic Rainbow: An Introduction to Television. Pyramid Films, 1977. 16mm 23 min. color.

Sheldon Renan's comprehensive film about TV and its dimensions, narrated by Leonard Nimoy, traces the history of TV, its physical principles, and the mechanism of broadcasting. It should be helpful for its visual explanation of such systems as cable TV, cassette recording, and microwave. A handbook by David Sohn accompanies the film series The Television Workshop, of which this is part. The other five films in the series might also be useful in courses covering the history, technology and current developments in television: *Televisionland,* by Charles Braverman; *Basic TV Terms: A Video Dictionary,* by Sheldon Renan; *Making of a Live TV Show,* by Charles Braverman; *The Television Newsman,* by Charles Braverman; and *Sixty Second Spot,* by Harvey and Dotty Mandlin.

Friendly, Fred W. *Due to Circumstances Beyond Our Control.* Random House, 1967; Vintage, 1967, pa.

An insider's look at the inside. Analyzes the operations

and problems of television news and public affairs programming at CBS. Useful especially for high school social studies, English and journalism curricula.

Greenfield, Jeff. *Television, the First Fifty Years.* Henry A. Abrams, 1977.
An artbook on television, so visually opulent (with over 500 lavish illustrations) and so informative and gracefully written that it has usefulness far beyond the usual coffee table book. But it is expensive, so you may be wise in looking for it on remainder shelves, or probably later as a reprint trade paperback.

Haratonik, Peter and Laybourne, Kit, eds. *Video & Kids* (Radical Software, Vol. II, No. 6), Gordon and Breach (One Park Ave., New York, N.Y., 10016), 1974, pa.
A nice collection of articles about the creative uses of video by elementary and secondary school students, contributed by a variety of individuals working with video and kids. Arranged in three sections: What Matters Most —a collection of concerns; Things to Do with Kids—a portfolio of video activities; and What's Doing—descriptions of video programs throughout the country.

Harmonay, Maureen, ed. *Promise and Performance: Children With Special Needs.* Newtonville, Mass.: Action for Children's Television, 1977.
This is a guide to the use of TV programming for and about children who have disabilities. It's aim is to illustrate how TV can be used to make presently handicapped children more acceptable to their peers. Included are views of psychologists, social scientists, educators and medical professionals as well as producers, researchers and educational consultants involved in the design or production of TV programs for handicapped children. Topics cover the mentally retarded, deaf and hearing impaired, children in hospitals, child development and parent education, among others.

Harwood, Don. *Everything You Always Wanted to Know about Videotape Recording.* 2nd ed. VTR Publishing Co., 1975, pa.
A good way to review what you think you know about the technical aspects of portable video. The Question/Answer format gets down to very specific aspects of equipment features, operations, and maintenance. Handy as a trouble-shooting reference book too.

Johnson, Nicholas. *How to Talk Back to Your Television Set.* Little, Brown, 1970. Bantam, 1970, pa.
Written by the youngest and most controversial member ever to serve on the Federal Communications Commission, and while he was a member, this inquiry into television's performance found TV dangerously inadequate. Unlike most critics of the medium, Johnson offers some tough-minded and concrete proposals for reform, including advice for discontented citizens. There is hope.

Kaye, Evelyn. *The Family Guide to Children's Television: What to Watch, What to Miss, What to Change and How to Do It.* Pantheon, 1974, pa.
Great for parents *and* teachers, this is practical and applicable advice by a co-founder of ACT (Action for Children's Television), the citizens' activist organization. It provides an overview of how TV programming for chil-

dren fits into the business of broadcasting, what's wrong with most of the programming, and how it can be changed for the better. It has its own valuable resource directory.

Kosinski, Jerzy. *Being There.* Harcourt, 1971. Bantam, 1972, pa.
How would someone behave when faced with the real world after having grown up and been "nurtured" in only two environments—television and an enclosed garden? This brilliant short novel is the story of such a man (named Chance) and how he survives in our world while possessing only those two metaphors for existence. A modern day *Pilgrim's Progress* or *Candide.* Suitable for high schools.

Kuhns, William. *Exploring Television.* Rev. Ed. Loyola University Press, 1975, pa.
No other work comes close to this publication. It is indeed "an inquiry/discovery program aimed at helping people to understand, analyze, criticize, evaluate, and judge the experiences they have had in front of the TV set." A work-text, it is well suited for fifth and sixth graders, the level commercial TV seems to aim at. The companion paperbook *Teachers Guide* is essential. It provides background information, guidelines to the text, resource listings, and some educational philosophizing.

Leibert, Robert M., Neale, John M., and Davidson, Emily S. *The Early Window: Effects of Television on Children and Youth.* Pergamon, 1973, pa.
A report on all studies, up to 1973, concerning the effects of this ubiquitous medium. It includes surveys by private individuals and by the federal government, and compares networks and FCC regulations.

Lesser, Gerald. *Children and Television: Lessons from "Sesame Street."* Vintage, 1975, pa.
The inside story of *Sesame Street* by that show's educational director and one of its chief architects. He presents the ideas that went into the series, the problems overcome, and the insights about children that emerged.

Mander, Jerry. *Four Arguments for the Elimination of Television.* Morrow, 1978.
A formidable case against TV by an activist researcher and founder of Public Interest Communications. Contending that TV is far from neutral, Mander shows how TV is "an instrument of sleep teaching" and a narrow channel through which perception and information may not pass, and most knowledge useful to human understanding of the complexities of existence cannot be conveyed at all. Whatever its content, he says, TV has a numbing, dehumanizing effect on people, and the problem is TV itself. TV is non-reformable, for its technology predetermines its content. Provocative reading.

Mattingly, Grayson, and Smith, Welby. *Introducing the Single-Camera VTR System.* Scribner, 1973.
A very basic technical manual. Easy to read and follow, but uninspiring.

Melody, William. *Children's Television: Economics of Exploitation.* Yale University Press, 1973, pa.
Commissioned by ACT, this study focuses on the economic aspects of commercial children's TV and their rela-

tion to FCC public-policy options. The author demonstrates that so long as administrators control programming, they will respond to their own vested interests and not to the needs of children.

Mitchell, Wanda. *Televising Your Message: An Introduction to Television as Communication.* National Textbook Co., 1976, pa.

A high school text for a course in *studio television* (not video) production. The author seems to have little knowledge or interest in portable video technology, so you may not find this book helpful. However as a text or reference for those teaching studio production, it is useful.

Murray, Michael. *The Videotape Book; A Basic Guide to Portable TV Production for Families, Friends, Schools and Neighborhoods.* Bantam, 1975, pa.

A gentle, well written introduction to portable video. It offers a brief history, basic technical information and production guidelines, and good descriptions of uses of video in education, health, the arts, and community work. Instructions are greatly simplified and the reading level is easy, making the book attractive as a classroom reference for secondary school students.

Potter, Rosemary Lee. *The New Season: The Positive Use of Commercial Television with Children.* Charles E. Merrill, 1976, pa.

Starting with the assumption that commercial TV is a sustained interest of most children, Potter presents a curriculum guide for elementary school teachers on using commercial TV as a tool for learning. Of particular interest are sections on determination of reality/fantasy and on recognition of class character traits.

Prete, Anthony, ed. *Media & Methods; Exploration in Education.* October 1977. North American Pub. Co., 1977.

Starting with Prete's own editorial, "Who Controls the Tube?," this issue of the magazine is packed with solid and thoughtful articles about the current state of the art/industry, and with some prognostications about the future of video. Included are: "The Impact of Home Video on the Schools," by Ken Winslow; "The Snarls Are Still There," by Susan Bistline, about off-air taping problems; "Using Video for Teacher (and Student) Training," by Robert Allender and Jay M. Yanoff; "Buying Video Equipment—Guide for the Thrifty," by Jon T. Powell; "The New Literacy: From the Alphabet to Television," by John Culkin; and "Unplug the Book, Not the Set," David England's response to Marie Winn's provocative anti-TV book, *The Plug-in Drug (q.v.).*

Price, Jonathan. *Video Visions: A Medium Discovers Itself.* New American Library, 1977, pa.

This is an excellent account of the educational, therapeutic and artistic explorations of video since its arrival as a portable medium in the late sixties. Price covers documentary and community access video and profiles the work of many video artists: he devotes one chapter to video pioneer Nam Jun Paik. With its informative and anecdotal style, this illustrated study is a fine intro to video history.

Robinson, Richard. *The Video Primer: Equipment, Production and Concepts.* Links Books, 1974, pa.

This may be the best overall guide to operating video equipment. It covers not only the basic camera and recorder but also the associated equipment, such as lights, sound equipment, and multi-camera setups. The author conveys a sense of excitement about the potential of video. Included are valuable appendices: sample shooting schedule and script, where to buy equipment, a selected bibliography, etc.

Schorr, Daniel. *Clearing the Air.* Houghton, Mifflin, 1977.

The former CBS reporter gives his personal story and a reporter's-eye view of secret government activities in Watergate, intelligence agencies, assassinations and attempted assassinations, and questionable media interference. If for no other reason, this book is essential reading for Schorr's account of his decision to disclose the House Intelligence Committee's Pike Report that led to his confrontation with Congress and eventual dismissal from CBS, and to his eloquent defense of the reporter's obligation to protect his sources. But what makes this book so apposite to Doing the Media perhaps is his fascinating descriptions of how television news works (chapter 2, "Stand-Ups and Take-Outs") and the power, pressures, and pre-eminence of television on our society (chapters 12 and 13, "The Sole Proprietor" and "The National Séance").

Schramm, Wilbur, Lyle, Jack and Parker, Edwin B. *Television in the Lives of Our Children.* Stanford University Press, 1961, pa.

One of the first studies undertaken on the impact of the medium—now a classic. Over 6000 children of different ages, sexes, economic and cultural backgrounds were studied in terms of viewing habits, attitudes, and perceptions, and a tremendous body of data was generated. While many of the specifics may be dated, the questions and ultimate recommendations are still viable.

Shamberg, Michael and Raindance Corp. *Guerilla Television.* Holt, 1971.

This large format paperback handbook to "alternate television" presents the counter-culture's concerns about and activities with television and videotape—TV and VT. The hip, self-conscious rhetoric of a few years ago does not hold up well, but most of the ideas and the research and the layout are very sharp. Recommended to any teacher wanting to learn about all sides of television in our society. For students too, but you should be prepared to deal with the possible reactionary criticism from those quarters who may find some illustrations and language offensive.

Shanks, Bob. *The Cool Fire: How to Make It in Television.*
Norton, 1976. Vintage, 1977, pa.

A combination of personal anecdotes, television history, and case studies on the industry, written by one of the most successful TV producer/directors of the past decade. A comprehensive, coherent study of the inner workings from someone who knows that business inside-out. Particularly valuable for students in high school or college for its realistic approach on how to break into the field. Also includes excellent chapters on such aspects as the rating system, technology and equipment, TV script-writing, and the possible future of cable and cassette video.

Spolin, Viola. *Improvisations for the Theatre.* Northwestern University Press, 1963.

An indispensible guide for teaching dramatic skills, this work includes tested improvisational techniques and the author's personal philosophy. Recommended for its applicability to video making.

Videofreex. *The Spaghetti City Video Manual.* Praeger, 1973.

Probably the most technical of all the handbooks/manuals on portable video, this is useful to nontechnical people too because of its readability, wealth of illustrations, and coverage. Contents: basic theory of how video equipment works; how to diagnose, isolate, and repair common equipment problems; basic maintenance, from head cleaning to more complicated procedures like changing belts, adjusting camera tracing, and replacing a camera's vidicon tube.

Winn, Marie. *The Plug-In Drug: Television, Children and the Family.* Grossman, 1977.

The thesis of this study simply stated is that it's not "what" children watch on television, but rather that they watch it at all that affects their development. Citing numerous examples from the popular press along with data from research reports, the author argues against all television programming. She confronts such topics as television and reading, viewing patterns and child behavior, changing family relationships, and a general approach to children's development. A challenging if not altogether radical thesis, and not as extreme in its condemnation as Mander *(q.v.)*. Important reading for parents and teachers alike.

Youngblood, Gene. *Expanded Cinema.* Dutton, 1970.

In the past few years a dedicated group of artists have been working creatively with image making in the video process. Their orientation is as artists. This book is about that movement. It may still be the only one of its kind, and it is very good. It begins with a discussion of film, and its movement into pure video art is slow and complete. Though not easy reading, its perceptions about the world of video and the world created by video are worth the effort.

Zettl, Herbert. *Television Production Handbook.* 3rd ed.
Belmont, Calif.: Wadsworth Publishing Co., 1976.

Often used as a text in university television production courses, this could be helpful for the high school student or teacher as a comprehensive reference work on studio production, including both technical and aesthetic aspects.

SOUND

Aside from books and magazines for technicians and hi-fi buffs, there are few, compared to those for the visual media, print resources on sound study and production for the general student or teacher. Sound is only beginning to grow as a field of study and bibliography, so keep an eye out for anything new. The following list excludes strictly technical materials.

Barnouw, Erik. *A History of Broadcasting in the United States.* 3 vols. Oxford University Press, 1966–1970.

The definitive study and comprehensive history of radio and television. For the reference collection and the serious student doing historical research in broadcasting.

Bliss, Edward, Jr., and Patterson, John M. *Writing News for Broadcast.* Columbia University Press, 1971.

An introductory text for the college student, but useful for the high school student wanting a good book on techniques of writing news for radio and TV.

Brodkin, Sylvia Z. and Pearson, Elizabeth J., eds. *On the Air: A Collection of Radio and TV Plays.* Scribner's, 1977, pa.

There doesn't seem to be any basis for selecting the eight complete scripts composing this collection, but the book can be useful as a sampling of actual scripts. Includes two original old-time radio serials, two radio plays adopted from literature, and four television scripts.

Diamant, Lincoln, ed. *The Broadcast Communications Dictionary.* Hastings House, 1974.

A handy, authoritative reference book that puts technical terms (over 2000) in context with common and slang speech in the broadcasting industry. Covers six major areas: broadcast programming and production; broadcast equipment and engineering; talent; advertising agencies and clients; TV and radio broadcasting; government, trade and associated industries.

Field, Stanley. *Professional Broadcast Writer's Handbook.*
Blue Ridge Summit, Pa. TAB Books, 1974.

All the essential ingredients or formats for writing radio or TV scripts are presented in this reference book, with numerous examples of actual working scripts and the author's personal experiences. Advice on breaking into the business of writing, the technical terminology, how to do a documentary, series plays, religious and children's shows, news programs, commercials, copyrights, markets, public broadcasting—all treated clearly.

Hilliard, Robert L., ed. *Radio Broadcasting: An Introduction to the Sound Medium.* 2nd ed., rev. & enl. Hastings House, 1974.

An introductory text for serious students. Includes recent developments, new programming formats, sample scripts, notes, illustrations, bibliographies.

Hilliard, Robert L. *Writing for Television and Radio.* 3rd ed. rev. & Enl. Hastings House, 1975.

A widely used text and home study book by the chief of the Educational Broadcasting Branch of the FCC. Covers latest developments in programming concepts and broadcasting techniques—production, commercials, news and sports, documentaries and features, talk and game shows, music and variety programs, children's programs, women's programs, ethnic and minority programs, information and educational programs, drama, and professional opportunities. Also has sample scripts and exercises for application and review.

Kintner, Robert E. *Broadcasting and the News.* Harper, 1965.

A pioneering view of radio and TV news. Again, useful for background information.

Lichty, Lawrence W. and Topping, Malachi C. *American Broadcasting: A Source Book on the History of Radio and Television.* Hastings House, 1975, cloth and pa.

A collection of about 100 readings with reference information, statistics, illustrations, chronologies, and bibliographies, making this a useful addition to the reference shelf.

Linton, Dolores, and David. *Practical Guide to Classroom Media.* Pflaum/Standard (now CEBCO/), 1971, pa.

Two chapters in this book are especially useful for sound study: Chapter 7, "Tape"; and Chapter 8, "Radio, Records and the Rock Scene."

Lipton, Lenny. *Independent Filmmaking.* Rev. ed. Straight Arrow Books, 1975, pa.

Chapter 7, "Sound and Magnetic Recording," is an excellent source of technical information on many aspects of sound and recording. Written for nontechnical readers, it has a casual style and is easy to understand.

Mendelsohn, Harold. "Listening to Radio." In Dexter, Lewis A. and White, David M., eds. *People, Society & Mass Communications.* Free Press, 1964.

A classic article in the study of the effects of radio on people's lives. Deals specifically with the personal functions that radio performs for us often at a level beyond our awareness.

Nijsen, C. G. *The Tape Recorder: A Guide to Magnetic Recordings for the Non-Technical Amateur.* Drake, 1971.

A comprehensive, well illustrated, fairly up-to-date book written in clear, nontechnical language.

Nisbett, Alec. *The Technique of the Sound Studio.* 3rd rev. ed. Hastings House, 1974.

The authoritative standard work for the professional working in sound, and a reference volume useful and readable for the nontechnical person too.

Nisbett, Alec. *The Use of Microphones.* Hastings House, 1974.

A good basic guide to microphones and their use for monophonic sound in radio, television, and film. For the beginner, yet a handy reference for the working professional. One of the publisher's series of Media Manuals.

Poteet, G. Howard. *RADIO!* CEBCO/Standard, 1975, pa.

A large format paperbook that can be used as a student text in a course or a unit on old-time radio, written in a reading level that seems about right for junior high school. It's a good overview of the entire subject, though not in much depth. A Teacher's Guide is also available, but the package needs to be supplemented by recordings of old radio broadcasts and further exploration into the subject.

Schwartz, Tony. *The Responsive Chord.* Doubleday, 1973. Anchor, 1973, pa.

You cannot do better than this book to begin your sound study. Schwartz's book is *essential reading.* It places sound study well within a communication theory based on a clear understanding of our electronic environment. One chapter is devoted to classroom learning, "Education in the Global Village."

Tall, Joel. *Tape Editing.* New Hyde Park, N.Y.: ELPA Marketing Industries, n.d.

A handy little pamphlet and interesting source for the latest techniques and ideas in physical editing and splicing.

The Tape Recorder. Austin, Tex.: University of Texas, Visual Instruction Bureau, n.d.

A pamphlet aimed directly at classroom teachers. Not very imaginative, but helpful: Part One describes the application of the tape recorder and its applicability in numerous classroom activities at all levels of instruction; Part Two explains the features of both reel and cassette recorders. Included are sections on recording techniques, editing and duplication, and general maintenance procedures.

Recordings

Old-Time Radio. Many of the radio dramas and comedies recorded during the thirties and forties have been reissued. Any record store should stock some of these. One company that has reissued many is the Radiola Company, P. O. Box H, Croton-on-Hudson, N.Y. 10520. And North American Radio Archives (P.O. Box 11962, Reno, Nev. 89510) also has hundreds of old radio shows, scripts, and a newsletter. Write for information on materials and membership.

Oral History. There are some 12,000 taped interviews to be found in 388 institutions in the U.S. They are listed and annotated in a reference book found in most libraries: Meckler, Alan and McMullin, Ruth, *Oral History Collections* (Bowker, 1975). For an enlightening and provocative discussion by a disparate group of professional practitioners, two 60-minute audiotapes are available from Precedent Pub. Co.: *"It's Not the Song, It's the Singing"—Doing Oral History: A Panel Discussion,* featuring Jan Vanisa, Saul Benison, Dennis Tedlock, Ron Grele, and Studs Terkel.

Sound Effects. Many record companies sell sound effects records, which can usually be found in your local record store. One company that carries a large line of such albums is Audio Fidelity Enterprises, Inc., 221 W. 57 St., New York, N.Y. 10019. Write for their listing of *Library of Sound Effects Records.*

Tony Schwartz. Though Tony Schwartz has not published any recordings recently, at least ten of his records can be purchased from Folkways Records, 43 W. 61 St., New York, N.Y. 10023. Write for the price listing. You may find his *The Sound of Children* especially helpful.

Music. Having trouble finding your way through the Schwann and Harrison record and tape catalogs? There's help for classical music selection: Halsey, Richard S. *Classical Music Recordings for Home and Library,* American Library Association, 1976. This is a library reference tool that is indispensible for private collectors, teachers, librarians, and radio station program directors. It is a 4000-item discography coded by listening level (elementary, secondary, advanced), aesthetic significance, and relative popularity. Notable, generally recommended, or best versions are cited for each title, as well as running times. Includes Gregorian chants and medieval, choral, orchestral, keyboard, experimental, and electronic works, and chamber music, orchestral pieces, operas, arias, art songs, and symphonies. Additionally it provides advice on purchasing, cataloging, and on appraising listening components. The appended glossary of audio terms is also useful.

OTHER MEDIA

D'Amico, Victor and Buchman, Arlette. *Assemblage.* Museum of Modern Art, 1972.
Among the many helpful and beautiful publications issued by the Museum, which was in the vanguard of the visual media, this one treats the reintegration of art and environment.

Liliberte, Nochan and Kehl, Richard. *100 Ways to Have Fun with an Alligator—and 100 Other Involving Art Projects.* Blauvelt, N.Y. 10913: Art Education, Inc., 1969, pa.
Practical projects kids can handle. Representative of the kinds of publications you can seek out from the arts and crafts communities and adapt to media arts programs.

Mincom Division. 3M Company. *Creative Teaching with Tape.* St. Paul, Minn. 55119: 3M Company, 1970.
The 3M Company and other large communications, computer and electronics companies produce a number of public relations and teaching booklets that innovative teachers can use with children and young people in a media arts program. This one was popular, and you are advised to seek out others.

Projectionists' Programmed Primer. Muncie, Ind. 47306: Ball State University Bookstore, Dept. M, 1976, pa.
An illustrated, simplified, self-instruction book on the principles of motion picture, opaque, overhead, slide, and filmstrip projection—designed especially for school use. (The bookstore also has another self-teaching book you may find helpful: *Mounting and Preserving Pictorial Materials,* which covers dry mounting, cloth backing, laminating, and inexpensive framing of pictures and objects).

Rosen, Stephen. *Future Facts: A Forecast of the World as We Will Know It Before the End of the Century.* Simon and Schuster, 1975.
Television was conceived in 1884, but wasn't seen by most people until 1947. Similarly, photography suffered a time lag from its conception, in 1782, to its realization in 1838. This book, one of the spate of futurist books, assembles an encyclopedic preview of products, services, processes and ideas that are likely to succeed when they appear—sooner than you think. Prominent among them are items in communications and information.

Schultz, Morton J. *The Teacher and the Overhead Projector.* Prentice-Hall, 1965.
Although this is now somewhat outdated and out-of-print, you might find a copy in your curriculum or education library. Still a useful reference.

Wigginton, Eliot, ed. *The Foxfire Book,* Nos. 1–4. Doubleday/Anchor, 1975–
Combining photography, audiotape, videotape, and print, and using their community (especially its elderly residents) as a resource in oral history, these compilations by the high school students at Rabun Gap-Nacoochee School in Georgia capture and document the reminiscences, dying crafts, and character of the people who live in rural Georgia near the school. The publications evolved

from the Foxfire project directed by Eliot Wigginton, the high school journalism teacher (see also *The Foxfire Fund,* listed in the "Organizations" section). The Foxfire phenomenon has spread to *Salt,* a magazine published by students at Kennebunk High School in southern Maine, and to *Bittersweet* magazine by students at Lebanon High School, Missouri. *The Salt Book* and *Bittersweet Country* will be published in 1978 (also by Doubleday).

Workshop for Learning Things. *Cardboard Carpentry Workshops.* Watertown, Mass. 02172: The Workshop, n.d., pa.

Workshop for Learning Things. *Further Adventures of Cardboard Carpentry.* Watertown, Mass. 02172: The Workshop, n.d., pa.

These two booklets are full of information about the apt use of cardboard as a versatile material and supply many details about the use of tools on cardboard, plus over 300 drawings and photographs.

Workshop for Learning Things. *Fragments.* Watertown, Mass. 02172: The Workshop, n.d., pa.

Not quite a book, but a pack of 158 cards, that grew out of a course about looking and seeing. Each card suggests an activity for a single person or group that moves towards looking more carefully at ourselves and our environment.

Workshop for Learning Things. *Label Press.* Watertown, Mass. 02172: The Workshop, n.d., pa.

Lots of suggestions on ways to print with label presses —those handy machines that extrude a tongue of colored plastic with raised white letters. This booklet was written by sixth graders who invented many of the procedures described.

CURRICULUM DESIGN

Curriculum and Media

Baker, D. Philip. *School and Public Library Media Programs for Children and Young Adults.* Gaylord, 1977, pa.

This volume shares the programs and ideas of 50 public libraries and school media centers. Each uses media in creative or exemplary ways with children and young people.

Boyle, Deirdre, ed. *Expanding Media.* A Neal-Schuman Professional Book. Phoenix, Ariz.: Oryx Press, 1977.

This reader is designed to answer some of the philosophical and practical questions raised by newer media in their broad applications to libraries. The 45 articles cover philosophy, programming, selection, and production of films, slides, audio cassettes, videotapes, photography, and other media forms in various library situations.

Cianciolo, Patricia. *Illustration in Children's Books.* 2nd ed. Wm. C. Brown, 1976, pa.

This is one of the few books available that takes a serious look at what wonderful visual materials are available in children's books, a visual medium too easily ignored by the classroom teacher. The author discusses, in detail, the wide variety of techniques and materials used by artists and illustrators, and the many different types of illustrated and picture books from which teachers, media specialists, parents, and child and adolescent readers might choose. She makes a strong plea for accepting diversity, yet presents sound considerations for determining quality and for developing in both children and teachers an attitude of critical evaluation of the illustrations produced. Chapter 4, "Using Illustrations in the School," offers practical curriculum applications and specific classroom activities. The extensive annotated bibliographies make this book useful also as a library reference and selection tool. The whole book is worthy of attention for filmmakers, especially animators, and for visual literary programs.

Davis, Ruth Ann. *School Library Media Center: A Force for Educational Excellence.* 2nd ed. Bowker, 1974.

Intended as a practical, in-service guide for educators and librarians, and also used as a textbook for some school library science courses, this book focuses on the library media center as an integral part of various curriculum programs. Included are discussions of the criteria and procedures for evaluating a school library media program, the role of the center's staff, team teaching, independent study, and a wealth of illustrative figures, tables, and checklists.

Estes, Glenn and Hanigan, Jane Ann. *Media Facilities Design.* American Library Association, 1978.

This welcome addition to the literature of school facilities presents the design components of a media center with a strong emphasis on facilities required for multimedia uses.

Gillespie, John T. and Spirt, Diana L. *Creating a School Media Program.* Bowker, 1973.

Aimed primarily at media librarians but of interest to teachers and administrators, this book gives helpful information for organizing and administering a successful media program in the usually understaffed, underbudgeted single school. It includes illustrative tables, checklists, and exhibits, and also has appendixes of actual selection policies in two school systems. As with most books on library media centers, this one emphasizes materials and programs, not equipment.

Gillespie, John T. *A Model School District Media Program.* American Library Association, 1977.

Since its early development of a media program in the 1960s the Montgomery County (Maryland) Public School system has been admired, studied, and frequently imitated. This book is an in-depth case study of that program, its evolution and operating procedures. It describes the history and functions of each media department in the school district. Included are discussions of personnel duties, job descriptions, budgets, services, policies and procedures, present problems and future plans, plus evaluations for each program. The book also contains organizational charts, outlines of inservice courses, evaluation criteria for reviewing media, and a sequential media skills teaching schedule. This unique volume holds much material that can be used directly or be modified for use in individual schools and in other school district media centers.

Houk, Annelle and Bogart, Carlotta. *Media Literacy: Thinking About It.* Pflaum/Standard (now CEBCO/), 1974, pa.

Literacy is defined here as independent behavior consciously shaping and being shaped by media of all kinds. The book contains practical suggestions for dealing with media and kids of all ages.

Katz, John Stuart. *Perspectives on the Study of Film.* Little, Brown, 1971.

An anthology of writings about what to teach and how to teach the study of film (which in most cases also means "media"). These readings present some thoughtful approaches used by successful media educators.

Linton, Dolores and David. *Practical Guide to Classroom Media.* CEBCO/Standard, 1971, pa.

A valuable book based on experience and written with a feeling for the problems and potential of media in the curriculum. It is a practical, straightforward look at what's needed philosophically and technically to launch activities in photography, film, television, and sound.

Maynard, Richard, ed. *Mass Communications Arts.* Vol. 1: *Sound and Sight;* Vol. 2: *Messages and Meanings.* Scholastic, 1975, pa.

These collections of readings are designed to supplement a high school level course. Most of the selections are current and interesting, and the layout and graphics are appealing and involving. *Sound and Sight* covers radio, records, rock, visual perception, art, photography, and movies. *Messages and Meanings* deals with newspapers and magazines, television, advertising, and propaganda.

McLaughlin, Frank, ed. *The Mediate Teacher: Seminal Essays on Creative Teaching.* North American Publishing Co., 1975.

This is a first-rate anthology of writings arguing that young people need competencies in a new spectrum of survival skills that reflect contemporary American culture, its machinery, and its materials. Assuming that teachers must adapt a new style if they expect to become more than functionaries, the authors urge teachers to welcome new media as allied agents so that the transition from teacher-centered to learner-centered instruction can become a reality.

Morrow, James and Suid, Murray. *Media & Kids: Real-World Learning in the Schools.* Hayden, 1977.

A series of curriculum ideas whose purpose is to allow young children to learn about media by active participation with various media tools. It contains some excellent ideas and curricular approaches. The introductory essay, however, which establishes the authors' philosophy,

seems to miss the point and unfortunately sets up an arbitrary dichotomy between various approaches to the use of media with children.

Nickel, Mildred L. *Steps to Service: A Handbook of Procedures for the School Library Media Center.* American Library Association, 1975, pa.

With the diminishment of staffing, especially in elementary schools, this practical down-to-earth manual of recommended procedures for setting up and maintaining a school library media center is a source of immediate help and guidance. Even if you have the staff, it is useful as an instructional and procedural handbook for paraprofessionals, clerks, aides, volunteers, and neophytes who should find it invaluable in assisting them in performing assigned duties in the media center.

Padgett, Ron and Zabatsky, Bill. *The Whole Word Catalogue 2.* McGraw-Hill, 1977, pa.

A collective effort by the poets, novelists, musicians, and media artists who make up the Teachers and Writers Collaborative, an innovative organization formed to foster creative writing activities through interaction between professional writers and children, and then expanded to include activities in film and video. Written in an informal style, this is an immensely valuable resource for the development of activities to foster and stimulate children's creative development. Also includes basic technical information in such areas as purchasing video equipment, doing your own printing, and creating puppet theater. Excellent annotations for books and recordings.

The Role of the Librarian in Media. 2 filmstrips with records or cassettes, and complete manual. Miller-Brody, 1976.

An in-service program to introduce the purpose, value, and components of a contemporary school media center, with emphasis on facilities, personnel, selection, organization of services to students and faculties. The well-photographed visuals and well-organized script include expansion of production facilities to encourage more student-made materials, increased use of the computer and information retrieval systems, computer-assisted instruction, management by computer, and adaptation of television for new uses. If your school has no or an inadequate media center, this program may be helpful as a dramatic representation of what is possible and available. It was prepared by three experienced Virginia practitioners: Beverly Bagan, supervisor of Richmond Public School Libraries; Amy Bradner, assistant supervisor of school libraries and textbooks, State Dept. of Education; and Dorothy James, library media specialist, Salem Church Junior High School, Chesterfield.

Schillaci, Anthony and Culkin, John, eds. *Films Deliver: Teaching Creatively with Film.* Scholastic, 1970, pa.

A landmark compilation of the best screen education articles of the sixties. Though written for high school teachers, it contains much that is useful on the elementary school level. Useful for discussion of why the movement seemed to decline in the 1970s.

Schrank, Jeffrey. *Teaching Human Beings: 101 Subversive Activities for the Classroom.* Beacon, 1972, pa.

Named a *Media & Methods* Maxi Award winner in

1973, this book is meant for teachers and students interested in changing education, for those who "have learned that the river can't be pushed, that love and caring are more important than any grade or degree, and that even schools can be places for growth."

Schrank, Jeffrey. *Understanding Mass Media.* Amphoto, 1976.

In this highly graphic book Schrank attempts to communicate an understanding of the mass media as a course of persuasion and education. While some discussion of technique is included, it is primarily an analysis of the mass media as a social and cultural influence. The Media Lab is an outstanding feature, teaching students to monitor and report their time in relation to their use of media in everyday life. Useful with junior and senior high school students.

student reader, *The Media Reader;* and a teacher guide for the reader. Altogether they form a total media study program for grades 9–12. Individual chapters in the text can also be teamed with corresponding chapters of the logbook and reader to provide a complete minicourse for the study of selected media. This experiential program was awarded the *Media & Methods* Recommended citation and voted the 1975 Maxi Award.

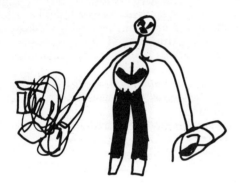

Library Reference and Selection Tools

AAAS Science Film Catalog. Ed. and comp. by Ann Seltz-Petrash. American Association for the Advancement of Science, and Bowker, 1975.

The most comprehensive (but not selective) annotated listing of its kind, this acquistions guide identifies some 5,600 films dealing with pure, applied, and social sciences that can be bought, rented, or borrowed from 150 U.S. producers/distributors. One section lists films for elementary students, and the other section films for junior high age–adult. Arrangement is by Dewey Decimal Classification, but full selection and ordering details, indexing, and directory information are included to help the user find desired information.

American Association of School Librarians and the Association for Educational Communications and Technology. *Media Programs: District and School.* American Library Association, 1975, pa.

Outlines the national standards for school library media programs on the district and individual school levels. The book includes specifications for personnel, operations, collection development, and library facilities.

American Film Institute. *Guide to College Courses in Film and Television.* Acropolis, 1975, pa.

A biennial compilation, arranged alphabetically by state, profiling all the colleges and universities offering a degree, a major, or a strong emphasis on courses, consortia, facilities and libraries in film and/or television. Also includes separate lists of foreign schools offering film and TV courses, schools by degrees offered, schools by major areas of concentration, and schools with media study courses for teachers.

Artel, Linda and Wengraf, Susan, eds. *Positive Images: A Guide to Non-Sexist Films for Young People.* San Francisco, Calif.: Booklegger Press, 1976.

An evaluative guide to 400 films, videorecordings, slides, filmstrips and photographs for preschool through grade 12.

Audio-Visual Equipment Directory. 22nd ed. National Audio-Visual Association, Inc. 1976/1977.

This is a buyer's guide to currently available audiovisual equipment, including 16mm and 8mm film projectors, recorders, multimedia systems, duplicators, among others. Information on the use, selection, purchase and maintenance of equipment also includes addresses of manufacturers and equipment dealers. This book is updated annually.

Audiovisual Market Place 1977: A Multimedia Guide. Bowker, 1977, pa.

This is a guide to 5000 firms and individuals that produce, supply or service audiovisual learning materials. Information on periodicals, reference books, associations, awards and other pertinent sources related to the production or distribution of audiovisual materials and equipment is listed. Updated annually.

Bauer, Caroline Feller. *Handbook for Storytellers.* American Library Association, 1977.

The most complete handbook available on storytelling, this is a beautiful and practical book for teachers, librarians, and community center programmers. All media having possible use in storytelling activities are described in detail—book illustrations, felt and magnetic boards, films, puppetry, music, magic, games, riddles, rhymes. The storyteller is taught not only how to create these media but also how to use them, how to plan story programs, what voice techniques to use, how to select tellable tales, and how to find the stories and the story-aids.

Boyle, Deirdre and Calvert, Stephen, eds. *Children's Media Market Place.* Gaylord, 1978.

This soft-covered directory provides media resources for children, including publishers, audiovisual producers, children's television programs, periodicals for and about children, juvenile book stores and book clubs, school and public library media selection centers and personnel, organizations, and a calendar of events, among other features.

Brown, James W., ed. *Educational Media Yearbook 1977.* 4th ed. Bowker, 1977.

This handbook of information begins with brief essays on developments in educational media. The best features are the directories of educational media organizations, media references, and funding sources. This annual also includes a directory of publishers, producers, and distributors.

Brown, Lucy Gregor. *Core Media Collection for Secondary Schools.* Bowker, 1975.

This directory lists some 2000 nonprint materials for grades 7–12, arranged alphabetically by title under subject headings based on the Sears List. All materials listed had received favorable reviews in professional journals or were listed in catalogs of schools judged to have outstanding media collections. Besides the usual bibliographic data, it identifies recommending sources and grade levels. There is a title index and a directory of producers and distributors.

Chisholm, Margaret E. *Media Indexes and Review Sources.* College Park, Md.: School of Library and Information Services, University of Maryland, 1972, pa.

An annotated list that evaluates media review sources and guides is featured in this source. Also included is a subject index.

Cianciolo, Patricia J., ed., and the Picture Book Committee, Subcommittee of the National Council of Teachers of English Elementary Booklist Committee. *Picture Books for Children.* American LIbrary Association, 1973, pa.

An annotated, carefully selected listing of picture books ranging from those for preschoolers to those for boys and girls in their teens. The 400 titles, representing a variety of artistic and literary styles, are listed in four groups: Me and My Family, Other People, The World I Live In, and The Imaginative World. Besides the usual bibliographic data, the age range of reader appeal or interest is also indicated. As an aid to classroom use, the annotations comment on the story or theme as well as art style and media used in the illustrations, and in some cases point out special classroom applications or reader interest. Like the author's more comprehensive work, *Illustrations in Children's Books* (listed in the previous subsection), the bibliography is useful for identifying readily available graphics for visual education and for comparing with the other visual arts.

Committee of the Young Adult Services Division, A.L.A. *Media and the Young Adult: A Selected Bibliography 1950–1972.* American Library Association, 1977, pa.

This bibliography examines 400 titles in six general research areas: attitudes of adolescents on subjects of interest to them; information-seeking behavior; media content; media use; impact of media; institutional services and access to media; and teaching strategies for media use and appreciation.

Diffor, John C. and Horkheimer, Mary Foley, eds. *Educators Guide to Free Films.* Educators Progress Service, Inc., 1977, pa.

This selected list of free films for use in schools provides information on sources and availability of each item listed. The guide is revised annually as are other "Free Guides" published by Educators Progress Service: *Educators Guide to Free Filmstrips; Educators Guide to Free Science Materials; Educators Guide to Free Social Studies Materials; Educators Guide to Free Tapes, Scripts and Transcriptions;* and *Elementary Teachers Guide to Free Curriculum Materials.*

Educational Media Catalogs on Microfiche. Olympic Media Information (71 West 2nd St., New York, N.Y. 10010), 1975–

An annual collection of the current catalogs of over 300 audiovisual software distributors, issued on positive NMA-format microfiches. Not a panacea for the problem of locating and getting, organizing and filing, and then up-dating all those catalogs, but this service makes an impressive start. The fiche are easy to use, and if you really want to get the hard copy of some or all of the catalogs, this tool should simplify your search for their names and addresses. The distributors selected are "the firms which sell, rent, or distribute on a free loan basis various films, filmstrips, videotapes, media kits, transparencies, slides, and other visual aids in current circulation among schools, universities, and businesses." The collection is offered on an annual subscription basis with a hard-copy index listing the location of distributors' catalogs by fiche and frame numbers.

Ferris, Bill and Peiser, Judy eds. *American Folklore Films and Videotapes: An Index.* Memphis, Tenn.: Center for Southern Folklore, 1977, pa.

Over 1800 films and videotapes which discuss the background and general history of the American folk experience or specific folk arts are indexed. Each entry includes information about the distributor and is briefly annotated. Annual supplements are planned.

Films for Children: A Selected List. 3rd ed. Children's and Young Adult Section of the New York Library Association, 1972.

A selected annotated list of 16mm films for children, with full ordering information.

Films for Hearing Impaired Children. Hyattsville, Md.: Prince George's County Memorial Library System, 1976, pa.

Includes more than 100 16mm films for use with hearing impaired children. Entries do not include captioned films for the deaf.

Gaffney, Maureen, ed. *More Films Kids Like.* American Library Association, 1977, pa.

This sequel to Susan Rice's *Films Kids Like* annotates 200 different short 16mm films for children ages 3–12. The book provides guidelines for screening films in classrooms and discusses Children's Film Theater approach. There is an appendix of films for preschool children and a subject index to films in both volumes.

Greene, Ellin and Schoenfeld, Madalynn. *A Multimedia Approach to Children's Literature: A Selective List of Films, Filmstrips and Recordings Based on Children's Books.* 2nd ed. American Library Association, 1977, pa.

A buying guide to a quality collection of book-related nonprint materials for use with children from preschool to grade 8. All items listed were viewed, read, and listened to by the selectors and were "child-tested." Especially useful for language arts, social studies, and storytelling programs, the list includes picture books, traditional and folk literature, literary fairy tales, fiction, the dramatic arts, poetry, and song, as well as materials concerned with the background of the books listed and their authors and illustrators. The guide includes author and subject indexes and a directory of the media distributors.

Kemp, Jerrold E. *Planning and Producing Audiovisual Materials*. 3rd ed. Crowell, 1975.

It's all here—basic and comprehensive descriptions and schematics of production with all basic media tools. What the volume lacks in conceptual pizzaz it makes up in nitty-gritty information. A good resource volume for those beginning to work with audiovisual gear—still cameras, video systems, audio recorders, and all the rest. There is little imagination but much practical assistance.

Kislia, J. A. *Let's See It Again.* Pflaum/Standard (now CEBCO/), 1975, pa.

This is an annotated listing of approximately 200 films that can be obtained at no cost but the return mailing. Films are listed both alphabetically and by subject, using Library of Congress and/or curriculum subject headings most useful for elementary and junior high school. Most film listings are followed by children's comments.

Limbacher, James L., ed. *Feature Films on 8mm and 16mm: A Directory of Feature Films Available for Rental, Sale and Lease in the United States 1977.* 5th ed. Bowker, 1977.

An annotated list of roughly 16,000 commercial films, documentaries, experimental films and animated films, with information on sources, running time, studio, director, actors, and distributors. It includes an index to film distributors by geographical area, an index to directors, and an index to film serials.

NICEM Media Indexes. Los Angeles, Calif.: National Information Center for Educational Media, University of Southern California.

NICEM indexes are a series of 14 bibliographic lists of media materials derived from a computer-based index system. Entries are listed alphabetically and by subject. Each indes includes a directory of producers and distributors. They include: *Index to Black History and Studies: Multimedia; Index to Ecology: Multimedia; Index to Educational Audio Tapes; Index to Educational Records; Index to Educational Slides; Index to 8mm Motion Picture Cartridges; Index to Health and Safety Education: Multimedia; Index to Overhead Transparencies; Index to Producers and Distributors; Index to Psychology: Multimedia; Index to 16mm Educational Films; Index to 35mm Filmstrips; Index to Video Tapes; Index to Vocational and Technical Education: Multimedia.* An Update Service is available by subscription for 4 bi-monthly volumes per year.

Parlato, Salvatore J., Jr. *Films Too Good For Words: A Directory of Non-Narrated 16mm Films.* Bowker, 1973.

A guide to 1000 non-narrated films for elementary school children to adults. Entries are arranged by title under subject headings and include ordering information.

Rice, Susan, ed. *Films Kids Like.* Published for the Center for Understanding Media. American Library Association, 1973, pa.

With a grant from the New York State Council on the Arts, the Center for Understanding Media established the Children's Film Theater in New York City. Screening of short films for children were followed by various activities, including discussion, creation of original soundtracks, painting, dancing, clay modeling, storytelling, videotaping and drawing on film. This book is a selected, annotated list of 225 of these "child-tested" short films, illustrated with film stills and reproductions of the young viewers' responses. Comments describe plot, suggested age level, running time, and distributors. A second edition, edited by Maureen Gaffney, was published in 1977 (See *More Films Kids Like*).

Rosenberg, Kenyon C. and Doskey, John S. *Media Equipment: A Guide and Dictionary.* Libraries Unlimited, 1976.

This encyclopedic dictionary of media equipment terminology is divided into two sections: an illustrated dictionary of 411 terms and a buyer's guide to media equipment which includes criteria for their evaluation and purchase.

Rufsvold, Margaret I. *Guides to Educational Media.* 4th ed. American Library Association, 1977.

This Sourcebook guide identifies and describes published catalogs and bibliographies on nonprint media. Entries are arranged alphabetically by title. A subject index is a useful addition.

Selected Films for Young Adults. Media Selection & Usage Committee, Young Adult Services Division. American Library Association. Annual, pa.

This annotated list of 16mm films recommended for use with young adults is selected from titles released in the U.S. during the previous year.

Sive, Mary Robinson. *Educators Guide to Media Lists.* Libraries Unlimited, 1975.

A classified guide to 270 instructional materials lists which describes curriculum subjects for preschool through grade 12. Grade level, subject, medium and title indexes are also provided.

Tillin, Alma M. and Quinly, William J., eds. *Standards for Cataloging Nonprint Materials: An Interpretation and Practical Application.* 4th ed. Washington, DC: Association for Educational Communications and Technology, 1976, pa.

The first section outlines the basic cataloging rules that apply to all types of nonprint materials. In section two, these basic rules are applied to specific media. This volume can be used in conjunction with the revised *Chapter 12* of the *Anglo-American Cataloging Rules* (American Library Association, 1975), which is also recommended for the AV reference collection.

van Orden, Phyllis, ed. *Elementary School Library Collection: A Guide to Books & Other Media.* 10th ed. Bro-Dart Foundation, 1976.

This annual covers available materials for school media collections, preschool through grade 6. Annotations offer full bibliographic data, reading levels and recommended acquisition phase.

Wall, C. Edward and Schwartz, Ellie, eds. *Media Review Digest.* Parts I & II. Pierian Press, 1976/77

An annual index to reviews, evaluations and descriptions of all forms of nonprint media from over 60 periodicals and reviewing services. Part I covers films, filmstrips and miscellaneous media. Part II covers records, tapes, record awards and prizes.

Weaver, Kathleen, ed. and comp. *Film Programmer's Guide to 16mm Rentals.* 2nd ed. Berkeley, Calif.: Reel Research, 1975. pa.

This guide lists 10,000 nontheatrical 16mm films available for rental from 60 U.S. distributors. It is helpful because it not only provides alternate distribution sources but outlines different rental fees for the same film.

Wyman, Raymond. *Mediaware: Selection, Operation and Maintenance.* 2nd ed. Wm. C. Brown, 1976, pa.

This is designed to be used as a lab workbook in a college course on audiovisual technology. It should be useful to anyone who needs good information on the principles of operation, selection, and maintenance of audiovisual equipment. Because it deals in general terms rather than specific brands or models, it will not become quickly outdated. This is very helpful either as a handy reference or as a guide for someone who needs to learn about a wide variety of AV technologies.

Zornow, Edith and Goldstein, Ruth M., eds. *Movies for Kids: A Guide for Parents and Teachers on the Entertainment Film for Children 9 to 13.* Avon, 1973, pa.

This guide to 300 entertainment films for children includes descriptive annotations and evaluations, a list of film organizations, distributor addresses, a bibliography of 100 books about film, and a recommended list of film periodicals.

PERIODICALS

ACT Newsletter. Action for Children's Television, 46 Austin St., Newtonville, Mass. 02160. Maureen Harmonay, ed. 4/yr. $15, free to members.

Highlights activities of Action for Children's Television, a nonprofit organization working to encourage diversity and eliminate commercial abuses from children's TV.

Audiovisual Instruction. Association for Educational Communications and Technology, 1126 16 St., N.W., Washington, D.C. 20036. Howard Hitchens, ed. 10/yr. $18, free to members.

Provides current information on hardware and other resources. Features a monthly insert called "Learning Resources" which is designed for people working with kids and media, "people who need practical, workable (but reliable) suggestions to become better teachers and media coordinators."

AV Communication Review. Association for Educational Communications and Technology, 1126 16 St., N.W., Washington, D.C. 20036. 4/yr. $19.50, available at reduced rate for members.

This research-oriented journal for PhDs in communications is heavy going but occasionally includes something relevant for those engaged in media studies with children.

Booklist. American Library Association, 50 E. Huron St., Chicago, Ill. 60611. Paul Brawley, ed. 23/yr. $28.

In the principal book and media review journal of the American Library Association, the Booklist staff and experienced librarians, reviewers and media specialists select and review books and nonprint materials *recommended for library purchase.* It is considered an essential selection and buying guide for currently produced books, 16mm films, filmstrips, and other nonprint media for use in school libraries and in many public libraries.

Educational Screen & AV Guide. Scranton Publishing Co., 434 S. Wabash, Chicago, Ill. 60605. Joe Ziemba, ed. 12/yr. $6.

This journal spotlights the latest equipment, materials and innovations in the audiovisual field. In addition to articles which touch on children's media, there are 350 reviews included each year.

EPIE Report. EPIE Institute, 475 Riverside Dr., New York, N.Y. 10027. P. Kenneth Komoski, ed. 8/yr. $100.

Provides reviews of media equipment to aid in the responsible selection and use of curriculum products.

ETC. The Journal of the International Society for General Semantics. Box 2469, San Francisco, Calif. Neil Postman, ed. $10, free to members.

Formerly devoted almost exclusively to language, this twenty-year-old publication has turned its attention to the media environment created by radio, television, and film. Contributors include such notables as Margaret Mead, Marshall McLuhan and Nicholas Johnson.

Film Library Quarterly. Film Library Information Council, Box 348 Radio City Station, New York, N.Y. 10019. William Sloan, ed. 4/yr. $10, free to members.

Dedicated to promote the wider and more effective use of films and nonprint materials by public libraries, this quarterly features articles, news and reviews of films and videotapes.

Film News. Film News, 250 W. 57 St., Suite 2202, New York, N.Y. 10019. Rohama Lee, ed. 5/yr. $6.

This publication reviews films and filmstrips and audiovisual hardware along with editorials, feature articles and news reports.

Journal of Communication. Annenberg School of Communication, University of Pennsylvania, Box 13358, Philadelphia, Pa. $15, free to members of the International Communication Association.

An official publication of the International Communication Association, this journal presents research studies, book reviews and articles of interest to the academic community. It can also be a valuable aid to classroom teachers, helping them keep in touch with new developments. It is generally the most readable of the formal journals in this field.

K-3 Bulletin of Teaching Ideas & Materials. Parker Publishing Company/Prentice-Hall, West Nyack, N.Y. 10994. Anne Bravo and Paul Zajan, eds., 10/yr. $21.

Gives teachers new and ready-to-use ideas and materials for young children. Feature articles on children and media and teaching techniques for instruction are focused upon.

Landers Film Reviews. Landers Associates, Box 69760, Los Angeles, Calif. 90069. Bertha Landers, ed. 5/yr. $45.

This service provides in-depth reviews, evaluations and information on short films, documentaries and other, multimedia materials for all ages.

Learning, The Magazine for Creative Teaching. Learning, 1255 Portland Pl., Boulder, Colo. 80302. Morton Malkofsky. 9/yr. $12.

An attractively designed magazine filled with what is new in education—innovations, strategies, opinions, book reviews, and information on new hardware and software.

Media and Methods. Media and Methods, 134 N. 13 St., Philadelphia, Pa. 19107. Frank McLaughlin, ed. 9/yr. $9.

Media and Methods is "The Voice" of film and media teaching. It has achieved its place as the best journal in the field with over 10 yeas of provocative and wide randing articles. A list of back issues and articles is available and is worth looking over. Individual articles can be ordered. The magazine has an easy "infocard" system to provide access to information on new products. *Media and Methods* really is a must: it's in a class by itself.

Media Digest. National Educational Film Center, 4321 Sykesville Rd., Finksburg, Md. 21048. George Ulysses, ed. 4/yr. $6.

This broadside paper offers news about children and media with the view of exploring and enriching visual education and communication.

Previews: Audiovisual Software Reviews. R. R. Bowker Company, 1180 Ave. of the Americas, New York, N.Y. 10036. Phyllis Levy Mandell, ed. 9/yr. $15.

Previews reviews education media materials geared primarily for elementary and secondary school audiences.

PTST. Prime Time School Television, 120 S. LaSalle St., Chicago, Ill. 60603. 10/yr. $10.

Prime Time School Television reports on evening television to alert high school teachers about quality programs. Study guides, suggested activities and resource information are included.

Rockingchair. Cupola Productions, Box 27-K, Philadelphia, Pa. 19105. 12/yr. $6.95.

This monthly newsletter "for those who buy records" carries record reviews. School librarians and teachers may find this new periodical helpful.

School Media Quarterly. American Association of School Librarians, 50 E. Huron St., Chicago, Ill. 60611. Glenn Estes, ed. 4/yr. $15.

This journal of the AASL includes features on children and media, on administration of school media centers, collection development, news of school media and idea exchanges. Approximately 100 books, periodicals and audiovisual materials for professionals are reviewed annually.

Science Books & Films. American Association for the Advancement of Science, 1776 Massachusetts Ave., N.W., Washington, D.C. 20036. 4/yr. $16.

This magazine evaluates children's science books and films for appeal and accuracy; approximately 200 books and 250 films are reviewed annually.

Sightlines. Educational Film Library Association, 43 W. 61 St., New York, N.Y. 10023. Nadine Covert, ed. 4/yr. $15, free to members.

This quarterly presents articles which deal with developments in the nontheatrical 16mm film field and covers topics of interest to film librarians. It occasionally publishes special issues on children and film. A new supplement, *Young Viewers,* appears in each issue and is edited by Maureen Gaffney, director of the Media Center for Children.

Super 8mm Filmmaker. PMS Publishing Co., Inc., 145 E. 49 St., New York, N.Y. 10017. $9.

This is an appealing magazine with award-winning graphics. It is the only journal exclusively devoted to the uses, problems and potentials of Super 8mm film. Included are ideas for films and how to produce them, tips on production gimmicks, equipment test reports, and helpful question-and-answer columns.

Teachers & Writers Magazine. Teachers & Writers Collaborative, 186 W. 4 St., New York, N.Y. 10014. Miguel Ortiz, ed. 3/yr. $5.

This is a highly recommended journal which highlights the work of a non-profit collaborative founded on the premise that professional writers and artists working in schools could find new approaches to making the arts accessible to children.

Teachers Guide to Television. Teachers Guide to Television, 145 E. 69 St., New York, N.Y. 10021. Gloria Kirshner, ed. 2/yr. $4.

Aimed at helping teachers and parents relate valuable TV programs to a child's education, this journal has feature articles and news about children and media along with listings of children's books, media, lesson plans, and bibliographies.

TV Guide. TV Guide, Box 400, Radnor, Pa. 19088. 52/yr $13.56, or 30¢ at newstands.

This is the Yellow Pages of American TV Broadcasting. In the past few years the quality of the articles has improved greatly. A good buy.

Videography. United Business Publications, 750 Third Ave., New York, N.Y. 10017. Peter Caranicas, ed. 12/yr. $10.

Offers a broad range of information to video users, including tips and techniques for production, updates on new equipment and technologies, lists and reviews of video programs, interviews with video personalities, and in-depth features on the use of video in business, industry, education, government, medicine, entertainment, and the arts.

ORGANIZATIONS

Action for Children's Television (ACT), 46 Austin St., Newtonville, Mass. 12160.

A national organization of parents and professionals, working to upgrade television for children and to eliminate commercialism from children's TV. ACT was founded in 1968 and today has thousands of members across the country and the support of major institutions concerned with children. Write for information on membership, *ACT Newsletter* (see Periodicals), campaigns, research information, publications, film and library facilities.

American Center of Films for Children, Division of Cinema, University of Southern California, University Park, Los Angeles, Calif. 90007.

Affiliated with the International Centre of Films in Paris, the American Center of Films for Children encourages the production, distribution, and exhibition of high-quality films with entertainment value for children. They are currently working toward a revival of the Saturday matinee. Among the services provided is a clearinghouse of information on children's film, seminars for teachers, librarians, museum staff and the general public, and an

annual award ("Ruby Slipper") for filmmaking excellence in children's film. A Film Rental Library rents 25 films for children, kindergarten through grade 7.

American Film Institute (AFI), The John F. Kennedy Center for the Performing Arts, Washington, D.C. 20566

An independent, nonprofit organization serving the public interest, established in 1967 through a grant from the National Endowment for the Arts, to advance the art of film and television in America. AFI is involved in such projects as restoring and saving classic films, managing a Center for Advanced Film Studies in Los Angeles and a Directing Workshop for Women, and a publishing program that includes comprehensive film catalogs, books on films, *The Guide to College Courses in Film and Television,* and the magazine *American Film,* which is free to members.

American Library Association (ALA), 50 E. Huron St., Chicago, Ill. 60611

There are three divisions in this national organization of librarians which are specially interested in the young: Children's Services Division, Young Adult Services Division, and the American Association of School Librarians. These divisions sponsor workshops for teachers and librarians in media selection and services for the young. They publish recommended lists of books and films for children and young adults and two quarterly journals, *Top of the News* and *School Media Quarterly.* The parent organization is also concerned with media, and its monthly magazine *American Libraries* ($20/yr., free to members) has frequent articles relating to the media world and media products. The Association publishes the multi-media review magazine *Booklist* (*q.v.*) as well as books and pamphlets on library and media subjects.

Artists-in-Schools Program. National Endowment for the Arts, Mail Stop 608, Washington, D.C. 20506.

A national program funded by the National Endowment for the Arts and the U.S. Office of Education. The film component of this program is designed to provide interaction between a film or video artist and students and teachers in a particular school or school district. If you are a teacher, administrator or media educator and would like to know more about the program in your state, contact your state Arts Council directly.

Association for Childhood Educational International (ACEI), 3615 Wisconsin Ave., N.W. Washington, D.C., 20016.

Members represent "those concerned with children from infancy through early adolescence." The Association has a good publications list which will be sent along with membership information upon request. One publication, *Children Are Centers for Understanding Media,* was a joint project of ACEI and the Center for Understanding Media in 1973.

Association for Educational Communications and Technology (AECT), 1126 16 St., N.W., Washington, D.C. 20036.

A professional association of educators and others whose activities are directed toward improving instruction through technology. Active membership ($30 per year) includes an annual subscription to *Audiovisual Instruction.*

Association of Media Producers (AMP), 1707 L St., N.W., Suite 515, Washington, D.C. 20036.

A national trade association for producers and distributors of educational media, materials and related services. AMP works with educational organizations to improve educational curricula and methodologies, lobbies at state and federal levels to increase funding for educational media programs, compiles statistics on annual educational media sales figures, holds conferences and meetings, and maintains a noncirculating collection of members' catalogs. AMP also publishes reports, surveys, and policy statements (free to members and available for a fee to the general public).

Carnegie Council on Children, 1619 Broadway, New York, N.Y. 10019.

The Carnegie Council on Children examines the way children grow up in America to determine how contemporary society influences children's lives and attitudes about their future. The Council provides writers and producers of children's media with ideas and leads to a variety of research materials.

Children's Television Workshop (CTW), 1 Lincoln Plaza, New York, N.Y. 10023.

The producers of *Sesame Street* and the *Electric Company* publish the "CTW Research Bibliography" listing sources of formal research and other information related to their TV programs. Most of the sources are easily available in libraries, but some are unpublished and can be obtained through the workshop. For a free copy, write on school stationary and send to CTW Library.

Educational Film Library Association (EFLA), 43 W. 61 St., New York, N.Y. 10023.

EFLA is an active library organization that serves as a national clearinghouse for information about 16mm films and other nonprint media. EFLA is chiefly concerned with 16mm film production, distribution, and use in education, the arts, science, industry, and religion. The association's extensive activities include numerous publications, film evaluations, workshops, a reference service, and sponsorship of the annual American Film Festival. Membership rates vary for individuals, organizations and institutions.

Educational Products Information Exchange Institute (EPIE), 475 Riverside Dr., New York, N.Y. 10027.

EPIE disseminates descriptive and analytical information about instructional materials, equipment, and systems. Reports and newsletters are published for members. EPIE operates an Equipment Testing Laboratory and sponsors workshops on how to analyze instructional media.

Film in the Cities, 2388 University Ave., St. Paul, Minn. 55114.

This group provides education, exhibition, information, and equipment access to children, teachers, and the general public in support of media culture in Minnesota. Film and photography classes are taught in elementary and secondary schools in St. Paul and animation classes are given to Indian youth in Minneapolis. Film and photography programs are sponsored in community and state colleges and universities. Films, videotapes and photographs by and for children, aged 7–12, are available for rental.

The Foxfire Fund, Route 1, Rabun Gap, Ga. 30568.

This organization, begun by Eliot Wigginton, provides workshops to train high school students in every phase of operating a community magazine. The purpose is to preserve the cultural heritage of the Appalachian highland and help initiate research and publishing ventures on other culturally distinctive areas. A museum on Appalachian culture is planned. *Foxfire,* published quarterly, is their fine publication. Articles from the magazine were collected and published as *The Foxfire Book* (Doubleday) and became so popular, selling millions, that three more *Foxfire* volumes have emerged (also from Doubleday).

Information Center on Children's Cultures, 331 E. 38 St., New York, N.Y. 10016.

The center collects materials in English and other languages which deal with the daily life of children in the developing countries. Serves as a reference service by disseminating bibliographies about specific countries and international subjects as they relate to children. A circulating collection of children's art and photographs is available as well as an extensive noncirculating library of children's materials. Publications co-published with the U.S. Committee for UNICEF and other companies are available for purchase.

Media Action Research Center (MARC), 475 Riverside Dr., Suite 1370, New York, N.Y. 10027.

MARC researches television's effects on children. For $1, MARC will send summaries of research and a set of suggested guidelines for responsible use of TV in the home. Write for details on a new "TV Values Kit" designed to help groups study the impact of television. Information on violence, racial and sexual stereotyping, news and commercials are featured in the kit. MARC also sponsors workshops. MARC participated in the creation of the film, "TV, The Anonymous Teacher" which is available from Mass Media Ministries, 2116 N. Charles St., Baltimore, Md. 21218.

Media Center for Children, 43 W. 61 St., New York, N.Y. 10023.

This is a nonprofit organization which researches film with kids. Current main activities include: screening and testing of films for children in the Children's Film Theater project; organizing conferences and workshops on the production and effective use of superior films with young people; documenting the activities of the organization in *Young Viewers,* a supplement to EFLA's *Sightlines* magazine; and producing other publications such as Gaffney's *More Films Kids Like.*

National Audio-Visual Association (NAVA), 3150 Spring St., Fairfax, Va. 22030

A national association of audiovisual producers of materials and equipment. NAVA works to improve professional services and to solve problems affecting producers, distributors and users of audiovisual media.

Prime Time School Television (PTST), 120 S. LaSalle St., Room 810, Chicago, Ill. 60603.

PTST is a nonprofit orgainization that provides background materials and bibliographies relating to documentaries and specials on prime-time TV. The aim is to help teachers make the best use of programs in the classroom. PTST is featured regularly in *Media & Methods* magazine. Membership in the organization is $10 per year: members receive additional teaching guides, program calendars, and other curriculum materials.

Television Information Office, 745 Fifth Ave., New York, N.Y. 10022.

This office provides free information to the public, including students, about current programming. Information is, however, presented from the point of view of the commercial broadcasters since this service is supported by the National Association of Broadcasters.

Workshop for Learning Things, 5 Bridge St., Watertown, Mass. 02172.

The workshop is a wonderful teacher resource which develops learning things for children and offers workshops for teachers. Write for the catalog which describes all the materials, supplies, and publications available.

World Future Society, (WFS), 4916 St. Elmo Ave., Washington, D.C. 20014.

The Society has a resource catalog of books, magazines, learning materials, games, and cassettes available for a small fee, and also produces a bimonthly magazine, *The Futurist.* As part of their membership, WFS members receive the magazine and a regular bulletin sharing ideas and investigations of futurists.

Young Filmakers Foundation, Inc., 4 Rivington St., New York, N.Y. 10002.

This is a media arts resource center. Through the Media Equipment Resource Center (MERC), equipment is loaned free to qualified New York State artists and media and arts organizations. Services in film and video employing young professionals are available. Young Filmakers houses a Youth Film Archives which numbers more than 150 films made by people 8–20 years old.

Young People's Radio Festival, c/o Deborah Baker, National Public Radio, 2025 M St., N.W., Washington, D.C. 20036.

This is a national festival sponsored by National Public Radio and NPR stations throughout the country. It provides an opportunity for young people aged 6–18 to produce their own radio shows and air them for professional broadcasters. The best programs are awarded prizes and broadcast on public radio.

Youth Film Distribution Center, 43 W. 16 St., New York, N.Y. 10011.

This group distributes 16mm sound films made by young people and sponsors workshops for young filmmakers. They also provide speakers and make grants to young film producers. A catalog is available upon request.

MEDIA DISTRIBUTORS

FILM DISTRIBUTORS

ACI Media, Inc.
35 W. 45 St.
New York, N.Y. 10036

Adelphia Cinema
580 Lancaster Ave.
Bryn Mawr, Pa. 19010

Agency for Instructional Television
Box A
Bloomington, Ind. 47401

Aims Instructional Media
626 Justine Ave.
Glendale, Calif. 91201

American Cancer Society
219 E. 42 St.
New York, N.Y. 10017

American Educational Films
132 Lasky Dr.
Beverly Hills, Calif. 90212

American Fisheries Society
New York Chapter
P.O. Box 86, Colvin Station
Syracuse, N.Y. 13205

Association Films
866 Third Ave.
New York, N.Y. 10022

Atlantis Productions, Inc.
850 Thousand Oaks Blvd.
Thousand Oaks, Calif. 91360

Attica Films, Inc.
789 West End Ave.
New York, N.Y. 10025

Audience Planners Inc.
1 Rockefeller Plaza
New York, N.Y. 10020

Audio Brandon Films
34 MacQuesten Pkwy, S.
Mount Vernon, N.Y. 10550

Avco/Meredith Broadcasting Corp.
c/o Avco Broadcasting Corp.
1600 Provident Tower
Cincinnati, Ohio 45202

Bandelier Films, Inc.
2001 Gold Ave., S.E.
Albuquerque, N.M. 87106

Barr Films
P.O. Box 7-C
Pasadena, Calif. 91104

Beattie Productions
3 Englewood Ave., Suite 11
Brookline, Mass. 02146

Geoffrey Bell Productions
1007 Sutter St., #406
San Francisco, Calif. 94109

Benchmark Films, Inc.
145 Scarborough Rd.
Briarcliff Manor, N.Y. 10510

Best Films
P.O. Box 692
Del Mar, Calif. 92014

BFA Educational Media
2211 Michigan Ave.
Santa Monica, Calif. 90404

Blackhawk Films
2607 Eastin-Phelan Bldg.
Davenport, Iowa 52808

BNA Communications
9401 Decoverly Hall Rd.
Rockville, Md. 20850

Stephen Bosustow Productions
1649 Eleventh St.
Santa Monica, Calif. 90404

BP North American, Inc.
620 Fifth Ave.
New York, N.Y. 10020

Brigham Young University
Motion Picture Production Dept.
Provo, Ut. 84602

William Brose Productions, Inc.
3168 Oakshire Dr.
Hollywood, Calif. 90068

Billy Budd Films, Inc.
235 E. 57 St.
New York, N.Y. 10022

Cameo Cameras
Rt. 2, Box 130A
Waldorf, Md. 20601

Campus Films, Inc.
2 Overhill Road
Scarsdale, N.Y. 10583

Carousel Films, Inc.
1501 Broadway
New York, N.Y. 10036

CCM Films, Inc.
866 Third Ave.
New York, N.Y. 10022

Cecropedia
547 David Bldg.
1629 K St., N.W.
Washington, D.C. 20006

Center for Southern Folklore
3756 Mimosa Ave.
Memphis, Tenn. 38111

Centron Films
1621 W. Ninth St.
P.O. Box 687
Lawrence, Kans. 66044

Churchill Films
662 N. Robertson Blvd.
Los Angeles, Calif. 90069

Cine-Pic Hawaii
1847 Pacific Hts. Rd.
Honolulu, Hawaii 96813

Cinema Concepts, Inc.
91 Main St.
Chester, Conn. 06412

Cinema 5 Ltd.
595 Madison Ave.
New York, N.Y. 10022

Colonial Williamsburg Foundation
AV Distribution Section, Box C
Williamsburg, Va. 23185

Communetics, Inc.
485 Madison Ave.
New York, N.Y. 10022

The Company
7027 Twin Hills Ave.
Dallas, Tex. 75231

Concordia Publishing House
3558 S. Jefferson Ave.
St. Louis, Mo. 63118

Connecticut Films, Inc.
6 Cobble Hill Rd.
Westport, Conn. 06880

Contemporary Films/McGraw-Hill
1221 Ave. of the Americas
New York, N.Y. 10020

Coronet Films
65 E. South Water St.
Chicago, Ill. 60601

Counterpoint Films
14622 Lanark St.
Panorama City, Calif. 91402

Courter Films & Associates
RD #1, Box 355B
Columbia, N.J. 07832

Creative Film Society
7237 Canby Ave.
Reseda, Calif. 91336

CRM-McGraw-Hill Films
1221 Ave. of the Americas
New York, N.Y. 10020

Dana Productions
6249 Babcock Ave.
North Hollywood, Calif. 91606

Peter Davis
Brophy Rd.
Hurleyville, N.Y. 12747

Melvin Denholtz
114 W. Mt. Pleasant Ave.
Livingston, N.J. 07039

Directors' Studio, Inc.
20 West 43 St.
New York, N.Y. 10036

Documentary Educational Resources
24 Dean St.
Somerville, Mass. 02143

Eccentric Circle Cinema Workshop
P.O. Box 1481
Evanston, Ill. 60204

Education Development Center
39 Capel St.
Newton, Mass. 02160

Educational Film Systems
11466 San Vicente Blvd.
Los Angeles, Calif. 90049

Educational Solutions, Inc.
80 Fifth Ave.
New York, N.Y. 10011

Encyclopaedia Britannica Educational Corp.
425 N. Michigan Ave.
Chicago, Ill. 60611

Essentia
P.O. Box 129
Tiburon, Calif. 94920

**Far West Laboratory for Educational Research
and Development**
1855 Folsom St.
San Francisco, Calif. 94103

Film Images/Radim Films
1034 Lake St.
Oak Park, Ill. 60301

FilmFair Communications
10900 Ventura Blvd.
Studio City, Calif. 91604

Films for the Humanities
P.O. Box 378
Princeton, N.J. 08540

Films, Inc.
1144 Wilmette Ave.
Wilmette, Ill. 60091

Flower Films
11305 Q-Ranch Rd.
Austin, Tex. 78757

Franciscan Communications Center
1229 S. Santee St.
Los Angeles, Calif. 90015

General Motors Public Relations Library
General Motors Bldg.
Detroit, Mich. 48202

Granada Television Int. Ltd. (U.S.)
Suite 3468
1221 Avenue of the Americas
New York, N.Y. 10020

Allan Grant Productions
808 Lockearn St.
Los Angeles, Calif. 90049

Greystone Film
336 Bayview Ave.
Amityville, N.Y. 11701

**Group W - Westinghouse Broadcasting
Company**
90 Park Ave.
New York, N.Y. 10016

Grove Press, Inc.
53 W. 11 St.
New York, N.Y. 10003

Guidance Associates/Motion Media
41 Washington Ave.
Pleasantville, N.Y. 10570

Haida Films
69 Banstock Dr.
Willowdale, Ontario M2K 2H7

HAF-Alternatives on Films
311 Spruce St.
San Francisco, Calif. 94118

Handel Film Corporation
8730 Sunset Blvd.,
W. Hollywood, Calif. 90069

Harvard University
Graduate School of Design
Cambridge, Mass. 02138

Alfred Higgins Productions, Inc.
9100 Sunset Blvd.
Los Angeles, Calif. 90069

Peter Hoffman
c/o Yale Audio-Visual Center
59 High St.
New Haven, Conn. 06520

Hollywood Film Enterprises, Inc.
6060 Sunset Blvd.
Hollywood, Calif. 90028

Hornbein-Wood Films
Box 174
Lemont, Pa. 16851

Human Relations Media
39-41 Washington Ave.
Pleasantville, N.Y. 10070

Huszar Productions, Inc.
420 E. 55 St.
New York, N.Y. 10022

Image
3259 Prospect St., N.W.
Washington, D.C. 20007

Impact Films
144 Bleecker St.
New York, N.Y. 10012

Indiana University
Audio-Visual Center
Bloomington, Ind. 47401

Interland Film Corp.
799 Broadway
New York, N.Y. 10003

International Film Bureau, Inc.
332 S. Michigan Ave.
Chicago, Ill. 60604

International Film Foundation, Inc.
475 Fifth Ave., Rm. 916
New York, N.Y. 10017

Janus Films
745 Fifth Ave.
New York, N.Y. 10019

Journal Films, Inc.
909 W. Diversey Pkwy.
Chicago, Ill. 60614

Dennis Lanson
148 Valentine Ave.
Sparkill, N.Y. 10976

Lawren Productions
P.O. Box 1542
Burlingame, Calif. 94010

Learning Corp. of America
1350 Ave. of the Americas
New York, N.Y. 10019

Learning in Focus
230 W. 13 St.
New York, N.Y. 10011

Lewis & Neale, Inc.
634 Empire State Bldg.
New York, N.Y. 10001

LFA Films
470 Park Ave. S.
New York, N.Y. 10016

Eli Lilly & Co.
Indianapolis, Ind. 46206

Lisberger-Ladd Creations
133 Summer St.
Boston, Mass. 02110

Little Red Filmhouse
119 S. Kikea Dr.
Los Angeles, Calif. 90048

LSB Productions
1310 Monaco Dr.
Pacific Palisades, Calif. 90272

Lutheran Brotherhood
701 Second Ave. S.
Minneapolis, Minn. 55402

Macmillan Films, Inc.
34 MacQuesten Pkwy. S.
Mt. Vernon, N.Y. 10550

Marion Laboratories
10236 Bunker Ridge Rd.
Kansas City, Mo. 64137

Marquis Film Distributors, Inc.
416 W. 45 St.
New York, N.Y. 10036

Mass Communications, Inc.
25 Sylvan Road S.
Westport, Conn. 06880

Mass Media Ministries
2116 N. Charles St.
Baltimore, Md. 21218

Harold Mayer Prod., Inc.
155 W. 72 St.
New York, N.Y. 10023

Maysles Films, Inc.
1697 Broadway
New York, N.Y. 10019

McGraw-Hill Films
1221 Ave. of the Americas
New York, N.Y. 10020

Media Guild
P.O. Box 881
Solana Beach, Calif. 92075

Media Production Service
Georgia Center for Cont. Ed.
University of Georgia
Athens, Ga. 30602

Miller-Brody Productions
342 Madison Ave.
New York, N.Y. 10017

Mini Productions Inc.
192 Hyeholde Dr.
Coraopolis, Pa. 15108

Modern Sound Pictures
1402 Howard St.
Omaha, Neb. 68102

Modern Talking Picture Service, Inc.
2020 Prudential Plaza
Chicago, Ill. 60601

Modern Talking Picture Service
910 Penn Ave.
Pittsburgh, Pa. 15222

Modern Talking Picture Service
Free Film Library
315 Springfield Ave.
Summit, N.J.
Sales & Hdqs.
45 Rockefeller Plaza
New York, N.Y. 10020

Arthur Mokin Productions, Inc.
17 W. 60 St.
New York, N.Y. 10023

Morning Star Film Company
31 Essex St.
Cambridge, Mass. 02139

Museum Art School
Film Dept.
S.W. Park & Madison
Portland, Ore. 97205

Museum of Modern Art
11 W. 53 St.
New York, N.Y. 10019

NASA Jet Propulsion Laboratory
4800 Oak Grove Dr.
Pasadena, Calif. 91103

National Audiovisual Center
General Services Admin.
Washington, D.C. 20409

National Bureau of Standards
Room B-08
Administration Bldg.
Washington, D.C. 20234

National Conference of State Legislatures
1405 Bellows St.
Denver, Colo. 80202

National Film Board of Canada
1251 Ave. of the Americas, 16th flr.
New York, N.Y. 10020

National Geographic Society
Educational Films Div.
17 & M Streets, N.W.
Washington, D.C. 20036

NBC Educational Enterprises
30 Rockefeller Plaza
New York, N.Y. 10020

New Day Films
P.O. Box 315
Franklin Lakes, N.J. 07417

New Line Cinema
855 Broadway, 16th flr.
New York, N.Y. 10003

New Visions
P.O. Box 599
Aspen, Colo. 81611

New York University
Film Library
41 Press Annex, Washington Sq.
New York, N.Y. 10003

New Yorker Films
43 W. 61 St.
New York, N.Y. 10023

NHK International/Films, Inc.
1144 Wilmette Ave.
Wilmette, Ill. 60091

Niles Films
Box 1576-MM
South Bend, Inc. 46634

9th St. Productions
21 W. 9 St.
New York, N.Y. 10011

NTA Film Services
12636 Beatrice St.
Los Angeles, Calif. 90066

Oxford Films, Inc.
1136 N. Las Palmas
Los Angeles, Calif. 90038

Paramount Communications
5451 Marathon St.
Hollywood, Calif. 90038

Kit Parker Films
Carmel Valley, Calif. 93924

Peach Enterprises, Inc.
4649 Gerald
Warren, Mich. 48092

Pelikan Films
3010 Santa Monica Blvd., Suite 440
Santa Monica, Calif. 90404

Pennsylvania Dept. of Education
Box 911
Harrisburg, Pa. 17126

Pennsylvania State University
Audio-Visual Services
Willard Bldg.
University Park, Pa. 16802

Perennial Education, Inc.
1825 Willow Rd.
Northfield, Ill. 60093

Perspective Films
369 W. Erie St.
Chicago, Ill. 60610

Phoenix Films, Inc.
470 Park Ave. S.
New York, N.Y. 10016

Picture Films Distribution Corp.
43 W. 16 St.
New York, N.Y. 10011

Polymorph Films
331 Newbury St.
Boston, Mass. 02115

Prentice-Hall Film Library
Englewood Cliffs, N.J. 07632

Princeton University
Princeton, N.J. 08540

Productions Unlimited
40 W. 57 St.
New York, N.Y. 10019

Psychological Cinema Register
Audio-Visual Services
The Pennsylvania State Univ.
University Park, Pa. 16802

Pyramid Films
P.O. Box 1048
Santa Monica, Calif. 90406

Quality Productions
256 S. Robertson Blvd.
Beverly Hills, Calif. 90211

R & A Films
9 E. 63 St.
New York, N.Y. 10021

Radio & Television Commission
Southern Baptist Convention
6350 W. Freeway
Ft. Worth, Tex. 76116

Rainy Day Films
23 18 Ave.
Venice, Calif. 90291

Gerald J. Rappoport
159 W. 53 St.
New York, N.Y. 10019

rbc films
933 North La Brea Ave.
Los Angeles, Calif. 90038

Reel Images
456 Monroe Turnpike
Monroe, Conn. 06468

Rembrandt Films
267 W. 25 St.
New York, N.Y. 10001

ROA Films
1696 North Astor St.
Milwaukee, Wis. 53202

Richard A. Sanderson
4502 Sierra Dr.
Honolulu, Hawaii 96816

Schloat Productions
150 White Plains Rd.
Tarrytown, N.Y. 10591

Scientificom
Div. of Mervin W. LaRue Films, Inc.
708 N. Dearborn
Chicago, Ill. 60610

Screenscope
Suite 2000
1022 Wilson Blvd.
Arlington, Va. 22209

Seashorse Films
P.O. Box 413
Remsenburg, N.Y. 11960

Serious Business
1145 Mandana Blvd.
Oakland, Calif. 94610

SIM Productions, Inc.
Weston, Conn. 06880

S-L Film Productions
P.O. Box 41108
Los Angeles, Calif. 90041

Harry Smith and Sons
525 Denison St.
Markham, Ontario L3R 1B8

Smithsonian Institution
14th & Constitution Ave., N.W.
Washington, D.C. 20560

Sterling Educational Films
241 E. 34 St.
New York, N.Y. 10016

I.F. Stone Project
P.O. Box 315
Franklin Lakes, N.J. 07417

Sunburst Communications
39-41 Washington Ave.
Pleasantville, N.Y. 10570

Super 8 Film Group
37 W. 20 St.
New York, N.Y. 10011

Swank Motion Pictures
393 Front St.
Hempstead, N.Y. 11550

TeleKETICS
1229 S. Santee St.
Los Angeles, Calif. 90015

Texture Films, Inc.
1600 Broadway
New York, N.Y. 10019

The Tom Thomas Organization
15 E. 48 St., #600
New York, N.Y. 10017

Robert Thurber
265 E. Argyle St.
Valley Stream, N.Y. 11580

Time-Life Multi-Media
Time & Life Bldg.
1271 Ave. of the Americas
New York, N.Y. 10020

Tribune Films, Inc.
38 W. 32 St.
New York, N.Y. 10001

Tricontinental Film Center
333 Ave. of the Americas
New York, N.Y. 10019

Twentieth Century Fox
P.O. Box 900
Beverly Hills, Calif. 90213

Twyman Films, Inc.
329 Salem Ave.
Dayton, Ohio 45401

Union Theological Seminary
3041 Broadway
New York, N.Y. 10027

United Artists
729 Seventh Ave.
New York, N.Y. 10019

United Learning
6633 W. Howard St.
Niles, Ill. 60648

United Nations
Radio & Visual Services
New York, N.Y. 10017

Universal/16
445 Park Ave.
New York, N.Y. 10022

University of Alaska
Northern Educational Research Center
Fairbanks, Alaska 99701

University of California
Extension Media Center
2223 Fulton St.
Berkeley, Calif. 94720

University of Pittsburgh
Communications Center
Pittsburgh, Pa. 15260

Varied Directions
Box 351
Croton-On-Hudson, N.Y. 10520

Vedo Films
85 Longview Rd.
Port Washington, N.Y. 11050

Vid Pic
2009 Baltimore
Kansas City, Mo. 64108

Viewfinders
P.O. Box 1665
Evanston, Ill. 60204

Vision Quest, Inc.
7715 N. Sheridan Rd.
Chicago, Ill. 60626

Walt Disney Educational Media Co.
500 S. Buena Vista St.
Burbank, Calif. 91521

Wardell Associates
49 Pinckney St.
Boston, Mass. 02114

Warner Brothers Film Gallery
4000 Warner Rd.
Burbank, Calif. 91505

Western Electric Co.
Motion Picture Bureau
195 Broadway
New York, N.Y. 10007

Weston Woods Studios, Inc.
Weston, Conn. 06880

John Wiley & Sons, Inc.
605 Third Ave.
New York, N.Y. 10016

WKYC-TV
1403 E. 6 St.
Cleveland, Ohio 44114

Wombat Productions, Inc.
Little Lake
Glendale Rd., Box 70
Ossining, N.Y. 10562

WRC-TV
4001 Nebraska Ave., N.W.
Washington, D.C. 20016

Xerox Films
245 Long Hill Rd.
Middletown, Conn. 06457

Yellow Ball Workshop
62 Tarbell Ave.
Lexington, Mass. 02173

Zipporah Films, Inc.
54 Lewis Wharf
Boston, Mass. 02110

VIDEOTAPE RECORDINGS DISTRIBUTORS/PUBLISHERS

ABC Merchandising Inc.
(subsidiary of ABC)
1330 Ave. of the Americas
New York, N.Y. 10019

Admaster Inc.
425 Park Ave., S.
New York, N.Y. 10016

Agape Productions
138 E. 93 St.
New York, N.Y. 10028

Agency for Instructional Television
(subsidiary of National Instructional Television)
Box A, 1111 W. 17 St.
Bloomington, Ind. 47401

Alternate Visions, Inc.
130 W. 86 St.
New York, N.Y. 10024

**American Cable Network Educators'
  Video Cassette Service**
701 S. Airport Rd., Box 936
Traverse City, Mich. 49684

American Educational Films
132 Lasky Dr.
Beverly Hills, Calif. 90212

American Video Network
660 South Bonnie Brae
Los Angeles, Calif. 90057

Ken Anderson Films
Box 618, 152 E. Winona St.
Winona Lake, Ind. 46590

April Video Cooperative
Box 77, Route 375
Woodstock, N.Y. 12498

Artcom
(division of LaRue Inc.)
708 N. Dearborn Ave.
Chicago, Ill. 60610

Associated Educational Materials Company
14 Glenwood Ave., Box 2087
Raleigh, N.C. 27602

The Athletic Institute
200 Castlewood Dr.
North Palm Beach, Fla. 33408

Audio Visual Productions
1233 N. Ashland Ave.
Chicago, Ill. 60622

August Films Inc.
321 W. 44 St.
New York, N.Y. 10036

Blue Hill Educational Systems, Inc.
52 S. Main St.
Spring Valley, N.Y. 10977

Blue Sky Productions
Box 548
Santa Fe, N.M. 87501

BNA Communications Inc.
(subsidiary of Bureau of National Affairs)
9401 Decoverly Hall Rd.
Rockville, Md. 20850

Borden Productions
Great Meadows Rd. P.O. Box 520
Concord, Mass. 01742

Brigham Young University
Green House
Provo, Utah 84602

Broadman Films
127 Ninth Ave.
Nashville, Tenn. 37234

Cambridge Book Company
488 Madison Ave.
New York, N.Y. 10022

Chamber of Commerce of the U.S.
1615 H St., N.W.
Washington, D.C. 20062

Chelsea House
70 W. 40 St.
New York, N.Y. 10018

Cinema Concepts, Inc.
Dept. VU.
91 Main St.
Chester, Conn. 06412

CK Communications
551 Fifth Ave.
New York, N.Y. 10036

Coe Film Associates
70 E. 96 St.
New York, N.Y. 10028

Columbia Pictures Cassettes
711 Fifth Ave.
New York, N.Y. 10018

Classroom World Productions
22 Glenwood Ave. Box 2090
Raleigh, N.C. 27602

Command Performance Video Network
(division of Educasting Systems, Inc.)
320 Interstate North
Atlanta, Ga. 30328

Communications Group West
6335 Homewood Ave. Suite 200
Hollywood, Calif. 90028

Community Development Foundation
48 Wilton Rd.
Westport, Conn. 06880

Contempo Communications Inc.
1841 Broadway
New York, N.Y. 10023

Control Data Corporation
Individualized Education Services
8100 34 Ave. S.
Minneapolis, Minn. 55440

Cornerstone Productions
6087 Sunset Blvd., Suite 408
Hollywood, Calif. 90028

Cornell University ETV Center
Van Rensselaer Hall
Ithaca, N.Y. 14850

Counselor Films, Inc.
2100 Locust St.
Philadelphia, Pa. 19103

Creative Media
820 Keosauqua Way
Des Moines, Iowa 50309

CRM/McGraw-Hill Films
1221 Ave. of the Americas
New York, N.Y. 10020

Custom Films, Inc.
11 Cob Dr.
Westport, Conn. 06880

Deltak
9950 W. Lawrence Ave.
Schiller Park, Ill. 60176

Lee Dubois Company
Box G
Hyannis, Mass. 02601

Education Development Center
55 Chapel St.
Newton, Mass. 02160

Educational Communication Association
822 National Press Bldg.
Washington, D.C. 20045

Edutronics Systems International Inc.
3425 Broadway
Kansas City, Mo. 64111

Electronic Arts Intermix, Inc.
84 Fifth Ave.
New York, N.Y. 10011

Electronic University
Box 361
Mill Valley, Calif. 94941

Encom, Inc.
4000 W. 76 St.
Minneapolis, Minn. 55435

Encyclopedia Britannica Educational Corporation
425 N. Michigan Ave.
Chicago, Ill. 60611

ETL, Inc.
1170 Commonwealth Ave.
Boston, Mass. 02134

Executive Videoforum, Inc.
200 Park Ave. Suite 303 East
New York, N.Y. 10017

Films, Inc.
1144 Wilmette Ave.
Wilmette, Ill. 60091

Films for the Humanities Inc.
Box 2053
Princeton, N.J. 08540

Flagg Films Inc./Bandera Enterprises
Box 1107
Studio City, Calif. 91604

Furman Films
3466 21 St.
San Francisco, Calif. 94110

Genesys Systems Inc.
1121 E. Meadow Dr.
Palo Alto, Calif. 94303

Global Village
454 Broome St.
New York, N.Y. 10002

Gratton Video Services Ltd.
711 Third Ave.
New York, N.Y. 10017

Great Plains National Instructional Television Library
Box 80669
Lincoln, Neb. 68501

Handel Film Corporation
8730 Sunset Blvd.
Los Angeles, Calif. 90069

Hartley Productions
Cat Rock Rd.
Cos Cob, Conn. 06807

Hewlett-Packard Company
1819 Page Mill Rd.
Palo Alto, Calif. 94304

Hunter & Hunter, Inc.
150 Fifth Ave. Suite 1101
New York, N.Y. 10011

IBM Data Processing
1133 Westchester Ave.
White Plains, N.Y. 10604

Indiana University
Audio-Visual Center
Bloomington, Ind. 47401

Instructional Television Center
Dallas County Community College District
12800 Abrams Rd.
Dallas, Tex. 75231

Integrative Learning Systems Inc.
326 W. Chevy Chase Dr., Suite 11
Glendale, Calif. 91204

International Communications Company
244 Thorn St.
Sewickley, Pa. 15134

International Film Bureau
332 S. Michigan Ave.
Chicago, Ill. 60604

Kaydan Records
(division of Stacy Keach Productions)
5216 Laurel Canyon Blvd., N.
Hollywood, Calif. 91706

Allan Keith Productions, Inc.
243 W. 56 St.
New York, N.Y. 10019

Lawren Productions Inc.
Box 1542
Burlingame, Calif. 94010

Library Filmstrip Center
3033 Aloma
Wichita, Kans. 67211

J. B. Lippincott
(Division of Higher Education)
E. Washington Sq.
Philadelphia, Pa. 19105

Marathon International
10 E. 49 St.
New York, N.Y. 10017

McDonnell Douglas Corporation
Film and Television Communications
2525 Ocean Park Blvd.
Santa Monica, Calif. 90406

McGraw-Hill Films
(Webster Division)
1221 Ave. of the Americas
New York, N.Y. 10020

Media Productions
6501 Winchester Ave.
Ventnor, N.J. 08406

Media One
10 Davis Dr.
Belmont, Calif. 94002

Memorex Corporation
1200 Memorex Dr.
Santa Clara, Calif. 95052

Metropolitan Pittsburgh Public Broadcasting Inc.
4802 Fifth Ave.
Pittsburgh, Pa. 15213

Milady Publishing Corporation
3839 White Plains Rd.
Bronx, N.Y. 10467

Modern Media Services
2323 New Hyde Park Rd.
New Hyde Park, N.Y. 11040

Monarch Releasing Corporation
330 W. 58 St.
New York, N.Y. 10019

Monumental Films Inc.
2160 Rockrose Ave.
Baltimore, Md. 21211

Motorola Teleprograms, Inc.
4825 N. Scott St., Suite 26
Schiller Park, Ill. 60176

National Education Association (NEA)
1201 16 St., N.W.
Washington, D.C. 20036

National Educational Media Inc.
15250 Ventura Blvd.
Sherman Oaks, Calif. 91403

National Geographic Society
17 and M Streets, N.W.
Washington, D.C. 20036

**Nebraska Educational Television Council for Higher
    Education Inc. (NETCHE)**
Box 83111
Lincoln, Neb. 68501

**New York State Colleges of Agriculture & Life Sciences
    & Human Ecology, Cornell University, Media Services**
201 Roberts Hall
Cornell University.
Ithaca, N.Y. 14853

Nightingale-Conant Corporation
6677 N. Lincoln Ave.
Chicago, Ill. 60645

Northern Illinois University
(division of Communication Services)
Altgeld Hall, Rm. 116
DeKalb, Ill. 60115

Ohio Historical Society
Ohio Historical Center
Columbus, Ohio 43211

Olympus Publishing Company
1670 E 1300 S.
Salt Lake City, Utah 84105

Our Sunday Visitor, Inc.
Noll Plaza
Huntington, Ind. 46750

Pacific Coast Community Video
121 E. De La Guerra St.
Santa Barbara, Calif. 93101

Parthenon Pictures
2625 Temple St.
Los Angeles, Calif. 90026

Perennial Education, Inc.
1825 Willow Rd.
Northfield, Ill. 60093

Pergamon Press, Inc.
Maxwell House
Elmsford, N.Y. 10523

Pictura Films Distribution Corporation
43 W. 16 St.
New York, N.Y. 10011

Playback Associates, Inc.
30 Rockefeller Plaza
New York, N.Y. 10020

Polymorph Films Inc.
331 Newbury St.
Boston, Mass. 02115

Prentice-Hall Media Inc.
(subsidiary of Prentice-Hall, Inc.)
150 White Plains Rd.
Tarrytown, N.Y. 10591

Professional Arts Inc.
Box 8003
Stanford, Calif. 94305

The Public Television Library
475 L'Enfant Plaza, S.W.
Washington, D.C. 20024

Purdue University
116 Stewart Center
West Lafayette, Ind. 47907

Purpose Film Center
(division of Parthenon Pictures)
2625 Temple St.
Los Angeles, Calif. 90026

Pyramid Films
Box 1048
Santa Monica, Calif. 90406

Raindance
71 W. Broadway
New York, N.Y. 10006

Ramic Productions
58 W. 58 St.
New York, N.Y. 10019

Ramsgate Films
704 Santa Monica Blvd.
Santa Monica, Calif. 90401

Reader's Digest
(Television Division)
200 Park Ave.
New York, N.Y. 10017

The Reading Laboratory Inc.
55 Day St.
South Norwalk, Calif. 06854

RMI Film Productions Inc.
701 Westport Rd.
Kansas City, Mo. 64111

S. C. Educational Television Commissi
2712 Millwood Ave.
Columbia, S.C. 29205

Salenger Educational Media
1635 12 St.
Santa Monica, Calif. 90404

William Schlottmann Productions
536 E. Fifth St., Suite 18
New York, N.Y. 10009

Scientifcom
(division of LaRue Inc. Communications)
708 N. Dearborn Ave.
Chicago, Ill. 60610

Al Sherman Films
Box 6, Cathedral Station
New York, N.Y. 10025

Smith-Mattingly Productions, Ltd.
310 South Fairfax St.
Alexandria, Va. 22314

Ken Snyder Enterprises
2032 Alameda Padre Serra
Santa Barbara, Calif. 93103

Southam Videotel Ltd.
1450 Don Mills Rd.
Don Mills, Ontario, Canada

Southern Baptist Radio & Television Commission
6350 W. Freeway
Fort Worth, Tex. 76116

Sterling Institute
2600 Virginia Ave., N.W.
Watergate Conference Center
Washington, D.C. 20037

Martha Stuart Communications
66 Bank St.
New York, N.Y. 10014

Sunburst Communications
39 Washington Ave.
Pleasantville, N.Y. 10570

TAD Products Corporation
TAD Institute
135 Cabot St.
Beverly, Mass. 01915

Teach 'Em, Inc.
625 N. Michigan Ave.
Chicago, Ill. 60611

Teletronics International, Inc.
231 E. 55 St.
New York, N.Y. 10022

Texas Instruments, Inc.
13500 N. Central Expressway
Box 5012
Dallas, Tex. 75222

Time-Life Video
Time & Life Bldg.
1271 Ave. of the Americas
New York, N.Y. 10020

Total Video Library Corporation
514 W. 57 St.
New York, N.Y. 10019

United States History Society Inc.
5425 Fargo
Skokie, Ill. 60076

United Synagogue of America
Department of Education
155 Fifth Ave.
New York, N.Y. 10010

University of Minnesota
Audiovisual Library Service
3300 University Ave., S.E.
Minneapolis, Minn. 55455

University of Missouri
Academic Support Center
505 E. Stewart Rd.
Columbia, Mo. 65201

University of Washington Press
Seattle, Wash. 98105

Unusual Films
Bob Jones University
Greenville, S.C. 29614

Valley Forge Films Inc.
Box K
Paoli, Pa. 19301

G. W. Van Leer & Associates
1850 N. Fremont
Chicago, Ill. 60614

VID PIC
2009 Baltimore
Kansas City, Mo. 64108

Video Tape Network
115 E. 62 St.
New York, N.Y. 10012

Videoplay Merchandising
1512 Merchandise Mart
Chicago, Ill. 60654

Visual Education Service
Yale University Divinity School
409 Prospect St.
New Haven, Conn. 06511

Visual Instruction Productions
(a dept. of Victor Kayfetz Productions, Inc.)
295 W. Fourth St.
New York, N.Y. 10014

Vocational Films
(division of Telecine Film Studios, Inc.)
111 Euclid Ave.
Park Ridge, Ill. 60068

Western Instructional Television, Inc.
1549 North Vine St.
Los Angeles, Calif. 90028

Ruth White Productions
(subsidiary of Rhythms Productions Records)
Whitney Building, Box 34485
Los Angeles, Calif. 90034

WOI-TV
Iowa State University
WOI Communications Center
Ames, Iowa 50010

Women Make Movies, Inc.
257 W. 19 St.
New York, N.Y. 10011

XICOM, Inc.
Clinton Woods
Tuxedo, N.Y. 10987

AUDIOTAPE DISTRIBUTORS

National Center for Audiotape
University of Colorado
Boulder, Colo. 80302

Pacifica Radio Network
5316 Venice Blvd.
Los Angeles, Calif. 90019

Jean Baity worked professionally in commercial, educational, and closed-circuit television after taking her degree in radio and television at the University of Michigan. When she was a Mamaroneck resident she volunteered her services to the Mamaroneck Media Project, for which she organized and trained other volunteers and generally lent her expertise to the development of the district's video and television studies programs, working with both teachers and students.

Ellie Waterston Bartow is a professional photographer and filmmaker. She served as consultant for the Center for Understanding Media and for its Mamaroneck Media Project. She was also filmmaking consultant for the artists-in-schools project in Montana.

Deirdre Boyle is a freelance editor and media columnist. She writes a featured column, "Media Minded," for *American Libraries,* edited *Expanding Media Services to Children & Youth* (Oryx Press), and co-edited *Children's Media Market Place* (Gaylord). An alumna of the Media Studies graduate program at the New School for Social Research, she has taught there too.

Bobbi Carrey is a professional photographer whose works have been exhibited and published widely. She developed the photography workshops for Workshop for Learning Things, and was photography consultant for the Center for Understanding Media. She has taught photography at Harvard University, at Concord Academy (Massachusetts), and at other institutions.

Pauline Cianciolo, is a freelance editor-publisher. She was editor-in-chief of R. R. Bowker Company's reference and professional books and previously headed the books, pamphlets, and audiovisual publishing program of the American Library Association. Also a former teacher and librarian, she practiced those professions at the elementary, secondary, and graduate school levels.

John Culkin is the director of the Media Studies program at the New School for Social Research in New York City, and has been executive director of the Center for Understanding Media since he inaugurated it in 1970. From 1964–1969 he directed Fordham University's Center for Communications. Dr. Culkin is an articulate evangelist for film and media studies, a popular teacher and speaker, co-author of *Films Deliver* (Scholastic) and *Trilogy* (Macmillan), and a frequent contributor to education, media, and national cultural affairs magazines.

Milo Dalbey is the media specialist for the elementary schools in the Mamaroneck School System in Westchester County, N.Y. He was the in-school coordinator for the Center's Mamaroneck Media Project. He has served on the faculties of the Media Studies program at the New School, of Virginia Commonwealth University, and in other institutions. He is an accomplished sculptor.

Jon Dunne is the director of public media for the Kentucky Arts Commission. He has directed media studies projects for the Philadelphia Public Schools system. He is also an independent filmmaker and a poet.

Todd Flinchbaugh is a filmmaker with an extensive background in animation. He was filmmaker-in-residence as part of the artists-in-schools programs in towns in Kansas, where he set up film production workshops for teachers and worked with student filmmakers. He also set up workshops for teenagers and adults in the San Francisco Bay area, where he is currently working.

Maureen Gaffney is founder-director of the Media Center for Children, New York City, and was previously a director of its predecessor, the Children's Film Theater, which formerly operated as a project of the Center for Understanding Media. She prepared the Children's Film Theater's second annotated filmography *More Films Kids Like* (ALA), and was coordinator of the 1975 American Film Festival. She is a leader of many workshops and symposia on films and media for children, and guest lecturer in media courses.

Robert Geller is the executive director of Learning in Focus, another offshoot of the Center for Understanding Media. He conceived and was executive producer of *Anthology: The American Short Story on Film*, the highly acclaimed PBS television series. Before that he was director of educational programs at the Center for Understanding Media and was dean of the Media Studies graduate program. His writings on media and education have appeared in *Media & Methods* and other journals.

Louis Giansante teaches courses in media design and sound in the Media Studies program of the New School for Social Research. He was formerly on the faculty of the Communication & Media Center in St. John Fisher College, Rochester, N.Y.

Don Kaplan teaches at the Bank Street College of Education and occasionally lectures at the New School for Social Research. He is also an actor in experimental theatre and a composer of music for dance and theatre. He has conducted workshops for many schools and organizations in the New York City area, and is a frequent contributor to education and media magazines, among them *Media & Methods, Learning* and *Music Educators Journal*.

Richard A. Lacey is an educational consultant and was formerly director of the Little Red Schoolhouse, an experimental school in New York's Greenwich Village. He has served as program officer in the education department of the Ford Foundation, lectures widely, teaches at the New

School for Social Research, and authored *Seeing with Feeling* (Saunders).

Gerry Laybourne is associate director of EPIE, a non-profit consumer agency for educational products and materials. She was a program director of the Children's Film Theater project. A former teacher she has written a number of articles with Kit Laybourne, her husband, on using media in the schools. She was the coordinator of the American Film Festival in both 1974 and 1976.

Kit Laybourne is producer of a pilot television program for the proposed PBS series *Mediaprobes*. Formerly director of research and publications at the Center for Understanding Media, he coordinated the Mamaroneck Media Project for the Center and edited its report in the earlier version of *Doing the Media*. He has made films and videotapes and has taught film, video, and media theory courses on elementary through graduate school levels. His most recent book is *The Animation Book* (Crown).

Ann Mandelbaum is a professional photographer whose work has been exhibited in New York galleries. She is a popular teacher of photography and has taught at the New School and elsewhere. She has also served as an artist-in-residence in a number of school programs.

Susan Rice is now a film writer. She worked with John Culkin on the Children's Theater project for the Center for Understanding Media, for which she prepared the first annotated filmography *Films Kids Like* (ALA), and co-edited *Children Are Centers of Understanding Media* (ACEI). She lectures widely and teaches film criticism at the New School when she is in New York. She is a frequent contributor to educational and media magazines, and was film critic for *Media & Methods*.

Georgeanna Spencer is an alumna of the Media Studies graduate program at the New School. An arts supervisor in School District 15, Forest Grove, Oregon, she lectures in the region on special arts and crafts techniques. She is an accomplished potter.

Kay Weidemann (Scott) is another alumna of the Media Studies graduate program at the New School. She was a research assistant for the Children's Film Theater and is currently director of media for Canisteo Schools System, in upstate New York.

Index

Index

AAAS Science Film Catalog, 184
Abstract animation, 75, 77, 85–87
ACT Newsletter, 187, 189
Action for Children's Television, 177, 189
Adams, Ansel, 169, 170
Advertisements (TV), 70–71
Africa on Film, 174
Alphabet, 5
Amelio, Ralph J., 171
American Association of School Librarians, 184, 189
American Broadcasting: A Source Book, 180
American Center of Films for Children, 189
American Council for the Arts in Education, 168
American Film Institute, 184, 189
American Film magazine, 189
American Folklore Films and Videotapes, 185
American Libraries, 189
American Library Association, 8, 187, 189
The American West in Film, 174
Amidon School, 175
Andersen, Yvonne, 82, 171, 176
Anderson, Chuck, 108, 176
Anderson, Rex, 170
Anglo-American Cataloging Rules, 186
Animated Film: Concepts, Methods, Uses, 173
Animation, 73–92
  abstract, 75, 77, 85–87
  cameraless, 74–78
  as a classroom technique, 73–74
  clay, 81
  cutout, 81, 82–83
  from discarded movies, 78
  felt, 82
  flip books, 82, 84, 175
  with overhead projector, 144–46
  representational designs, 75–76
  resources on, 171, 172, 173, 174, 175, 176
  scratch-and-doodle, 9, 74–78, 175
  setups for filming, 74, 78, 79, 80, 81, 82, 83
  silhouette, 85
  small objects, 80, 81, 86–87
  sound in, 76–77
  splicing film, 76–77
  still-scan, 78–80
  stop-action, 79–81, 172
  storyboard, 78
  synchronizing sound track with, 77
The Animation Book, 173
Animation: Learn How to Draw Animated Cartoons, 172
Anthropology and the media, 167
Arnheim, Rudolf, 167
Art & Visual Perception, 167
The Art of Walt Disney, 172
Artel, Linda, 184
Artists-in-Schools Programs, 189
Arts and education, 168
Aspect ratio, 58

Assemblage, 181
Association for Childhood Education International, 189
Association for Educational Communications and Technology, 184, 189
Association of Media Producers, 190
Audiotape, 131–34
  cassettes for, 131–32
  distributors, 201
  editors, 133–34
  erasing, 133
  reel-to-reel recorders for, 132
  transferring, 134
Audiovisual departments, 9
Audiovisual equipment, 184, 186
Audio-Visual Equipment Directory, 184
Audio Visual Instruction, 131, 187
Audiovisual Market Place, 184
Aural/visual awareness, 136
AV Communication Review, 187

The Babysitter, 95
Bad Dog, 97
Baity, Jean, 113, 203
Baker, D. Philip, 182
Ballad of Crowfoot, 39
Ballet Adagio, 68
Bank Street College of Education, 175
Barnouw, Eric, 176, 179
Barton, C. H., 172
Bartow, Ellie Waterston, 41, 48, 203
Basic TV Terms, 176
Bauer, Caroline Feller, 184
Begone Dull Care, 77, 175
Behavioral studies, application in video, 108–10
Behind the Camera, 172
Behind the Scenes at the Walt Disney Studio, 175
Being There, 177
Being with Children, 168
Belson, Jordan, 87
Benchley, Robert, 175
Bensinger, Charles, 176
Berarducci, Wilma, 175
Berner, Jeff, 170
Bigger and Better Enlarging, 170
Bittersweet Country, 182
Bittersweet magazine, 182
Black Men on Film, 174
Blair, Preston, 172
Bliss, Edward, Jr., 179
Blueprint paper, 16
  body prints, 17
Body silhouettes, 17, 38
Bogart, Carlotta, 183
Bogus films, 64
Bone, Jan, 172
Boogie-Doodle, 175
Booklist, 187, 189
Boyle, Deirdre, 166, 182, 184
Brainstorming, 90

Brakhage, Stan, 69, 168
The Brakhage Lectures, 168
Braundet, Pierre, 169
Braverman, Charles, 176
Breer, Robert, 87
The Broadcast Communications Dictionary, 179
Broadcasting:
  history, 176, 179, 180
  language of, 179
  news, 179, 180
  a simulation, 123
Broadcasting and the News, 180
Brodkin, Sylvia Z., 179
Brown, James W., 184
Brown, Les, 176
Brown, Lucy Gregor, 185
Bruner, Jerome, 167
Burder, John, 172
Butch Cassidy and the Sundance Kid, 68
Byrne-Daniel, J., 172

Cable television (CATV) (*see* Television, cable)
Calvert, Stephen, 184
Camera and Lens, 169
Camera effects (in filmmaking), 78
Camera Cookbook, 171
Camera obscura, 19, 22, 41
Camera photography, 28–36
  activities, 31–35, 37–39
  checklist of equipment and supplies, 36
  pre-camera warmups, 32
  (*See also* Photography)
Cameraless movies, 175
  scratch-and-doodle, 74–78
  screening techniques, 76
  sound in, 76–77
  using discarded 16 mm film for, 78
Cameras, film, 62
Cameras, photographic, 28–31, 169
  box (Brownie), 28–29
  cartridge loading, 29–30
  homemade, 9, 22, 23
  inexpensive, 11, 28
  instamatic, 29–30
  instant image maker, 30
  Leica, 171
  plastic, 28
  Polaroid, 170
  positions for holding of, 34, 35
  single lens reflex, 30
  twin lens reflex, 31
  view camera, 30, 33
  (*See also* Pinhole camera)
The Candidate, 174
Capriccio, 68
Cardboard Carpentry Workshop, 182
Caring for Photographs, 171
Carnegie Council on Children, 190
Carpenter, Edmund, 3, 6, 167
Carrey, Bobbi, 14, 37, 203
Cartier-Bresson, Henri, 170

Cartoon vegetable garden, 144–45
Cartooning for Amateur Films, 174
Cauntier, Julien, 173
Cel animation, 82, 84, 85, 174
Celluloid Curriculum, 173
Center for Advanced Film Studies, 189
Center for Understanding Media, 8, 14, 186
Changing bag, 10, 28, 29
Chaplin, Charlie, 91, 130
Chartpak, 24
Chewing face, 144
Chickamauga, 61, 69
Chiefs, 66
Child development, 168
Child study, 175
Children and Television, 177
Children as Film Makers, 173
Children's Film Theater, 93–95, 96–99, 185, 186, 190
Children's films, 185, 186, 187, 188, 189, 190
Children's literature, 182, 185
Children's Media Market Place, 184
Children's television, 5, 177, 189, 190
Children's Television: Economics of Exploitation, 177
Children's Television Workshop, 190
Child's Eye View, 175
Chisholm, Margaret E., 185
Ciancolo, Patricia, 182, 185
Ciancolo, Pauline, 166, 203
The Cinema as Art, 174
Citizen Kane, 173
Claro, Joseph, 176
Classical Music Recordings for Home and Library, 181
Classroom Cinema, 173
Classroom photography:
  resources for, 169, 170, 171
Classroom Projects Using Photography, 169
Clay animation, 81
Clio Award, 71
Clothes, for television performance, 116
Cockaboody, 98
Collage animation, 81
Collage with overhead, 142
Columbia Broadcasting System, 176–77, 178
Comic strips, 63–64
Coming to Our Senses, 168
Commercial photography, 44
Commercial television, 176, 177
Commercials (on television), 121–22, 130
Committee of the Young Adult Services Division, ALA, 185
Communication cubes, 147–48
Communications, 6, 167, 180
Composers of Tomorrow's Music, 135
Composition:
  in photography, 32, 42
  in sound, 137
Construction paper, 15
Contact paper, 17
Control room (television), 114
Cooke, Robert W., 169
The Cool Fire, 179
Cool Hand Luke, 174
"Cool" media, 5
Copy stand, 79
Core Media Collection for Secondary Schools, 185

The Craft of Photography, 171
Crazy Talk, Stupid Talk, 167
Creating a School Media Program, 182
Creative development in children, 183
Creative Film Making, 174
Creative Teaching with Tape, 181
Creative writing, 183
Creativity, 167, 168, 183
Critiquing film, 52, 88–92
Crow, Jeanne, 184
Crystallizing paint, 23–24
Cue sheet for television, 118
Culkin, John, 3, 183, 203
Cultures, environmental relations of, 4–5
Curriculum design and media programs, 155–58
  activities checklist for, 157–58
  diagnosing teaching environment for, 156–57
  format for writing of, 158
  integrating media arts with, 159–63
  method for constructing, 156
  resources for, 182–86
  uses for video activities in, 116–17
Curriculum Guide for Photographers, 169
Cutout animation, 82–83, 174
Cutout silhouette puppet, 142, 143

Daguerreotype, 41
Dalbey, Milo, 147, 159, 203
D'Amico, Victor, 181
Darkroom, photography without, 15
Davis, Phil, 169
Davis, Ruth Ann, 182
Daybooks, 39
deBono, Edward, 167
The Desert, 68
Design by Accident, 170
Design connection, 67
Design elements in film, 66–68
Designing with Light on Paper and Film, 169
Developing tank, 29
Diamant, Lincoln, 179
Diffor, John C., 185
Discovering the Movies, 174
Disney, Walt, 74, 172, 175
Documentary films, 65–66
Documentary photography, 38, 43–44
Documentary projects, 9
Documentary video, 106–8
Doskey, John S., 186
Dots, 176
Dramatic production (video), 105–6
Dramatic readings, 105
Dramatic skills, 104–6, 116, 179
Dream of Wild Horses, 63, 68, 69, 130
Due to Circumstances Beyond Our Control, 176–77
Dunne, Jon, 56, 203

The Early Window, 178
Eastman Kodak Company, 170, 173
Editing:
  audiotapes, 133–34
  film, 50–51, 57, 61–62, 66, 68, 76, 92, 172, 174, 180
  sound, 128
  tape, 180
  television, 108

videotape, 133, 134
Edmund Scientific Company, 23
Education & Ecstasy, 168
"Education in the Global Village," 180
Education through Art, 168
Educational Film Library Association, 61, 188, 190
Educational Media Catalogs on Microfiche, 185
Educational Media Yearbook, 184
Educational Products Information Exchange, 187, 190
Educational Screen & AV Guide, 187
Educational theory and practice, 168
Educators Guide to Free Films, 185
Educators Guide to Media Lists, 186
Educators Progress Service guides, 185
Eisenstein, Sergei, 87
Elam, Jane A., 169
Electric Company, 190
The Electronic Journalist, 176
Electronic media, 5
The Electronic Rainbow, 176
Elementary School Library Collection, 187
Ellul, Jacques, 167
Emotions, 109
Englander, David A., 172
Environments:
  for classroom learning, 153–54
  influence on the senses, 4–6
  for learning, 3
  media environments, 3–7, 8–15, 167, 171, 177
  for media arts programs, 152–53
  for teaching, 156–57
  relationship to cultures, 4–5, 190
Epic productions (in filmmaking), 70
EPIE Report, 187
Equipment check-out system, 54
Estes, Glenn, 182
ETC, 187
Everything You Always Wanted to Know about Videotape Recording, 177
Ewen, David, 135
Exotic Menus (film activity), 97–98
Expanded Cinema, 179
Expanding Media, 182
Experiences in Visual Thinking, 168
Explorations in Communication, 167
Exploring Television, 177
Exploring the Film, 173

Fabun, Don, 168
Face in the Crowd, 174
The Family Guide to Children's Television, 177
Family Way, 174
Fantasy play, 105
Feature Films on 8mm and 16mm, 186
Federal Communications Commission, 123, 177, 180
Feelies, 148
Feininger, Andreas, 169
Feller, Alan, 169
Felt animation, 82
Ferris, Bill, 185
Field, Stanley, 179
Film (filmmaking), 46–99
  activities for children after screening, 96–99

Film (filmmaking) *(continued)*
  animation, 73–92
  as art, 66–67, 167, 172, 174
  camera effects, 78
  for children, 93–95, 185, 186, 188, 190
  as communication skill, 71
  course in, 56–72, 184, 189
  critiquing, 52, 82–92
  curriculum uses of, 159–63, 173, 174, 175
  design elements in, 66–68
  documentary, 50, 53, 57, 65–66
  editing, 50–51, 57, 61–62, 66, 68, 172, 174,
      180
  epic productions, 70
  equipment, 174
  feature films, 172, 174, 186, 187
  form in, 67–68
  framing, 9, 58–61, 79, 91
  genres, 171, 173
  history of, 174
  Hollywood and, 172
  language and terminology in, 49, 50, 55,
      172, 174
  logistics of, 53–54
  moods in, 69
  motion in, 67–68
  narrative, 50, 57, 60–61
  non-narrated, directory of, 186
  organization and structure of, 172
  positions for holding camera, 52
  resources on, 169, 171–76
  scheduling, 53
  screening, 9, 51, 82–92, 174
  silent, 173, 186
  single concept, 172
  sound in, 63, 69, 79
  splicing, 51, 61
  studio, 174, 175
  Super 8, 48–55, 63, 172, 173
  techniques, 56–72, 171, 172, 173, 174, 175
  titling, 53
  viewpoint in, 66
Film: A Montage of Theories, 173
Film: An Anthology, 174
Film as Art, 167
Film Attitudes and Issues Series, 174
Film cameras, 48–49, 172
Film cutters, 61
Film director's viewfinder, 63
Film discussions, 88–92, 94, 96, 173
Film distributors, 192–97
Film festival, 54
Film in the Cities, 190
Film in the Classroom, 171
Film leader, 24
Film Library Quarterly, 187
Film News, 188
Film projector, 77
Film programs, 7–15, 93–99, 168, 185, 186,
    187, 188
Film Programmer's Guide to 16mm Rentals,
    187
Film: The Creative Eye, 174
Film study, 88–92, 172, 173, 174, 183, 184,
    189
The Filmic Moment, 171
Filmmaking for Children, 174
Filmmaking in Schools, 173
Filmographies, 184, 185, 186, 187, 188
Films Deliver, 183

Films for Children, 185
Films for Hearing Impaired Children, 185
Films Kids Like, 94, 186
Films on filmmaking, 171, 175
Films Too Good for Words, 186
Filmstrips:
  making, 26, 27–28
  projector for, 10, 26–27
Finch, Christopher, 172
The Fine Print, 170
Fischinger, Oscar, 87
Flinchbaugh, Todd, 85, 86, 204
Flip book, 82, 84, 85, 174, 175
Found sound, 137–139
  discography of, 138
*Four Arguments for the Elimination of
    Television*, 177
The Foxfire Book, 181–82
The Foxfire Fund, 190
Foxfire project, 108
Fragments, 182
Framing:
  in filmmaking, 9, 58–61, 63, 79, 91
  with overhead and opaque projectors, 143
  in photography, 32, 39, 42, 43
Frank Film, 63, 130
Frederick, 98
French Embassy, 38
Friendly, Fred W., 176–77
Frontiers of Photography, 171
Frye, R. A., 169
Fuller, Buckminster, 167
Further Adventures of Cardboard Carpentry,
    182
Future Facts, 181
Future studies, 170, 181, 191
The Futurist, 191
Futurist music, 135

Gaffney, Maureen, 96, 185, 188, 204
Games in doing video, 104–6
Gaskill, Arthur L., 172
Geller, Robert, 7, 204
Geographical Fugue, 137
Gerbner, George, 167
Gessner, Robert, 172
Giansante, Louis, 126, 131, 204
Giardino, Thomas, 172
Gillespie, John T., 182
Gilmour, Clyde, 175
Glass, 66
"Global Village," 4, 127, 180
The Golden Fish, 61, 92
The Golden Web, 176
Goldstein, Ruth M., 187
Grafilm, 172
Graphic notation for sound, 135, 137, 138
Graphic poetry, 138
Greene, Ellin, 185
Greenfield, Jeff, 177
Guerilla Television, 178
*Guide to College Courses in Film and
    Television*, 184, 189
Guide to Film Making, 174
Guide to Videotape Recording, 176
Guides to Educational Media, 186

Hal in the Classroom, 171
Hall, Edward T., 4
Halsey, Richard S., 181

Handbook for Storytellers, 184
Handbook of Super 8 Production, 172
Hanks, Cheryl, 168
Haratonik, Peter, 177
Harmonay, Maureen, 177
Harwood, Don, 177
Hat, 66
Headcracker Suite, 68
Help My Snowman Is Burning Down, 61
The Here's How Book of Photography, 169
High Noon, 174
Higher education courses in media, 184,
    189
Hilliard, Robert L., 180
*A History of Broadcasting in the United
    States*, 176, 179
*History of Photography: 1839 to the Present
    Day*, 170
The Hole Thing, 170
Holland, Vicki, 169
Hollis, N. Todd, 171
Hoos, Gunther, 172
Hoppity Pop, 175
Horkheimer, Mary Foley, 185
"Hot" media, 5
Houk, Annelle, 183
The House, 61
How to Animate Cut-Outs, 172
How to Do Tricks in Amateur Films, 172
*How to Make and Use a Cartridge Pinhole
    Camera*, 169
How to Photograph Your World, 169
How to Read a Film, 174
How to Shoot a Movie Story, 172
How to Talk Back to Your Television Set,
    177
Howard, Margaret, 172
The Hunters, 4
Hustle, 174

I Think They Call Him John, 66
Illustration in Children's Books, 182
The Image Empire from 1953, 176
Images of Man, 170
Imogen Cunningham, 68
Improvisations, 38, 104, 105, 179
Improvisations for the Theater, 104, 179
In the Kitchen, 61
Independent Filmmaking, 173, 180
Information Center on Children's Cultures,
    190
An Interview with Norman McLaren, 175
Interviews, 106, 107, 108, 116, 120–21, 129
Introducing the Single-Camera VTR System,
    177
Isolation booth, 109
It's Not the Song, It's the Singing, 181
It's So Simple: Click and Print, 171

Jacks, 133
Jacobs, Mark, 169
La Jette, 39, 61, 66
Jigsaw puzzles, 99
Jodoin, Rene, 87
Johnson, Nicholas, 122, 177
Johnson, Ron, 172
Journal of Communication, 188
Journalism and broadcasting, 179, 180
Junkyard, 61

K-3 Bulletin of Teaching Ideas & Materials, 188
Kaplan, Don, 135, 204
Kaye, Evelyn, 177
Kemp, Jerrold E., 186
Kennebunk High School, 182
Kindergarteners as animators, 83, 86
Kindergarteners as photographers, 45
Kinestasis films, 86–87, 174
Kintner, Robert E., 180
Kislia, J. A., 186
Kodak (*see* Eastman Kodak Company)
Kokrda, Ken, 169
Kuhns, William, 167, 172, 173, 177
Kung Phooey, 72

Label Press, 182
Lacey, Richard, 88, 152, 173, 204
Lampsan, Nancy, 169
Landers Film Reviews, 188
Lange, Dorothea, 170
Language and communication, 167, 168
The Language and Thought of the Child, 168
Larson, Roger R., Jr., 173
Lateral Thinking, 167
Laybourne, Gerry, 96, 204
Laybourne, Kit, 7, 56, 73, 103, 119, 155, 173, 177, 204
Leaf, 66, 130
Learn to See, 170
Learning, the Magazine for Creative Teaching, 188
Lebanon High School, 182
Leibert, Robert M., 177
The Leica Manual, 170
Leonard, George B., 168
Lesser, Gerald, 177
Let's Make a Film, 82, 171
Let's See It Again, 186
Letter from Siberia, 66
Levinson, Ralph, 169
Library reference and selection tools, 184–87
Library of Congress, Prints and Photographs Div., 38
Library of Sound Effects Records, 181
Lichty, Lawrence W., 180
Lidstone, John, 173
Liepmann, Lise, 168
Life Library of Photography, 171
Light and Lighting, 169
Light drawings, 17–18, 39
Light-sensitive papers, 14, 15–17
Light shows, 146
Lighting (for television), 114
Liliberte, Nochan, 181
Limbacher, James L., 186
Linton, Dolores and David, 131, 180, 183
Lipton, Lenny, 173, 180
"Listening to Radio," 180
Literature of the Screen Series, 174
Loneliness of a Long Distance Runner, 174
Looking at Photographs, 170
Loops, 175
Lopate, Philip, 168
Lowndes, Douglas, 173
Lyons, Nathan, 170

MacCann, Richard D., 173
McKim, Robert, 168
McLaren, Norman, 77–78, 87, 175
McLaughlin, Frank, 183
McLuhan, Marshall, 4–6, 126, 167
Madsen, Roy P., 173
Make Your Own Animated Movies, 171
Making It Move, 174
Making of a Live TV Show, 176
Manchell, Frank, 173
Mandelbaum, Ann, 14, 204
Mander, Jerry, 177
Mandlin, Harvey and Dotty, 176
Marble, 98
Marinetti, F. T., 135
Mass Communications Arts, 183
Mass media, 3, 180, 183, 184, 185
Mass Media Ministries, 190
Mattingly, Grayson, 177
Maynard, Richard, 173, 174, 183
Meadows Green, 68
Meaningless texts (in sound), 135
Measuring standard for film frames, 75
Meckler, Alan, 181
Media Action Research Center, 190
Media & Kids: Real-World Learning in the Schools, 183
Media & Methods, 131, 178, 188, 190
Media and Symbols, 167
Media and the Young Adult, 185
Media arts programs, 152–63
    curriculum design for, 155–58
    environments for, 152–54
    integrating with curricula, 159, 161–62
    model (K-6), 160–62
    resources on, 167–68, 182–87
    team planning in, 155
    (*See also* Media studies programs)
Media catalogs, 185, 186
Media Center for Children, 188, 190
Media Digest, 188
Media directories, 184, 185
Media education courses and programs, 8, 184
Media environments, 3–7, 8–15, 167, 171, 177
Media equipment, 9–11, 184, 186, 187
Media Equipment: A Guide and Dictionary, 186
Media Equipment Resource Center, 191
Media Facilities Design, 182
Media in the classroom, 183
Media Indexes and Review Sources, 185
Media Literacy, 183
Media Programs: District and School, 184
The Media Reader, 184
Media Review Digest, 187
Media studies programs, 1–11, 150–63
    curriculum and, 150–63
    education in, 9, 184, 189
    equipment and software for, 9–11
    funding of, 9–11
    planning of, 8–9
    rationale for, 7
    resources on, 167–68, 182–91
    role of parents in, 9
    role of teachers in, 9
    role of library media center in, 9
Media terminology, 55, 179, 186
The Media Works Program, 184

The Mediate Teacher, 183
Mediaware, 187
Meiselas, Susan, 170
Melody, William, 177
Mendelsohn, Harold, 180
Messages and Meanings, 183
Messiaen, Olivier, 135
Microphones, 180
Mr. Smith Goes to Washington, 174
Mitchell, Wanda, 178
Mixed media, 111, 129–30, 143, 146, 148
Model K-6 Media Arts Program, 160–62
A Model School District Media Program, 182
Mole and the Chewing Gum, 98
The Mole and the Lollipop, 95
Monaco, James, 174
Montgomery County (Maryland) Public Schools, 182
Moods of Surfing, 63
Moon drawings, 39
More Films Kids Like, 94, 185, 190
Morrow, James, 174, 183
"Most of the Pictures Came Out Real Well," 171
Mounting and Preserving Pictorial Materials, 181
Mouris, Frank, 130
MOVE, 175
Movement in film, 67–68
Movie Machines, 175
Moviemaking Illustrated, 174
Movies [*see* Film (filmmaking)]
Movies and How They Are Made, 173
Movies for Kids, 187
Movies: The Magic of Film, 172
Movies with a Purpose, 172
The Moving Image, 172
The Moving Picture Book, 173
A Moving Picture Giving & Taking Book, 168
A Multimedia Approach to Children's Literature, 185
Multiple exposure, 32, 43
Multiple projections, 146
Mumford, Lewis, 167
Murray, Michael, 178
Music:
    recordings of, 132
    resources, 136, 181, 183
    as sound, 135–38
    for television, 115–16

Nanook of the North, 4
National Audio-Visual Association, 190
National Film Board of Canada, 77, 175
National Public Radio, 191
National Society for the Study of Education, 167
The Negative, 169
The New Season, 178
The New York Times, 37
The New York Times Encyclopedia of Television, 176
Newhall, Beaumont, 170
Newscasting, 107, 176, 177, 178
Newton High School, 175
Nibbelink, Don, 170
NICEM Media Indexes, 186
Nickel, Mildred, 183

Night and Fog, 39
Nijsen, C. G., 180
Nine Variations on a Dance Theme, 68
Nisbett, Alec, 180
Noise, 135–38
Non-portable television, 107–8
Non-sexist films, 184
Notation (sound), 136–38
Nothing But a Man, 174

O'Brien, James F., 170
Observation techniques, 98
Occurrence at Owl Creek Bridge, 61
Oh! What a Blow That Phantom Gave Me, 167
Olson, David R., 167
Olympiad, 66, 68
Olympic Media Information, 185
Omega, 62, 68
On Photography, 168
On the Air, 180
100 Ways to Have Fun with an Alligator, 181
101 Experiments in Photography, 171
Opaque projector, 9, 64, 67, 143
Optical devices, 11, 22, 23, 36
Optical sound track, 77
Oral history, 108, 181, 182
Oral History Collections, 181
Orange and Blue, 130
Organizations on media, 189–90
Oscillations, 145
Other Voices in the Wilderness, 63
Overhead projector, 9, 10, 64, 66, 142–46, 181
Overlays, 82, 84
Overture Nyitany, 98

Padgett, Ron, 183
Paik, Nam Jun, 178
Painting with the Sun, 170
Paper Movie Machines, 175
Parlato, Salvatore J., Jr., 186
Pas de Deux, 62, 68
Patch cords, 133
Peace, 61, 63
Peiser, Judy, 185
Pen Point Percussion, 77, 175
People, Society & Mass Communications, 180
Perception (see Senses and perception)
Perception and Photography, 171
Periodicals, annotated list of, 187–189
Photograms, 169
Photograms, 14–19
   equipment and supplies for, 36
   objects for, 15, 16, 18
   papers for, 15–17
   processing, basic, 14–15
   processing with blueprint paper, 16
   processing with construction paper, 15
   processing with repro-negative paper, 16–17
   processing with photographic papers, 17
   resources on, 169
   samples of, 14, 15, 16, 18
   self-portraits, 39
   special effects and techniques, 17, 38, 39
   texture in, 39
Photographers on Photography, 170

Photographic chemicals, painting with, 18–19
Photographic essay, 40
The Photographic Experience, 169
Photographic painting, 17–19
Photographic papers, 17
Photographic Tools for Teachers, 169
Photography, 169
Photography, 12–45
   activities, 37–39
   as art, 44, 168
   cameraless, 14–27, 169
   color, 169
   commercial, 44
   documentary, 38, 43–44
   enlargement, 170
   future of, 171
   history of, 41–42, 169, 170
   introducing, 11, 14
   lighting, 42, 169, 170
   of people, 33, 43, 170
   processing steps, 29, 30
   resources on, 168, 169–71
   technical aspects of, 42–43, 169, 170, 171
   techniques, 169, 170, 171
   terms, 42–43
   35mm, 170
   three dimensional, 39
   (*See also* Camera photography; Photograms; Pinhole camera)
The Photography Catalog, 170
Photography in Focus, 169
Photography in the Classroom, 169
Photography: Simple and Creative, 169
Piaget, Jean, 168
Picker, Fred, 170
Pictorial vocal writing, 135
Picture Books for Children, 185
Picturing People, 170
Pigs, 66, 130
Pincus, Edward, 174
Pinhole camera, 19–23
   activities with, 21–23
   directions for exposures, 20
   equipment and supplies, 36
   films for, 20
   as filmstrip projector, 26–27
   as filmstrip viewer, 22–23
   how to make camera, 19–20
   optical devices, 22–23
   photos from, 20–21
   processing exposed film, 21
   resources on, 169, 170
   sizes and shapes of, 19, 22
   as slide viewer, 22–23
Pirsig, Robert M., 167
Pixillation, 81, 174
Planning and Producing Audiovisual Materials, 186
Playacting, 99, 105–6
Pleasure dome, 148–49
The Plug-In Drug, 178, 179
Point of View (film activity), 97–98
Polaroid Corp., 39
Pollack, Jackson, 87
Portable VTR, 103–12
Portraiture:
   photographic, 33, 38, 39, 43, 170
   sound, 129

Positions for cameras:
   film, 52
   photography, 34, 35
Positive Images, 184
The Post-Industrial Prophets, 167
Postman, Neil, 167
Poteet, G. Howard, 180
Potter, Rosemary Lee, 178
La Poulet, 61
Practical Guide to Classroom Media, 131, 180, 183
Pratella, F. B., 135
Prete, Anthony, 178
Previews, 188
Price, Jonathan, 178
Primitive sounds and music, 135
Prime Time School Television, 190
The Print, 169
Print-making, 39, 169, 170
Print media, 5
Printing-out paper, 15–16
Privett, B., 174
Production crew (television), 114, 117
Production sheet for filmmaking, 79, 80
Professional Broadcast Writer's Handbook, 179
Profile puzzle game, 145
Profiles, video, 120
Processing photographs without darkroom, 29, 30
Projectionists' Programmed Primer, 181
Projection paper, 17
Promise and Performance, 177
Propaganda on Film, 174
PTST (Prime Time School Television), 188
Pulling Together (film activity), 98–99
Puppets:
   animated, 81, 144–45, 174
   cutout silhouette, 142, 143
   shadow hand, 143
   video show, 116

Quinn, Thomas, 168
Quinley, William J., 186
Quiz on films for children, 94–95

Rabun Gap-Nacoochee School (Ga.), 181–82
RADIO!, 180
Radio:
   effects of, 180
   history of, 176, 179, 180
   old-time, 180, 181
   plays, 129, 179
   public, 191
   recordings of programs, 181
   resources on, 179, 180, 183, 191
   script, 130
Radio Broadcasting, 180
Read, Herbert, 168
Rear screen projections, 85, 107, 146
Recordings:
   of children, 181
   classroom applications of, 180
   for film, 180
   of music, 181
   of old-time radio, 181
   oral history, 181
   reviews and discographies of, 188
   of sound effects, 181
   techniques in, 181

Recycled media, 9, 143, 144
The Red Balloon, 93
Reiniger, Lotte, 82
Reisz, Karel, 174
The Reluctant Dragon, 175
Renan, Sheldon, 176
Repro-negative paper, 16–17
The Responsive Chord, 126–27, 180
Rice, Susan, 93, 186, 204
Robinson, Richard, 178
Rock scene, 180, 183
Rockingchair, 188
The Role of the Librarian in Media, 183
Role-playing, 91, 92, 110
Rosen, Stephen, 181
Rosenberg, Kenyon C., 186
Ruby Slipper Award, 189
Rufsvold, Margaret I., 186
Rynew, Arden, 174

The Salt Book, 182
Savage Innocents, 174
Scenario, 57, 70
Schafer, R. Murray, 136
Schillaci, Anthony, 183
Schoenfeld, Madalynn, 185
Scholastic's Concerned Photographers
        Program, 170
*School and Public Library Media Programs
        for Children and Young Adults*, 182
School librarian/media specialist, 9, 153,
        182, 183
*School Library Media Center: A Force for
        Educational Excellence*, 182
School library media centers, 9, 11, 182,
        183, 184, 185, 187, 188, 189
School Media Quarterly, 188, 189
Schooling, 7
Schramm, Wilbur, 178
Schrank, Jeffrey, 183, 184
Schultz, Morton J., 181
Schwartz, Ellie, 187
Schwartz, Tony, 126–27, 127, 128, 180, 181
Science Books & Films, 188
Science fiction film, 171
Scratch-and-doodle filmmaking, 9, 74–78,
        175
    on clear leader, 75–76
    on opaque leader, 76
    setup for filming, 74
    synchronizing sound track, 77
Screenplay, 70
Scripts:
    filmstrip, 26
    radio, 130, 179, 180
    shooting, 57, 70, 92, 106
    television, 107, 114–15, 179, 180
Seeing with Feeling, 89, 173
SEG (*see* Special effects generator)
Selected Films for Young Adults, 186
Self-portraits (video), 109–10
The Selling of the Pentagon, 66
Senses and perception, 3–7, 57, 62–63, 168,
        171
Serenal, 175
Sesame Street, 5, 74, 177, 190
Sets for television, 113–14, 116
Setups for filming:
    clay animation, 81
    with copy stand arrangement, 79

cutout animation, 82, 83
flip books, 85
still-scan, 78, 79
stop-action, 80
Super 8, 74
with tripod arrangement, 79, 83
Seven Authors in Search of a Reader, 69
Shadow hand puppets, 143
Shamberg, Michael, 178
Shanks, Bob, 179
Short films, 93–99, 173, 185, 186
Short Films for Discussion, 173
Shull, Jim, 170
Sightlines, 188, 190
The Silent Language, 4
Silhouette animation, 82, 85, 143
Simon, Sidney, 110
Simulations:
    broadcasting, 122
    television, 121
Siskind, Aaron, 170
Sive, Mary Robinson, 186
Six Penguins, 98
Sixty Second Spot, 176
Ski the Outer Limit, 68
Sky, 61, 63, 66
Slide making without camera, 9, 23–24, 25,
        36, 143
Slide mounts, 24
Slide/tape making, 11, 24–28, 38
Slides, lifted, 148
Slides, recycled, 148
Small objects in animation, 80, 81, 86–87
Smallman, Kirk, 174
Snyder, Norman, 170
Society, effects of mass media on, 167
Sohn, David A., 174, 176
Sontag, Susan, 4, 6, 168
Sound, 124–38
    activities, 127–30
    basic equipment and skills, 131–34
    editing, 128
    environment, 126–28
    in filmmaking, 52–53, 63, 69, 76–77, 79,
        130
    monophonic, 180
    as music, 130
    as noise, 127
    perception of, 127–28
    portraits, 129
    quality, 127
    recordings, 180–81
    relation to image, 136–37
    resources on, 180–81, 183
    in video, 110–11, 130
Sound and Sight, 183
Sound collage, 130, 132
Sound effects, 127, 181
The Sound of Children, 181
Spaghetti City Video Manual, 179
Sparrow, 172
Special effects generator, 108, 114, 119
Spencer, Georgeanna, 142, 204
Spirt, Diana L., 182
Splendor in the Grass, 174
Splicing film, 51, 61, 62, 76–77
Spolin, Viola, 104, 179
*Standards for Cataloging Nonprint
        Materials*, 186
Stanley, Robert, 173

Starr, Cecile, 174
Stars and Stripes, 175
The Starter, 70
Steinmetz, Andreas, 112
Stella, Frank, 87
The Sting, 172
Stephenson, Ralph, 174
Steps to Service, 183
Still photography (*see* Camera photography)
Still-scan animation, 78–80
    with photographs as image source, 78
    notation system for, 79
    production sheets for, 79, 80
    setups for, 78–79
Stop-action animation, 79–81, 172
Storyboarding, 9, 57–65, 78
    basic storyboard, 58–59
    as communicator, 78
    design storyboard, 66–67
    documentary storyboard, 64–65
    dream storyboard, 68–69
    framer for, 58
    narrative storyboard, 59–61, 63–64
    notation system, 78
    with photographs, 57–59, 64–65
    production sheet, 80
    relationship to still-scan animation, 78
    samples of, 49, 58, 59, 60, 65, 67, 69
    for Super 8, 49
Storytelling, 184
Studio proof paper, 14, 15
Studio television, 113–18
Suid, Murray, 170, 174, 183
Sun-prints, 14, 15
The Super 8 Book, 173
Super 8 filmmaking, 11, 48–55, 63
    camera, 48–49
    resources on, 172, 173, 187, 188
    storyboarding, 49
    synchronizing sound with, 63
Super 8mm Filmmaker, 188
Szarkowski, John, 170

Taffy pull, 99
Talbot, Daniel, 174
Talking face, 144
Tall, Joel, 180
Tape Editing, 180
The Tape Recorder, 180
The Teacher and the Overhead Projector,
        181
Teachers:
    as resources, 154
    roles in media studies programs, 9
    self evaluation of, 153, 156
    as team member, 153, 155
    training in media, 8, 184, 189
Teachers and Writers Collaborative, 183,
        188
Teachers & Writers Magazine, 188
Teachers Guide to Television, 189
Teaching Film Animation to Children, 82,
        171
Teaching Human Beings, 183–84
The Technical Manifesto of Futurist Music,
        135
Technicas & Civilization, 167
The Technique of Editing 16mm Films, 172
The Technique of Film Editing, 174
The Technique of the Sound Studio, 180

The Technological Society, 167
Televising Your Message, 178
Television:
  alternate, 178
  as a business, 122, 176, 179
  cable (CATV), 122, 176
  children's, 177, 178, 187, 188, 189, 190
  commercial, 176, 177, 190, 191
  commercials on, 70–71, 121–22, 130, 177
  as communication, 3, 178
  crews, 114, 117
  criticism of, 177, 178, 179, 188, 189, 190,
      191
  cues for, 118
  as educator, 5–8
  effects of, 3, 7, 176, 177, 178, 179, 190
  as entertainment, 176
  environment, 3, 5, 7, 177
  films about, 176
  history, 176, 177, 178, 179
  as industry, 176, 178, 179
  networks, 176–77
  news, 176, 177, 178
  occupations in, 179
  plays, 179
  programming, 116–17, 176, 177, 187, 189,
      196
  public, 176
  resources on, 176–79, 189, 190, 191
  studies, 119–22, 177
  studio, 113–18, 176, 178
  techniques, 114, 118, 179
  viewing environments, 120
  viewing habits, 3, 7, 120–21, 177, 178, 179
  (*See also* Video)
Television in the Lives of Our Children,
    178
Television Information Office, 191
Television journalism, 176, 178, 179
The Television Newsman, 176
Television Production Handbook, 179
Television: The Business Behind the Box,
    176
Television, the First Fifty Years, 177
The Television Workshop series, 176
Televisionland, 176
Texture (in photography), 34, 39, 42, 43
That's Me, 174
Theater games, 104–5
Themes Two, 173
Tillin, Alma M., 186
Time Is, 61, 62, 68
Time-lapse animation, 80–81
Time-Life Books Editors, 171
Time Piece, 61
Titling:
  for film, 53
  for television, 115

Toch, Ernst, 137
Top of the News, 189
Toward a Psychology of Art, 167
A Tower in Babel, 176
Toys, 66
Transparent contact paper, 24
Tripod (for film), 51–52, 79, 83
Trojanski, John, 174
Tube of Plenty, 176
Tug-of-War game, 98, 105
TV: Behind the Tube, 176
TV Guide, 121, 189
TV, The Anonymous Teacher, 190
TV Values Kit, 190

U-film, 24
Unanswered Question, 66
Understanding Mass Media, 184
Understanding Media, 4, 167
Understanding the Film, 172
UNTITLED, 175
Up Is Down, 62
Up the Down Staircase, 174
The Use of Microphones, 180

Valdes, Joan, 184
Valse, 137
Values Clarification, 110
Values study, 91–92, 110, 191
van Orden, Phyllis, 187
Vaseline self-portraits, 38
Very Nice—Very Nice, 66
Vestal, David, 171
Video, 101–22
  activities, 104–12
  art, 110–12, 178, 179
  discussions, 112
  equipment, 103–4, 114, 178, 179
  feedback, 110, 111
  history, 178
  profiles, 120–21
  programs in elementary schools, 116–17
  projects, 176, 177
  resources on, 176–79, 189, 190
  teaching of, 176
  techniques, 114–16, 176, 178
  (*See also* Television; Videotape recording
      system)
Video & Kids, 178
Video Power, 176
The Video Primer, 178
Video Visions, 178
Videofreex, 179
Videography, 189
The Videotape Book, 178
Videotape recording system (VTR):
  classroom activities for, 103–12
  editing in, 133, 134

resources on, 176, 177, 178, 179, 181
  use of in film discussion, 90
Videotape recordings
  distributors/producers, 197–201
Viewfinder, 63
Viewpoint (in film), 66
Visual arts, 185
Visual literacy, 57
  resources for, 167–68, 169, 171, 182, 185
Voices in the Wilderness, 61
Vorkapitch, Slavko, 87
VTR (*see* Videotape recording system)
VU meter, 132–33

Wall, C. Edward, 187
War of the Worlds, 162
Weaver, Kathleen, 187
Weidemann, Kay, 96, 204
Welles, Orson, 162
Wells, H. G., 162
Wengraf, Susan, 184
Wentz, Bud, 175
Weston, Edward, 170
When Pictures Began to Move, 173
When Words Sing, 136
White, Minor, 170
The Whole Word Catalogue 2, 183
Why Man Creates, 68
Wigginton, Eliot, 108, 181–82
Winn, Marie, 178, 179
Word notation, 135–37
Words, for musical purposes, 136
Workshop for Learning Things, 21, 171, 182,
    191
World Future Society, 191
Writing for radio and television, 179, 180
Writing News for Broadcast, 179
Wyman, Raymond, 108

Yellow Ball Cache, 176
Yellow-Ball Workshop, 171, 176, 181
You and Creativity, 168
Young Filmmakers, 173
Young Filmmakers Foundation, 191
Young People's Radio Festival, 191
Young Viewers, 188, 190
Youngblood, Gene, 179
Your Child's Sensory World, 168
Youth Film Archives, 191
Youth Film Distribution Center, 191

Zabatsky, Bill, 183
Zakia, Richard D., 171
Zebras, 98
Zen and the Art of Motorcycle Maintenance,
    167
Zettl, Herbert, 179
Zornow, Edith, 187